T0385679

The Authenticity Industries

THE Authenticity INDUSTRIES

Keeping It "Real"
in Media, Culture, and Politics

MICHAEL SERAZIO

Stanford University Press
Stanford, California

Stanford University Press
Stanford, California

Printed in the United States of America on acid-free, archival-quality paper

Library of Congress Cataloging-in-Publication Data
Names: Serazio, Michael, author.
Title: The authenticity industries : keeping it "real" in media, culture, and politics / Michael Serazio.
Other titles: Keeping it "real" in media, culture, and politics
Description: Stanford, California : Stanford University Press, [2024] | Includes bibliographical references and index.
Identifiers: LCCN 2023017239 (print) | LCCN 2023017240 (ebook) | ISBN 9781503635487 (cloth) | ISBN 9781503637290 (epub)
Subjects: LCSH: Popular culture—United States. | Authenticity (Philosophy)—Social aspects—United States. | Authenticity (Philosophy)—Political aspects—United States. | Authenticity (Philosophy)—Economic aspects—United States. | Authenticity (Philosophy) in mass media. | Mass media—Social aspects—United States.
Classification: LCC E169.12 .S44 2024 (print) | LCC E169.12 (ebook) | DDC 306.0973—dc23/eng/20230428
LC record available at https://lccn.loc.gov/2023017239
LC ebook record available at https://lccn.loc.gov/2023017240

Cover design: Jason Anscomb

For my friends, the good Company who've kept me laughing all these years and who—despite what the next 300 pages argue— have always seemed truly authentic.

Contents

The Authenticity Industries

INTRODUCTION

XXXXXX

Our Enduring Quest for Authenticity

This above all: to thine own self be true,
And it doth follow, as the night the day,
Thou canst not then be false to any man . . .
—POLONIUS, *Hamlet*, act 1, scene 3

Authenticity. If you can fake that, the rest will take care of itself.
—SETH GODIN, marketing guru[1]

A few decades into the twenty-first century, America obsesses over authenticity.

It can be felt in contexts far and wide, in cultures high and low, and is affirmed as both profound and superficial. It animates thirty years' worth of reality TV programming and fuels the explosive popularity of TikTok. It characterizes former president Donald Trump's willful disregard for political correctness (and spelling, grammar, and punctuation), as it did the vague vibe that more voters could see themselves cracking a beer with George W. Bush than with Al Gore. It inspires giant corporations toward political activism in ways that few brands dared before and buttresses a multibillion-dollar influencer industry of everyday folks shilling their friends with #spon-con. And in pop music, it is cited as the source of Bruce Springsteen's blue-collar credibility as well as hip-hop's doctrinaire injunction to "keep it real."

But authenticity is not actually real.

Or, at least, it doesn't exist objectively—that is, as some quality inherent in anything complimented as such. In the examples above, and many more to follow, this book will show how authenticity gets *made*, by talking with producers who cast reality television, technologists who design social media platforms, music industry leaders who manage artists, advertising executives who strategize brands, influencers who pose with products, and political consultants who run campaigns. *These* are the professionals who construct, communicate, and accentuate authenticity on behalf of their clients. And this book is a study of the mediated work they do behind the curtain.

The "mediated" part will be foregrounded throughout, because staging authenticity is, paradoxically, a project of creating that which seems *unmediated*. Social media's intrusion into any and all walks of life and work amplified this imperative—and scaffolded the architecture to enable it—but the yearning has been many decades in the making, pre-Friendster.

Back in the 1960s, one philosopher lamented how society had devolved from a more authentic lived experience into a passive, screen-dependent one.[2] Around the same time, another public intellectual similarly warned of a growing spectacle of "pseudo" events: news, images, and celebrity affairs concocted for the sake of the camera-world.[3] They were reporting from the dawn of a new TV age. A half-century later, as social distancing further atomized humanity amidst a global pandemic, our Zoom and FaceTime sessions fulfilled these bleak prophecies rather literally. Lives once lived in three dimensions were suddenly rendered depthless.

The pursuit of authenticity is, therefore, an effort to recover what remains human within us, at a time when society, commerce, and technology are grafted onto how we interface with the world. Authenticity asks what fundamentally drives us: internal, autonomous stirrings of self-actualization or acquiescence to social decorum and material needs? The more public that once-private lives become, the more that market logic seeps into our thinking and relations, the more that sameness and predictability are offered up by cultural environments—the more we're left searching for something "real" to grab onto and predicate an identity upon.

Authenticity is, therefore, nothing short of the central moral framework of our time: a quasi-religion for self-discovery; a way of coping with the conditions, anxieties, and external pressures of contemporary reality through ideals and pretenses of higher purpose and inner meaning. And an industry stands ready to sell us *precisely* that product.

Get Real

Throughout those early decades of the twenty-first century, the signs of that authenticity obsession dotted the media landscape, in ways both silly and revealing.

Time magazine, venerable scorekeeper of mainstream zeitgeist, declared it one of ten world-changing ideas.[4] In Netflix's *The Circle*, a reality show where new neighbors interact only online for competitive ratings—a meta-meditation on social media posturing—slicked-back bro Joey Sasso chalked up his victory to effortless authenticity: "I didn't have a strategy because I just always knew I had to be myself and I don't want to overthink anything."[5]

NBA legend LeBron James scored props for not outsourcing to his publicity team those "authentic" Instagram glimpses of his backstage life (lip-syncing raps! texts from Mom!).[6] An *Adweek* cover profiling actress Jennifer Lopez as "Brand Visionary" feted her in all the clichéd puff-piece ways—"both glamorous and authentic . . . appealingly aspirational and accessible"—with the star singing along: "I'm real. That was important to me—to stay connected to my roots and not ever change or make what people said or thought about me influence who I really was inside."[7] Even Buckingham Palace started angling for "more authenticity" online, posting childhood photos of Queen Elizabeth and home interiors kept hidden for decades.[8]

Among celebrities, authenticity was aesthetically affirmed through acts of disclosure, imperfection, and relatability: late-night comedians broadcasting nationally from their living rooms and TV stars unabashedly owning naturally gray roots and makeup-free selfies on social. This "aspirational realness" defined certain beauty and fashion brands, shooting models in "everyday places [like] urban street corners with parked cars and trash bags in full view."[9]

In journalism, *Vice*'s CEO touted authenticity as their "magic elixir," and former CNN head Jeff Zucker explained the network's tonal shift away from sober impartiality to more opinionated content, informal language, and "emotional rawness" likewise: "One of the things I've tried to encourage is authenticity and being real. If we pretend not to be human, it's not real."[10]

Out in Silicon Valley, a certificate of blockchain-based authenticity for nonfungible tokens drove digital art prices skyward, while a disposal camera emulator app, backed by lucrative venture capital, recreated the serendipitous delight of documenting nightlife escapades—authentically unfiltered, in the moment, rather than trying to perfect the performance of them with retakes and retouches.[11] More successful still, tens of millions of Gen Zers downloaded an app enjoining them to "BeReal" by showing friends just how mundane everyday lives could be.[12]

Within management journals, scholarly articles about authenticity more than doubled in the 2010s and a healthy portion of *Forbes'* SEO content mill proselytized its market value.[13] Facebook executive Sheryl Sandberg leaned into the trend, stressing that "leaders should strive for authenticity over perfection."[14] Even formal faith could not resist the seductive gospel: "In the search for sharing, for 'friends,' there is the challenge to be authentic and faithful, and not give in to the illusion of constructing an artificial public profile for oneself," Pope Benedict exhorted. "Everyone is confronted by the need for authenticity."[15]

In the past decade, *failures* of authenticity abounded as well: Scarlett Johansson was cast as the Japanese lead in a manga adaption; the Oberlin College cafeteria slapped pulled pork and coleslaw on ciabatta and called it a "banh mi"; and an Oprah-endorsed bestselling novel about Mexican migrants, written by a White lady, flubbed key details.[16]

Online, bunk circulated swiftly and convincingly. There was, of course, the great 2016 election disinformation crackup, wherein Russia seeded actual "fake news"—not to be confused with Trump's hijacking of the phrase for *unflattering* news—which Facebook and Twitter decried an "inauthenticity" problem.[17] Domestically, hundreds of "pink slime" propaganda operations popped up, posing as independent local news sites.[18]

Voice falsification was possible using as little as sixty seconds of machine-learned listening and the democratization of AI-deepfake tools heralded plausible video imitations of not just Barack Obama and Mark Zuckerberg—as early viral hits demonstrated—but any celebrity or noncelebrity who one might have pornographic imagination for.[19] In advance of the 2020 election, one tech nonprofit launched the emblematically named "Reality Defender" digital scanning tool to detect and expose such meddling: "The line between the real and fake is rapidly vanishing with enormous consequences to our society and democracy," its press release lamented.[20]

Indeed, as media scholar Gunn Enli forewarned, the more "unreal, staged, and manipulated" our mediated culture becomes, the greater the hope that authenticity might quench a thirst for what had been lost.[21] But what do we actually *mean by* authenticity—what does it signify on its own and how does it signify for us?

Defining Qualities of an Evasive Ideal

This panoply of examples, many previewing what later chapters will elaborate on, shows how slippery it is to categorize authenticity, as well as its ubiquity and centrality. It encompasses both Sarah Palin's hockey mom shtick and Bernie Sanders' undeterred legislative consistency; the Volkswagen Beetle's hippie roots and Harley Davidson's leathery ethos; Johnny Cash and Deepak Chopra; dive bars and farmers markets and greasy spoons; Bhutan, Cuba, and Williamsburg, Brooklyn. (Well, probably not Williamsburg anymore—Bushwick, maybe? Bed-Stuy?)

A brief taxonomic detour might help—mapping, theoretically, how scholars from varying disciplines have tried to nail down this mercurial term over the years. Rich Silverstein, creative director of a prominent San Francisco ad agency, similarly sputters when I ask him to define authenticity: "It immediately feels right in the gut—it's just immediate. It's just—there's no words for it, because you feel it."[22] And yet a semiotician as skilled as Silverstein surely can't shrug off as ineffable what also happens to be the first commandment of his life's work, advertising.

Etymologically, the word originates from the Greek *authentes*, which translates to "master" or "one acting on [one's] own authority"—a heritage of self-actualization we'll see traced through more recent contexts, in part because quelling suspicion of motives is essential to authentic performance and therefore key to the industrial work staging the appearance of it.[23]

In distant centuries, the term retained a more formal or technical quality, likely owing to its museum use: Was this artistic object, created by Vermeer or Matisse, really what it claimed to be and thus worth paying for?[24] This first kind of authenticity can be evaluated factually by experts based upon an indexical link to the referent represented and, thus, a point, place, or person of provenance it emerges from.[25] This is taken up, strategically, by the authenticity industries in their efforts to affirm the ideal origins of a client entity.

On the other hand, authenticity can be aesthetically approximated rather than verifiably absolute: It can fit our sense of what something seems like it *should* be rather than *actually*, necessarily, being that. Rather than binary, authenticity here is iconic, sensory, and subjectively graded, usually based upon stylized cues: Does the entity fit observers' abstract expectations and projections for the form or genre?[26] For example, if that *Old Guitarist* really is a Picasso, how come the perspective isn't cubistically deformed like we're used to seeing?

Authenticity, though, doesn't just hang on a wall, drape from one's shoulders, or sit on a dinner plate; it's also expressive in a social sense. This second kind of authenticity identifies an "original and unadulterated selfhood" and rejects "any force or process that separates or alienates the individual from their true identity, character, or sense of purpose," as scholars summarize.[27]

An authentic speaker sounds uncontrived, natural, spontaneous—never giving a performance and always delivering from some core experience of the world.[28] Reflecting this, the literary critic Lionel Trilling severs sincerity from authenticity, with the former term ("a congruence between avowal and actual feeling") capturing the ideal of presenting yourself honestly in public as you truly are.[29] Such is the fine line, we'll see, that politicians, reality stars, and you—across all your social media accounts—must navigate.

Along with those aesthetic affectations and that interpersonal integrity, authenticity might, third and finally, be emphasized in terms of motivational autonomy: How much does behavior seem to stem from extrinsic forces, like punishment or reward, rather than inherent inclinations and personal passions?[30] Philosopher Charles Guignon categorizes this as the "master dichotomy" of modernity: "What is inner is what is true, genuine, pure, and original, whereas what is outer is a mere shadow, something derived, adulterated and peripheral. . . . To be authentic, you must be in touch with what lies within, that is, the inner self, the self no one sees except you."[31]

Authenticity is tallied here as fidelity to one's internal compass and values rather than adapting identity to cultural norms or outright greed.[32] A work of art, for example, is authentic if it is uniquely true to itself: accommodating the independent muse of a single-minded creator; transgressing accepted formulaic limits as needed; and surely never done to appease any buyer or collector.[33] We'll hear this rhapsodized by rock stars and rappers alike in chapter 3.

Treating prior scholarship as word-salad thesaurus, authenticity registers across a wide range of overlapping synonyms, alphabetically assembled here: amateur, communal, consistent, craft, credible, direct, ethical, faithful, genuine, honest, human, innate, innocent, intimate, legitimate, naïve, natural, nonconforming, nonstandard, ordinary, organic, original, pure, raw, real, rooted, simple, sincere, spontaneous, traditional, true, unadulterated, unaffected, uncorrupted, unfiltered, and, of course, unmediated. The persistence of those "un-" prefixes attests to authenticity so often being a term of contrast: a positional social good, endlessly Othering, to delineate difference among people's penchants and practices (especially consumer) and hierarchically implying judgment.[34]

"You can only truly be an authentic person," the cultural critic Andrew Potter wittily discerns, "as long as most of the people around you are not."[35] Ironically, then, for all its self-aggrandizing claims to deep durability, authenticity is ever-unstable—"a relative concept which is generally used in absolutist terms"—both contextually dependent and subject to the vagaries of time and taste.[36]

Perhaps above all, authenticity must be *effortless*: "a self that appears to simply *be*, rather than a self that is accomplished," for to expose that labor of authenticity calls into question the claim of accomplishment as well as our collective faith in the concept itself.[37]

Rather impishly, that's exactly the ambition of this book.

Jean-Jacques Rousseau Can't Even

How did authenticity get here? When did it get here? Thousands of years ago, it would have had decidedly little use. Identity was so intertwined with and foreordained by family, tribe, and gods that a person wasn't even seen as independent from that interlocking cosmos of belonging.[38]

The philosopher Charles Taylor dates authenticity's conceptual birth to the late 1700s, when Enlightenment individualism fused with the soul-archaeology of the Romantic era.[39] Personal aspiration no longer had to be sacrificed, self-lessly, at the altar of some prevailing, sacred social order; thanks to Martin Luther, God Herself could be found one-on-one, outside the cathedral, in the stillness of contemplation, in the hush of an inner voice and the feelings that it stirred.[40]

Around this time, as interiority was established as a legit spatial-psychological domain, the self, itself, emerged as an "autonomous noun" and got imprinted on the cultural and physical landscape: autobiographies, introspective literature, portraits for posterity, individual plates and chairs at meals, and private rooms within the home.[41] On the plus side—for the Romantics—came a philosophical license to zealously defend that self against any external forces that might impede creativity, freedom, and actualization; alas, this came at the cost of a complete collapse of the hierarchy of meaning-making institutions and the shared social sensibilities structured by them.[42] You were now on your own, authenticity shrugged—for better or worse.

If anyone would've swooned at that prospect, it was the patron saint and intellectual godfather of authenticity, Jean-Jacques Rousseau. Though he apparently never uses the term directly, it undeniably animates his being and informs his core ideas: the embrace of an essential inner light; misgivings about societal strictures; nostalgia for childhood spontaneity; and veneration of capital-n Nature.[43] His most famous phrase—"man was born free, and he is everywhere in chains"—often shorthands an entire philosophical schema and telegraphs his low regard for repressive rules and social decorum.[44]

Rousseau contributed vitally to that introspective turn in human culture— liberating self-discovery as morally righteous duty, rather than being molded by outside pressures, and expressing yourself "openly, with full candor, and without any embellishing or editing."[45] As he autobiographically confesses, "Thrown, in spite of myself, into the great world, without possessing its manners, and unable to acquire or conform to them, I took it into my head to adopt manners of my own, which might enable me to dispense with them."[46] This is just a grandiloquent, eighteenth-century version of the reality TV cliché, "I didn't come here to make friends."

In delineating the real from the artificial, what matters most for Rousseau— and what we'll hear echoed, especially in later chapters on political communication strategy—was *feelings*, not rationality.[47] For just as children, in their purity, have yet to learn the "perfidious veil of politeness" that civilization imposes, so, too, should adults aim to emulate the supposedly noble savage, outside of or predating corrupt modern life and its culturally refined customs.[48] A solitary life, off-the-radar, perambulating Walden Pond, is about the best one can salvage.[49] Admire those who seem motivationally sovereign: those defined by "perfect autonomy of [their] consciousness," without regard for others or outside demands.[50] All of this, by the way, makes the truly authentic person a real jerk to deal with.

Yet Rousseau's impulses are, nonetheless, understandable, given the pressures of modern life, which would have been first crystallizing around his time. For authenticity, as a concept, was produced by and reacting to changes in the Western world in the eighteenth and nineteenth centuries: "the slow recession of belief in a cosmic order with fixed and unquestionable roles, the countervailing idea of individual selfhood . . . the rise of capitalism and wage labor, the growing authority of science and Enlightenment appeals to rationality," as scholars Meredith Salisbury and Jefferson Pooley summarize.[51] In particular, urbanization, commercialization, and industrialization—that trifecta of modern woe to be disentangled shortly—contributed to the increasing centrality of authenticity within lived experience.[52]

Perhaps *that* was the ideal that could help piece back together a Humpty Dumpty sense of self—a lost wholeness, a coherence fragmented by these forces.[53] The anxieties impressing upon authenticity would only increase in the past hundred years, becoming, by midcentury, "the defining concept" of the era."[54] And Rousseau's ideas remain the still-timeless wellspring for appreciating authenticity's appeal within and against contemporary culture: the starting point, philosophically, for venerating spontaneity, emotion, and unfiltered engagement with the world.

Backstage Scheming with the Two-Faced Self

"While 'the savage lives within himself, [the] sociable man, always outside himself, can only live in the opinion of others.' "[55] So sneers Rousseau, who gazed back upon the "natural state" of our ancient ancestors with wondrous envy: Their limited contact with each other, in the epoch of hunting and gathering, limited the benefit of chasing distinguishing qualities for tribal admiration.[56] Then the development of cities, in the history of humankind, introduced the weight of anonymity: "People were no longer quite sure where they belonged, what their futures held for them, or who their neighbors were," the anthropologist Charles Lindholm writes, a diagnosis as relevant today as centuries ago. "They had begun the irreversible plunge into modernity, which can be succinctly defined as the condition of living among strangers."[57]

Seeds of doubt sprouted about the "staged, prepared, and performed" character of *inauthentic* communication in those public spaces.[58] One's true self could only be found in private life, set apart from the "artificial existence" of "playing games and reciting lines."[59] Rousseau reserves special disgust for those unoriginal, "other-directed," conformist types: those "whose whole being is attuned to catch the signals sent out by the consensus of his fellows . . . to the extent that he is scarcely a self at all, but rather, a reiterated impersonation."[60] The poet Oscar Wilde likewise grieves, "Most people are other people. Their thoughts are someone else's opinions, their lives a mimicry, their passions a quotation."[61]

For half a century, scholars have drawn upon the ideas of sociologist Erving Goffman to map these dynamics, and his work remains inimitable to understanding authenticity, in large part because routine habits on social media render explicit his pre-digital insights about everyday life. Goffman furnished this enduring metaphor about human experience: that our interpersonal interactions are like theater, projecting particular versions of ourselves for particular audiences based upon the roles we assume appropriate.

To influence others' impressions, we scheme these frontstage "performances" decorously—acting one way in front of a boss, another way in front of a child—while privately backstage (among intimate associates or simply by ourselves, in our own minds), that charade might well be contradicted or even castigated.[62] Absent any such "pretense and superficiality," this backstage entices: "It is here that illusions and impressions are openly constructed. . . . Here the performer can relax; he can drop his front, forgo speaking his lines, and step out of character."[63] Here the authenticity industries researcher snoops.

Because of that, backstage access must be jealously guarded, lest audiences catch a glimpse of the true(ish) self of the performer—and the more famous a person is, the less time and space they tend to be afforded for social seclusion.[64] Yet this "informal, familiar, relaxed" version of the performer is also what the authenticity industries increasingly try to *perform*: frontstaging the backstage, if you will, especially as media tools afford and audiences demand something more "real" behind the pseudo-event.[65] The more that content from private life is both possible for public view and (for now) still generally assumed innocent—rather than calculated—the more that mundane and vulnerable revelations staged there can authenticate those with instrumental ambitions.

Thus, this book follows in the tradition of applying Goffman's theories of microsocial interaction to entire fields of image-making collective labor like entertainment, technology, advertising, and politics.[66] Throughout, I'll shorthand this problem as the "two-faced self," contrasting my interviewees' counterefforts to stage their clients as "real"—meaning (projected as) the same both on- and offstage.

Yet because authenticity needs to seem effortless, the blood, sweat, and tears of all that self-work has to remain invisible, if the actor is to come off as "natural."[67] You could call this strategy "performing-not-performing," where a person always seems to be themselves, no matter who they're conversing with.[68] This, by the way, is why politicians forever face dubious audiences, assuming the same scripted speech has been given before: Extemporaneity, by contrast, indexes sincerity, so it's a great plan to come across as impromptu.[69]

As chapters 1 and 3 will show, this also holds true in entertainment, namely the artistic ideal of expunging the opinions of others and society in order to "let the unconscious creative process work itself out."[70] As rapper Method Man righteously avers: "Basically, I make music that represents me. Who I am. I'm not gonna calculate my music to entertain the masses. I gotta keep it real for me."[71]

Cash Rules Everything Around Me

"What is authentic?" novelist Michael Crichton asks. "Anything that is not devised and structured to make a profit. Anything that is not controlled by the corporations. Anything that exists for its own sake, that assumes its own shape."[72]

This second lament of inauthenticity—one that I'll term "marketplace motives" throughout the book—has centuries-old roots, much like the two-faced self. One might trace it back to the development of capitalism itself, and the attendant estrangement of societies, where meaning was evacuated from work, save for the necessary paycheck it produced.[73]

Such alienation stems from the feeling that we really only relate to one another through the nihilistic mechanisms of the marketplace and the "devilish autonomous energy" of money—an *inauthentic* energy "that was seen to change everything into something it was not," as Karl Marx bemoaned.[74] Work, moreover, often demands a two-faced self, suppressing resentment and shamming servility to supervisors, while an authentic self is "not defined by your job, or your function, or your role," TV psychologist Dr. Phil consoles. "It is all your strengths and values that are uniquely yours and need expression, versus what you have been programmed to believe that you are 'supposed to be and do.'"[75]

But the wonders that paycheck can buy! Wouldn't consumption—a Netflix binge, an overnight Prime delivery, some nice avocado toast—feed the hunger for authenticity, even if our roles in the means of production didn't? Alas, the Frankfurt School, a group of Marxist philosopher-critics, suggest no such satisfaction, savaging the culture industry: for in pursuing the lowest common denominator for mass audiences, media content gets homogeneously churned off assembly lines and panders rather than enlightens—an "organ of soft domination"—lulling the proletariat into docile conformity.[76]

For these dissenters, authenticity was forever tainted by "the logic and constraints of capitalism, a force that was determined to process and standardize art, products, and services at the expense of their genuine and original qualities."[77] Consumer culture might tantalize gratification, but it delivers only "store-bought baubles" that are "pre-packaged, mass-produced, and shallow"; Amazon offers speedy, never existential, fulfillment.[78] And the more lonely and alienating working lives become, the more junk is bought to placate an insatiable inner being.[79]

For shopping sheep, it's a never-ending, unscratchable itch: "members of the herd, cogs in the machine, victims of mindless conformity [who] lead vacuous, hollowed-out lives ruled by shallow, materialistic values."[80] The quest for authenticity is, then, a countercultural yearning to experience individual identity *outside* the spectacle of commodities—which cues, in turn, the marketplace's effort to satisfy those alternative longings, often through craft production pretenses, as we'll see in chapter 4.[81]

This has also defined creative desires in the myth of an independent bohemian genius uncorrupted by compromising commercial constraints.[82] We see it in the adoration of entrepreneurialism that fetishizes the "free" laborer side-hustling their way to the American Dream, one Uber fare at a time.[83] In social media and influencer practices of later chapters, these values presume a continuum with the creativity and amateurism of authenticity located at one end and the promotion, commerce, and professionalism of capitalism diametrically opposed at the other.[84] As media scholar Sarah Banet-Weiser notes, all this makes for an uneasy tension between art's innocent ambitions to achieve "enlightenment, transcendence, and the sublime" and the market economy's grubby, greedy goals of profit, through that which is "planned, fake, calculating, and marketed."[85]

This formulaic quality of cultural production—hedging against the risk of all-too-frequent flops in the entertainment business—conscripts and contains the authentic "singularity" of a given work and the authentic inventiveness of its artist, whose ambition ought to be as "self-defining" as the opus generated.[86] Ironically, of course, artists whose authenticity is beyond reproach can actually bag *more* money for their work, but once it appears they're doing it for the dough—and not "*from the heart*"—it costs both cred and cash.[87]

To be sure, critics have been slagging "selling out" for nearly two centuries, when capitalism and industrialization intruded upon the tradition of aristocratic patronage and creators suddenly had to concern themselves with, and contort themselves to, popular preferences.[88] It plagues allegations of abandoning values for wealth or power in politics, and these allegations persist as loudly in chapter 3's world of pop, where fans sweat beloved musicians chasing mainstream popularity, "going commercial," and abandoning die-hard loyalists who loved the first album before they blew up.[89]

Whether it's a candidate for office or a rocker onstage, a shared suspicion holds that someone "who should be trusted to act independently is no longer doing so."[90] To be authentic, then, is to reject bourgeois benefits—to remain "a nonconformist, a solitary rebel at odds and out of step with the mainstream," never allowing "creativity to atrophy in the name of comfort and security."[91]

Yet while marketplace motives recur throughout, as a mistrust the authenticity industries must strategize around, this book also interrogates whether "selling out" still has any currency as a catchphrase or underlying concept of derision, now that we're so steeped in neoliberal logics. It assumes a binary of authenticity versus complicity, when selling out has adeptly replenished capitalism's co-optation of counterculture for several decades.[92] Indeed, the landscape illustrated in the chapters that follow show advertising infiltrating social media feeds, political activism, and interpersonal relations, even as it tries to "blend in" with that native content and those experiences.

When market mentalities are ubiquitous within and inextricable from those culture industries, when "commercialization and self-branding are hardwired into the technologies made for self-expression," and when Gen Z seems to shrug about the trade-off, selling out no longer retains the same meaning, much less fortitude to preserve non-market-based spaces and motivations.[93] If resistance to selling out is a luxury relic of an earlier, less ad-choked era, how can one afford *not* to sell out these days?

Rage Against the Machines

If inauthenticity bedevils interpersonal interactions (i.e., the two-faced self) as well as acts of creation (marketplace motives), it also maps onto a third suspicion: mass-produced homogeneity. I'll shorthand this problem throughout the book as "technological standardization." As with other themes in the chapter, this, too, traces distant historical and theoretical lineage, namely sociologist Max Weber diagnosing disenchantment with rationalization, scientific modernity, and the loss of supernatural wonderment.[94]

Nineteenth-century industrialization—in work, especially, but with a logic of reason spilling over into other arenas of human experience—framed efficiency, automation, and quantity as unsurpassed values.[95] The writer George Orwell observed, "Machines have become a modernist habit of the mind," such that even if you smashed them to bits—as the Luddite weavers famously did—they'd be swiftly restored, having prevailed in our cultural sensibility as the correct way to do things.[96] Weber's world-weariness longed for a lost Eden—technological civilization had severed human "contact with the earth and the rhythms that our ancestors had," misguidedly dominating nature in both the countryside and the deep recesses of the soul.[97]

Central to these anxieties about industrial inauthenticity is the ubiquitous uniformity it produces. It becomes ever harder to suss out what's "real" when an original copy of some cultural artifact can be forever cloned, with ever greater digital fidelity.[98] The Frankfurt School fretted over this as well, terming the authenticity of such an artifact "aura," or belief in the "charismatic radiance [that] emanates from the singularity of the work" itself—that is, the handmade, unique, moral authority of an artist's creation.[99]

Aura is what, theoretically, compels tourists to crowd a Louvre gallery where the Mona Lisa hangs, even when the tacky replication of her image is easily available on key chains and mouse pads and beer koozies. How, then, can authenticity be based upon being "one of a kind" if the gift shop shows there's plenty for sale?[100]

That loss of aura is not just visible—and regrettable—in the standardization of singular artifacts but across whole landscapes of life: the stultifying ennui of nondescript office parks, suburban tract homes, and casual dining chains. Inauthenticity lurks in the fear and loathing of every city becoming Disney's Celebration, Florida: a "community" master-planned and prefabbed to chipper, generically dystopian extremes.[101]

Franchising, in particular, telegraphs McWorld alienation, for corporations tend to breed formulaic operations, the erosion of local neighborhood character, and the primacy of profits.[102] Because of this, corporations have been desperate for authenticating social legitimacy since their inception a century ago, and much early public relations sought to bequeath a "soul" upon these faceless monoliths—a task we'll see extended in the brand politics of chapter 4, now that the soul needs to have a say about hot-button issues.[103]

All of this unsettles: In the wake of authentic local spaces bulldozed by homogeneity, it's hard to know *where* we are, at any given time, which, in turn, makes it hard to know *who* we are.[104] Against that angst, cultural theorist Andreas Reckwitz diagnoses societies in thrall to "singularities"—that is, nonstandardized objects, spaces, and experiences that fulfill cultural and emotional yearnings rather than the functional needs that assembly lines might once have simply satisfied.[105] The interchangeability of much of our lives' surroundings suggests an unsettling emptiness beneath.

Travel often sells itself as existential solution, beckoning with exotic, undiscovered alternatives more distinct and traditional than the usual routine.[106] Travel bloggers, for example, tout their "inner self-realization" and flex like backpacking Rousseaus: "The choice to leave everything behind is presented as an act of rebellion against the social norm."[107] Yet even tourism is, itself, an authenticity industry, happy to commodify and cater to that experience, stocking trinkets of local culture to show the squares back home that you went on a trip—even if your modern-day Magellan is just grabbing a few snow globes at Hudson News before the flight boards.[108]

Meanwhile, the inauthenticity of technology plagues us, as human experience seems ever more governed by interaction with algorithms, Big Data, and artificial intelligence. Some of these anxieties are, as elsewhere, far from novel. Ever since AOL began rewiring life in the 1990s, there's been a pervasive, and mistaken, assumption that what's online is fake and what's offline is real: "On the internet, nobody knows you're a dog," in the conventional wisdom of the *New Yorker*'s cartoon canine.[109]

Nonetheless, the more virtual that everyday experience becomes, crescendoing with the pandemic, and the more that "post-human" lives merge with machines, thanks to technological augmentation, the more we seem to crave authentic alternatives.[110] Tallying a decade's worth of scams, grifts, and "alternative facts"—so many online, from Trump's disinformation trolls to WeWork and Theranos start-up flameouts to fraudulent social media bots to a Fyre Festival fiasco—*New York Times* columnist Farhad Manjoo summarizes the lessons of the 2010s: "Almost nothing is as it seems. Doubt everything. Trust no one."[111]

Contra these forces of technological standardization, a series of aligned authenticity archetypes entice. One that will recur, especially in discussions of social media amateurism and multinational brand identity, is that of the "craft" ideal—a longing for the nonindustrialized, handmade, and traditional that is somehow morally superior to the mass-produced.[112] Here, the artisanal affects authenticity—a premodern purity of spirit and wholeness of purpose rather than being engineered for profit, imbuing a product with aura, just as it did with sacred art.[113] Aesthetically, as we'll see throughout later chapters, a "rough cut" beats a polished one if something or someone needs to seem more realistic.

In winemaking, for example, impersonal scientific and industrial methods are downplayed in favor of a production ethos more simple, random, and intuitive: "When the grapes are ready, they're ready," a vintner shrugs to branding scholar Michael Beverland, unperturbed by modern bustle and showcasing an embrace of slow quality over speedy quantity.[114] Likewise, the family-run business, the mom-and-pop diner, the locally sourced food supply—all these are accompanied by adjectives of authenticity admiration: sentimental, organic, low-impact, nonhierarchical.[115]

There's a healthy market for goods that, being unique, can reflect the uniqueness of consumers and narcissistically differentiate them from the homogenous masses (slandered, per youth slang, as "basic bitches").[116] From IPA beers to vinyl albums to indie cinema, what's local and uncommercialized counters the onslaught of globalized, corporatized sameness.[117] Before furniture became industrially manufactured, for example, marble and refined wood elicited fashionable envy, but once "anything could be made to look like anything else," a more natural, rustic look ascended as aesthetically authentic among tastemakers; better still nowadays, "a table hammered together in the garage" by some DIY hobbyist.[118]

And the pursuit of authenticity is arguably fiercest within those niches where mass-produced, multinational competitors vie for market share.[119] This is one reason that product personalization purportedly persuades. If purchasing for identity, an unfinished item to be tailored uniquely—whether that be a Build-a-Bear or Tesla—can better express ourselves as real than some "off-the-shelf" SKU.[120] Authenticity thus spins stories of craft tradition and anti-commercialism, because these are savvy ways to sell us stuff—that, ultimately, frustratingly, anyone else can buy just as easily.[121]

An Edenic Fable

To summarize, then, authenticity responds to this threefold estrangement of modern life: alienating urbanization (i.e., being unknown and surrounded by strangers, with whom social rules must govern two-faced-self conduct); alienating capitalism (i.e., having to constantly sell ourselves to survive, being motivated by marketplace needs); and alienating industrialization (i.e., lives and spaces calibrated and homogenized by technology and machinery to bland effect).

A similar distillation defines authenticity as that which is not "of man" (i.e., "*qualifying* one's choices by the norms of society"); not "monetary" (i.e., "*commercializing* any activity"); and not "mechanical" (i.e., "*altering* the natural order").[122] This alliterative trifecta of woe—man, money, and machine—represents that which the authenticity industries have to compensate for in producing media and culture for disenchanted audiences, consumers, and citizens. And all of this underscores a nostalgia intrinsic to authenticity for what feels adrift in our contemporary world.[123]

Edenic analogies abound, as summarized by the cultural critic Andrew Potter: "In the beginning, humans lived in a state of original authenticity, where all was harmony and unity. At some point . . . we became separated from nature, from society, and even from ourselves. . . . Our great spiritual project is to find our way back to that original and authentic unity. . . . Modernity is the reason we have lost touch with whatever it is about human existence that is meaningful."[124]

Efforts to recover that authenticity have persisted across time and space. For example, in the late 1800s, when more "authentic" lifestyles were receding from view, the folk museum was invented to preserve rituals and traditions.[125] The appeal of authenticity also registers in the conservation of small-town Main Streets, the restoration of faux-old architecture, and in country music's cowboy archetype—"a self-reliant . . . child of nature, unfettered by the constraints of urban society."[126]

Contemporary consumers gravitate toward authentic "symbols of agrarian simplicity (organic beets, folk music)" and "the gritty charms of proletarian life (Pabst Blue Ribbon beer, trucker hats)," urban sociologist David Grazian observes.[127] "Organic" acts as moral halo, whether stamped explicitly on foodstuffs or evoked vaguely by cultural artifacts (e.g., *MTV Unplugged*), warding off suspicion of technological standardization.[128] And authenticity courses, leisurely, through the Slow Food movement, contrasting the "existential anomie" of mechanized McWorld habits that eat away at both physical health and communal traditions—this, a subset of the larger Slow Movement that stands athwart our manic capitalist culture of speed, productivity, and abundance, yelling, "Unplug!"[129]

Authenticity aspirations are hardly exclusive to the Western world: Witness the antimodern, separatist purity of Wahhabi ideology and the Islamist implementations and critiques espoused by Al-Qaeda and ISIS.[130] And the hippie cosplay mecca that is Burning Man annually serves up the fullest gemeinschaft experiment in authenticity, contra capitalism: forbidding sales, masking logos, and enforcing a barter economy to temporarily restore a space for artistic expression, countercultural exchange, and spontaneous community.[131] Society (and clothing, as I understand it) too often gets in the way of that.

A Cartography of Authenticity, From the Margins

Where does authenticity come from? That Burning Man takes place off-the-grid, in a remote Nevada desert, feels apropos, for authenticity has a distinctly spatial bias worth mapping. This continuum is found across social, pop, political, and geographic contexts: It pits mainstream versus subculture; mediated versus underground; centrist versus polarized. The edges and margins of these various life-worlds are where authenticity remains most fertile relative to the phony masses who play it safe in the middle in their fandom, consumption, and voting habits.

Media theorist Sarah Thornton evokes a similar set of binaries: "the esoteric versus the exposed, the exclusive versus the accessible, the pure versus the corrupted, the 'independent' versus the 'sold out.'"[132] Ironically, then, a mohawked punk at CBGB and a Brooks Brothers–clad activist at CPAC talk and think in the same underlying terms, even as they have decidedly different attitudes toward, well, everything.

To that end, authenticity ever Others: romanticizing a simplistic, "uncorrupted" representation of what's foreign or countercultural from a "Western, white, middle-class" backdrop.[133] Squalor supposedly, misguidedly, authenticates—a "bohemian rhapsody" to a less hygienic, willfully imperfect lifestyle pose, perversely fixating on "hardship and disadvantage" to generate "status, prestige, or value" within the economy of cultural and geographic legitimacy.[134]

Ever since suburbia took shape in the postwar years—with its tract housing and homogenous conformity—Levittown has been synonymous with middle-class anomie: "fake, artificial, unreal, and ersatz, offering a mere simulacrum of real living to people who are either too dim or too brainwashed by advertising to know better," tallies one summary of those snobby judgments.[135]

By contrast, deindustrialized, dangerous, and diverse downtown neighborhoods furnish the exploitable aesthetic difference (and cheap rents) for modern-day slumming Rousseaus—edge-worlds garnering buzz before inevitable gentrification and displacement by real estate developers and bougier brunch joints.[136] Manhattan's SoHo was the O.G. textbook example of this, where once-abandoned factories gave way to avant-garde galleries that gave way to chain pharmacies.[137]

Some of the same geographic and socioeconomic biases of authenticity pervade cultural expression, particularly pop music. Midcentury jazz and beat scenes were born of nonconformity, bequeathing an indie ethos idealized for decades hence.[138] Country music corroborates its "southern, working-class, rural, and unschooled" origins with "real music about real life for real people"—in contrast to high-falutin' folk who put on airs (i.e., the inauthenticity that comes with the trappings of wealth).[139] And like blues before it, hip-hop's authenticity is steeped in origin stories of racial marginalization—a meta-"Message," from Grandmaster Flash onward, that threads itself through nearly all rap.

It, too, has spatial authenticity, anchoring itself in the "street"—a term used to signal the geographic, communal roots of the art form, as well as the symbolic point of "keepin' it real," from which to measure potential sellout distance (and also partly explain why so many artists namecheck their native neighborhoods in rhymes).[140] 2Pac's rejoinder to haters in his 1996 hit, "I Ain't Mad at Cha," embodies the legitimizing power of one's mailing address: "So many questions, and they ask me if I'm still down / I moved up out of the ghetto, so I ain't real now?"[141]

Similarly, in the art world, gallery organizers might embellish the rough, squalid edges of an artist's biography ("from gang membership to mental disabilities"), even if they hail from "stable, middle-class families," to help exoticize their creations from mainstream culture.[142] The work of Shepard Fairey, Banksy, and others evinces this "cultural capital of the street," increasingly leveraged to more staid branding schemes.[143]

As that last example suggests, authenticity is commodifiable, even as— and precisely because—it is born of the absence of those marketplace motives. Within the trend-spotting business, detailed in chapter 4, the cool rebel has long been hunted along exotic societal edges and economic margins.[144] Alas, as *New Yorker* staffer Malcolm Gladwell's puzzled some three decades ago, "the act of discovering cool is what causes cool to move on"—a problem only exacerbated in the years since by the speed at which internet culture moves.[145]

In chasing external motives (money, popularity, acceptability, etc.), any previous internal authenticity gets watered down—a softer, safer version of the original, co-opted and peddled to the masses.[146] This continuum from pure integrity to calculating compromise holds as true in rock music as in electoral politics: Pink Floyd's *The Piper at the Gates of Dawn* is to *Dark Side of the Moon* is to *The Division Bell* as Bernie Sanders' single-payer, Medicare-for-all is to the public option is to Obamacare.

And authenticity, in the end, doesn't *have* an endpoint: It doesn't stay put; it's not permanent; it's restless, squirrelly, transforming with the times. Today's authenticity is tomorrow's ersatz; yesterday's effortless is today's trying-too-hard. Such dynamism, such evasiveness shows up most palpably in the landscapes of fashion, travel, and urban development, but also weighs upon technological platforms, electoral seasons, and consumer goods.

Facebook was authentic once, as was George W. Bush and Starbucks—and probably still are, to some people, in some ways. But there's no guarantee they'll always be. That's not how authenticity works.

Telling Origin Stories

One practice, shown throughout the book, is to scheme and stage an "aura of genealogical authenticity"—or, put simply, the origin stories of clients (e.g., musicians, brands, politicians, etc.).[147] This often anchors them geographically in "contrast to the apparent placelessness" of standardization and duplication; alternately, it can emphasize an originating point in the past.[148] Such "traditionalizing" can also aim to connect clients to classic production techniques and formulas as well as histories and spaces from a way of life receding from view, thus satisfying that nostalgic hunger.[149] "Inventing" tradition, through ritual and symbolism borrowed from the past, legitimates individuals, actions, or solidarities during eras of disruption and transformation—and those seem to be constant in the modern world.[150]

A "coherent biographical narrative" can also secure genealogical authenticity, especially in an era when identity remains so central to our politics and culture.[151] Audiences seemingly *need* to see themselves reflected in mediated forms (e.g., reality TV star, pop artist, consumer brand, elected leader, etc.) if those forms' authenticity is to be believed, and we'll see interviewees laboring to this end throughout the book.

Moreover, because "authenticity equals ancestry," the former is frequently judged by proving lineage with the latter—biography imbuing ensuing content with meaning and legitimacy.[152] Thus, identity politics are forged by "imagined 'authentic' group identities" and afforded to leaders who can model those "alleged characteristics of the group"; battles pitched over identity politics frequently boil down to who has "the right to speak authentically" on behalf of the group.[153]

Recent failures in this regard include the author of *American Dirt*, Senator Elizabeth Warren's purported Cherokee DNA, and Rachel Dolezal's NAACP leadership masquerade. In Hollywood, Native American and Muslim American consultancies help films stage appropriately "authentic" representations of those co-cultural groups.[154] "If you have a gay character [in a show or film], you have to have someone who's gay [involved in the production] . . . You need somebody there who knows what it feels like to be that person," declares the co-creator of *Glee* and *Pose*, crystallizing conventional authenticity industry wisdom.[155]

Yet this logic applies to historically White, straight genres as well: Audiences for country music, for example, expect those stars to be true to their lyrics—"men and women who could just as well be farmers, truck drivers, construction workers, housewives, or hairdressers," for their "ordinariness" gives them license to seem real in performance, as we'll see demanded of and staged for reality stars, politicians, and influencers alike.[156]

Authenticity operates within racialized and gendered confines, as shown throughout the book, with certain identities privileged, traditionally, for retaining the authority to define authenticity and therefore benefit from it. This is acutely apparent in the double bind that female politicians face, most conspicuously in 2016's US presidential showdown, detailed in chapter 7—when supporters and press alike exalted Donald Trump for "telling it like it is," while seizing upon Hillary Clinton's presumed façades.

Chapter 5 analogizes this tension to female social media influencers burdened by a pressure to come across as authentic yet also curate their beauty through filters and other postproduction techniques not expected of male counterparts; that is, if authentic masculinity is more able to indulge unrefined performance, authentic femininity has been granted the privilege much less often, which adds to the already exhausting costs in those social spaces. And as chapter 3 demonstrates of blues and hip-hop, African Americans' experience of marginalization is treated as a fount of authenticity—even as it is "yet another trope manipulated for cultural capital."[157]

Thus, while birthright makes for "the easiest sort of authenticity work," in terms of granting representational license, it also sets up a "cruel trap," where an individual's ambition—artistically or politically—is hailed when relayed from their demographically native turf, but also often pigeonholed to that ascribed group identity.[158] In the Trump era, especially, identity politics became a defining, ubiquitous, contentious force in American culture: "a tool for equality, or a means of exclusion . . . a rallying cry for America's minorities, or a torch lit by white nationalists," as *New York Times* critic Carlos Lozada summarizes.[159]

Authenticity is, in turn, a means of exercising power: It is how institutions convince groups and individuals of the legitimacy of their machinations or render rivals' ambitions unacceptable.[160] Edward Bernays, public relations' godfather, understood the importance of authenticity as essential to governing the masses "invisibly" by engineering their consent.[161] But authenticity is equally important to individuals: a "moral quest" to discover a stable identity within the fluid chaos of the postmodern world—when doubts abound about divining real from fake.[162]

That authenticity quest is, above all, spiritual. For in the absence of durable metanarratives—be they religious or political—that guide one through life and civilizations through history, and the abandonment of trust in externally sourced motives, the struggle for meaning becomes "interiorized" and authenticity an effort to locate the "God within."[163] Thus, all that "quasi Biblical jargon of authenticity" venerating "unity, wholeness, and harmony" offers, often unknowingly, a "religious way of thinking" for believers otherwise "disenchanted" with institutions that would have traditionally provided those ideals, but have either abandoned them or seen them wither into irrelevance.[164]

Authenticity tells us how to live our lives—not just in spite of, but *because* of the cynicism of our media age.[165] "Our demand for authenticity is partly a response to living in a fake, constructed world, to being manipulated over the airwaves at every moment of the day, to the way virtual communication is cutting out human contact," writes David Boyle, a British journalist. "[We] judge the authenticity of things and ideas by whether or not they are human-scale . . . rather than trying to squeeze us into whatever shape is most convenient for the factory, machine, or computer. . . . Authenticity may mean natural or beautiful, it may mean rooted geographically or morally, but behind all that it means human."[166]

Hence, survey research by leading pollster John Zogby finds that "desire for authenticity" tops the list of Americans' political and cultural preferences.[167] Powerful entities in media, culture, and politics recognize that yearning: "The rapid pace of social, political, and technological change has clearly increased the consumer's need for *authenticity*," acknowledges the CEO of Nestle, a capitalist colossus whose humungous, homogenous output simultaneously contributes to the problem it wants to solve.[168]

The book is a study of those purported and projected solutions.

Method Acted

With this scholarship as backdrop, authenticity can be defined as both a wanderlust for liberation from the woes of modernity (i.e., the two-faced self, marketplace motives, and technological standardization)—one might call this *existential* authenticity—and a savvy strategic presentation by media-makers, businesses, and politicians to satisfy this powerful existential urge—one might call this *mediated* or *produced* authenticity. Paradoxically, there is an intricate industry to concoct authenticity, and authenticity is one of humankind's enduring core virtues and identities that cannot be counterfeited.[169]

It is, therefore, both authentically felt and authentically faked: a moral ideal, rooted in the yearnings of Rousseau onward and presumed within the modern subject, and also contrived for them as audiences, consumers, and citizens. This makes it an unmanageable quality: sought out because, by definition, it cannot be rendered, even as my interviewees here elaborately scheme it so.[170]

Authenticity draws upon symbolic resources that help people establish how real or false a representation ought to be considered.[171] Yet it is not *just* discursive and adjudicating; authenticity is also, as this book tracks, theatrical and industrialized. *Someone* is supplying those resources—symbolic engineers, you might call them—and they are fashioning authenticity, every day, in entertainment, technology, advertising, and politics.[172] It is both "constructed and constructive," and having spent the preceding pages scaffolding the latter—unpacking, at times abstractly and theoretically, that existential authenticity—the chapters that follow will excavate, empirically, the former and detail the dimensions of mediated or produced authenticity.[173]

What, then, is it that professionals in these authenticity industries actually *do*? They pitch shows and cull casting calls; they design websites and manage bands; they make ads and pose with products; they run campaigns and write speeches. But even this panoramic depiction of content creation across contemporary contexts runs narrow and procedural. Media scholar David Hesmondhalgh's canonic categorization of *Cultural Industries*—"institutions most directly involved in the production of social meaning"—points toward the bigger picture and upshot.[174]

These professionals formulate and shape representations, discourses, practices, and settings that allow individuals and communities to position themselves in the world and define their identities.[175] The authenticity industries represent a slice of those wider cultural industries or, perhaps more accurately, a lens through which to view a slice of that work. To be certain, in the process of generating and circulating symbolic texts in politics, advertising, and pop culture, none of the folks interviewed here would consciously consider themselves part of an "authenticity industry," even as I hope to make the case that such a frame fits their output in revealing ways.

Again, we often mistakenly perceive authenticity as an innate quality in the mediations encountered—in part, because innateness, without the appearance of mediation, is essential to authenticating those claims. But this variety of industries, ironically, "invest their lifeblood in producing the very authenticity they tell us cannot be manufactured."[176] It might seem natural, uncontrived, and innate, but that's because it's been *orchestrated* to seem so: It is media work that labors to seem effortless; puppetry that effaces its own fingerprints; encoding that denies anyone ever wrote a script for the performance. The book thus hunts for how that authenticity is "staged, fabricated, crafted, or otherwise imagined" by such industries of media and culture.[177]

Other scholars' phrases effectively, even sardonically, capture the conceit here. Media scholar Jefferson Pooley coins "calculated authenticity" to describe microlevel machinations of interpersonal interaction (i.e., the self-work of performance and promotion, the conscious con-job behind our backstage curtains), which is mapped onto industrial-level schemes in these pages.[178] Another analogous turn of phrase is "strategic authenticity," something often seen on social media that's applied across contexts here.[179] And "fabricating authenticity" is offered by sociologist Richard Peterson, who pioneered the template for cultural production research of it.[180]

This book departs from that industrial perspective, a valuable lens for understanding media products—and how symbolic creators imbue them with meaning—and, yet, an approach less utilized than textual analysis or effects studies.[181] Following the work of media scholar Vicki Mayer, I look at "how specific production sites, actors, or activities tell us larger lessons about . . . culture," gathering the routines, rituals, and processes of these professionals and how political, economic, and technological pressures shape their labor.[182]

Because these various media industries (music, advertising, politics, etc.) face tumultuous economic, cultural, and technological challenges, authenticity is eyed lustily by those who produce content as a "realistic" solution to them. Moreover, these professionals themselves often see authenticity *as* real, even as we discuss, at length, the means by which they labor to make their clients *seem* real; quoting their representations of their work does not imply taking their claims at face value. (Moreover, access to these production spaces is tough to finagle, which explains the relative paucity of studies of them, and, as Mayer cautions, there's often a difference between what subjects say and what they actually do; my hopes for getting out into the field to observe sites and events, triangulating in-person, were dashed when the pandemic crashed down and forced remote, socially distanced conditions.[183])

For in manufacturing that authenticity through mediated domains, it is, again, a task of effortless effort: making sure that audiences believe the front-stage is real and, frankly, not a stage at all—that the thing being done for their benefit doesn't seem "fraudulent, manufactured for some ulterior purpose, or contrived."[184] Authentic might thus be "the most *inauthentic* word" in the English language—its invocation causing a knee-jerk twitch of skepticism among onlookers.[185] And yet, "far from being expelled, authenticity operates at the core of mass cultural production, its energy strictly and scrupulously contained to generate the power that the system requires"—burnishing products', politicians', and pop cultures' distinctiveness in the marketplace to quench the assumed authenticity thirst of consumers.[186]

Others have blazed this path of study before. Most consequentially, *Authentic*, by media scholar Sarah Banet-Weiser, theorizes the ambivalent experience of brand cultures—a compromising space defined by neither consumer autonomy nor corporate incorporation—while this book, less concerned with the creativity of cultural fandom, drills down on the "how to" of production-side practices.[187] I follow the methodological lead of Banet-Weiser, who conducted interviews in the early 2000s with advertisers, updating conversations with that community and widening to other professional circles in media and politics.

Equally indispensable, Gunn Enli's *Mediated Authenticity* tallies case studies from textual analysis and distills the core aesthetic characteristics of authenticity that will be detailed here from behind-the-scenes: spontaneity, confessionalism, ordinariness, and imperfection, among others.[100] She introduces, in short, a "genre system" for authenticity—particularly in how it *looks*—which I build upon in showing how it gets *made*.[189] Enli's closing line—counseling future research on "how media constructs its illusions of authenticity, and how the authenticity contract is renegotiated in new media"—represents, aptly, the starting point of departure.[190]

Similarly, I extend Richard Peterson's conclusion that managing the semblance of authenticity is "the central work of creative industries"—not just in country music as he studied, or other forms of entertainment like reality TV and pop music, but also in the technology, advertising, and politics explored in these pages.[191] As such, there will be a fair amount of intertwined dot-connecting here across domains and examples—from Hillary Clinton to TikTok, from the Wu-Tang Clan to *The Real Housewives*—following scholarly advice to identify "connections across media industries and move out of the largely siloed study" of them heretofore.[192] These investigations have become ever more urgent as social media, in particular, has afforded and necessitated more "professionalized" and "manipulated" strategies there.[193] And though scholars often stress authenticity's backstage definitions, empirically they are more oriented to frontstage examinations of it.[194]

To access that backstage, I relied overwhelmingly on in-depth interviews with those professionals whose work takes place there. Over the course of eighteen months in 2019 and 2020, I reached out, by e-mail and through online sites, to 277 potential contacts (i.e., people and organizations) and ultimately secured 79 interviews lasting 58 hours.

From media and pop culture, explored in part I of the book, the 28 participants included reality TV producers and casting directors, assorted tech company leadership, and artist management and music label executives. From advertising and consumer culture, explored in part II, the 25 participants included chief strategy officers, chief creative officers, influencer firm CEOs, and social media creators themselves. From electoral campaigns and political culture, explored in part III, the 26 participants included campaign managers, communication directors, advertising and digital specialists, and other senior advisors and strategists. In a few instances, interviewees could actually speak to multiple genres of authenticity industry work: a reality TV producer–turned–political ad-maker; a record label talent manager–turned–campaign advisor; and a branded music director–turned–social media business executive. (A complete listing of names, titles, dates, and lengths of these 79 interviewees is available in the appendix.)

Of these different industries in media, culture, and politics, I probably had the hardest time getting current or former representatives from Silicon Valley firms to talk with me, presumably because there's just too much money to lose there in violating nondisclosure agreements. I also occasionally drew upon material, as it was especially relevant, from more than a hundred other interviews I've conducted in the last decade for research previously published on guerrilla marketing, political consulting, and brand journalism.

Although the aforementioned job titles are indicative of widely varying domains, I came to each interview with a fairly stable set of questions: Why is authenticity an important quality in your field? What strategies or tactics can help emphasize the authenticity of the people or companies that you work for? How do different platforms and contexts (and especially social media) require different approaches to authenticity? How do you scheme the appearance of informality, spontaneity, or backstage lives and spaces? Which aspiration takes priority in your strategy and messaging output: emotion or reason? In what ways do you try to communicate the origin stories (i.e., places, histories, demographic identities) of your clients? Have you ever attacked the inauthenticity of a rival in your field? How do you try to distance your client—be it person or company—from the perception of inauthentic influences (e.g., the two-faced self, marketplace motives, and technological standardization)?

The number of interview questions that begin with "how" reflects the operational orientation of this inquiry. In some cases, the interviews might well have been considered "leading," in the sense that I took for granted—as seen in the phrasing of those questions—the importance of authenticity as a moral ideal, its simultaneous construction by producers, and the relevance of other dimensions informed by the research literature (e.g., economic pressures, staging self-presentation, anchoring genealogy, etc.). Generally, any qualitative inquirer—be they academic or journalistic—has a sense of the patterns they're looking for before setting out; otherwise they'd be lost amid the deluge of data in the field.[195]

Moreover, if, as the old cliché goes, all you have is a hammer and everything looks like a nail, then I fully concede—as a production studies scholar—much of mediated culture tends to look like strategic calculation and projection. I make no claim or attempt to understand how *audiences* processed or were in-fluenced by these tactics—that is, whether the produced authenticity shown in the chapters that follow actually satisfies the existential authenticity discussed previously—but I'll be eager to learn from those better equipped down the road who can elicit those findings.

I augmented these interviews by reading widely on the subject of authen-ticity. More than two hundred academic books and articles that buttress the intellectual backbone of this work (and inform this chapter, in particular) were drawn from diverse disciplines, and the reader of footnotes will already notice sourcing from scholars not just in my native communication, media, and cul-tural studies but also in sociology, philosophy, management, and technology.

Of course, this being a study of media production, various outlets in the trade press also regularly furnished illustrative examples and quotes that I've tracked or searched for in *Ad Age*, *Adweek*, *Billboard*, *Campaigns & Elections*, *Digiday*, the *Hollywood Reporter*, and *Variety*—not to mention relevant cov-erage from the popular press (the *New York Times*, the *Washington Post*, the *Boston Globe*, *The Atlantic*, *New York*, *Politico*, *Vox*, *Slate*, *Vanity Fair*, *Wired*, etc.). Although this coverage was sought out for its relevance to the book's cen-tral questions and themes, it shouldn't be mistaken for formal textual analysis: Many of these articles simply helped fill in the gaps where interview access fell short—but conspicuous developments or examples still needed to be invoked within the narrative—or were used to prepare more informed, specific ques-tions with those interviewees who did agree to participate.

Finally, the project retains an unavoidably US-centric perspective—a limitation this author notes with lament. Partly that is the product of native circumstances, but also, given the unusually wide scope of domains yoked together here and the sheer volume of examples summoned—just *within* that domestic context—a more internationally inclined book would both lack the savvy depth of familiarity needed to land those connections and be even hope-lessly longer than this already is. I will therefore make a number of claims about authenticity that are mostly circumscribed to American media, culture, and politics, with the humble hope that readers external to that setting find evidence of thematic overlaps from their own experiences as audiences, con-sumers, and citizens abroad.

Authenticity Industry Orientations

The book is written in a fashion that aims to build linearly, with concepts in ear-lier chapters informing later ones (e.g., the notion of social media's "rough cut" ideal showing up in political campaigns), but a reader could skip around, fol-lowing this introduction, without much confusion. Thematic coherence, rather than chronological precedence, takes priority in the storytelling: that is, while I seek, whenever possible within chapters, to structure the presentation so that earlier examples come before later ones, it is more important to group evidence together around common conceptual patterns and ideas. And, frankly, there's also an unavoidable interlocking quality to much of this material—where dis-entangling a later chapter on influencers from an earlier one devoted to social media might seem redundant—but they're partitioned and treated discretely enough to save you from slogging through overly long chapters.

The first part of the book foregrounds how authenticity looks and oper-ates within media and popular culture. Our starting point is reality television, where, perhaps more than in any other entertainment genre, authenticity has been venerated as vital to success, so chapter 1 investigates how it's actually strategized by producers who cast, shoot, and edit popular shows like *Jersey Shore* and *Keeping Up with the Kardashians*. Because relatability and intimacy ascended as cardinal virtues of celebrity, interviewees seek to frame audience *identification with* rather than *adoration of* the ordinary "stars" they shape—and all the better if these folks hail from marginalized origins. As TV pro-fessionals try to excavate that "realness"—from ethnographic sampling to surveillance camerawork to confessional arrangements—authenticity produc-tion has to self-efface its own presentations. Their schemes are meant to coax out uninhibited, emotional self-disclosure—a participant with no backstage to retreat to, their once-private lives put out for public viewing—but counter-vailing trends in the calculated pursuit of fame make that un-self-conscious authenticity harder than ever to harness and project.

Social media—effectively, reality TV for and by all of us—carries forward these logics, ideals, and expectations into digital domains. Chapter 2 shows how tech companies design their platforms to demonstrate and facilitate gen-uine self-performance from users: As we produce content for them, they hope to induce authenticity from us. An amateur model has long populated these spaces: everyday individuals, rather than professional media companies, cre-ating and circulating popular content, innocented by the apparent absence of marketplace motives. We see creators spilling their mundane, backstage lives in bathroom-mirror selfies onto apps owned by gargantuan corporations that cling, conveniently, to garage-myth origin fables. The "rough cut" emerges here as the key principle for achieving aesthetic authenticity: a low-production-value formula that seems spontaneous, unfiltered, and, hence, unmediated as seen in the glitchy imperfection of YouTubers like Emma Chamberlain and TikTok's sloppy informality (relative to Instagram's obsessively manicured sheen). And yet Silicon Valley has also had to authenticate its own inexorable creep toward commercialization—as both hobbyist creators professionalize, while professing and producing amateurishly, and platforms implement native ad structures to blend in with the "real" content in news feeds that appears less marketplace motivated.

Those marketplace motives have long loomed in popular music, the story of chapter 3, where authenticity is widely acclaimed—from fawning *Billboard* profiles to my interviews with artist managers and label executives. Authenticity is, here, foremost an *artistic* ideal: It ignores societal strictures and capitalist imperatives; courts one's own Rousseauian muse for self-expression (and, in turn, fan identification); and navigates the cultural tensions of mainstream versus underground in folk, rock, and punk scenes. Edge-worlds abound with assumed authenticity, as do professionals' efforts to authenticate the spatial and socioeconomic origins of star clients there—from Bon Iver's PR team scripting a debut album winter isolation story to hip-hop's street team seeding strategy. Indeed, it was hip-hop that pointed the way toward commercial embrace—an indispensable recourse once digital distribution decimated record revenues and hastened the need to accept "selling out" through sponsor partnerships and even entire labels financed by brands like Mountain Dew. Today's pop music industry-wide shrug about the defense of authenticity reveals it was a pretense of privilege all along—and as the business ramparts fell apart and commercialization washed in, so, too, were the norms of artistic high-mindedness forced to concede to capitalism's burdens.

The second part of the book examines advertising and consumer culture to see how authenticity works commercially and how commercials work authentically. Chapter 4 begins with today's advertising industry upheaval, as digital interactivity subsumes the dependability of mass broadcasting, Generation Z craves authenticity (like timeless youth narratives before them), and my interviewees go cool-hunting for it, increasingly via online data-streams. Here, too, marketplace motives blatantly bedevil the advertisers' challenge—hence their "cool sell" ambition to self-efface rational, product-utility appeals—but so does the technological standardization of the McWorld products being peddled. We'll see efforts to humanize them though craft posturing and brand-anchoring identity origins, from Starbucks' localizing schemes to moralizing histories of humble, mom-and-pop founders (rather than faceless corporate chains). More conspicuous of late, "purpose-driven" poses have ignited political controversy: from anti-Trump Super Bowl ads to Pepsi's gauche Black Lives Matter piggybacking to the quasi-feminism espoused by Dove and Gillette. These commodity activism campaigns—and their Madison Avenue authors—seek to imbue consumer choice with the authenticity of moral authority, fill the vacuum of lost faith in other societal institutions, and respond to newly politicized cultural domains in hyper-polarized times.

Those are, however, mostly manifest as traditional 30-spots. Back on social media, influencing became one of the hottest categories among the authenticity industries in the last decade; chapter 5 opens by tracing the long history of this multibillion-dollar market from World War I propaganda through to TikTok's Charli D'Amelio. The chapter illuminates behind-the-scenes processes—from engagement metrics obsession to output exhaustion—in creating less-scripted, seemingly "real" tableaus of increasingly backstaged lives and embedding products "naturally" for brands (that are, nonetheless, inevitably marketplace motivated). A central tension is that of corporate control versus creative autonomy: that is, how much influencers are allowed to produce sponsored postings off-script. Micro-influencers—some with as few as a thousand followers—are increasingly enlisted, because their familiarity, believability, ordinariness, and unpolished self-aesthetics help navigate the delicate balance of #spon-con ratio and reaffirm authenticity's amateur ideal. The whole scene is built upon an ideology of aspirational labor, an economy of gig-hustling, and a marketized mentality of self-branding and points toward, once more, a commercialization of once-authentic exercises (not to mention an infestation of fraudulent followings and bought bots). As in pop music, "selling out" isn't defined by insulation from the marketplace—or fidelity to some higher calling—but, rather, by not shilling for uncool brands within it.

Part III of the book turns to the production of electoral campaigns and American political culture, where authenticity is as critical as it is complicated. Chapter 6 briefly tours the rise and dominance of performative ideals like intimacy, ordinariness, and spontaneity in this space—archetypes inherited from the environmental conditioning of reality TV and social media culture. Also foregrounded here are the countervailing pressures that threaten to compromise political authenticity: namely, a two-faced candidate self, torn between base purity and centrist accommodation in polarized times, and marketplace motives, post–*Citizens United*, where small, grassroots donors scan as more authentic than backroom billionaires. Talking with some of the most influential political consultants of the twenty-first century, I tally their tactics to authenticate: from ad cliches in "realistic" settings like the Main Street diner and factory floor to backstaging lifestyle habits and press access (e.g., the un-poll-tested "Straight Talk Express") to anchoring identity origins with rural, small-town bias (e.g., the Texan-ization of Yalie George W. Bush by spotlighting ranch hobbies). All this, however, represents the triumph of Rousseauian indulgence at the expense of Enlightenment sobriety: a politics of style for emotional engagement and consumer self-discovery, not rational petition and voter self-governance—because rationality is calculated and, thus, inauthentic—and a politics where the sign-value of candidates has, superficially, eclipsed their use-value.

Continuing with politics, populism animates and is animated by the ideals of authenticity, and chapter 7 disentangles the nationalistic substance and rhetorical style defining this recent tide. Within digital politics, especially, populist authenticity has been mythologized and strategized: from Howard Dean's blogger-netroots run through to Michael Bloomberg's army of meme-making influencer shills, we've seen crowdsourced flows, displaced journalists, increased output, and rough cut aesthetics (especially given pandemic-era production constraints) all forcefully operative. These dimensions set the stage for Donald Trump's emblematic triumph over Hillary Clinton: his raw, coarse, emotionally viral performance of authenticity (via both sloppy, amateurish social media style and incendiary, anti-PC substance) besting an opponent more scrutinized for calculating, two-faced-self reinvention (via sexist undercurrents) than any woman in political history. Still, for all his anti-establishment posturing, Trump ultimately delivered big for economic elites by talking like a blue-collar boor; a cultural populism that enabled policymaking detrimental to the very working-class folk who supposedly swooned to it.

Before setting off, one last quick tip of the hand here: Nearly every one of my interviewees agreed that authenticity was an important aspiration for their clients, and even those who did not use that specific term recognized its relevance; there was, however, some divergence throughout as to whether authenticity could be strategized, coached, or emphasized (which is, essentially, the book's thesis) or whether it just needed to be naturally in existence already.

That's perhaps a chicken-or-egg question that the reader can judge when this case rests. It is nonetheless telling that a similar set of queries about authenticity could be posed to the casting director for *Jersey Shore*, the director of monetization at Facebook, Bruce Springsteen's longtime manager, the head of brand strategy at Ogilvy, the vice president of global creative at Starbucks, Donald Trump's press secretary, and Howard Dean's 2004 campaign manager, among others . . . and they would all have much to say, in similar terms, despite having little ostensibly in common with each other. That, to me, shows how authenticity threads itself constantly, obsessively, throughout our media, cultural, and political life.

Let's tug at that thread a little and see what unravels.

xxxxxxxxxxxxxxxxxxxxxxxxxxxxxxxxxx

MEDIA *and* POPULAR CULTURE

ONE

Casting Reality Television

Stages of Self-Disclosure

> **Real people should not be on television—it's for people like us,**
> **people who have trained and studied to appear to be real.**
>
> —GARRY SHANDLING, comedian host at the 2000 Emmy Awards[1]

> **Good TV is someone who doesn't know that they are giving you good TV.**
>
> —ROBYN KASS, *Big Brother* casting director[2]

If ever there was an emblematic ingenue of authenticity for the reality TV era, she was, arguably, the first character introduced in the first episode of a show of this type: Julie from season 1 of *The Real World*.

Audiences meet this sweet-faced, plainly dressed nineteen-year-old with a lilting twang in her Alabama home as departure approaches to the exciting Big Apple up north. She declares to the camera, in the opening minutes, a vow of fidelity, an oath of aim that every reality TV producer hopes to coax out of their subjects: "I just hope when I go to New York, I learn a lot about myself."

Her stiff, overbearing father regards the nosy camera—zooming in and out in that early '90s fashion, from weirdly canted angles that announce "edgy"— with flitting glances of suspicion. A glimmer of emotion breaks his glower as youngest daughter departs: "I believe I can shed a tear." Landing in the noisy, crowded metropolis, Julie meets her roommates, many pursuing bohemian dreams of their own—the writer, the rapper, the model, the painter—much like Julie, who aspires to dance despite her father's admonition to pursue a *sensible* career in computers.

With that, a new era of media-culture commenced, MTV's catchphrase marching orders soon to define the sensibility of most all reality programming that followed: "to find out what happens when people stop being polite and start getting real." The two-faced self, that durable fact of social interaction articulated by sociologist Erving Goffman, was put on notice. In the thirty years since *The Real World* debuted, intimacy and relatability ascended as cardinal virtues of celebrity; they also help define and are defined by the production of media authenticity, perhaps here more so than in any other entertainment genre.

But how is that actually strategized by those who cast, shoot, and edit these enduringly popular programs? How is "realness" excavated from and presented on behalf of participants? By examining the industry schemes to achieve *identification with*—rather than *adoration of*—these stars who are shaped, we'll see an effort to frontstage the backstage, in Goffman's conceptual terms.[3] It is an ambition and technique that informs social media, marketing, and politics alike in coming chapters.

The Real World's Julie just wanted to discover herself—which philosopher Jean-Jacques Rousseau ordains as moral imperative and industry showrunners envision as "good TV." The more *unstaged* that process appears, they assume, the more convincing and popular the product.

Wither Fame, Whither Fame?

Just as authenticity had little meaning or value before modernity, so, too, did celebrity. For millennia, the social world was hierarchically ordained: You inherited your lot in life, a fixed order of fate, fame-wise, that involved little in the way of self-definition, much less popular aspiration. With industrialization and urbanization, the prospect of mobility beckoned, albeit freighted with the anxiety of existential uncertainty.[4]

Yet fame—the state of being *known*—could repair the plight and plague of modern anomie, offering an experience not unlike authenticity, for the basic allure of celebrity is that they're "somehow more real than we and that our insubstantial physical reality needs that immortal substance," cultural historian Leo Braudy observes. "Fame is a quiet place where one is free to be what one really is, one's true, unchanging essence."[5]

Most people are, in the eyes of the world, just anonymous, "demographic aggregates," while celebrities can express their identities "quite individually and idiosyncratically" and those selves are legitimated as their image multiplies.[6] Braudy estimates that, until the medieval period, the average person saw maybe a hundred others in their entire lifetime.[7] A brisk Instagram scroll tallies that figure before many people get out of bed in the morning—this parade of stranger faces triggering some impotent unease of being unknown oneself. Most vitally, along the y-axis that is eternity, fame issues a siren call to somehow cheat death—a delusive, godlike yearning that summons seekers, a permanence of self that proffers some stability of identity when other dependable institutions for that have withered away.

Over the last century, however, fame got flipped upside-down. In the heyday of the Hollywood studio system, celebrity was carefully manicured and "micromanaged" at a reverent remove from the public; "perfection, glamour, and distance" defined traditional fame and the entertainment industry's publicity machines policed those boundaries aggressively.[8] Similarly, when Madame Tussaud's first museum opened in London, ropes kept visitors at a distance from the wax figurines and photography was prohibited, enforcing awestruck.[9]

By contrast, today's celebrity is far more open, ordinary, and proximate—thanks largely to the trends of reality TV explored in this chapter and social media in the next. It is, if not democratic—as cultural studies scholar Graeme Turner nuances—certainly "demotic," in terms of being of the common people.[10]

Film fame once vaulted stars onto giant public screens, but television's living room intimacy made them minor and mundane; then television bifurcated, with complex, prestige TV franchises aiming high culture while reality and talk shows went low.[11] Each new platform delegated fame in more egalitarian ways and the same technologies that empower common folk to chase renown also cheapen its value and destabilize its structure: 15 minutes to all, as Andy Warhol allegedly forecast, becomes 15 seconds on TikTok (to 15 people, probably). Today's celebrities lack the breadth, depth, and length of their media-world predecessors; they are comparatively disposable.

Hence the dawn of microcelebrity, a label initially coined to describe "camgirls," those women who began broadcasting their lives over the internet in the early aughts.[12] Alice Marwick, social media scholar, shows how the mentalities, habits, and performances of these (otherwise oxymoronic) "niche famous" proliferated in the years since, treating networked friends as fans, indulging relentless self-promotion, and packaging one's online persona as a brand.[13]

Microcelebrity also demands that the D-lister be "more available and more 'real'" than movie stars of old and, vice versa, formerly celestial bodies must now stoop to more "direct, unmediated relationships with fans."[14] Increasingly, paparazzi pursued and magazines presented them as "just like us."[15] Together, such "unexceptional people" gaining fame and stars being banalized is, in the judgment of cultural sociologist Joshua Gamson, the defining feature of celebrity in the past few decades.[16]

Whereas fame was once reserved, theoretically, for an "elite" class of individuals, it's now distributed widely and without regard for standards or merit; Paris Hilton, heiress-turned–sex tape starlet, may well have been first "human pseudo-event" to usher in this era.[17] Such notoriety is often necessary: exposing "tragedy, unpredictability, and spontaneity" in one's life, the kind of infamy that more rarefied stars of yesteryear could keep secret from public view.[18] Reality TV has, in particular, been castigated as trashy, shameless, and exploitative for gatekeeping access to casting based upon an applicant's willingness to participate in such humiliations.[19] Not calling those aspirants "talent," even on contest shows, further emphasizes their amateur status—their value being "only one step removed" from the audience watching.[20]

All of this makes for less-famous famous people. *American Idol*'s first season got more voters than the previous US presidential election and only the Super Bowl topped *Survivor*'s finale in viewership—a time, one could argue, of peak mass-culture—but subsequent installments of both franchises dwindled to a fraction of that market share.[21]

Television, one Gen Zer griped to the *New York Times*, is mainly made "by old people for old people," while YouTube and TikTok are "by teenagers for teenagers"—platforms where intimacy and relatability, confined to previously private spaces, defines celebrity norms and expectations.[22] As ratings for the 2021 Oscars plunged to record lows, one study found the top 10 influencer accounts on YouTube and Facebook reached 150 million unique monthly visitors—more than twice the number of the top 10 TV-personality accounts (i.e., Jimmy Fallon, Ellen DeGeneres).[23]

None of that fragmentation doused fanaticism for fame; one Pew survey of millennials during their formative years found that half felt "becoming famous" was one of the most important life goals (and another poll found that about half of these people thought they actually *would*).[24] Social psychologist Jean Twenge variously dubbed these American youth cohorts *Generation Me* and *iGen* to capture, as she sees it, the wildly entitled expectations about fame and the attendant self-absorption that stems from that.[25]

Such widespread hopes for celebrity are surely conditioned by platform affordances (i.e., the do-it-yourself opportunism of social media that bypasses gatekeepers) and, in turn, populate an inexhaustible supply of potential talent for reality TV.[26] "The audience that watches [our] show," says one *Real World* co-producer, "think that they have a chance to be on it."[27] That is, as we'll see here, by design.

Some point to *Cops*, the dystopian ride-along panorama of policing practices, as the advent of the genre spreading across prime-time schedules.[28] Documentary film equally lends itself as obvious forerunner, long capturing ordinary people's lives in everyday settings, as does *The Real World*, widely credited with establishing *cinema verité* observational style, first-person confessional interludes, and interwoven character narratives.[29] The burst of reality programming that ensued in its wake came from a confluence of economic, technological, and cultural factors.

The first generation of studio-audience talk shows, which overtook the daytime reign of soap operas, laid the foundation for the feel of televised authenticity: Phil Donahue, Sally Jessy Raphael, and, above all, Oprah Winfrey—many known, "intimately," by first names alone—coaxed out parasocial attachments from overwhelmingly female audiences, while wringing human-interest angles from broad social problems.[30] As channels multiplied, so did competitors, with more than two dozen daytime talk shows vying in the 1990s, before reality supplanted that genre's centrality in the aughts.[31]

Penny-pinching TV executives swooned to this cheap content (no actors! no writers! no sets!), which cost, on average, a third less than scripted alternatives, squeezing out unionized crews below the line and higher-priced, agency-affiliated talent above it; befitting neoliberal economics' pursuit of flexible, dispensable labor, writers' guild strikes further galvanized interest in expanding the genre.[32] In addition, regulatory change in the early '90s repealed rules on financing and syndicating in-house shows, though most reality programs remained independently produced and then sold to networks.[33]

Meanwhile, web interactivity and camera-phone ubiquity nurtured narcissistic norms of exhibitionism—blurring together the logic, participation, and interplay of reality TV and social media genres.[34] As celebrity authenticity came to depend upon identification—"performers [who] speak as rather than for their audience"—their "ordinariness" became the "essential programming strategy."[35] How, then, do producers of that content pursue those ideals tactically?

Mapping, Excavating, and Staging Authenticity

"Many shows are looking for what they think would make good television." Mark Burnett, the Emmy award–winning producer of *Survivor* and *The Apprentice*, then clarifies in a *New York Times* interview: "But my primary concern is authenticity."[36]

Among my own interviewees, this ambition was widespread. Danielle Gervais, casting director for *Pawn Stars*, uses or hears the term "thirty times" a day, says it "influences everything," and has become even more central to overcome escalating audience skepticism.[37] Sheila Conlin, who helped develop *Hell's Kitchen* and *Nanny 911*, venerates authenticity as the "pinnacle" of her work, likening it to the effortless, organic, and raw: "It's a naturalness. . . . You cannot teach someone how to be themselves. . . . And then if you get people [who] already know how [reality TV] works, then there isn't any spontaneity."[38]

Through the nineties and aughts, reality TV producers refined an analog approach to finding that authentic talent, in contrast to more recent digital means. This demanded "boots on the ground" and one-on-one enlistment—hustling flyers and business cards by hand and spreading the word at office park lunch tables, self-help meetings, college bars, grocery stores, nursing homes, and strip clubs.[39] It meant hitting up radio and TV stations in promising markets to do casting call shout-outs, taking out classified ads, and querying local film commissions about subculture hot-spots. It included soliciting friends of friends, through pre–social media grassroots networks: "If you don't know someone, your sister will, or your mother will, or your grandmother, or your neighbor," as Conlin cajoled.[40]

Gervais likens the process to journalism—"walking around, meeting people," cultivating sources, reading the news, trying to get the pulse of a beat or bureau. For one season of *Queer Eye*, she sent a scout to the same sad mall in Kansas City every single day for two weeks, prowling (successfully, in turned out) for just the right zhlub who gave off "a slobby first impression."[41] *America's Next Top Model* recruiters likewise leer after teens at gas stations, amusement parks, and big box stores: "I always feel like Target is a gold mine," one noted.[42] Doron Ofir, casting associate for *The Amazing Race*, sees the process as an "anthropological and sociological experiment," and would lean on insider informants, a la ethnography—"natives . . . hired to scout among their own kind."[43]

Then, at auditions, Ofir switches disciplinary hats: "You have to break the person down to their core and then rebuild them to who they once were. I'm not turning them into who I want them to be—I'm just allowing them to be who they really are. So, in a weird way, I play psychologist, but I'm not looking for, like, lifelong hurt or trauma. What I'm looking to do is: What really makes you tick? And why do you do what you do? And 'who' are you doing?"[44]

Applicants are asked not just to describe themselves but also how *friends* would describe them and whether the latter are accurate assessments, as refracted through the social looking-glass. If a finalist successfully makes it through the canvassing and filtration stages of casting, background checks ensue: calling up those friends and family to triangulate claims and calling in (real) psychological and medical evaluators to pin down personality projections. Ideally, authenticity is marked by a "roughness around the edge" and a "rawness" to how one looks and talks, including colorful accents to indicate geographic origins.[45]

Gradually, like everything else in the world, these IRL ("in real life") techniques became augmented and then fully subsumed by internet convenience. Less lurking at nightclubs and pounding the pavement for fresh faces; no need to have audition tapes snail-mailed or hundreds of hopefuls stacked in-person at open calls.

Shannon McCarty, who cast *The Real World* and *The Biggest Loser*, recalls how social media platforms enabled age- and location-based targeting of profiles; concurrently, interviews on Skype, FaceTime, and Zoom meant those boots on the ground could be stashed away in a closet.[46] One Bravo casting director, for example, used the Instagram hashtag #alwaysabridesmaidneverabride to trawl hundreds of photo leads, commenting on users' posts to solicit interest in what later became a show premise.[47] Social media also buttresses background checks, offering assessment and affirmation of online self-presentation.[48]

All of this helped make the casting process cheaper and quicker—though not necessarily better at strip-mining that authenticity. On one hand, filter- and edit-savvy young people are well trained in staging a highlight-reel lifestyle for followers, but, an *Amazing Race* casting director cautions, "That's not who they are. . . . [So] I look at their room. I look at their house. I look at all the things they're not expecting me to."[49] Plus, many of the subcultures with the *most* authenticity retain it precisely because of how they live their lives *offline*: "How are we going to find the best possible cast for the show, the most authentic cast, the most [type of] a cast that hasn't already been on TV?" asks Gervais. "Like, if we're looking for blacksmiths in the Ozarks, you're not gonna find those people necessarily on Instagram."[50]

In that, the notion of genealogical authenticity, introduced in the opening chapter, resonates extensively within reality TV. It's not just that location becomes a metaphorical "character on the show," as in Gervais' *Clash of the Ozarks* miniseries; it's that those ideal origins should be imprinted on the actual characters as an authenticity watermark, evinced by her casting strategy for *The Real Housewives of New Jersey*: "They sort of embrace what people believe about New Jersey," she says. "Like, you could mute them for a moment, look at them, and sort of see the pride just to feel that that is where they're from."

An equally famous Garden State example here is, of course, *Jersey Shore*, the ensemble assembled by Ofir in lineage with the "Guido" stereotype he affectionately categorizes Italian Americans that he grew up with in the tri-state area.[51] Seeking inspiration, Ofir, a former nightclub doorman, went to The Sound Factory in midtown Manhattan to scout those in thrall to DJ Boris, then "king of the Guido scene," and found "wife-beaters, big hair, gold chains, [and] fist pumping their faces off" to thumping house—all hallmarks of the aesthetic and lifestyle that would define *Jersey Shore*: "So, now, I'm swimming in a pool of the archetype or stereotype I'm looking for." That logic of genealogical authenticity begat a frenzy for wacky geographic subcultures across the US, many of which Ofir eagerly supplied: *#RichKids of Beverly Hills, Floribama Shore, Party Down South, The Vineyard*, and so on.

Why, one magazine profile of Ofir asks, do reality stars "from the margins of society resonate so strongly with the mainstream"—from *Honey Boo Boo* to the *Duck Dynasty* family?[52] It's because of authenticity's spatial bias, where "class conventions" as much as geographic origins signify genuineness—both within reality TV and across American life.[53]

"Even a politician who comes from nothing versus somebody who was [born with a] silver spoon. . . . People naturally give more credibility to the candidate that came from nothing," explains Julie Pizzi, a reality TV studio executive, foreshadowing logic and strategy seen in later chapters on political communication. "Same with cast members. . . . People root for them more, because they feel compassion [and] can identify with somebody who comes from nothing."[54]

In short, Horatio Alger bootstraps authenticate: Hence, *American Idol*'s fondness for emphasizing the ordinariness of contestants' lives—to engineer audience identification with them and reaffirm faith in the allegedly democratic selection process.[55] Ordinary, of course, is economically determined and indicative: a marker of "misfortune or disadvantage" more often than "prosperity or privilege."[56] On MTV, for example, *Jersey Shore* nudged the reality genre toward vulgar, lower-class imperfection relative to its more perfectly coiffed, glossy predecessor, *The Hills*—a fitting zeitgeist comedown from aughts prosperity to Great Recession slumming.[57]

Those genealogical biases of authenticity find an industry cynically pursuing ideal origins that tend to be less than ideal, socioeconomically speaking: Hollywood cameras seeking simplicity, weirdness, even squalor from edge-worlds and parading it for audiences who—producers assume—find the lack of affectation endearing. This scouting work "converts [a] real person into an objectified type," often stereotypically so, doting on "familiar cliches about identity" that translate easily to media markets; seeking notice and validation, but with limited means of accessing the TV stage, auditionees trade their embodied emotion as the only "raw material" available (a theoretically "democratic" form of capital).[58] Marginalized participants, whether by race or class, might fantasize these opportunities as empowering, but the imbalance ultimately tilts in favor of those who determine how their lives will be packaged for gawkers.

Once on set, a variety of techniques can coax out authenticity. In some cases, "reality" is assumed to emerge if you simply capture enough raw footage: "Constant surveillance assures that cast members are no more and no less than who they appear to be."[59] This relentless observation, argues pop culture scholar Rachel Dubrofsky, validates that authenticity by measuring how well participants maintain a consistent self on camera and off, behaving "naturally" under contrived surveillance.[60] (Social media, as we'll see in the next chapter, imports these technologies and ideals into one's own "normal" daily life and living space.) Reality makeover shows, in particular, teach neoliberal lessons about constant self-monitoring and discipline toward entrepreneurial empowerment for women and girls.[61]

Ideally, producers want 24/7 stationary-camera coverage if the show takes place mostly within a fixed setting like a house, such that, if the crew goes home and drama unfolds, they don't have to ask participants to—inauthentically—reenact the performance the next day.[62] This, however, adds up to thousands of hours of leftover material from a single season that editors must sift through (and adds the authenticity challenge of "picking exactly what shot to sell [a] character," while maintaining fidelity to the totality of that captured self).[63] Another issue emerges when narrative sequences aren't later spliced with fidelity to exact chronological order—perhaps montaged, with liberties, to heighten emotion or drama—but characters' social feeds have already tipped off audiences about what happened when during those many months of filming.[64]

As Erika Bryant, co-executive producer for *The Real Housewives of Atlanta*, explains to me, this surveillance strategy wears people down, eventually eroding the two-faced self and leaving the show with the authentic *non*performance she needs: "At a certain point, the cameras do become the wallpaper. . . . There's cameras watching you nonstop. And, so, when you're in the moment, you're living it—you're just in it. . . . I think it makes you more who you are."[65] (Interviews with sorority sisters on one MTV reality show clarify that it's not so much that the cameras are forgotten, but that they "grew used to having them around" to the point that the cameras "became familiar fixtures."[66])

By downplaying the production apparatus (i.e., making equipment and crew as "invisible" as possible), a more "uncensored" glimpse of selves is on display—precisely *because* they don't seem to be anxious about managing audience impressions and can betray those authentic "moments of truth."[67] One trick—of dubious ethics—involves telling people who tend to clam up that the cameras are just there for casting purposes, even though it's already the first day of shooting.[68]

Here, again, the power imbalance tips its hand in favor of producers rather than participants—whose guilelessness about these tricks to reveal their authenticity is precisely the reason many made it through auditions; in other words, if they were savvy enough to know how the staging works, they wouldn't deliver the unstaged self that shows seek. Normally, says Jacob Lane, a co-executive producer on *Keeping Up with the Kardashians*, it takes a few weeks of shooting "to get those real emotions because they let their guard down" and "their internal monologue starts to come out a little bit more," at least beyond the usual initial (inauthentic) polite pleasantries.[69] And Lane attends to authenticity not just in the sheer quantity of that footage but in the *quality* of it as well: "For the longest time, it was always in reality TV. . . . If someone starts screaming or they start crying . . . from another room, we're going to follow the cameras into the room, because we're catching the moment as it happens. And that sort of 'dirty' camerawork . . . searching for the action as it's happening, because we're catching that moment and trying to make it feel as authentic as possible. . . . It's okay to leave the dirty camerawork in—you want to see the whip-pans to people."

Yet as bigger show budgets and more equipment became available, multiple cameras could be stationed in that hypothetical other room to nail "the perfect shot" rather than relying on a clunkier, shakier one. Lane believes, however, that that comes at a cost of selling authenticity to savvy audiences (ever suspicious of staged drama), who would puzzle over, "Why do you always have the perfect shot of someone screaming?" (i.e., Was this planned?) This led Lane's crew to reconsider and opt for a "rougher cut"—a concept introduced in the next chapter—as more indexical of authenticity, even though they have the means of capturing a well-lit, better-filmed, crisper audio version; by sometimes shooting fights on *The Kardashians* from only one vantage point (rather than in both rooms), "it made it feel more chaotic" and thus "real."

Unlike, say, the refined cinematography of scripted entertainment—where, with perfectly positioned cameras, "you know where [the characters] were going"—with reality, "the cameraman—the note I normally give is, like, we shouldn't be omnipotent," Lane says. "We should try and follow as much as possible, so that it feels like—as the audience—we are following what's happening, as opposed to knowing what's going to happen."

In short, if it seems staged—not just in the *non*performances but in the very film grammar itself used to capture them—it seems inauthentic. For as scholars Laura Grindstaff and Vicki Mayer summarize, "ordinary performances on-camera necessitate ordinary production practices off-camera," blurring amateur and professional distinctions to convince audiences of the reality of the conceit.[70]

This is not to say that, behind the scenes, certain rather inauthentic—not "of the moment"—techniques weren't being employed. *The Real World*'s Shannon McCarty explains that sometimes the term "ice" would have to be shouted when producers—for whatever inconvenient reason—needed cast members to stay silent or chitchat on innocuous topics unrelated to the narrative or scene, until filming could restart.[71] An inversion of "ice," where *characters* can get the show to stop filming them, was divulged in season 10 of *The Real Housewives of Beverly Hills*, when Denise Richards broke the fourth wall by shouting "Bravo!" (the cast used the network name if the cameras came on before they were ready for them), thereby revealing her awareness of being on a show.[72]

In other cases, some foresight is required—not necessarily staging scenes, per se, but planning and talking with casts about which locations need to be shooting-ready for the unscripted behavior that could unfold. *The Kardashians*, for example, don't employ full-time surveillance, which means Julie Pizzi, their production company president, has her team set up times with the family to map out where drama might go down.[73] Although she, like others, adamantly denied to me that performances are scripted, another interviewee admitted that producers can "make suggestions into people's minds through interviews" and, in competition shows, challenges (particularly unexpected ones) can jump-start the spontaneity and tension needed.[74]

Given that it was one of the earliest and most successful examples of reality programming in the 1990s—winning an Emmy a half-decade before the genre was explicitly honored as such—it's worth lingering on *Taxicab Confessions* as a case study for details of technique revealed by creator and producer Harry Gantz.[75] The HBO show captured hidden-camera conversations—by turns, tragic, graphic, and funny—with passengers riding late at night in New York City. That nocturnal, seemingly anonymized setting (with its rearview-mirror eye-contact, not so different from a Catholic confessional) turned out to be vital to elicit authenticity: "At the end of the night . . . they felt more vulnerable," one driver explains. "They felt like they were never gonna see me again, so they didn't care what I thought and could open up."[76]

Befitting authenticity's spatial orientation, the taxi cruised to "seedy" places and picked up "the dispossessed and often unseen," and Gantz takes special pride in crafting one of the earliest shows to give voice to the transgender and sex worker community, long mocked by media outlets.[77] (He also notes that, as reality TV became more popular and widely understood, it became harder to secure releases from once-naïve riders, now wary of the "Franken-editing" they saw manipulating on other shows.) And those "stranger" intermediaries coaxing out the authenticity had to be well chosen: Gantz preferred female drivers, assuming that riders would self-disclose more, and an eager listener's deep curiosity about people—hesitant to interrupt, gently midwifing pregnant pauses—as well as a willingness to frame open-ended questions without implying advance judgment.

Gantz's team would trail the cab in a surveillance van, monitoring the conversation and suggesting angles in the driver's earpiece: "We were trying to find a way that we could encourage people to open up and tell their story in a way that was unadulterated," he recalls. "I heard more stories than an eighty-year-old psychologist. But we always felt that our goal was to get something that authentically portrayed the emotional life of these riders."

Reality casters have been called "emotion experts" for just this reason: skilled at managing and harnessing others' affect (not to mention their own, by "feeling" just the right amount); "connecting, bonding, sympathizing, befriending, cajoling, mollifying, pressuring, cheerleading, and guilt-tripping" to satisfy industry necessities; and making pals in order to make the deal, then handing them off to the production pipeline.[78] For both the daytime talk shows of the '90s and reality conceits in the decades since, this emotional labor undergirding media production fell disproportionately to White women and gay men; as media scholar Vicki Mayer points out, this is due to stereotypes of these groups being "naturally communicative, flexible, empathetic, and detail-oriented multitaskers."[79] Emotional authenticity is, in this framing, distinctly feminized work.

The Ideals of (and Schemes for) Self-Disclosure

What conclusions might, then, be drawn about the schemed nature of authenticity within reality television? Above all—and especially against the disingenuous, diplomatic two-faced self—authenticity is defined here by acts (though ideally not "performances") of *self-disclosure*.

Rousseau himself might have been pleased by the antics of *The Apprentice*'s Omarosa, *Jersey Shore*'s Snooki, and *The Real World*'s Johnny Bananas, feeling that authenticity collapses "one's outer appearance and inner sentiments, to be 'true' to oneself."[80] For the eighteenth-century philosopher, confessing inner depths was the enduring ideal, even if it meant going against societal norms.[81] Such disclosure also proves pivotal, as media scholar Sarah Banet-Weiser saw, to sharing on social media, sans artifice, and the subsequent self-branding ideologies made possible, all explored in later chapters.[82] But that starts with reality TV upholding and perpetuating a presumed binary governing authenticity: "the natural side of life as *pure*, *spontaneous*, and *innocent*, whereas the social or public side of life is seen as *calculating*, *contrived*, *tainted*, and so *deformed* and *fallen*."[83]

Thus, seeming—if not provably *being*—"true to yourself" is perhaps the highest compliment for reality TV participants, and research confirms audiences enjoy these shows more when stars seem like they're "not fake."[84] By contrast, says *The Real World*'s McCarty, former cast members who get angriest about their edited portrayal are those "who have not really looked as deeply into themselves" and done the work of honest self-introspection.[85] "Reality TV has always been looking into a mirror that most people don't get to see," she adds.

The accomplishment of this authenticity is intertwined with five ideal adjectives that recur throughout later chapters: It is unfiltered, confessional, emotional, relatable, and effortless.

Authenticity must be uninhibited in the sense that it cares not for the kind of impression management that sociologist Erving Goffman discerned as rife across interpersonal experiences. Authenticity's aesthetic is, instead, raw, unscripted, spontaneous—even lacking self-control, as media scholar Gunn Enli enumerates.[86] Thinking back on his pioneering *Taxicab* show, Gantz would use whatever means possible "to create an environment in which people felt comfortable to get something off their chest, which connected in a society that felt inhibited by what they could say and who they could be."[87] Reality producers try to cast seemingly transparent people who lack any sort of "internal governor"—that inner voice that keeps the peace by biting your tongue when you can't say what you really want to say, be it crass, crazy, or comical.[88]

"People that are most successful within the genre are the open books," *Queer Eye*'s Danielle Gervais explains to me. "You're looking for people who are not editing what is coming out of their mouth. . . . Having someone who's guarded in that way can be difficult . . . because they're constantly having to overthink, like, 'Oh, did that come out okay?'"[89] This also means there can be no "backstage" to retreat to, no skeletons safely stashed in a closet somewhere. The omniscient eye of reality TV production wants *most* to find that which the participant *most* hopes to keep hidden, because that's where authenticity resides: beneath the veil of decorous upkeep.

"It's one of my first questions: 'Are you willing to share every aspect of your life?'" *Jersey Shore*'s Doron Ofir asks of candidates, noting that otherwise "you're not authentically right for the show."[90] Partly that's because those deepest secrets—"like, I was in recovery and I was addicted to meth for twelve years"—are often vital to explaining the formation of a person's character; partly, too, because, given the digital trail of lives led on social media nowadays, fan bases will ferret them out anyhow.[91]

Another interviewee elaborates: "Something that can shut an [audition] interview is, 'I don't want to talk about that.' . . . If you're going on a show where somebody is going to follow you for weeks or months, kind of everything needs to be on the table. . . . People, the audience, whoever, will recognize if something's being hidden. . . . It's like an investigation, you know, when police are trying to figure out what's happening. . . . If you're trying to hide something, whatever you're trying to hide, the light is going to get shown on that."[92]

A police interrogation is an apt metaphor here, for "confessionality" very much also defines the structure and ideals of reality TV's authenticity strategy. In that sense, the title of Gantz's show—*Taxicab Confessions*—was neither accidental nor ancillary to the ambition:

> The show hit a chord with our collective unconscious in our society, because we live in such an inhibited world when it came to sharing our personal lives, our inner life, our dark side—whatever you want to call it. There used to be frameworks for that in religion—whether that's literally the [Catholic] confessional or whether that's testifying in the Baptist church, where you go down and, in front of the entire congregation, confess your sins. And the onset of people moving to cities and living alone and being isolated and [having] to be careful about what you say at work, because of the political correctness

police, and just feeling like your inner life really has a very limited space to exist in. . . . This was a way to get stuff off your chest that kind of fulfilled this inherent need that we have that had lost an outlet in society. And so that's the reason that I think many people signed [the consent form to use their conversation]. . . . They wanted the world to know what happened to them and they felt like this was their only outlet.[93]

Around the same time on *The Real World*, a similar confessional monologue trope was being developed—a genre technique that's essential to excavating emotional authenticity from participants, not least because, in its fourth-wall-breaking style of direct address, it feels intimate and *unmediated*.[94] The confessor might, technically, be talking to a producer—though "[we're] just like, 'don't talk to us—go talk to a camera'"—but it scans, on screen, as the confidences of a close friend, namely because it's often "stuff that they don't have to say out loud to the entire cast."[95]

Nonverbal accompaniments can index the authenticity sought: biting nails, looking down or away—"that's saying something and we'll try to use that behavior to sell some of that."[96] For one *Real Housewives* offshoot series, producers opted to film the confessional commentary on-the-spot rather than after the action, heightening the assumed authenticity because, as *New Jersey*'s Melissa Gorga put it, "Half the time you're a little tipsy [while filming], but you say whatever you really feel in the moment."[97]

In vino veritas—and when this formal device (or adult beverages) is unavailable, confession takes some on-set cajoling by a producer who might be privy to intimate details elicited in the audition phase from a cast member who's since gotten cagey and cold feet about sharing them again. All such bespeaks the producers' power and calculations in unearthing the uncalculated from subjects.

"It takes a lot of effort to be like, look, this [topic] is one of the reasons that you're here, because if this is [making you] hysterical or whatever—you got to do it, you got to say it. You said it to us before," explains Adam Reider, a producer on *Survivor*. "We didn't pressure you to say it [then] and, now, you can't be all worried about how you're going to seem—because this is you."[98] Recalling work on *Revenge Body*, a Khloé Kardashian makeover show, Sheila Conlin says that meant coaching out "some deep, dark secrets" about abuse and abandonment.[99]

Real Housewives' Erika Bryant spins this, understandably self-servingly, as the work of psychological growth, consoling cautious cast members that "if you can open up and really just express . . . what we talked about off-camera, what I know is going through your mind, it really is going to be a weight off your shoulders."[100] Such is the therapist façade commonly adopted by the caster—by turns, "social worker" and "life coach"—touting cathartic "self-knowledge, self-acceptance, and well-being" and, of course, fame, if they just let it all out in public view.[101] Because that's what good TV demands.

Through this unfiltered expression and intimate confession, the reality genre exhumes and exports emotion—that authentic byproduct of the heart, unrestrained by a calculating, inauthentic mind. To be certain, the television industry has long exploited those who could wear emotions on their sleeve; sociologist Laura Grindstaff, in an ethnography of daytime talk shows, calls this the "money shot"—that moment when participants, in response to shock or grief, surrender to overwhelming, volatile, emotional performance (which, being emotional, does not scan as "performance" in the impression management sense).[102] As she phrases it, "Emotion puts 'the real' in reality TV"—differentiating amateur from professional because, again, that's all the former has to offer as exchange value in the fame marketplace.[103] And while emotional reserve has, historically, defined wealth and Whiteness, unrestrained "expressivity" has been associated with people of color, women, and blue-collar populations: to hold it in is seen as classy; to vent it out, trashy.[104]

The Real World's Shannon McCarty says this is the most important thing that reality scouts look for: not just big emotions—although those are certainly welcome as punchy preview clips—but access to any and all emotion.[105] This takes prep, of course: laying the groundwork for that affective performance in a preprogrammed fashion that nonetheless scans as spontaneous.[106]

The confessional monologue device is certainly one space where emotions from that "true self" can "run free," and showcasing "painful experiences" in those intimate interludes is part of the production of authenticity.[107] Having an actual professional counselor on hand can also help, as was the case in the early years of *The Real World*, when a PhD in clinical psychology ran audition interviews.[108] Moreover, emotion endears: Jacob Lane suspects that, from his work producing *The Kardashians*, Khloé's penchant for not holding back generated the most audience connection.[109]

Thus, relatability defines a fourth dimension of reality television's authenticity conceit: trying to get viewers to see *themselves* in the cast. "If you're doing your job and producing a great show. . . . You want [the audience] sitting there to go, 'Oh my God, I could do that,'" explains Conlin. "Or, 'Oh my God, does she remind me of me.' Or, you know, your mother or brother going, 'Oh my

God, you look like her—you sound like her.'"[110] Here, again, reality TV (and, later, social media) helped redefine fame: Microcelebrities judged by a different, lower standard relative to A-listers, where familiar normalcy is corroborated by audiences seeing and assuming they have "lifestyle, shared experiences, and inner life" in common.[111] We'll see this imprinted on political strategy in later chapters.

On some level, it should be cautioned, this is tautological: Because reality TV usually focuses on the everyday lives of average folks rather than the otherworldly feats that movie stars perform, identification arrives that much easier. Yet even those real celebrities—as in the *truly* first-name famous, like Leo and Scarlett and Meryl—have long been subject to familiarity and likeability for economic value; this is what the "Q score" was specifically developed to measure.[112] Moreover, casting can signal the assumed audience niche: a "proxy" stand-in, on-screen, who casters believe, in aggregate, will deliver ratings and revenues to the program.[113]

Finally, and maybe most ineffably, reality TV authenticity must seem, for lack of a better word, effortless—the kind of "good TV" that the *Big Brother* casting director fetishizes in the chapter epigraph. *Queer Eye*'s Danielle Gervais illustrates here how casting looks for people not trying to give what they believe she wants: "Even a first interview, you feel like they're self-editing. As they're speaking, they're almost talking their soundbites. . . . That can be a bit of a red flag or people that are telling you things that they think we want to hear. They're trying to fit into these quote-unquote, like, 'reality TV boxes'" of character types.[114]

On the hunt for authenticity, producers desire, instead, those who seem natural, "with no or few signs of premeditation or self-consciousness"—a candidate none "too controlled, or seem[ing] staged and preplanned in their performances," which, again, should not seem like performances at all.[115] The scholar Grindstaff frames reality as "self-service" TV celebrity for this reason: Non-actors can walk in and deliver a performance not simply in spite of—but *because* of—their lack of training, credentials, and talent.[116] However: "If you want to be on TV consistently, and you're forever trying to get on a reality show, you're probably not what I'm looking for," *Jersey Shore*'s Doron Ofir explains.[117] "I tend to find people who don't want to be on TV. . . . They just happened to embed themselves in a world that I'm incredibly interested in."[118]

Alas, this goes against something fundamental to human nature that Goffman charted: "In our natural lives, whether you're going for an audition or a job interview, even like a college interview, what you're trying to do is fit what they're looking for. So very few people show up, you know, not really caring and just, like, saying what they mean," explains *The Kardashians'* Julie Pizzi, even though that's exactly what she wants: "somebody who's not trying to fit what they think we're looking for."[119] Susan Boyle, the unlikely star of season 3 of *Britain's Got Talent*, offers an exemplar of this: her authenticity affirmed by a spontaneity, a naiveté, a conspicuous lack of glamour—a "human rough cut" of sorts.[120] Reality TV seeks that self "unapologetically" unchanged, by either a calculating participant or production refinement.

The Aftermath of Reality's Authenticity

"Each time I am (or let myself be) photographed, I invariably suffer from a sensation of inauthenticity."[121] So said French philosopher Roland Barthes about a decade before *The Real World* hit the air, foreshadowing the main paradox of reality TV's arc: a genre of authenticity production has found it increasingly difficult to excavate the very ore that long defined it.

Early seasons of, say, *Big Brother* and *Survivor* featured contestants much less savvy to producer preferences or the tricks to grab screen time.[122] (Daytime talk in the '90s wised up in a similar way, the more well-known it got: One *Ricki Lake* producer estimated that, at the show's peak, a third of the guests might have been faking their stories to get on-air.[123]) My interviewees sketch an evolution of the genre: from its origins where those coming from Very Serious Documentaries pioneered fly-on-the-wall programming—a "Wild West" period of authenticity—to an explosion of cheap, slapdash, increasingly inauthentic conceits implemented in the aughts.[124] They also claim the pendulum might be swinging back again in the last decade, driven by millennial and Gen Z demand for less "overly produced" shows as well as new market entrants like Netflix and Amazon with the bandwidth to provide them. But the challenges remain acute for producers who must program for "most people [who] believe all reality is fake"—convincing them that it's not.

Because behavioral motives are central to adjudicating authenticity (i.e., are ambitions and actions intrinsic or extrinsically influenced?), so, too, have those proven key for professionals judging reality TV talent. "Part of our casting process is distilling people that want to be famous from people that authentically—*authentically*—want this [show] experience and they're showing up as their authentic selves," explains Pizzi, adding that background checks and psych evaluations can help pin this down.[125]

Obviously, few will openly, gauchely admit, "I want to be the next Kardashian, you know, I want to be rich and famous," and notoriety is often an unavoidable externality, but, for casting directors, it can't appear like the over-riding impulse.[126] *The Real World*'s McCarty tracks a career-long trend (that she finds particularly annoying) whereby auditionee goals seem to have mor-phed from the comparatively "real" to the effectively pseudo-evented: "In 2005, people, you know, students' bucket lists were still like, 'I'd like to climb Mount Kilimanjaro.' And now it's like: 'I want to be on a reality show.' 'I want to be a TikTokker, an Instagram influencer.'"[127] Many even come in openly promising her, "I'm going to get you great ratings."

Auditionees imitating *former* reality stars is an especially vexing, inauthentic trend that producers face. Women, in particular, often "automatically think if you're loud and obnoxious or if you're opinionated that makes you a better unscripted candidate," but an inauthentically outspoken façade will fade under the klieg-lights of 24/7 filming: "They can't maintain that bitch level, because they're not really a bitch," quips *Survivor*'s Adam Reider, who relies on intersti-tial interactions during phone call scheduling or in the waiting room to gauge if they "suddenly flip the switch" into what's assumed desirable.[128]

One dead giveaway of inauthenticity is anything that sounds too prepared, not least given the nature of the genre and its ideals of spontaneity: "You'll get some interview bites from people . . . that sound sort of scripted and, like, 'Why would they say it like that?' I mean, it sounds like the perfect soundbite and those are the right words that we would normally use, but it just doesn't feel right," puzzles *The Kardashians*' Jacob Lane. "It doesn't feel authentic to, like, the way they would actually talk. It sounds like they're on a reality show. And, so, we should not use this."[129]

Much better, for the purposes of authenticity, is a rougher-cut version of themselves, a self that's not angling so hard: "There's nothing more painful than seeing someone who's trying to act like they think they should be," says *Queer Eye*'s Gervais. "Whereas somebody who makes mistakes, who has a flub or two, but they're still themselves"—that's preferable.[130]

This has also gotten harder the more that young people have grown up watching reality TV—perhaps unknowingly internalizing those tropes and clichés, which sound inauthentic to older ears but may well scan genuine to Gen Z.[131] It's further complicated by operations like the New York Reality TV School, which, starting in the late aughts, offered techniques to "unlearn" those assumptions about what showrunners wanted so aspirants "could play them-selves with greater authenticity."[132] Online, sites collate casting calls, instruc-tional clips, and training tips for the hopeful aspirant.[133]

"Those are people I'm not interested in," scoffs *Jersey Shore*'s Ofir. "What I'm looking for is people who have the gift to be able to self-express themselves without sounding like an Instagram or a dating profile." He adds, "Everything is [now] about self-marketing. So, the authenticity is there, sort of, but it is now hidden [behind] a brick wall of whatever their brand is. And this starts at the age of ten now."[134]

Inextricable here is, of course, the rise of social media influencers, a phenomenon taken up expansively in chapter 5. By the end of the 2010s, nearly every major TikTok creator and content collective had entered into conversations about a more traditional reality show.[135] Networks and streaming outlets obviously recognize the potential value in crossover stars bringing built-in eyeballs with them.[136] (Although the evidence seems, as yet, inconclusive, notes one interviewee: "We have the saying of, like, 'followers don't always follow."[137])

This is no different than casting a celebrity in a sitcom or an athlete in an ad, adds Pizzi, who met with Sway House and Clubhouse, but found marketplace motives dominated too much of their thinking, at a cost of authenticity: "They want to show the business of making these [TikTok] videos as opposed to the personalities and personal lives of the characters," which she was seeking.[138]

In other cases, influencer opportunities represented the ideal *outcome* for reality participants; McCarty found that the majority of those she'd assembled for *The Circle* had abandoned their original professional endeavors in favor of "being themselves on Instagram" (which, cyclically, "influenced" the ambition of those trying out for season 2).[139] Even though the delusion is probably widespread that one can parlay reality stardom into post-show fame and fortune, rare is the Snooki who can package a lifestyle for 14 million followers on Instagram Stories rather than MTV.[140]

The problem, moreover, with casting big-time influencers is that, being self-aware, they tend to resist the virtues of spontaneity that reality TV has long harvested and showcased. "[They] sort of have a shtick, a story—something that they sort of address the audience with that often doesn't read very authentic to begin with," explains Pizzi. "To sort of strip that away so that they can show up, like, really vulnerable and raw and not so polished . . . actually really takes some time in training."[141] Typically, the cold calculation of personal branding—and the marketplace motives it is inextricable from—gets in the way of the influencer being "real": both "living in the moment" and relatable to audiences in the nonperformance of ordinariness.[142]

"They've figured out their brand and they are hard in on it. Like, let's say it's a bodybuilder and, you know, they're known for their biceps. Guess what they want to talk about all the time?" notes McCarty, who gets annoyed when networks push for including influencers. "[They] spend so much of their lives thinking, 'I'm going to live my life so that I can post about this,' rather than the other way around. . . . I don't want to watch somebody who's so aware of their own content."[143]

That same problem tends to bedevil reality show alums, Ofir adds: "I'm not interested [in them], because now they're no longer who they were before they were that—and that's when I want to find them," he says, adding later, "Once they realize they are liked [for something], they have to keep up with it," trying hard (inauthentically) at what came more naturally before. "The reasons that they are put on a show to begin with is usually the same thing that destroys them later."[144]

His point is one that will recur throughout the book: If media authenticity is defined by its apparent *lack* of mediation, then the media representation of it tends to despoil it being convincingly, enduringly authentic, forcing producers to look elsewhere for less corrupted alternatives. This is authenticity's dynamism; this is its restlessness in mediated culture. And as casters scour for those identity representations as a commodified source of industry profit—objectifying "real" people as products—they represent how affective, precarious, flexible, always-on, and often invisible labor powers more and more of advanced capitalism.[145]

For more than three decades, reality television has established these cultural principles of authenticity: that we should identify with as much as revere the renowned; that being unfiltered and confessional are the best ways of being true to yourself; and that we must trust the unrestrained heart rather than the conniving mind. Genre producers often excavate that authenticity, genealogically, from geographic and class-based margins and then try to coax out self-disclosure by effacing the media apparatus that makes it available to audiences—for the best performances of authenticity don't front like performances at all.

These principles of media logic inductively categorized here from reality TV will be carried forward and illuminated in other contexts like pop music, advertising, and politics. For as those decades of unscripted selves have piled up—and as stardom has been brought down to earth and smashed into a thousand D-list fragments—authenticity has become that much more evasive in the self-consciousness of those selected for its stage. Turns out, the more that "reality" is sought, the more it runs the risk of being faked.

TWO

xxxxxx

Social Media Designs

The Amateur Ideal

Authenticity is absolutely the key to a great tweet.

—DICK COSTOLO, former Twitter CEO[1]

Social media, to date, has largely been the
domain of real humans being fake.

—ALEXIS OHANIAN, co-founder of Reddit[2]

At the close of 2006, when *Time* magazine named "you" its "Person of the Year"—and appended a mirror surface to the computer screen on the issue's cover to drive home the point—it reflected not just an individual reader, gazing into the digital future, but a massive shift in the information environment.

The editors didn't yet have the now-ubiquitous phrase "social media" to draw upon—"user-generated content" and "Web 2.0" being terms of the time— but they nonetheless signaled how blogs, MySpace, YouTube, and Wikipedia would reposition the amateur from the margins of culture to its center.[3] That amateur ideal, as I'll reference throughout the book, has both been defined by and helped define authenticity in the two decades since—an ideal based upon everyday individuals, rather than professional media companies, creating and circulating popular content.[4]

Technology conditioned this cultural logic and fueled its hype. If broadcasting monolithically organized mass media for much of the last century, networks decentralized that power in ours.[5] As content traversed those pathways, often evading traditional gatekeeper judgment (albeit not its algorithmic equivalent), its viral quality—feeling "discovered" and "serendipitous"—also made it *seem* somehow more authentic and credible.[6]

Blogging, arguably the first form of social media, established the parameters and pretenses of this amateur ideal: free of corporate control, expressing "immediate, 'pure' reactions rather than rehearsed or calculated statements," as media scholar Gunn Enli describes, and, by being participatory and collaborative, also supposedly democratizing the "means of media production" to produce more authentic representations online.[7]

To blog, then, was to reject both the two-faced self and marketplace motives: posting on one's own behalf—indulgently idiosyncratic and openly biased—rather than fronting (and thus faking) as the objective voice of a staid news outlet, much less someone with commercial concerns.[8] And this was true not just of citizen journalists and blogosphere pioneers like Instapundit, Daily Kos, and Wonkette but equally of producers of lifestyle content. Travel bloggers hyped humble roots, tantalizing readers to follow in their flip-flopped footsteps; leading fashion bloggers alike posed as down-to-earth folk, renouncing the usual trappings of status symbols.[9]

YouTube, especially, claimed the mantle of viral populism. In *Videocracy*—a title aggrandizing with egalitarian pretense—Kevin Allocca, its head of culture and trends, argues that democratizing distribution sparked unprecedented cultural creativity, because the content is not "defined by the few with the economic means" to circulate it: "One of the many unusual experiences you have as a YouTube employee," he writes, "is the day you realize that you and your colleagues do not actually control the thing you are building together."[10]

This, of course, conveniently ignores the decisive power of the algorithm—programmed by humans, with all their flaws and biases, yet effacing those beneath the objective sheen of mathematical machinery. Still, myths need not be true in order to take hold. Users are told that their "empowering" engagement propels the amateur popularity of ordinary people (Rebecca Black! Damn Daniel! The Ice Bucket Challenge!) rather than the conspiring forces of corporate gatekeeping and information scarcity—that techno-democracy, not capitalism 2.0, rules social media.[11]

Allocca likens YouTube to the "folk art" of commoners, pre–Industrial Revolution and pre–mass media, before companies, elites, and professionals took over leisure time and delivered "bland and homogenized" content out of *broad*cast necessity.[12] (And even as companies, elites, and professionals seized upon YouTube in the years since its birth, many of the most popular videos remain, basically, amateurish productions—either authentically or by imitation.[13]) Not coincidentally, amateurism emerged as a concept in reaction to nineteenth-century industrialization and characterized dilettantes dabbling in off-hours spare time: activity done for its own sake rather than requiring economic reward.[14]

In sum, amateurs are essential to networked spaces just like the audience was the target for decades of broadcasting attention; they represent what's trending at the "grassroots" level, supposedly decentralized from power and indifferent to marketplace motives, an artless autonomy substantiating authenticity as content creators.[15] Tech companies celebrate and cozy up to that amateurism—framing their (professional, industrial) designs as ethical, idealistic, and innocuously embedded among users doing it for love, not money.[16] As Julian Assange, founder of Wikileaks, wryly quips to the *New Yorker*, "Everyone is an amateur in this business."[17]

How that business took shape is the story of this chapter.

Model Amateurs

In the years since *Time* fêted "you" 2.0, social media companies jockeyed to hype their own platforms as more authentic than competitors'. One clever study scoured the promotional pablum, CEO platitudes, and app store copy from Friendster onward, finding that nearly every site dotes on the same rhetorical clichés—like "real life" and "genuine"—as a means of defining itself against the purported phoniness of *other* sites.[18] But this might well be the narcissism of tiny differences at work: Copycatting took hold in social media design just as it had dictated decades of formulaic mass media content.

By early 2020, Twitter began testing Fleets, a copy of Instagram's Stories, which was itself ripped off from Snapchat; Snapchat developed Spotlight, comparable to Instagram's Reels and YouTube's Shorts, all of which were an attempt to fend off TikTok, itself a reincarnation of Vine, before it got bought by Twitter. As one *Wired* staffer snarked, "Which major platform has a news feed, disappearing posts, private messaging, and a live broadcasting feature? That would be . . . all of them."[19]

If the endgame is engagement—and it is, because that drives advertiser revenues—then every minute spent on TikTok comes at a cost to Facebook, Twitter, and so on. The tactics to keep us glued to our phones can feel downright nefarious in their addictive design, exploiting weaknesses in human psychology: the slot machine–dopamine rush that jolts us with unpredictable notifications; the likes, comments, and tagging that prey upon our desire for affirmation and belonging; the auto-play and endless feed-scrolling that militate against self-control; and the lure of personalizing our devices and tailoring their output so that it more closely mirrors our sense of self.[20]

Virtually everything on every social platform worth its salt has been A/B tested to make sure you spend more of your time on it.[21] And if that effort is successful, it's because they've also crafted what feels like an "authentic" place to spend that time. By 2020, Americans averaged an estimated 90 minutes per day thereabouts—a figure that only further skyrocketed with the onset of the pandemic.[22]

We should, therefore, scrutinize these platforms not as "neutral stages of self-performance" but, as new media theorist José van Dijck warns, "the very tools for shaping identities" and "normative behavior."[23] How, in other words, do social media sites try to demonstrate to their users what authenticity looks like and how to perform it themselves? For instance, by tallying followers and likes and stamping them on our accounts so prominently—metrics that could just as easily and modestly be stashed backstage—tech companies define success when using their products and encourage us to produce more content (i.e., our mediated lives) for ever larger audiences (i.e., our "friends").[24]

An introductory example, drawn from Instagram, might be instructive. Bailey Richardson's job, when hired as one of the first ten employees, was to manage the start-up's blog, suggest other follows, and curate—handpicking rather than algorithmically—the @instragram feed, which would grow to 600 million followers by 2023.[25]

But she was also, in effect, cultivating the community and culture of the platform and inducing its output by trying to establish norms around an aesthetic of accessibility and authenticity. Company decisions, she tells me, were obviously based upon "the ways we wanted people to share." And early on, Richardson wanted to emphasize that Instagram was a space for amateurs, not professionals, in what she modeled via the official channels. Thus, she would *only* feature people taking cellphone photos:

> We wanted it to be something that would make sense to someone who's new to the platform. So, if we had someone who was taking pictures with, like, an insane camera or, you know, with incredible depth of field or zoom capacity or something like that—that would be really confusing for someone who just, like, has a phone and doesn't understand how that got onto the app. The earliest days of thinking, in some ways, about authenticity, was really just about the actual hardware. . . . It should be taken with your phone; it should be from your perspective. And I think that's, like, the bare minimum of authenticity.[26]

Even as more professional photographers flocked to the app, she spotlighted (and thus rewarded and encouraged) their more pedestrian scenery rather than jaw-dropping tableaus: "We were sort of trying to represent—not the lowest common denominator, but the most accessible sort of denominator of how to make content."

Additionally, she claims, the site did not fall over itself early on to promote the output of celebrities (e.g., boosting their photos or suggesting them as follows) in the way that other social networks gave blue-checkmark types the white-glove treatment, because their lives could seem remote to amateurs, dousing participatory interest: "If you're already famous, that doesn't mean you made interesting content on Instagram; it doesn't mean that you actually made content that other people would want to mimic or mirror."

Content made by celebrities—or other elites and professionals, for that matter—elicits more suspicion than that of amateurs, as TikTok's brand partnership director, Hudson Sullivan, explains: "When people see something that's polished, they assume it's been constructed; it's been delicately crafted. There's this inauthenticity to it, because it's, like, well, they have a professional shoot. And that was staged; that is fake," he says. Creators should, instead, "focus more on these smaller, more relatable moments that are shot in a way that just makes people feel like, 'Wow—that actually happened!'"[27]

The tension between professional legitimacy and unencumbered amateur license represents authenticity's fulcrum here: a trade-off between perfected quality and democratized dabbling.[28] In a book on social media entertainment, scholars Stuart Cunningham and David Craig explain that elite media's long-standing legacy of "fictionalized abstraction from the everyday and encrusted barriers to entry" gives off a vibe of artifice.[29]

YouTube's Allocca echoes this in conversation: "One of the ways to boil it down is through the levels of mediation that the content goes through," he explains. "Amateur" signifies "a person has shot the thing themselves, and posted the thing, which means there's no layer besides the platform . . . between the creator and the viewer." A TV show, on the other hand, has "a hundred people between you and the person who made the thing"—from writers to camera operators to executives to advertisers—and "they actually shape what the person on the camera can or can't say."[30]

Thus, the timeless tale told of Web 2.0, from bloggers onward: an old media stereotyped and scorned as "corporate, bullying, exploitative, elitist, and anti-democratic" set against new media that postures as "grassroots, collaborative, independent, customizing, empowering, and democratic."[31] Unlike professionals, marketplace motives do not blemish the amateur, who innocently, romantically—albeit precariously—toils away at autonomous self-realization, without money or its strings attached, and wins the credibility prize of authenticity.

Tech companies *themselves* undertake these contortions when they embrace the "garage myth" origin story. That is, by emphasizing in corporate narratives that, say, Apple and Google started in a messy home garage or that Mark Zuckerberg and Bill Gates dropped out of college, they position the company in lineage with amateur ideals. (Even Silicon Valley's informal, fleece-forward fashion announces humble origins: Zuck's iconic hoodie, worn seemingly whenever he's not being grilled at congressional hearings, looks like the sort of Saturday casual get-up one might wear while cleaning the yard.)

Rich Silverstein, an advertising creative director, recalls posing then-CEO Carly Fiorina literally in front of the Palo Alto garage where HP was founded for one commercial.[32] That spot starts with grainy archival footage of a decaying, barn-like structure, her voiceover narrating: "This is the workshop of radicals—a one-car garage where two young men with five hundred dollars in venture capital invented an industry. . . . The original start-up will act like one again," she proclaims. Said "start-up" wound up bringing in $63 billion in annual revenues. Not bad for a day's fun.

"[That] tells a whole slew of people that if they have an amazing idea and no money and no connections, they can someday maybe make it, too," Yael Cesarkas, another Bay Area–based ad industry executive, notes of this creation-story cliché. "It's like from nothing to something, right? That anyone, any guy in the hoodie that drops out . . . that can be you, too."[33]

The garage myth is useful, strategically: American Dream in architectural shorthand, ratifying an often-misplaced faith in the wide-openness of class meritocracy. And, maybe more pivotally, it blunts the impression of marketplace motives, at a time when, circa 2021, the market cap of FAANG stocks (the acronym for leading US tech companies) had soared to a modest $7 trillion.[34] These idealized origins, from the alleged margins, assuage antitrust-agitating anxiety about the unchecked political, economic, and cultural power of corporate entities of unprecedented size and scale.

If you can picture a young Jeff Bezos in a tiny home office, you might be less defensive about his company devouring the entirety of American retail. If you recall the most famous Super Bowl commercial of all-time—a *1984* allusion where a lone figure rebels against mindless automatons in an IBM-dominated dystopia—you might still be inclined to think of Apple as scrappy upstart rather than the most valuable company in history. These are postures of humility by capitalist institutions that function as anything but.

"The garage mythology is about humanizing the brand, right? It's about making technology and the scale of what they do and what they touch feel, like, homegrown and local and friendly or everyday," explains Chris Cummings, a chief strategy officer who consulted on some of that same mythology for General Electric. "A lot of those big brands and those big corporations want to operate small, want to think small, want to act small, want to behave small. . . . There's authenticity in that smaller feels so much realer."[35] No one should, of course, confuse Amazon or Facebook for "small," though that is precisely what garage-myth authenticity hopes to convince us.

Single-Identity Authenticity

Identity has been aptly called the "primary commodity of the social media culture industry," which means that, like reality TV studios, this industry must design to produce that commodity, also through genuine self-disclosure.[36] This further erodes what's considered public and what should be kept private. One study of the most popular YouTube channels, for example, finds that when vloggers reveal their personal lives, they're rated as more authentic.[37] Such "authenticity work" necessitates inviting audiences backstage, behind the curtain, to offset suspicions of a scheming two-faced self; media scholars Brooke Duffy and Emily Hund term this the "visibility mandate" of social media, an overriding imperative to "put oneself out there."[38] And the more you divulge, the more "real" you make yourself for the surveillance capitalism that profits from that (non)performance.[39]

Such self-disclosure shows up in all kinds of ways online. YouTube's Allocca reports that, to court teen fans, in particular, transparency and sharing vulnerability is practically a prerequisite for success on the platform.[40] Likewise, influencers who sprinkle in "tidbits of curated intimacy" from their backstage lives—say, scenes of children and pets—project relatability, which, as we'll see in chapter 5, can then be sold onward to brands and advertisers.[41] In that sense, "filler material" anchors authenticity: the "raw, unfiltered, spontaneous" interludes of daily life from domestic contexts—"purposefully mundane and inane"—that demonstrate microcelebrities are, indeed, just like us.[42]

Vloggers' popularity depends upon staging such authenticity, where sociologist Erving Goffman's distinction between front and back spaces of self-performance withers away with each banal, "slice of life" divulgence.[43] For beauty genres featuring makeup preparation or shower routines, we see the self being assembled, cosmetically, rather than the finished (two-faced) product required for public display. For example, Luhhsetty, a beauty vlogger, netted 5 million views for video of her hair and legs being washed; JoJo Siwa, another YouTube personality, racked up 23 million to watch her brushing teeth and applying makeup.

Revealingly, bathrooms—that most intimate of home spaces, where the self is exposed in all its unvarnished, embarrassing authenticity—figure prominently on TikTok, especially among popular collaboratives like Hype House, partly chosen for its bathroom size and abundant mirrors.[44] Few examples better embody the private-going-public quite like this trend, as mirrored selfies shot there, with their low production value and unstaged ordinariness, tend to outperform non-bathroom-setting footage: "Knowing how to film yourself speaking with a cellphone in a bathroom mirror is a new skill to be mastered," explains one social media strategist. "It's part of the craft."[45]

Even among gaming vloggers, a great deal of self-disclosure and personal information is expected (the filler material overlaid to gameplay), perhaps owing to the fact that influencer talent is based less upon storytelling mediation— absent production crews and editors—and more on charismatic personality.[46] For "real" celebrities (i.e., movie stars) as well, pressure has mounted to casually self-disclose on social—offering "the impression of candid, uncensored looks" into backstage lives, creating the "illusion of intimacy" and *im*perfected selves.[47] (Seeing celebrities interact with each other online further indulges the illusion that we're getting some sort of an insider glimpse of relationships otherwise remote to fans.[48])

Pivotal to social media authenticity, like reality TV before it, is the somewhat paradoxical obligation to not seem like you're trying for it, for authenticity can never come off as instrumental; per Rousseau, it must exist only for itself.[49] Yet because every profile is, inherently, a deliberate affectation and curation of the hoped-for frontstage impression, all that blood, sweat, and tears of self-presentation has to be rendered invisible, or it will scan as inauthentic if the creator seems like they care about the audience reaction or have worked hard (or falsely) to project themselves there.[50]

Thus, spontaneity—or at least the façade of it—is key to authenticating those performances of self-disclosure, not least given that these sites function as machines of "calculated authenticity," structured for premeditated mediations.[51] For bloggers and microbloggers alike, that "real self" is established by constant, instinctive status updates rather than the edited, delayed texts posted to traditional media formats.[52] Twitter, in particular, has sold itself as the "guardian of real-time authenticity"—its immediate ephemerality a supposedly more realistic representation of any given moment than the "plodding, packaged deliberation" about it.[53]

"Context collapse" complicates these calculations. That's the scholarly term for how social media tends to break down boundaries between diverse, offline social networks, reassembling them into a single audience, now numbering your best friend, grandmother, and boss, all of whom observe the performance of a suddenly singularized self—and often, in turn, resulting in a self-censored, inoffensive, "lowest-common denominator" version that's safe for those various eyeballs, if not all that authentic-seeming.[54] Facebook, maybe more so than any other tech company, impelled that context collapse, partly because its success depended on designing a platform that induces an online performance of a "true" offline self.

Those norms were, in fact, embedded within design choices. Zuckerberg famously made plain his disregard for our multistage, two-faced selves in an oft-quoted line: "You have one identity. The days of you having a different image for your work friends or co-workers and for the other people you know are probably coming to an end pretty quickly," he declared, dancing on the grave of Goffman's theory. "Having two identities for yourself is an example of a lack of integrity."[55] Thus, "single-identity authenticity" became the social network's initial market strategy, with registration and onboarding rhetoric steeped in claims and commands to that end.[56]

The design choice may well have been critical to Facebook vanquishing its closest early competitors, Friendster and MySpace, and the company benefited from being able to draft off .edu email addresses as the gatekeeping mechanism for sign-ups (originating with Ivy League exclusivity and trickling outward). "The .edu email system served as this authenticating clearinghouse," explains Tim Kendall, who served as Facebook's director of monetization in its first decade. "Really, users zero through ten million were all verified and authenticated by the .edu email system, [while], you know, MySpace had fifty-seven Jennifer Anistons."[57]

Identity is perhaps the most lucrative commodity you can trade in. As Sheryl Sandberg crowed to a tech conference in 2008, "We've taken the power of real trust, real user privacy controls, and made it possible for people to be their authentic selves online. And that is what we think explains our growth."[58] (Within two presidential election cycles, Russian trolls would make a mockery of this boast.)

This was, moreover, no average network system to draw from: College students, Kendall notes, circulate within "the most socially dense environment that probably exists in America."⁵⁹ As such, "even though there was the virtual and then the real, because the real was so socially dense, it made it difficult to make shit up in the virtual, because you have this feedback loop in the real that was incredibly tight and fast because of the density." The development of News Feed as an early innovation, aggregating profile status updates into a single homepage flow, amped up authenticity strategizing and altered the history of human behavior. Kendall adds:

> Now I can disclose and now I get that my disclosure gets put in a contest with lots of other people's [disclosures] and then the algorithm picks the winner. . . . [We] created this sort of popularity contest via NewsFeed, absolutely. . . . It's like, I can take the picture that sort of accurately illustrates my vacation or I can take the picture that . . . is airbrushed and makes it look like I have the most incredible time and that picture is going to do better in NewsFeed. . . . That feedback loop also, I think, further amplified disclosure and sort of induced and incentivized disclosure as well.

Perhaps even more than Facebook and its competitors, dating websites—which nearly a third of Americans have used—shoulder the burden of inducing authentic self-disclosure, so I reached out to Sam Yagan, co-founder of OkCupid before running Tinder and Grindr.⁶⁰ He recalls how, in the 1990s, online dating retained an undesirable stigma, perhaps owing to the falsity of usernames and other means of inauthentic representation. "You [were] sort of invited to assume an identity different from your own when you log into your [dating] account," he notes—a backdrop they designed and strategized against.⁶¹

Thus, when, say, Tinder piggybacked on Facebook's authenticity checkpoint for account sign-ups—forcing behavior to be tacked against and influenced by preexisting network identity—"people felt like these [other] people were real. And so, okay, this isn't the stories you used to hear from about online dating of, like, you meet someone and it's some serial killer," he says. "This is actually Sam and Sam actually went to Harvard and, you know, Sam has thirty-six friends in common or whatever. . . . Then you're like, well, if he wants to get set up for a drink, maybe that's okay."

Hence, Tinder's tagline ("like real life but better") sold authenticity to users as practice and product—with consistency countering cultural anxieties about dating being "virtual or separate from everyday life."⁶² Ultimately, all online communication bears the burden of proof in this vein: It must compensate for the absence of face-to-face veracity by demanding real names and profile photos lest that canine in the old *New Yorker* cartoon succeed in his boast, "On the internet, nobody knows you're a dog."[63]

The Rough Cut

What, then, characterizes the aesthetic of authenticity on social media? I would call it the "rough cut"—a concept that will diagnose a broad formula of strategies seen across pop culture, advertising, and politics in coming chapters. Media scholar Gunn Enli similarly casts authenticity as a production genre, encompassing everything from tiny tweaks to lighting and sound to major editing alternations.[64] The ambition is, paradoxically, to make media that seems unmediated, because the mediation process is implicitly antithetical to authenticity.

Thus, if, in the last chapter, TV reality had to seem "found rather than produced," so, too, should amateur creators appear to lack the professional talents "to manufacture the things they depict" and instead "merely record" them, with comparative naiveté.[65] Spontaneity, again, defines authentic output, as media scholars Meredith Salisbury and Jefferson Pooley observe: "a social-media presence that comes off as effortless, carefree, and/or indifferent to audience reaction," concealing "forethought and planning," and evinced by postings and photos that don't appear too "fussed over."[66]

A short-lived, mid-2010s app called Beme allowed users to share five-second disappearing clips that couldn't be edited or previewed before upload so as to capture a more "real-life, real-time interaction"; the start-up wanted "to calculate the sensation of uncalculatedness [and] engineer unenginereedness."[67] A decade later, its chart-topping descendent, BeReal, fulfilled the promise of this premise, with 56 million downloads notifying users at random times each day to snap an immediate selfie for friends, sans filters, retakes, and poses to showcase mundane, unflattering lives; countless articles heralded BeReal as the triumph of intimacy, imperfection, and authenticity and, of course, competing platforms attempted to copy the feature.[68] This necessity of spontaneity also translates to writing online, as informality of prose and outright grammatical and spelling typos, rather than conniving, corrected calculation, are thought to signal authentic expression; as a certain former US president demonstrated, detailed further in chapter 7, this can provide a contrast to the usual "overly managed" politician profiles.[69]

YouTube, maybe as much as any site, influenced the aesthetics of rough cut authenticity: messy in both its cinematography and editing norms. "The mistakes—the kind of, you know, off-kilter angle, these are other things that also contribute to that idea of, 'Oh, this is a real person,'" explains Allocca, its head of culture and trends. "A lot of the successful YouTube creators leave in their mistakes—they edit them in."[70]

Examples of this technique—an ironic aspiration toward imperfection—abound. They include "grainy or blurred footage and 'clumsy' editing" and casual, impromptu, or outtake "filler" scenes in between the primary thrust of a video topic.[71] For instance, one "Pillow Talk" installment from beauty YouTuber Michelle Phan finds her opening up about the dark poetry she wrote as a teen and leaves in a car horn interruption outside her home. Because the vlogging ideal is "liveness, immediacy and conversation," established by a single camera in an ordinary setting, a creator must be transparently self-referential about the production apparatus—all connoting "an anti-professional sense of the real."[72]

This rough cut is both stylistic in its unfiltered ambitions—people "going out of their way to make their photos look worse," one internet reporter observes—as well as substantive, as when, say, a creator opens up candidly about mental health struggles.[73] One mid-pandemic trend found users earning thousands of likes for self-diagnosing psychological pathologies and openly announcing their worst personality peccadillos on TikTok and Twitter (e.g., "My toxic trait is my sadness turns into destructive anger").[74] As one teen told *The Atlantic*, "It's not cool anymore to be manufactured"—hence, the "realness" that the authenticity industries attempt to manufacture.

If one had to identify a poster child for the rough cut aesthetic and ethos, it might well be Gen Z icon Emma Chamberlain, who perfected, imperfectly, a skittery, slapstick vlogging style of jarring edits, subtitle typos, surreal distortions, conspicuous zooms, and corny sound effects. Inheriting reality TV's penchant for plotless minutiae (and served with a healthy dollop of neuroses and self-referentiality), Chamberlain's "I Made Myself Dinner" garnered 10 million of her nearly 1 billion views for a riveting travelogue to her grocery store and kitchen.[75] She establishes authenticity through sloppy self-presentation: "enlarging a pimple on her forehead, putting reverb on a burp, slowing down her voice and replaying when she said something particularly dumb," *New York* magazine observes, and "editing her content in a way that shows 'flaws' and paints a 'relatable' portrait."[76]

To be certain, all that seeming sloppiness takes serious precision: Chamberlain estimates that she'll spend as many as thirty hours editing a single clip.[77] (The extensiveness of this editing might be inversely proportional to the depth of narrative it conveys: the former working to compensate for the absence of the latter.) Still, with the ease of app-based tools like transitions, lip syncs, and green-screening, this editing doesn't aim for seamlessness—which usually helps maintain the conceit of fictionalized mass media stories—but rather disruption, announcing itself openly via "distortions, filters, and overlaid text."[78] Add in deliberately debased audio, flub takes, and shaky camera close-ups and you get an "anti-Instagram perfection movement" and "anti-premium aesthetics," as Allocca summarizes it.[79]

Indeed, Instagram, as it evolved in the last decade, often represents the aesthetic antithesis against which other platforms measure their authenticity. Those glossy, perfectly manicured tableaus the app became infamous for, ironically, run contrary to early design intent; Bailey Richardson, an early employee, describes how speedy, efficient upload was the original engineering imperative—particularly given network and software torpor, circa 2010— but that, upon Facebook acquisition, they discovered, "in fact, people spent a shitload of time, like, editing their picture and deciding on their caption and choosing a filter"—all hallmarks and machinations of *inauthenticity*.[80] (Filters themselves—now both ubiquitous and seen as visually disingenuous—were developed "on a whim" and implemented only at the behest of the founder's wife, but drove many early downloads to improve smartphone camera quality.)

Sun-kissed, faux-nostalgic hazes enveloped user output, along with envy- and eyeroll-inducing, faux-humility hashtags like #blessed appended to far-flung travels and mouth-watering food porn.[81] Among filters, the warm, washed-out, vintage Polaroid look attempted to recover "aura"—that "language of photographic imperfection"—and thus an analog rebuke to the technological standardization afforded by and witnessed in crisp, icy, digital pics.[82] #NoFilter caveats even arose as an authenticity *backlash* to all those ostensibly posed lifestyles on what became a premium channel, stylistically speaking.[83] Facetune, which enables magazine-quality photoshopping, topped paid-app charts and netted $200 million in venture capital.[84] (If any platform deserves the wry judgment of the earlier epigraph quote—that social media has largely been "the domain of real humans being fake"—it's Instagram.)

While professional media long made audiences—namely, female audiences—feel inadequate about their bodies and lives, social media now ginned up much the same anxiety, what with its parade of FOMO highlights from friends and quasi-friends; in response, to feign relatability, prominent

Instagrammers interspersed more pedestrian pics ("making dinner, rinsing with Listerine") among their glam scenes of "floating in the Aegean Sea [and] sunbathing on a yacht."[85] Couture even turned toward unaffected affectation, with Instagram's fashion director claiming that "blurry photos that give users a behind-the-scenes look" perform the best metrics: "The fashion industry has been invested in making hyper-produced content and controlling everything, [but] what does well on Instagram are the outtakes."[86]

As Instagram ossified these aesthetic expectations, Snapchat proffered an alternative of informality and, hence, authenticity. The company announced its position contra Insta's "carefully curated, finely filtered, and generally up-tight gallery show" in its first blog post: "Snapchat isn't about capturing the traditional Kodak moment" (a reference that surely sailed well over the heads of its teenage user base).[87] Still, by offering the option of sharing photos that disappear, it sold spontaneity and candor through ephemerality, lowering the stakes and contrasting the "museum-like" look that other services pressured.[88]

In turn, Instagram tried to chill: Users toyed with "finsta" accounts, shared only with close pals for sillier, shameless (more "real") imagery; opted for "'meta selfies' that make the behind-the-scenes work visible"; and deliberately blurred photo dumps of random images rather than aiming for fussed-over masterpieces.[89] Meanwhile, the company copy-and-pasted Snap's innovation, launching Stories, which "emphasize who you are, not necessarily who you wish to be seen as"—disavowing the inauthenticity of two-faced selves that get manipulated and manufactured online.[90]

TikTok further exploited this trend at decade's end, becoming the first non-Facebook mobile app to surpass 3 billion downloads and dethroning Google as the most trafficked internet domain.[91] Its brand partnership director, Hudson Sullivan, trumpets this—admittedly self-servingly, though not necessarily incorrectly—as a victory over fakery: "[Instragram's] basically almost designed to make your friends jealous. . . . It kind of makes me depressed a little bit sometimes when I go on Instagram and I feel, like, 'Oh, I'm not fit enough. I'm not successful enough'. . . . You go to [TikTok] and it's more people giving you a portal into their everyday lives. . . . You get the sense that people are just sharing more of their sort of real life, everyday experiences. It's not overly polished; it's raw; it's zany. But, most importantly, it's authentic."[92]

That framing frequently shows up in the hype by and about TikTok, but a global Nielsen study did find that more than half of users trust others "to be their real selves" on the platform—a survey figure that Instagram would be hard-pressed to reach.[93] As one venture capital investor put it in a tart Substack take: "Where Instagram filters in 2011 made everyone beautiful, TikTok filters in 2021 make everyone ugly."[94]

The medium may well be the message here: Because TikTok video is formatted vertically (per smartphone handheld habits), it gives off a more amateur vibe than the horizontal alternative, which visually inherits the orientation of screens for professional content at movie theaters and living room TVs.[95]And the app's biggest stars, like Charli D'Amelio, excel at relatability, with dance moves choreographed to give an "offhand, casual quality," making her seem more "approachable" than skilled competitors.[96] Her sometimes-paramour and fellow TikTok celebrity, Lil Huddy, testifies to imperfection's viral value: "The weird people get the furthest on the internet."[97]

During the depths of the pandemic—when best lives couldn't really be lived outside of lockdown and sweatpants chic reigned—TikTok furnished a platform for casual honesty and saw engagement rates skyrocket. Instagram, naturally, attempted to rip this off by deploying a Reels option for short clips set to music.

A Feed Just "For You"

Social media authenticity also leans heavily on direct address, especially in online video meant to contrast the fictional narratives of traditional media: breaking the fourth wall, forthrightly, and shrugging off the conceit that the audience somehow isn't actually there. One YouTube Creator Academy tutorial explicitly recommends "talking to viewers in an authentic way on camera" so as to give fans "access to the real you."[98]

Decades of television undoubtedly conditioned these patterns and reflexes of parasocial connection: eye contact with news anchors; increasingly informal language; confessional tropes in reality programming; and the way that, at home, the viewing experience tends to blend in with ordinary routines.[99] Selfies, which represent the still-photography equivalent of vlogging's direct address, must abide by similar expectations—being ratified, positively, when they seem casual, intimate, unedited, and capturing a real moment rather than staging an artificial one.[100] Authenticity is, once more, an effortless achievement: A photo *shouldn't* look like a pseudo-event that exists only to be captured, even though that's inescapably what selfies are.

In sum, social media celebrity demands what cultural studies scholar Mingyi Hou calls "staged authenticity"—offering an "intimate and private self" who interacts with fans to show they have much in common and, in fact, are no better than them.[101] Michelle Phan, the beauty vlogger, has thus likened herself and fellow creators to "friends, brothers, or sisters to the audience" rather than idols.[102] And one survey of teens found that YouTube stars were seen as "more authentic, approachable, and influential" than their mainstream equivalents.[103]

For vloggers, this relational labor of fan feedback can take up half their time and, because a standardized response scans as inauthentic, it's "nonscalable" interactivity, to say nothing of the in-person meetups and event invites which also maintain that appearance of familiarity.[104] "You have this expectation [on YouTube] that [creators] need to . . . be in the comments and responding to the comments," Allocca tells me. "When you watch a movie, like, the director doesn't come out afterwards and ask you what you thought. . . . That builds a relationship with the viewer [who has] some investment in what's created, and you also feel like you're a part of the content."[105]

Most memes have long hinged on a similar adaptability: the degree to which the user is able to see *themselves* reflected in some joke or trend determines their virality (a logic seen in how reality TV participants are cast in the previous chapter).[106] Opportunities to join in have driven everything from Ice Bucket challengers to "Gangnam Style" dance imitators; more recently, TikTok videos employ conversational grammar, with volleying emulations, sea shanty duets, and personal twists, thanks to a speedy, user-friendly interface built for green screens, background music, and meme-mimicking.[107] BuzzFeed, in particular, pioneered a web publishing model that involves dumping a variety of content, absorbing the data of what gets shared most, and then tailoring future content accordingly, which can be more spontaneous, reactive, and thus authentic to audiences.[108]

In that sense, algorithms themselves might be thought of as cogs in the authenticity machine: trying to get the right "feeling" content in front of the right people so that the platform feels personalized and genuine to them. Echoing descriptions of YouTube as a "giant crowdsourcing exercise," Allocca notes how machine learning processes would model and auto-play those relevant videos based upon metadata and user habits.[109] This, rather distressingly, contributed to problems of polarization and extremism as users get "rabbit holed," by design, down crazy content streams.[110]

Twitter faced some of the same challenges of algorithmic authenticity, according to Alex Roetter, former senior vice president of engineering, who framed his job as a "giant info retrieval problem," sifting through and funneling the most approachable, pertinent content—against a deluge of voluminous alternatives—via iterative improvements to someone's timeline.[111]

This, he explains to me, was especially critical in the immediate hours and days after a sign-up—"We have to get you a Twitter that works for you. . . . We have to get you following people you're going to care about immediately," before it's a dead account—training the algorithm to take whatever minimal information might be available about the user (in some cases, name and IP address alone) to customize and maximize attentiveness, using lookalike populations as a crutch.[112] He also endeavored to juice user output, since "almost no one tweets"—truly, a mere fraction of total accounts—such that "when you author something, [we're] getting other people to favorite it or react to it, so you're not tweeting into a void."

TikTok's algorithmic innovation—topically populating feeds biased less toward follower counts in a creator's social graph, like Instagram, and more off content trending (AI-extrapolated from captions, hashtags, and sounds) and engagement rates (e.g., likes, comments, lengths viewed)—seems to reward newcomer uploads who can score hundreds of thousands of likes if the clip is strong enough; it fosters the indulgence, as *Ad Age* put it, "that anyone can become a breakout star."[113] Hudson Sullivan, a brand partnership director at the company, furthers underscores the populist pretense here: "On TikTok, you can have little to no following, but if you're producing great content, the app will make sure that that content gets seen by a lot of people. And, so, we use the expression 'democratizing creativity' a lot, you know, in terms of our pitch stacks."[114] Not coincidentally, "democratizing creativity" was also the authenticity conceit of YouTube's *Videocracy* years earlier.

The Market Value for True Selves

Authenticity is, alas, still commercially motivated here—for as media scholars Meredith Salisbury and Jefferson Pooley cleverly put it: "One person's expressive self-fulfillment is another's profit margin."[115] That's certainly been long true for dating websites; as OkCupid's CEO Sam Yagan summarizes, "You give us data. We give you dates."[116] (He neglected to add, "Advertisers give us money!")

Yagan co-founded the website to contrast with predecessors like eHarmony and Match, designing an algorithm that funneled and targeted based upon *user*-submitted questions, rather than relying upon company-determined (less authentic) queries; the platform also allowed users to rank, weight, and skip, and required them to suss out an ideal pairing—"empowering each person effectively to create their own, you could say, authentic, or at least self-driven or self-written matching algorithm."[117] They also mined for correlations to flag and offset disingenuous answers in match confidence intervals, based upon data from millions of others' members: "If someone is answering these questions highly irregularly," Yagan explains, "there's a chance of this person who's trying to not be authentic." He adds, "We spent a lot of time incentivizing people to give us a lot of information." If a user didn't, their matches would be tattooed— quite deliberately and conspicuously—with a "0% confidence" caveat.

"Nobody wants a big zero next to their profile. So, people immediately said, 'Okay, well, I'm going to start answering more questions.'" Divulging more and getting better dates, "You start to realize, 'Wait a minute—this works. I give OkCupid some data about myself, I reveal myself, I disclose, and I find people.'" And even if he can't recall explicitly using the word "authenticity" within internal company conversations, "I have to understand something authentic about you in order to make an authentic match. So, we did spend a lot of time trying to figure out how do you learn who someone is. And, to that extent, I think we were very much in pursuit of determining one's authentic self."

For social media companies, authentic expression from transparent, uniform user identities makes for better data to mine and sell; the more connected and communicative that participants are within a given platform, the more lucrative that platform's market share.[118] This is the essence of social psychologist Shoshana Zuboff's notion of surveillance capitalism: the technologies that capture, predict, and modify individual behavior have, not coincidentally, become some of the most valuable money-making assets known to humankind.[119]

Google birthed this business model at the turn of the century, instrumentalizing human activity and monetizing information architecture—and its logic informed all the Big Tech ambition that followed to hoover up as much social knowledge as possible.[120] Thanks to "pervasive computer mediation," Zuboff argues, almost every aspect of the world (and people's lives) becomes "visible, knowable, and sharable"—feeding advertiser frenzy and shaping civilization.[121]

This also partly explains Facebook's disinformation panic. In response to an infestation of election interference by nefarious political actors, detailed more in chapter 7, Facebook doubled down on the feature that catapulted it past MySpace a decade earlier: policies to affirm accounts aren't from faked identities. Expunging nearly 3 billion fake accounts in 2017 and 2018, it added an "Authenticity" entry to its community standards, declaring: "We believe that authenticity creates a better environment for sharing."[122]

However, as legal scholar Sarah Haan shrewdly discerns, "Authenticity provides significant *business* value. . . . [It helps] Facebook quantify and surveil users, fix fees for advertisers, measure user growth, and develop accurate machine learning."[123] In other words, its Big Data panopticon *needs* truthful inputs, lest someone's misrepresentation (around, say, age or interests) glitch the microtargeting systems that ensure a smooth and assured ad-buy marketplace for custom audiences.[124] One trillion dollars in market cap, at peak, depended on it.

Amateurs Go Pro

As social media matured over two decades, opportunities for amateurs to professionalize grew considerably. Creative across platforms and, in some cases, globally popular, these jack-of-all-production-trade entrepreneurs could churn out content quickly and cheaply, pioneering a new route to media work and fame with fewer barriers to entry while clinging to authenticity as a core ideal.[125] VidCon, held annually in Anaheim, swelled to become the premier confab for this sub-industry, as one-third of tweens hoped to make a career as a YouTuber.[126]

All this reshuffled the power, financing, and participation within traditional screen industries toward streaming and social platforms, as professionals integrate amateurs into their systems, imperatives, and business models.[127] Meanwhile, those social media entertainers—many of whom began tinkering, for fun, with self-taught video creation as a hobby in adolescence, with no designs on income much less a viable career path, and thus exercised more creative control over their output than professionals—must now contend with that long-standing specter of inauthenticity: marketplace motives.[128]

Beauty vloggers, in particular, were at the monetization vanguard, aligning easily with fashion and consumer brands; similarly, internet stars like Grace Helbig and Lilly Singh gradually graduated to traditional TV shows.[129] Both the pandemic stoppage of formal shoots and the Gen Z-resonance of influencers (able to continue production independently) pushed Hulu and Netflix to chase TikTok headliners like Charli D'Amelio and Addison Rae for projects.[130] Late-night TV already harbored a convergent, symbiotic relationship with amateur internet video—taking cues from trending topics, pillaging for quirky clips, and seeding their own professional content back into the space.[131] And platforms themselves had to allocate funding to prolific creators to keep their confines vibrant: $1 million per day to launch Snapchat's Spotlight rollout; $100 million for Shorts on YouTube; and a cool $1 billion of Meta money for Facebook and Instagram creations.[132]

Again, though, amateurs are valued (by audiences and professional industries alike) precisely *because* they come across as doing it for love, not money, which means that industries can embed their designs on money and power, while shrouding them with an egalitarian, populist sheen—crowdsourcing promotional machinations through a TikTok creator, a basement tweeter, a YouTube cineaste.[133] This renders black-and-white distinctions between the amateur and the professional increasingly irrelevant, given co-creative arrangements: "The reality-TV celebrity, the social media user, the blogger, the citizen journalist, the hacker, and the media intern are all roles performed somewhere between the lines of paid/unpaid [and] authorized/unofficial," as digital culture scholar Caroline Hamilton tallies.[134]

One of YouTube's very first stars exemplified this mold: lonelygirl15. The web series, launched a mere year after YouTube's founding, chronicled the bedroom-based video diary of a teenage girl thrust into a bizarre family cult; it played her fictitious background and adventures as real, before being exposed as a hoax. Greg Goodfried, co-creator of lonelygirl15, cast his YouTube project in lineage with previous real-or-fake entertainment like *Gulliver's Travels*, *The War of the Worlds*, and *The Blair Witch Project*: "lonelygirl15 was the very beginning of user-generated content—users having the power to upload to a service and millions of people being able to go to it and watch it and you wouldn't know. You're not on alert if this is real or not."[135] (Goodfried also pioneered proto-influencer opportunities, with the paid integration of Hershey's and Neutrogena products woven into the storyline.)

YouTube's Allocca adds, "Audiences were so drawn to people sharing themselves honestly in front of the camera, they rarely even question the authenticity of the motives behind it. . . . lonelygirl15 became part of a larger trend of productions built around transparency and reality (even when fabricated)."[136] Yet some fans eventually felt betrayed by the *inauthenticity* of the scheme, which had to reconcile the apparent technical savvy of the production and the star's purported amateurism.[137]

Precisely for that reason, as amateurs and amateur platforms increasingly professionalize, they cling to conceits—technological or economic—that reaffirm their original amateurism, and even as production quality can "afford" to get better (financially, if not in terms of relatable credibility), it's sometimes made to seem worse or, at least, raw, spontaneous, unfiltered, or ordinary.[138] Thus, "symbolic amateurism" fronts the pose of a naïve nonprofessional (e.g., "commercially disinterested and emotionally invested") to seem like marketplace motives aren't, inauthentically, determining the content.[139]

Seeking to avoid emulating professional media, the manager for one YouTube sketch comedy channel explains, "We hired actors. We wrote scripts. We had full-scale productions. But we didn't want it to look like a television show or movie. We wanted it to look just slightly out of reach from what the audience does."[140]

Elsewhere, Instagram's Bailey Richardson notes a filter trend, at one point, of photographers using professional cameras but debasing them with smartphone-style lenses to seem more basic.[141] And, similarly, in developing a YouTube show for DreamWorks, Allocca recalls long debates about how to retain the "YouTube-y" aesthetic: "The point was to make it feel, well, real. The aesthetic of YouTube is about stripping away the artifice that prevents us from connecting with the things people make, the people who make them, and the other people who watch them."[142]

Advertising Goes Native

As these amateurs increasingly professionalized over two decades, so, too, did the platforms themselves. While bloggers in the early years concerned themselves little with advertising, today's social media is choked with it.[143] And though brands initially relied upon organic distribution and fingers-crossed viral seeding, platforms converted that early reach to pay-for-play, having realized they were giving away valuable inventory.[144]

Alas, even as corporations sought to capitalize on creators' connection with followers, they had to seem sidelined to that primary, authentic relationship.[145] Around the time his $7 million in earnings was revealed by a Swedish newspaper, PewDiePie, a leading YouTube gamer, solemnly vowed, "My goal is not to make money."[146] YouTube's Allocca confirms that fans are often shocked to discover the sums earned by vlogging stars: "Money breaks what we might here call the 'fifth wall': our belief that the personalities we connect with are 'just like us' and that our relationships with them are just as intimate as the ones we have with our real-life friends, most of whom aren't making millions."[147]

Michelle Phan, an equally famous YouTuber, exemplifies these tensions in her seventh-most watched video, "Why I Left," which narrates her life's story in animated pastels: from bright-eyed kid scampering around her mom's nail salon to dropping off the med school path to pursue beauty vlogging ("creating these videos didn't feel like work," she revels), and, ultimately, monetizing that popularity and heading to Hollywood. A classic "Cinderella story," as others have observed, of becoming one of the biggest beauty vloggers on the internet—seemingly naïvely—and establishing a template for influencer marketing.[148]

Yet throughout that clip, she interlaces an authenticity lament about marketplace motives—that money can't ultimately buy happiness—even from her glittery heights of digital fame. "Once I was a girl with dreams who eventually became a product," she mourns—estranged from her constantly selling self, imprisoned by the vanity of metrics. "The life I led online was picture perfect but in reality, I was carefully curating the image of a life I wanted—not had," she says, ventriloquizing a generation raised on Instagram and nodding along.

In order to find inner peace, she goes full Rousseau: back to nature—in Rousseau's native Switzerland, no less—a place with "no WiFi, no distractions—just me and my thoughts." And, having found herself, she concludes the clip with a pitch for a new cosmetics site she's launching. Call that two birds with one stone: self-actualization *and* synergistic product line expansion, the moral purity of the former veiling the grubby instrumentality of the latter.

As each platform commercialized in different ways and at different times, one common commandment threaded throughout: Advertising must not look like advertising, lest it despoil the space as inauthentic.[149] Tim Kendall, who joined Facebook in 2006 as director of monetization, confirms that, because authenticity was so critical when they first started inserting ads into NewsFeed, they opted against industry-standard banners and instead required a Facebook proprietary format "more congruent with the style and aesthetic" of the site; this, one might say, represented the birth of native advertising norms on social media.[150]

Indeed, Zuckerberg and Kendall apparently hand-approved every single ad that appeared, rather than automating as has defined the operation, trillions of times over, in the years since. He describes this process and the aspirations over the course of an interview:

> We didn't allow, like, exclamation marks and we didn't allow brands to go crazy. . . . We just didn't want it to be visually disruptive to the feed. . . . "Be a part of the conversation" versus interrupting it. . . . The top-line point was these are the kinds of things that people are reading in NewsFeed and [here's] how you might make your content congruent with that. . . . Most of the organic content on Facebook was often of people and so we did encourage advertisers to make your photograph content more on people versus products. You know, don't toss your brand at people, indiscriminately.

Similar ambitions and anxieties emerged at Instagram around its inclusion of advertising. Early on, co-founder Kevin Systrom would also approve, one by one, the commercial imagery and copy "so it felt super Instagrammy . . . in line with other things that you might see in your feed," according to Bailey Richardson, an initial employee there.[151] The very first Instagram ad was, in fact, a bit of a failure to that end: a close-up of a gold Michael Kors watch in crisp focus, while a plate of macaroons is hazily blurred out in the background, the depth of field inauthentically betraying that an amateur's mobile phone could not have captured the shot.

Richardson left the company shortly after it was purchased by Facebook, fearing that the "intimacy, artistry and discovery" would be corrupted by the tech goliath. "There was so much pressure to do things that 'scaled,' to use the Silicon Valley buzzword," another early employee noted. "But when you have over a billion users, something gets lost along the way."[152]

That "something" is authenticity—a casualty here of both marketplace motives and the technological standardization that, as the introductory chapter explained, defines any industrial scaling process. Chasing addictive usage, Facebook's influential growth team dissected and streamlined the Instagram app toward higher follower counts, larger networks made up of weaker ties, and more time sucked away from users by pushing notifications about friend activity and photo-tagging to prompt "emotional anxiety." Richardson notes that the "photos of you" tab was one of the stickiest, most visited parts of the app and therefore highly effective in keeping people coming back: "As humans, we're so neurotic about whether or not we're loved or what our status is—it's a never-ending well to tap into."[153]

All this helped turn Instagram from a $1 billion investment by Facebook— monopolistically cutting off a potential rival—into a $200 billion valuation.[154] Five years after Facebook launched sponsored posts there, nearly 4 million were circulating, with Instagram ads accounting for almost a quarter of the parent company's revenues, though Systrom shrugs, "The thing I'm bummed about is Instagram feels less authentic over time."[155]

Over at Twitter, many of the same concerns persisted. Sometime after Alex Roetter arrived at the company in 2010, he built out the ad system and began the "controversial" process of inserting them in timelines, obsessing over dozens of metrics to ascertain if commercial content was souring the quality and volume of user experience: "We were always worried about [the following]: If we show you too many ads, your usage might decrease."[156]

At the same time, he was also trying to pin down what made for effective Twitter advertising to coach those best practices with brands—"be an authentic voice, talk directly to people, don't have the marketing bullshit speak, do things on Twitter that differentiate yourself from the usual television ad"—because "that made them successful, so they would spend more money with us." Oreo's

13,000-retweeted "You can still dunk in the dark" wisecrack during the 2013 Super Bowl blackout became the holy grail case study of real-time adaptability (i.e., as a message, it didn't seem prepackaged and standardized) and noninstrumental intent (i.e., as a pitch, it didn't sound like a hard sell). Roetter elaborates:

> It's really more about this authentic, in-the-moment, short half-life [content]—you can't show the same ad on Twitter every day for a week. . . . [In that example, Oreo seemed less like] a multinational corporation; they're like my funny friend from college. . . . [*Later in the interview, he adds,*] The things that make advertisers successful on Twitter are very similar to the things that make [verified account holders] very successful that are very similar to what makes ordinary people very successful: Be unfiltered; don't be overly polished. Don't perfectly craft every sentence—typos are okay. The real-time nature of the content matters more than the polish. . . . You don't want to come off as overly commercial, even though you're an advertiser.

Even more recently, the pandemic platform *du jour*, TikTok, charted much the same path, both strategically and rhetorically, co-opting the rough cut for corporate ends. Hudson Sullivan, brand partnership director there, tells me that successful ad engagement is partly driven by bespoke content native to the app; BMW, for example, can't just repurpose a highly polished 30-spot as it might across other social spaces: "That's not what the community is there for—they want to see the raw moments . . . the behind-the-scenes."[157]

This is not, it surely goes without saying, a premium brand's instinct. Hence, the app has been more popular with prosaic brands like Mountain Dew and Chipotle and participatory strategies like Procter & Gamble's #DistanceDance challenge, encouraging pandemic social distancing via a gently gyrating Charli D'Amelio.[158] Given its perplexing aesthetic style—one that "does not lend itself to easy commercial interruptions," as *Ad Age* lamented—and complex advertising structure, TikTok has given away astonishing amounts of free media inventory to hesitant corporations to get them to test out the platform and defect from social network rivals.[159] (By 2024, TikTok was estimated to earn $24 billion in ad money, rivaling YouTube's haul.[160])

Those hashtag challenges represent a signature product and enable less sexy brands like Lysol to create content around, say, proper handwashing: "If you're a dishwasher detergent company or you make toilet bowl cleaner or a paper towel or something like that, how are you marketing your product on Instagram? People aren't there to, like, interact with those types of products and brands and stories, because it's your life's highlight reel. And the toilet bowl cleaner doesn't make the cut into your life's highlight reel," quips Sullivan. "Whereas TikTok, it's really more about people giving you this window into their everyday lives."

Over the course of an interview, Sullivan elaborates on how these rough cut aspirations can position brands more authentically:

> Very often [on TikTok], it'll take me eight or nine seconds to be like, "Oh shit, this is an ad." . . . We just launched a campaign this summer, which has the tagline, "Don't make ads; make TikToks." . . . [We] encourage brands to stand shoulder-to-shoulder—you know, think about it as more like peer-to-peer marketing versus this brand that's marketing down to their legions of potential consumers. . . . The more raw it is, the more, you know, real it feels, the more—I think the word that comes to mind is "relatable." . . . We often use the word "vulnerability"—encouraging brands to be vulnerable. Kind of poke fun at themselves; not be afraid to upload something that's got a small mistake in it or something like that. Some little screw-up—because people actually respond really, really well towards brands that are willing to be a little self-deprecating.

It's a pretense, of course, as is so much in this "genuine" space. Social media companies have countless designs on our lives. Among their most consequential, if subtle, is designing platforms that demonstrate and facilitate self-performance. In that, they teach us what authenticity means and looks like on second screens, just as reality television modeled it for the TV screen.

Few ideals are fetishized more than authenticity; YouTube executive Kevin Allocca calls it "one of the cliché terms of the decade" in his orbit, the word that industry-types reach for when they're grasping to try to articulate the aspiration for a given project or start-up. This is partly because "we began to value the genuine and transparent at a level we didn't before" and also because, on his site especially, a commenter is quick to shout out "FAKE" within minutes of a dubious upload.[161]

Social media is thus defined by an authenticity that is "simultaneously promised, demanded, and disputed" based upon the dynamics illustrated in this chapter: amateurism unencumbered by marketplace motives; self-disclosure from a presumed single identity; rough cut aesthetics biased toward informality and imperfection; and a mandate to personalize content, either parasocially or algorithmically.[162] Some of the most powerful companies in human history depend upon this process—trying to coax this behavior from us as their principal ambition for the environments they create. And this is, not coincidentally, essential grist for the mill of surveillance capitalism: Authenticity shows the self, on social, in full view, not trying to make a buck, which makes it possible for Google and Facebook to make many bucks.

Questions of how to live authentically, in the 2020s, are therefore pretty much inextricable from the "authentic" management of one's online self: Are our deeply personal disclosures honest or faked? Are we posting from a place of autonomous self-determination or are we just trying to rack up views, likes, and ad dollars? Do we truly stand for ourselves or are we in a pseudo-event pose just to please the audience?[163]

The best, "honestly," don't overthink it: "At the end of the day, you want to act like yourself, not somebody else," TikTok's Lil Huddy counsels aspiring social media stars in an MTV interview. "Make it you. Make it authentic."[164]

THREE

XXXXXX

Pop Music's Sponsorship Play

The Art of Selling Out

The fact is, I can't fool you, any one of you. It simply isn't fair to you or me. The worst crime I can think of would be to rip people off by *faking it* and pretending.

—KURT COBAIN, Nirvana frontman, in his suicide note[1]

When product endorsements first came on the scene, there was a dividing line—if you went that route, you were selling out. In modern times, the stigma of endorsements has pretty much disappeared.

—JON LANDAU, Bruce Springsteen's manager and co-producer[2]

Authenticity has always been an obsession in pop music.[3]

From blues and folk to rock and rap, artists, critics, and fans alike have endlessly hungered for the "real" and rejected that which sounds, looks, and above all, *feels* "contrived, pretentious, artificial, or overly commercial."[4] In 1953, country music's leading producers told *Billboard* magazine that "authenticity, authenticity, and originality" were foremost in scouting talent; four decades later, those pressures appear to have been weighing on Kurt Cobain, right before he put a 20-gauge shotgun to his head, as evidenced by the above note.[5]

As seen in reality TV and social media, authenticity is vigorously venerated among music industry professionals: "Authenticity is probably the mainstay of what we do. . . . The organic nature of it is at the forefront of every decision we make," vows Josh Sunquist, co-manager of indie folk act Bon Iver.[6] Janet Billig Rich, who helped manage Smashing Pumpkins, Jewel, and others, echoes, "It literally has to come from their, like, breath—you can't make someone authentic that they're not. . . . People see it—there's something like it that comes from their gut."[7] Yet taking that authenticity at face value misses the work that these interviewees do to construct it for onlookers.

Pop music journalists routinely buy what the authenticity publicity machine is selling, whether in their overall story framing or in quoted declarations of an artist's integrity and sincerity.[8] Thumbing through a few hundred pieces in *Billboard* from the last two decades, common tropes include an artist discovering themselves, staying true to their vision, or spinning real stories in their work. We hear of Lizzo's journey to self-actualization: "I wanted to be like [another star]. But at a certain point, it's like, 'Bitch, you not him. You got to find you.'"[9] There's an Atlantic Records executive disavowing any two-faced self from Cardi B: "When I met her, she was the same person you saw on social media and TV."[10]

Authenticity's insistence on self-disclosure, that project and principle of reality TV, gets admiringly reported in the "unguarded," "raw honesty," and "messiness" of R&B's Kehlani—who Instagrammed herself from the emergency room following a suicide attempt—and the "total transparency," "unpretentious candor," and "little tolerance for fakeness" that pop singer Demi Lovato exudes online, chronicling her bipolarity, alcoholism, eating disorder, and rehab stints.[11]

Elsewhere, authenticity is defined by purity and singularity of vision: an alleged unwillingness to chase trends to win fame or fortune, as touted by label presidents for EDM DJ Deadmau5 ("If [the VMAs] had asked him to do something that was against his artistic principles, he would have refused; he could care less that it was MTV.") and soul star Robin Thicke alike ("If we catch hit records, we catch hit records. The main thing is that he sticks to who he is.").[12]

Even alt-popper Lana Del Rey—who, ironically, reinvented her earlier Lizzy Grant birthname stage persona by wiping it clean from the internet—sings from this Whitman hymnal: "My little heart's path has such a distinct road that it's almost taking me along for the ride. Like, 'I guess we're following this muse, and it wants to be in the woods. OK, I guess we're packing up the truck!' It's truly ethereal and it's a huge pain in the ass."[13]

Authenticity, *Billboard*'s reportage further suggests, can derive from informal settings (Billie Eilish recording in her brother's bedroom); impulsive spontaneity (Ariana Grande conjuring "Thank U, Next" in a "weeklong blitz"); plumbing one's own lived story (Lil' Baby's drug dealing); and being able to *actually* write, sing, and play one's own instruments (which famously shredded Milli Vanilli's cred).[14] As pop-rapper Mike Posner pledged, authenticity is "the most important word in my life. Once I lose authenticity, I've lost everything. I'll quit."[15]

As we'll see in this chapter, the more that commerce and capital encroaches, the more necessary these declarations become.

Courting the Muse Within

Within music culture, authenticity is defined, foremost, as a set of artistic ideals: creativity as means of self-definition, arising from and arousing feeling, and unbound by society's strictures or moralities.[16] This bohemian exemplar rebels against norms, pursuing truth and beauty; follows an inner light, giving voice to boundless depths; and indulges B-side filler in concert rather than just mailing in the hits.[17] Intrinsic motivation, rather than courting favor from outer direction, should seem to drive decision-making, much as Jean-Jacques Rousseau might have mandated.[18]

Jon Landau, Bruce Springsteen's longtime consigliere, describes to me this restless disregard for popularity that guarantees authenticity: "When the artist becomes unpredictable, searching for new ideas, not trying to imitate past successes, the audience will realize that they're dealing with a person of substance. Conversely, artists who are too interested in chart positions, sales figures, concert grosses will tend to project—they tend to be the pretenders."[19]

The creative ideal is unselfconscious, guileless—mystical, even: Whence does The Muse arrive and to where might it take the artist to pour forth an unadulterated vision?[20] "The real music comes to me, the music of the spheres, the music that surpasses understanding . . . I'm just a channel," rhapsodizes John Lennon, words evasive as plumes of incense and hash. "I transcribe it like a medium. I have nothing to do with it."[21] Or as rapper Method Man summarizes: "Basically, I make music that represents me. Who I am. I'm not gonna calculate my music to entertain the masses."[22] No two-faced self; no marketplace motives here.

Rousseau would have surely approved of self-expression so "instinctive and unstudied," so spontaneous and devoid of artifice, so lacking in backstage calculations that it might be characterized as performing-without-performance, just like what the reality TV casters sought out in chapter 1.[23] Indeed, Rousseau adored music as humankind's "natural language, unmannered and unsophisticated," for precisely that reason: It transmits directly to the soul, without the abstraction of language or civilization interfering.[24]

Centuries later, the artist who seems to lose control onstage, impulsively—think here of, say, The Who's Keith Moon thrashing his drum kit into oblivion—appears more authentic than one that executes a concert plan cleanly.[25] The tortured genius has no "internal governor" advising decorum—again, as reality television also seeks from its participants.

In the '60s and '70s, Lennon and other classic rockers shaped this archetype of unrepressed soul-baring, and the darker those recesses, the more authenticity assumed to be excavated.[26] A life lived along the edges—chronicling vulnerability to nocturnal, even "self-destructive" extremes—has also biographically authenticated artists from Billie Holliday to Hank Williams.[27] Curiously, unlike other forms of media and culture, the identity and lifestyle of the musician has to be authentic to their output; that is, a novelist, filmmaker, or actor need not have lived their characters and stories quite as much as expected of songwriting counterparts.[28]

Jeff Castelaz, former president of Elektra Records, explains to me: "Every actor who stars in a movie is constantly trying to remind the public that who they play on screen is not who they really are. Every rock singer spends their life trying to convince everybody that they are who they say they are." Castelaz then jokes, "Everybody [in music] is trying to be as authentic as possible, which is why when we find a rock star who you find out went to fucking Exeter or something, it becomes a real issue of authenticity."[29]

These stirrings have folkloric roots set against the many plagues of modernity tallied in the introduction: commerce, technology, mass production, homogeneity.[30] Folk culture—historically, an oral tradition among close-knit tribes, with no thought of remuneration—exudes, synonymously, the authenticity of amateurism.[31] Folk music retains an "aura" that defies mechanical assembly, from artists who could convey (or, at least, feign) sincerity of purpose, obfuscating tip jar or royalties check.[32] And because it celebrates the humble commoner, the identity of the performer becomes central to that authentication.[33] Seeger and Guthrie and Dylan ought to at least *seem* like they could have been riding that jalopy out of Oklahoma with the Joads.

This is because music helps fans locate and validate their *own* identities—a theme of authenticity interwoven throughout the book—most especially for young fans and those within distinctive subcultures.[34] Fans *consume* music, yes, but they want it to feel like something more than mere market exchange, and authenticity, theoretically, can bridge that empty gap of capitalism with meaning and affirmation.[35] You achieve authenticity between fan and artist, one label executive suggests, by "being reachable, being touchable, being real."[36] Castelaz thus uses social media platforms to show backstage tour-life minutiae from his bands and to "reflect the audience back to audience," as he put it:

> Deeply authentic artists are channeling their actual lives, their pain, the mysteries of their lives, the un-dealt-with traumas. . . . In other words, people whose lyrics in melodic and rhythmic sentiments mirror my own, saying things that I need to say, but never could really figure out how. . . . [*Later in the interview, he adds,*] Music is not entertainment for me. Music is, like, I fucking cut my arm open and the blood of The Smiths comes out and the blood of Pearl Jam comes out . . . I bleed their colors. Then when I'm at the concert and I see a photo of a concert that I was at on their socials, I go, like, "Fuck, man—that crowd is me! That's my people. . . . No one else in the fucking world matters on that night—everyone's [there] I need to be who I am."[37]

Declarations of Independence

Alas, so many of these ideals of authenticity run aground, as ever, on commerce. What gushes from Castelaz's veins is—for EMI or Warner Music Group—but a mark on a financial ledger somewhere, within a capitalist industry that prefers "cultural commodities that will 'sell themselves.'"[38] Therein lies the timeless duality of pop music: a vessel for the authentic expression of identity and community, and simultaneously an audio widget to rake in profits; pitting artist against ownership and die-hard, deep-cut fan against mindless Top 40 follower.[39] Artists, paradoxically, make music they surely want the world to hear, but can't be seen embracing the "corporate beast" gatekeepers who make that a reality.[40]

The tension between mass media and authentic subculture calibrates these whims of taste. A hip underground is forever fleeing the mainstream, which threatens to turn the lights on in seedy spaces and expose the obscure.[41] In typical subculture framing, popularity and purity are not just antithetical, they're inversely correlated: The bigger the act, the less "ownership" a fan can feel for it.

"When something's on the radio, it's for everybody. It's *everybody's* song. Like [someone who says], 'This is my song' [of a radio hit]—[I'd reply], 'That ain't your song, it's everybody's song,'" sneers one member of the (decidedly radio-unfriendly) horrorcore Insane Clown Posse in a *Frontline* documentary interview. "But, to listen to ICP, you feel like you're the only one that knows about it."[42]

Thus, "alternative," as a concept and term, arose in the late '60s to describe a counterculture music style that rejected aesthetic strictures and compromise with a self-serious purity that Rousseau might have admired.[43] From origins in Boomer rock, it seeped across genres to punk, grunge, and rap alike, and was subsumed, semantically, by "indie" in the aughts. By contrast, across that arc of time, pop shallowly borrowed from whatever's trendy to gain mass appeal.[44] And so goes the theory of cultural co-optation: the market diluting street creativity and dulling the sharp blade of artistic edge; the early rebel paving the way for later conformity.[45] Online life accelerated this cycle to hyperdrive, as few trends can stay undetected by TikTok's all-seeing algorithmic eye.[46]

Some of this tension, too, hinges on record labels. As much as any medium (i.e., books, television, etc.), independence is ideologically revered within music distribution, emancipating the art from oligopolies that care more for profit than aesthetic or political purity.[47] The industry was, historically, dichotomized into indies and majors: the former distrusting authority and upholding principles like divine inspiration, local fetish, proletarian credibility, and middlebrow loathing.[48] "Indie labels were craft beer and the major labels were Miller Genuine Draft," likens Lucas Keller, whose company had produced nearly a quarter of Top 40 songs at one point in the late 2010s. "[Indies] would spend less money, but they've put a lot of TLC into working with these artists."[49]

Indies cultivated this reputation for authenticity because of their structural position against capital pressures: smaller-scale organizationally, lower-risk financially, hands-off artistically, and therefore adaptably catering to niche tastes.[50] Rap indies, in particular, got valorized for being supposedly "closer to the street" than White executives could credibly claim.[51] "Indie integrity" is a bind: Go platinum with a major at the cost of coolness and credibility or stay stuck selling slow in the "alterna-ghetto."[52] And meddling by a major, according to one interviewee, is no myth: "You're signed to a major label, you take a lot of money. They want to have a say in, you know, your process . . . 'Make it a hit; revise this song; edit it; try this; try that; let's a bring in a producer.' That's all real stuff."[53]

Bethany Klein, a pop culture scholar who literally wrote the book on *Selling Out*, unpacks the nuance of her title concept: It's the amateur opting for more professional instrumentation; switching genres to chase fads; collaborating with lame mainstreamers; or "watering down" output into a "less challenging" format.[54] All such machinations scan as a bid to widen the buying market, which risks backlash from fans who had steeped their subculture identity in the previous, uncompromising style.[55] This moral panic became acute in the

'80s and '90s when indie acts like Nirvana and Green Day stood charged with trading up to conglomerate labels in order to, presumably, broaden appeal.[56]

Some of these assumptions, to be sure, remain unfair: "Too often music artists get hemmed in by things that they said in their first few years, maybe over their first couple albums. The public is very unforgiving about allowing musicians to evolve," notes Castelaz, who ran Elektra Records.[57] Evolution looks two-faced when a fan has bet their soul on earlier artistry—even if Dylan going electric at Newport Folk Festival was arguably the *un*popular move to make, evinced by the boos. Still, as another interviewee acknowledges, "Chasing success by changing to try to keep up with the times never passes the sniff test."[58]

Making Rock-Solid Authenticity

Perhaps in no genre have these pretenses of authenticity been more fervently devout than within rock. Already by the 1960s, pop had become rock's boogeyman Other: a hater epithet for depthless, phony, mass culture (and a gendered one at that, given the long-standing critique of female pop stars as overly ersatz).[59] Rock ideology put a Romantic, masculine premium on creativity, integrity, individualism, and rebellion; "'real' rock musicians," as pop scholar Matthew Stahl summarizes, "were to distance themselves (symbolically, at least) from the culture industry, look inside themselves for inspiration, write music and lyrics that reflected their inner states, and sing and play these songs themselves."[60]

Rock venerates "unmediated expression"—like reality TV and social media in previous chapters—in that the artist should convey maximum emotion unencumbered by the limits of communicative or performative encoding.[61] Above all, this ideology must not be for sale: an anticommercial, even anticapitalist badge of honor to be worn on the rocker's sleeve—or, in the case of an April 1992 *Rolling Stone* cover, Kurt Cobain's T-shirt that pouted, "Corporate magazines still suck."[62]

Punk inherited this ethos, and all the usual authenticity aspirations and affectations: an amateur ideal born of outsider freedom, from "below," from the margins; a recalcitrant questioning of authority and protest of social conformity, especially popularization at the expense of purity; and a need for the individual to *be themselves*, above all, with pissy kvetching about "selling out" when that's betrayed.[63] Preferring DIY rawness to slick production, sincerity trumped skill: Here's three chords, now form a band, as the proto-meme famously held.[64]

The nature of instrumentation also seems to matter for claims to authenticity. Live performance is seen as more real, its unmediated immediacy demonstrating artistic bona fides.[65] One interviewee recalls countless conversations about how to capture the "visceral live" sound of a client band from a propulsive concert hall while recording in a comparatively dead studio setting.[66] Alternately, a quieter, acoustic format, following folk legacy, can reinforce rocker authenticity, as flashy image and production wizardry get stripped away.[67] And rock ideology loves to see the artist sweating, grinding it out with "visible physical effort" on display at, say, a three-hour-plus Springsteen marathon.[68]

The *Sturm und Drang* that befell Dylan at Newport was, if not about technological standardization, then surely technical augmentation: machines treated as the ghosts that haunt authenticity. Whether it be an electric guitar or synthesizers, these scan as unnatural, illicitly enhancing playing talent, and impeding some kind of "real," human-to-human connection.[69] One study found that audiences preferred the imperfect, rough cut percussion of live musicians over the "too precise," computerized drum machines that can nail a beat without betraying any rhythmic flaws.[70]

Disco faced this bias in the late '70s: scorned as shallow, manufactured, repetitive, femme, and escapist (i.e., *anti*reality).[71] Its DJ-driven stepchildren—the EDM family of house, techno, drum'n'bass, and others—caught some of that "it's not real music" flak, though ravers discriminated in turn, drawing lines between the authentic, obscure underground and Moby lamely licensing his many *Play* smash-hits.[72]

In that, authenticity is, once more, subjective: a slippery "moving target," an "unstable value."[73] Moreover, as this book argues, it is both makeable and fakeable—a "con game" with stereotypical tropes in staging stars.[74] Whether bands hailing from middle-class suburbia but slumming in seedy clubs or street musicians in old Europe serenading with rote playlists on bygone instruments, authenticity can be tailored to meet fan expectations as needed.[75]

"I fake it so real that I'm beyond fake," alt-rocker Courtney Love once apparently joked.[76] Her wry sentiment applies even more aptly to that most plastic of genres, boy bands, whose authenticity has been doubted—albeit not necessarily by swooning youth—from the Monkees' fabrication through to NSYNC (a gendered disregard, it should be noted, toward acts with mostly teen-girl fan bases).[77]

To formulate musical authenticity, a number of industry stakeholders play a role: Writers conjure tunes they assume seem "real" enough; record companies whittle down the most plausibly successful of them; promoters affix convincing imagery and identity to artist; radio programmers adjudicate what gets airplay; and, finally, if fans buy the bit, countless more imitators are ordered up, restarting the cycle again.[78]

Sociologist Richard Peterson illustrates how early country music manufactured authenticity as formulaic template.[79] Because few *real* cowboys and hillbillies fiddled and sang, the malleable performers who took center stage had to be fabricated through rural, primitive signifiers and genre norms.[80] So they donned ten-gallon hats and scuffed-up boots; faked beards and blackened-out teeth; accented a rural Southern drawl during informal stage banter; and hailed proudly from humble hometowns and blue-collar backgrounds—projecting a "down-to-earth, average person . . . modest and much like their fans in interests and beliefs."[81] These identities could be wholesale invented: Pee Wee King, frontman for the Cowboys of the Golden West, was really Frank Kuczynski of Wisconsin and Dollie and Millie Good didn't hail from Muleshoe, Texas, but rather the tumbleweed-less East St. Louis.[82]

Nearly a century later, from starkly different electro-pop confines, Charli XCX fumed to *NME* magazine about her label pushing much the same posturing on her:

> There is this quest at the moment for authenticity within all art, but particularly in music. There's this stigma of, "They don't write their songs, they're not real." I think that transferred to the way labels wanted artists to be on social media. I remember having a meeting with my record label where they were like, "We just need you to post every Tuesday about your flaws and maybe you could post some pictures with dogs." I stormed out. I was like, "This is fucking ridiculous!" It was crazy. That's not real.[83]

Street Cred

Autobiographical and geographic origins are often an effective way to authentically anchor a pop star, much as seen with reality TV casts. My interviewees elaborated on a variety of angles they'd used to this end. "When you're introducing an artist . . . where someone is from is like 90 percent of who you are," notes Janet Billig Rich, A&R manager and label executive. "Where they went to school or where their parents are from or what their lineage is—you'd always want to use things that you could sort of make a hook. . . . You say a town and immediately, you know, a reader can sort of frame up where [the artist] is from."[84]

She adds that, pre-internet placelessness—where anywhere can be anywhere—geography mattered even more to artistry, because a band might be shaped, insularly, by local scenes and venues that came to define them. "The artist's place of origin is unimportant. The fact that they come from some place in particular and that it becomes part of their work is of great importance," nuances Jon Landau, whose client Bruce Springsteen based a career on this, from his debut *Greetings from Asbury Park, N.J.* onward.[85]

"We do a lot of work in country music, among other genres, and that doesn't only connote place of origin—it also comes with a whole lifestyle, you know, football and tailgating and hunting and fishing and camping," says Matt Ringel, managing partner at New Era Media and Marketing. "That's where the notion of authenticity resides."[86] Another interviewee who represents several Dutch DJs recalls stationing Oliver Heldens on a traditional, flat-bottomed boat floating around the Amsterdam canals for livestream sets during pandemic lockdowns to visually emphasize that place of origin.[87] And, similarly, Steve Rifkind, who launched Wu-Tang Clan, notes that because music videos early in a rapper's career often must shoot on a shoestring budget, it's the norm to "shoot it in your hometown so you could have the hometown supporting you."[88]

Brands are even hip to this strategy, with 1800 Tequila sponsoring a "Back to the Block" series that showcased Travis Scott and other hip-hop artists returning to play their hometowns and Bud Light sponsoring a Lady Gaga dive bar tour: "The key element we take into account is authenticity," Anheuser-Busch's chief marketing officer commented. "She wanted a project to go back to where everything started."[89]

An especially apt example of this mythmaking can be found in Bon Iver's debut album, *For Emma, Forever Ago.* Following the breakup of his band and girlfriend, and battling mono and the usual quarter-life existential dread, indie folk singer-songwriter Justin Vernon went full *Walden*: retreating to an isolated cabin in northern Wisconsin; hunting food, splitting logs, hunkering down for winter; and summoning, therapeutically, a critically acclaimed nine tracks of hushed, wounded, acoustically strummed, falsetto wailing. Rousseauian muse beckoned and he answered its call: "Words like 'decision' and 'intention' aren't words that float in my head because I just went . . . I knew I wanted to be alone," Vernon explains, and "the songs began spilling out" (authenticity being the absence of deliberation).[90]

Kyle Frenette of Bon Iver's management team very much wanted to append that whole backstory to the album: "It wasn't planned. The goal was to hibernate," his press release begins, a document replete with authenticity nods. "He escaped to the property and surrounded himself with simple work, quiet, and space. . . . The record was created entirely by Vernon with nothing more than a few microphones and some aged recording equipment."[91]

For music journalists, themselves forever hankering for authenticity, Vernon's tale was irresistible, chockful of these origin details that Frenette's team furnished—like building a recording studio "three miles from the house I grew up in, and just ten minutes from the bar where my parents met," and then staying Midwest humble rather than decamping for fancier zip codes when he'd hit it big.[92] Vernon, in fact, literally stamped a Wisconsin-shaped tattoo on his breastplate shortly after *For Emma* blew up to "reaffirm what was important to him."[93]

The most authentic origin stories often emanate from edge-worlds. These can be literal, in the case of the icy tundra of that Wisconsin winter, where Vernon cosplayed Whitman. These can also be socioeconomically hardscrabble edge-worlds, given the misguided bias that there's "something innately authentic about the lives and music of the poor and downtrodden, and that this music emerges fully formed from the soul, from deep wells to which the affluent no longer have access," as pop analysts Hugh Barker and Yuval Taylor write.[94] It is, assumed, in other words, that marketplace motives pollute those deep wells.

This has long defined blues, for example. Urban sociologist David Grazian charts tourists' pursuit of it, slumming southward across Chicago: to dingy and dilapidated dives, off-the-beaten path, with cheap booze and unschooled performers, searching for "rugged authenticity suggested by images of poverty and blackness."[95] Such fetishism is undoubtedly racially tinged, with Black blues seen as the most "genuine" American music sound and audiences *expecting* performers to be Black for believability's sake.[96] "They think a black band is more *real*, more *authentic*," one white guitarist shrugs.[97]

Another traditionally African American music genre, hip-hop, has similarly steeped itself in dictates about being true to the street.[98] Taking stock of street art's capital value—one of the four core elements of hip-hop along with MCing, DJing, and breakdancing—media scholar Sarah Banet-Weiser observes that "street," like "urban," semantically functions as code for Blackness: conjuring "danger, transgression, and racialized constituencies."[99]

Other scholars have defined hip-hop authenticity by what it is *not*: "being soft, following mass trends [of] commercial rap music, and identifying oneself with White, mainstream culture that is geographically located in the suburbs."[100] No phrase articulates this fidelity more conspicuously than hip-hop's oldest proverb (and this book's cheeky subtitle): keeping it real. The saying is invoked to resist conformity to external forces and remain true to one's roots (communally, geographically, aesthetically, and so on).[101]

As in blues, Blackness has long been assumed essential to rap legitimacy—the chief genre for bearing witness to and voicing critique of racial oppression and injustice.[102] Even when less overtly political, hip-hop heads expected that an artist would speak "to real people in a real language about real things," as the editor-in-chief of *Vibe* puts it.[103] "Sellout" itself tracks linguistically racial, as the insult for "disassociating oneself from 'blackness'"—from plantation-era slaves who snitched out emancipatory schemes to more recent milquetoast elected representatives who betray political interests.[104] And White appropriation looms, the industry specter having snatched Black sound (and its authenticity) for White performers, audiences, and profits from Elvis Presley onward.[105]

Origins authenticate: Well-worn phrases like "back in the day" and "old school" testify to nostalgia for a time before widespread popularity, before commercialization.[106] Such is the "originalist" bias of authenticity: that how hip-hop—and individual artists—started determines their lien on keeping it real.[107] This formula for street cred often entails autobiographical testimony of crime, drugs, and racism: "50 [Cent]'s authenticity [comes from] being shot nine times and being the underdog and being blackballed and surviving that and coming back," notes James Cruz, artist management executive at Combs Enterprises, who helped stage the Queens rapper in a Reebok commercial regaling that brush with death.[108]

That social realism of dramatic gang life got pushed to ever more graphic edges once hip-hop recognized it could cross over to pop audiences if it flexed as sufficiently hard and real.[109] And local, too—what is *Straight Outta Compton* but a righteous declaration of authentic origins? To "rep," in rap, is to represent, geographically, one's home hood, as when an Atlantic Records executive praises Cardi B as "the people's champion," the ten-times platinum lyricist being just barely "removed from the Bronx projects."[110] That posturing is most pivotal when an artist blows up and sells big: Don't be fooled by the rocks that J-Lo got, she soothingly reassured listeners, she was still just Jenny from the block. No marketplace motives here!

Still, some of this can be fronted. Run-DMC hailed from middle-class origins, but "looked at that [ghetto] life like a cowboy movie. . . . We could talk about those things because they weren't that close to home," Rick Rubin, their Def Jam producer, admits to a *Vibe* editor.[111] White rappers, in particular, have had to smooth over perceptions of illegitimacy: Vanilla Ice outright invented biographical details, while Eminem treated his Whiteness, head on, as the *impediment* to gaining respect while foregrounding his impoverished upbringing as solidarity with those marginalized.[112]

In other instances, authenticity can be simulated through marketing distribution. Because the "street" is, again, so central to hip-hop lingo and aspiration, Steve Rifkind, CEO of Loud Records, helped pioneer "street teams"—the word-of-mouth means of seeding buzz and absorbing feedback about new releases on college campuses, at pickup basketball games, and in neighborhood barber shops.[113] Rifkind's innovations point toward hip-hop's enduring comfort with commerce.

Early on, recalls James Cruz, an executive at Diddy's company, hip-hop wised up about its own equity value, incorporated more corporate logic, diversified into fashion lines, and eagerly name-checked sponsors: "Managers got smart and hip to the fact [of] Run-DMC holding up an Adidas sneaker at Madison Square Garden in front of 18,000 people.... People started to see, 'Oh, there was money to be able to get there.'"[114] That track, "My Adidas," foreshadowed cutting deals without the stigma of selling out—where inauthenticity was not about partnering with brands but with the *wrong* brands.[115] Hence, Ice Cube shilling for St. Ides malt liquor was actually "keeping it real," while MC Hammer got dragged for doing a cheesy KFC spot.[116]

By 2017 a roundtable discussion featuring Kurtis Blow, Soulja Boy, and A$AP Ferg concluded that selling out was largely "irrelevant," in terms of commerce, although it still held currency as a way of slighting someone who forgot their roots.[117] As artists became comfortable seeing *themselves* as brands, Cruz married clients like 50 Cent to Pontiac ("it made sense—it's driven and it's fast") and Vitamin Water ("it was authentic—the guy worked out, he looked strong").[118]

With entrepreneurial hustle as candid and timeless as the American Dream, 50 had already announced his unrepentant ambition to *Get Rich or Die Tryin'*.[119] No shame there, unlike some genres: "[Rappers] embrace making money in a way that we [rockers] could never do," laments Peter Mensch, who ran AC/DC, Red Hot Chili Peppers, and other hard rock acts. "[Rockers] came out of an era that said, 'We don't embrace the culture of making money.' Even though we enjoy making money."[120] As times changed, when the money stopped coming in, that affectation of protestation ceased as well.

Now Brought to You By

David Bason, then A&R coordinator for RCA Records, crisply recalls the moment around the turn of the century when a lawyer friend invited him over, pulled up Napster, and downloaded the entire catalogue of his client, Dave Matthews: "He's like, 'It's over. It's all over.'" Bason immediately scheduled a meeting with the president of the label, demoing the same for his dumbstruck boss: "He was like, 'Do you have a solution for that?'" Bason shook his head. "And he's like, 'Well, until you have a solution, can you not bother me with this?'"[121]

The music executives had caught their first terrifying glimpse of the industry's fate as online piracy took a wrecking ball to their business model. Napster beget imitators, which beget lawsuits, which beget tinkering with distribution (iTunes), format (unbundling), and revenue alternatives as CDs went the way of Sam Goody and Tower Records.[122] The music business would hemorrhage $20 billion in annual sales decline during the first two decades of the millennium.[123] What could recoup the shortfall?

Licensing had been a viable option since the early '80s, when Pepsi paid Michael Jackson $5 million to turn "Billie Jean" into an ad jingle.[124] Yet though artists with credibility—even rock-solid credibility like the Rolling Stones, who sold "Start Me Up" to Microsoft—might pad traditional record revenues with 30-spot royalties, a taboo lingered that this was somewhat gauche and lame.[125] In an ironic coincidence of turning points, the same year Napster launched, Moby set a record for licensing all eighteen tracks from *Play*—the disruptive future ushered in by the former necessitating recourse suggested by the latter.[126] Apple's hip cachet further normalized the trend, spotlighting cool up-and-comers like the Vines and Feist in its 30-spots.[127]

Thus, a once-novel alternative became a "commonsense" fixture in the 2000s, as music scholar Leslie Meier chronicles, with product placement mushrooming in lyrics and videos and corporations headlining festivals alongside fan favorites.[128] Reba McEntire became the gender-bending face of KFC; Brad Paisley's Nationwide croon crawled into countless ears on commercial repeat; and 73 million Super Bowl viewers saw the marriage of Busta Rhymes and Mountain Dew that my interviewee, James Cruz, brokered ("[he's] boisterous, loud, aggressive, colorful—all the things Mountain Dew was").[129]

That exposure has been as important as the financing. In the aughts, brands as the "new radio" took hold as meme: the means to circumvent the usual label-FM-MTV gatekeeping troika that was creaking anyhow in a fragmented digital landscape.[130] Artists got an infusion of capital, brands an infusion of credibility—parasitically piggybacking those vessels and spaces for authenticity that couldn't survive economically on their own any longer, as media scholar Nicholas Carah frames the transaction.[131] And because people find their identity in music, there's corporate value there, too—especially as hard-sell ad techniques and contexts falter—with local scenes and beloved artists seen as especially fertile to mine for transferable loyalties.[132]

"[Music] is in someone's ears and brain and bloodstream. If you look at the nature of the relationship that musicians have with their fan bases, that's the relationship that these brand programs are really looking to be a part of," explains Matt Ringel, who manages such partnerships.[133] Citi, for example, tried to "inject emotion into the financial services category"—about as unsexy as a field gets—by borrowing from Van Morrison and the Pixies.[134] Similarly, Intel attempted to link its rather abstract microchip product to M.I.A. and David Bowie.[135]

All this adds up to some $2 billion annually that brands now pour into the music industry for tours and venues like State Farm's #HereToHelp lounge at Bonnaroo and the Pepsi Zero Chill House at Lollapalooza, as well as use in ads, shows, and video games.[136] Live Nation reports matching almost a thousand brands—from traditional players like beer, auto, and credit cards to newer entrants like CBD, B2B, online dating, and fast fashion—with an estimated 86 million fans, and the average music festival now counts more than fifteen sponsors.[137] For headlining artists, brand work might account for a fifth of their annual revenue.[138]

Ringel explains, in an interview, that it's a "bidirectional" process, whereby agencies sometimes approach artists or labels and, on other occasions, the artist's management reaches out in advance of a release or promotional opportunity; the range and depth of integration can include everything from a one-off private performance to an ad license to tour sponsorship to original content creation to product collaboration.[139] For example, Ringel negotiated a multiyear deal between Dave Matthews and DocuSign, where the jam band leader spoke and played at their global sales conference, did panels with the CEO, and hosted sign-ups for the product on tour.[140] For the many artists that Ringel represents, he conducts regular "brand questionnaires" to ascertain preexisting affection for beverages or clothing that can springboard conversations with those companies.

That also helps disavow marketplace motives: "It never starts with money. It starts with an area of shared interest," Ringel emphasizes. "Maybe it's an outdoor brand that the artist happens to have used their entire life. Artists want to get closer to that and also represent to their fan base, 'Hey, this is something that you need to know about me.' "[141] One country music client, Luke Bryan, already parked a Silverado pickup onstage at concerts and regularly name-checked the brand in interviews ("If you're a Bryan from South Georgia, you drive Chevrolet—and that's how it's been for generations")—all freely—before Ringel went to Detroit to consummate the financial relationship formally.[142] Similarly, because Nicki Minaj grew up wearing MAC, it supposedly made the collab "feel authentic" when she signed with the cosmetics retailer.[143]

The branding ambition here is to show without telling and to sell without selling; to allow capitalism to do its thing, without appearing to intrude on artist autonomy (or influencer autonomy, as we'll see in chapter 5).[144] "When we don't speak—when artists speak and we don't—it's way more powerful," says one shoe company representative overseeing a music alliance.[145] Hence, corporations aim to keep logos subtle and "naturally embedded" within spon-sored contexts, feigning disinterest about their own marketplace motives, lest the artist endorsement "look contrived," especially to savvy, skeptical youth consumers.[146]

That subtlety complicates the capacity to substantiate return-on-investment. After Scion plowed funding into tracks and tours for EDM DJs and grindcore groups, its head of music strategy shrugged, "There's no magic tool out there that says, 'Because you're associated with the Melvins, you're guaranteeing a certain amount of kids to sell a car.' "[147] Presumably, though, someone higher on the org-chart was looking for precisely that. Scion is, after all, still in the business of selling cars.

Yet Scion wasn't alone in positioning itself outright as a quasi-music label. Early in the 2010s, Converse opened Rubber Tracks, a hip Brooklyn studio where upstart hopefuls could book free recording time; the musicians owned the output and Converse just hoped a little buzz might rub off.[148] Elsewhere, TAG Body Spray partnered briefly with Def Jam to drop rap units and Bacardi inked a four-track EP deal with DJ duo Groove Armada.[149]

Most ambitious of all, though, was Mountain Dew's Green Label Sound venture, born to fill the vacuum of a collapsing music industry and assist artists in distributing their output via social media platforms.[150] Yet to "elevate and empower those artists in a really authentic way," as Hudson Sullivan, PepsiCo's head of the initiative, describes it, the soda brand had to low-key efface itself from the transaction:

Make sure that it's not: "Mountain Dew! Mountain Dew! Mountain Dew!" And be really subtle and really kind of choiceful in terms of how and where we decided to integrate branding. . . . We wanted it to feel like we could live authentically within these different subcultures and genres that our consumers were playing in. . . . [*He later elaborates:*] It was never going to be, "Well, how do we get, you know, Chromeo . . . to be, like, chugging a bottle of Mountain Dew in their music video or something like that." I mean, we did want the product to be incorporated, but we wanted to make sure that it came across as genuine.[151]

To make sure Mountain Dew was playing it "cool" enough—meaning both hip and understated—Sullivan leaned on focus groups with their 18-to-24-year-old Black and Hispanic target demo to grasp what came across in brand-music campaigns as authentic and what stunk of "selling out." Green Label netted 2 million downloads for its sixty-five singles and one full-length album—but no direct revenues—and claims it didn't infringe on creativity in trying to popularize their sound (which a "real" label might have).[152]

In the aftermath of digital upheaval, record labels now self-identify as "artist-focused global rights management companies" with 360-degree contracts to cover all these possible money streams.[153] The industry has pulled itself up from darkest financial days, thanks to streaming, which now makes up more than 80 percent of music revenues and saw Spotify paying out $5 billion to rights holders by decade's end.[154] This is, however, largely a "winner-take-all" economy—not that dissimilar from American capitalism broadly—wherein the top 1 percent of artists collects three-quarters of those dollars, given each track played online earns as little as one-tenth of a cent.[155]

Digital teams at music companies also keep a close eye on social trending patterns to see if artists can take part in a hashtag or dance challenge without it looking too "cringey."[156] In other cases, data might help foster a brand marriage, as one interviewee found when he licensed out client DJ Tiesto to 7-Up, after discovering that EDM over-indexed among Hispanic millennials that the soda brand coveted.[157] At minimum, nearly every brand deal now also includes a stipulation about the artist using social channels to sling spon-con.[158]

In a pop culture landscape where abundance is the defining feature of content—and some 60,000 songs get uploaded to Spotify daily—a great deal more promotional labor is required: from publicity to target marketing to data analysis to fan engagement across social media.[159] The same networked technology that decimated music corporations by enabling peer-to-peer file sharing became pivotal to musicians as their own distribution channels (music was vital to early MySpace, for example)—a pandemic-era necessity amplified with the complete shutdown of concert tours and the rise of more "authentic and intimate" livestreaming from cozy home quarters.[160]

Moreover, as we'll later see with influencers having to maintain some restraint in the ratio of organic-to-marketplace motivated social media output, so, too, must artists lightly intersperse tour promotion, merchandising shills, and branded content with "really personal and kind of non-salesy-type stuff," including informal backstage scenes, as one executive recommends: "People don't want to feel like they're getting upsold all the time—people hate that."[161] Still, when "you can't sell records," another interviewee summarizes, "an extra, added income stream . . . become[s] a main income stream."[162]

Who Wouldn't Sell Out?

"Sell out, with me, oh yeah / Sell out, with me tonight / The record company's gonna give me lots of money and / Everything's gonna be alright." So goes the chorus to a catchy '90s ska-punk ditty, foreshadowing the great shrug that befell music—and, maybe, culture more generally—in the decades since.

Pop had long anguished itself, uneasily riven by the dueling allegiances of independence versus industry, culture versus commodity: a product that forged identity and community, meaningfully, for fans—and profit, quantifiably, for bureaucratic business structures.[163] It thrived in both the wild abandon of Dionysian nightclubs and the pragmatic calculations of workaday spreadsheets. To be capital-A Art—creative, fertile, transformative—it ought only to exist external to the market, or so authenticity ideology dictates: "Art is something that is inherently part of the human condition and people have a need to express themselves and what comes out as art—that's not necessarily a financial thing," urges David Bason, a label executive. "All the finance around it is just, like, manufactured and there's a business, you know, parasitical or not."[164]

That idealism was born of '60s-era rock, which self-consciously tried to police its political and aesthetic integrity against moneyed influences.[165] Kurt Cobain himself—arguably one of the last inheritors of this righteous ethic—struggled, ambivalently, with these loyalties: yearning to become a legend but prickly toward the commercial-promotional infrastructure that could vault him there. "I don't blame the average 17-year-old punk rock kid for calling me a sellout," he commented in one *Rolling Stone* profile (the cover for which he wore that "Corporate Magazines Still Suck" shirt). "Maybe when they grow up a little bit, they'll realize there's more things to life than living out your rock and roll identity so righteously."[166] In this, he was foreshadowing the direction that pop culture and the music business would turn.

"When we started in the '90s, it was still considered sacrilegious to work with brands," the CEO of one of the most prolific music-marketing agencies admits.[167] More so, a naiveté about the whole business side of music-making could help authenticate a star. Bruce Springsteen initially signed a crummy record contract, which inadvertently burnished credentials that he was single-mindedly focused on his art, not its recompense; one of my interviewees, Jon Landau, was brought in as a replacement manager, allowing the Boss to delegate that "commercial dirty work" and preserving his reputation for "everyman" authenticity.[168] Another interviewee adds that such "dirty work" is a key aspect of the manager's job, converting muse to commodity: "I have to figure out a way to take your creativity and essentially sell it to people, you know, expose it to people so they'll line up behind your creativity or your authenticity and follow you to all the ends of the earth."[169]

For musicians who still bear the weight of rock ideology, even that one-layer-removed insulation from marketplace motives apparently does not always absolve unease about the art being sold at all. "Across the generations, they're handed down fucking weird guilt about not talking about money," explains Jeff Castelaz, who managed alt-acts Dropkick Murphys and Candlebox. "Guilt is about what I've done [as the artist]: 'I've taken your money for the concert ticket; I've taken your money for the T-shirt and the album'. . . . [The artist] would say, 'I feel low or tricky about this exchange.' "[170]

Those imperatives of capitalism might have left them feeling hollow and disgusted, yet what happens to that guilt when the money that triggered it melts into thin air? A reckoning, as one label executive explains, and a reconsideration: "Not only is [selling out] not worrying; it's not even a conversation anymore. . . . That's a really privileged way to look at the world. . . . There's an entire generation of people who came up [after] thinking that 'sponsor-powered by Geico'—fuck, who cares?. . . . If you're an artist and you're faced with either making a living or not making a living, getting through the tour or not getting through the tour, you might well wrap the damn bus with the fucking insurance logo."[171]

In short, thanks to upheavals in technology, economics, and culture, much of the stigma and angst of selling out—forever the crux of tension between art and commerce—has lifted and is now treated more as ideological relic.[172] "Maybe ten years ago, we could go on tour and play nothing that was sponsored," the lead singer of The Hives tells *Forbes*. "But nowadays, if we said, 'We don't play anything that's sponsored,' we'd get no shows."[173]

To be sure, it wasn't just the implosion of the music business revenue model that forced a capitulation of ethics. The uptick of commercial licensing in the '90s, when the industry was still flush, planted the seeds of this logic that would grow to ease the long-standing taboo.[174] With the business model now *depending* on what was once seen as debasement, distinctions between majors and indies also eroded.[175] Broader still, the relentlessness of promotional culture in the digital era probably bears some responsibility for changing attitudes.[176]

"I remember like coming up [in the '90s] and there used to be a term called, 'Yo, you're going to sell out,' you know what I'm saying? But I feel now it's the reverse," rapper Wyclef Jean tells *Ad Age*. "What brands now are looking for when I speak to them is relevancy within the culture."[177] Once-romanticized values of artistic insularity have given way to unabashed collaborative enthusiasm.[178] This makes Matt Ringel's job at a music-brand partnership firm that much easier: "Our artists' groups have grown up like anybody in a much more commercialized world," he notes. "It's just more accepted that it's just part of our everyday life. And this is what people do. It's not questioned in the same way."[179]

Is this, then, but the latest incarnation in the cycle of co-optation—in which *authenticity* itself is the product that gets bought and sold? New genres have long been born with starry-eyed ambition in which creativity is prized over commercial concerns, only to be inescapably commodified, tamed, and recycled back into the capitalist system: Classic rock spins this yarn of innocence lost, as did its punk and grunge after it.[180] Yet authenticity, I would argue, is not fully dead within these new market dimensions and norms; rather, authenticity is *still* demanded even in the midst of selling out.

Artists and brands alike have to double-down, rhetorically, on their commitment to authenticity when consummating commercial schemes: It serves as cover and reassurance that the thing which is being exploited will nonetheless be preserved.[181] Furthermore, being choosy about *which* sponsors you partner with also helps sell the sellout as *not* selling out and, across the table, brands alike dig that impression of restraint: It makes Pepsi feel special that Coke just wasn't enough of the "real thing" to win the courtship with Michael Jackson and helps the subtlety of the sell come across as convincing rather than contrived.[182]

Thus, when, say, alt-rockers Linkin Park boast that they have "turned down 100 deals" because of the band's "desire to stay true to its fan base," it makes becoming an eventual brand ambassador for Mercedes-Benz that much more credible.[183] Or take Springsteen himself, who studiously avoided licensing for decades, but finally gave in to Jeep for a 2021 Super Bowl ad—the commercial coyness rendering his promotional supply that much more in demand.[184]

"You don't just take anything, any money, any deal on the table—it's gotta make sense. You know, if you drink from every cup, eventually you're going to be poisoned," James Cruz, an executive at Combs Enterprises, evocatively puts it when asked about the rules for dealmaking.[185] Capitalism and commerce are, indeed, theoretically poison to maintaining authenticity.

But the problem, again, is not doing a deal—it's doing a deal with a brand that doesn't align with your own brand or overexposes yourself commercially: "You can only do so many spots for a corporate brand before people are just, like, 'Oh, you're just kind of lame,' " notes Lucas Keller, a label president.[186] And even that caution seems increasingly dated in a market-conditioned culture. As Hudson Sullivan, Green Label–turned–TikTok brand manager, concludes, "I don't see that sentiment nearly as much, because you have this influx of younger talent there that's like . . . 'Selling out—fuck yeah! Selling out is exactly what I want to do.' "[187]

×××××××××××××××××××××××

PART II

ADVERTISING *and* CONSUMER CULTURE

FOUR

xxxxxx

The Commercial Brand Sell

Humanizing the Corporate

Mass advertising can help build brands, but authenticity is what makes them last.
—HOWARD SCHULTZ, Starbucks CEO[1]

It's very hard for brands to communicate who they are when they're trying to sell you shit.
—JASON LONSDALE, Ogilvy head of brand strategy and planning[2]

On a sunny, pleasant day, as Black Lives Matter demonstrations have been building, a multi-culti coalition of protestors streams through downtown streets. They hold signs aloft with radical messages, rarely heard outside of Madison Avenue boardrooms—signs like, "Join the Conversation." A platinum-haired Kendall Jenner slinks about a photo shoot as the movement passes by; her curiosity piqued, her eyes searching, she tosses the wig and smears the lipstick from her face. This is a generational moment; she will answer the call of history.

She, too, will *join the conversation.*

Alas, the marchers run aground of a stone-faced police brigade. Who among them will be brave enough to step forward? Jenner parts the crowd, Pepsi can in hand, offering one officer this gesture of goodwill: She is Sadat recognizing Israel; John Paul II journeying to communist Poland.[3]

The cop's disposition melts away; he cannot help but sip and smile. The generations-long injustice of unarmed African Americans being murdered suddenly seems redressable. All it took, apparently, was high-fructose corn syrup.

The crowd cheers and dances, vaguely hip-hoppy. A tagline appears on screen: "live bolder, live louder, live for now."

Only two questions linger: What in the world was Pepsi thinking with this ad? And why did "authenticity" lead them there?

Upheavals Trending

Advertising in the twenty-first century has been a story of uncertainty and, often, desperation. A process that had been fairly stable and straightforward—make ad, place ad—got thrown into disarray by digital developments: the cratering of local newspapers, the commercial deprivation of streaming models, the deployment of filtering technologies, and the utter impotence of banner advertising. One industry cliché jokes that you've got better odds surviving a plane crash than someone clicking on your display ad.[4] "You have entire generations that are pretty much unreachable by paid media buys except for in new social feeds," says Barry Wacksman, R/GA's global chief strategy officer.[5]

Alas, on social, exposure to brand content became pay-to-play, as seen in chapter 2.[6] Google and Facebook hoovered up the majority of those online ad dollars and Fortune 500 multinationals fretted that Amazon's *un*branded, vertically integrated private label could destroy them overnight with a simple tweak to default search results. Simultaneously, PR firms made a "radical shift," gobbling up more creative agency business, while consultancies like Deloitte and Accenture touted their services' analytics advantages.[7]

All this drove advertisers' authenticity imperative, along with a fear that audiences aren't buying their BS anymore (if they ever really did)—a cynical mistrust assumed strongest among youth.[8] "[They] evaluate marketing with a far more critical lens than any generation that's ever come before," Hudson Sullivan, the brand partnership director at TikTok, tells me in a classic riff on the subject. "Being authentic is more challenging, because they're so quick to kind of see through certain tactics and kind of designate a thing as being inauthentic, a sellout."[9] By contrast, this Gen Z myth holds, "social discovery" authenticates: *happening upon* brand messages within native content (the next chapter's focus) rather than being *forced* to sit through a hard sell interruption.[10]

This is, however, a timeless, recurrent narrative. Before Generation Z supplanted millennials—and our now-cringe side-parts and skinny jeans—the ad industry told pretty much the same story about us: as tech-savvy, ad-skeptical, and hard-to-reach.[11] "Teens value authenticity highly. . . . With teens increasingly connected to each other and the world . . . word will spread fast when a campaign does not ring true or a brand does not follow through on its promise," one industry panel on viral marketing reported—*in 2004.*[12]

Arguably since the invention of "teens" as a market concept in the 1950s, "youth culture has always demanded what is 'real,' what is somehow 'on the street'"—an age cohort-wide quest for "self-actualization," in contrast to what is mass-marketed *to* them (and therefore intrinsically phony because of those contrivances).[13] That's why nurturing a pipeline of young talent is critical for an agency's survival: Twentysomethings on staff are, effectively, emissaries from that Land of Authenticity where "things that are happening in the life of a twenty-year-old that absolutely make no sense to me as a forty-year-old," one chief creative officer quips.[14] Cool, after all, ages about as well as milk left out.

Hence, the authenticity industries, especially the commercially inclined, must stay fresh on trends, for relevance makes products feel more "real" to consumers. Yet because that's an evasive charge, for half a century, a multimillion-dollar industry of influential boutiques has helped corporations keep up with the Joneses: analyzing, predicting, managing, and manufacturing cultural innovations.[15]

Media scholar Devin Powers charts these forecasting firms, often tasked with wrangling intractable youth markets, that became known for "cool hunting"—scouring tastemaker authenticity along the margins and converting that subcultural capital into cold cash for mainstream retailers.[16] As one prominent futurist summarizes: "The raw authentic is hunted down by cool hunters, snatched up, stripped clean, and mass marketed."[17] This is, in short, how culture "works" for capitalism.

Yet it requires a range of orientations and skills: from data sensitivity to pattern filtration to agile dot-connecting.[18] It zigs and zags with zeitgeist—tallying monumental social changes, demographic shifts, historic context, and useful "myth markets."[19] If such authenticity archaeology excavates effectively, the ad generated creates "mass intimacy," as one interviewee puts it: "An idea that everyone can feel intuitively, but it feels very specific and emotional to them. . . . Something truly insightful that cuts you to the core, that says, 'Yes, I know about that. And that—that is me.'"[20] Here, as throughout the book, identification is, ultimately, the industrialized product: the sense of self that has market value because it retains social value.

Historically, these techniques included macro and micro alike and both qualitative and quantitative digs into culture: purchased datasets, targeted surveys, focus groups, in-depth interviews, pop media charts—even eavesdropping on strangers on public transit.[21] Going from desk-based research into the field is framed as advantageously authentic, not unlike—in academia—an ethnographer insisting that participant-observation in a native's setting is more "real" than requiring that subject to submit to the external (albeit more objective, comparable) instruments of understanding that a social scientist might prefer.[22]

Meredith Chase, a trained anthropologist–turned–chief strategy officer, thus hypes her firm's in-home stalking and embedded shadowing: "We join the family breakfast table, hang out during homework time, go shopping together, hop into their social feeds and peek into their closets."[23] These, after all, are the spaces where authenticity is presumed to be found.

Over the past two decades, marketers increasingly viewed the boundless depths of online conversation to plumb genuine insights. From Google and Twitter trending data to text mining practices, this machine-augmented sifting through Big Data got framed as a route to the real.[24] One interviewee ratifies this as more "quantitatively valid," in the sense that Facebook's potential billion-plus sample size trumps any piddly survey extrapolation from yesteryear.[25] By the late 2010s, Facebook had opened its users' postings and comments to marketers who wanted to mine for reactions and insights into their products.[26] These online listening practices—unlike, say, an annual Yankelovich report—adapt to the speed of digital culture and absorb authenticity trends in real time.[27]

The problem with the cycle of authenticity is the same as the cycle of cool before it: as soon as capitalism attaches it to a commodity (whose purpose is, fundamentally, profit), it loses any distinction of realness that might exist external to marketplace motives.[28] Some say that authenticity simply *can't* be mass-marketed, because anything "mass" is too impersonal—too technologically standardized—to ever feel authentic to the target consumer.[29] Thus, if a niche brand catches popularity, it's sometimes vital to slow the diffusion of exposure—"cool selling," if you will, rather than crassly grabbing at all the market share that's possible, because it'll quickly feel mainstreamed and lose any cred of its authenticity roots.[30]

After all, a person who can just *buy* their way into the legitimacy of meaning that a subculture generates is, by definition, a poser; they are "outer-directed," faddish in the fashion of a two-faced self, rather than reflecting individualism, independence of taste, and inner authenticity.[31] Jean-Jacques Rousseau could never "find himself" at the mall; that's where authenticity goes to die.

Anthropomorphizing the Impersonal

As in earlier chapters and contexts, authenticity has also achieved clichéd ubiquity on Madison Avenue. It is "the contemporary advertising equivalent of the search for the holy grail"; the "cornerstone" of marketing strategy.[32] One interviewee says "authenticity" comes out of her lips, or from someone on her team, at least two or three times a day as their number-one strategic priority.[33] Another estimates that nine of every ten briefs from clients contain the word.[34] A search for "authenticity" in the Association of National Advertisers member content library yields no fewer than 1,300 entries.

It is routinely revered in trade mags like *Ad Age*, *PR Week*, and *MediaPost*.[35] Almost weekly, *Forbes* extolls its holiness with vapid headlines like "Why One CEO Says Brand Authenticity Is Not Optional" and "The Value of Authentic Entrepreneurship (And How to Make Sure You Fit the Bill)." In one entry, "The Importance of Building an Authentic Brand," a consultancy co-founder exalts its anti-two-faced ethos, amidst so much digital insincerity: "The greatest compliment that [your brand] can hear is that you are the same offline as you are online. . . . Authenticity, however, requires you to be truly vulnerable, allowing those who follow you [online] inside your world."[36]

One study found nearly 90 percent of consumers ranked authenticity highest among brand qualities in buying decisions, even more than product innovation or uniqueness.[37] And because brands deemed authentic can be sold at a premium and command more loyalty, managing consumer perception of that becomes a key advantage in the marketplace, even as its positioning there invalidates it.[38] Ironically, of course, all this veneration of "authenticity" as advertising's ethical ideal—and the industry's zealous pursuit of it—belies the true, polar-opposite nature of what's really going on: contrivance.[39]

Authenticity is also, not coincidentally, a post-industrialization term—a type of hype that only emerges in twentieth-century consumer culture and cannot be found in Victorian vocabulary about merchandise.[40] As early as 1908, Coca-Cola was already pitching itself as "genuine" to consumers—part of "manufacturers' efforts to persuade buyers that their brand was more natural, more located in history, or more pure" than competitors—and doubtless responding to anxieties of an era when factory-line products began filling home shelves.[41]

That technological standardization, and the homogenized culture that it produces, alienates shoppers seeking to avoid the feeling of being shepherded through checkout registers.[42] For an authenticity-seeking consumer who is "inner-directed," how, then, to find meaning—and oneself—in stuff that everyone else has?[43] From Harley-Davidson to the Volkswagen Beetle, from torn jeans to rare sneakers, the marketplace has tried to furnish "therapeutic" totems, assuaging anxiety about achieving autonomous self-definition through mass-produced goods.[44]

If successful, these brand icons offer symbolic anchors of mythic meaning.[45] For example, Apple has, over the years, catered to the "creative, anti-establishment" self-identity of its consumers, enabling expression of their "inner personal truth" through its gadgets, available to all but distinguished as uniquely "you" (unlike the lame, khakis-wearing, PC-avatar John Hodgman seen in their late-aughts 30-spots).[46]

"When you consume a brand, it's an extension of your own personal brand," explains Lesley Bielby, chief strategy officer for Hill Holiday, invoking her work for a casual dining client. "To see you sitting in a Ruby Tuesday versus seeing you sitting in a Chili's, they're going to have a different perception if they knew the whole brand story."[47] I believe this is what Freud meant by the "narcissism" of small differences.

Thus, brand authenticity operates as a "positional good"—a wedge offered to consumers to define themselves distinctly from others who buy indiscriminately.[48] Branding scholar Michael Beverland summarizes this as products based upon "commitments to tradition (including production methods, product styling, firm values, and/or location), passion for craft and production excellence, and the public disavowal of the role of modern industrial attributes and commercial motivations."[49] An authentic brand is rooted, variously, in particular geographies, purified ingredients, or unevolved designs; it adheres to artisanal, handmade, long-standing means; it's purpose-driven, by amateurs, for love not money, and never blandly standardized.[50]

"Brands have to have a voice; they have to have a character; they have to have morals," Rich Silverstein, creative director at Goodby Silverstein & Partners, tells me. "A brand is a living, breathing idea. And you don't want to open your house to a dishonest person."[51] For nearly a century—again, not coincidentally, when those impersonal, standardized, potentially "dishonest" objects began churning off assembly lines—corporations have eagerly contrived this widely shared delusion: that a brand is human, that a brand has a "soul."[52] (Or as animatronic presidential candidate Mitt Romney affirmed, testily, from the stump: "Corporations are people, my friend.")

This underpins the effort to affix immaterial qualities—feelings, values, personalities—to manufactured goods.[53] As media scholar Sarah Banet-Weiser underscores, branding is "now both reliant on, and reflective of, our most basic

social and cultural relations"—a means of making a capitalist commodity resonate with the buyer through these immaterial dimensions.[54]

Marketing scholars find that brands which exhibit "human-like characteristics" secure stronger, more authentic relationships with consumers, because people relate to them anthropomorphically.[55] Hence, Dunkin' Donuts
changing the name on its (standardized) 11,000-plus outlets to just "Dunkin'"
to "highlight how the brand was now on a 'first-name basis' with fans," even
giving away "handmade friendship bracelets" to commemorate the copyright
registry.[56] For most of our species' history, buying and selling was done face-to-
face; with industrialization, it got harder to judge the dependability of a faceless
corporation peddling mass-produced wares, yet we still longed for that assur-
ance.[57] Enter authenticity.

Don't Buy This Jacket

If, however, a brand aims for authenticity in order to sell product, it faces a fundamental, paradoxical challenge: It can't seem like it's trying to sell product.

Its motives must seem intrinsic (i.e., committed to the brand's essential
purpose or meaning) rather than extrinsic (pursuing its exchange value), and
that old cliché, "the customer is always right"—therefore fulfilling the desire
of others—indicates *inauthenticity* by pandering, two-facedly for profit, rather
than defending some innate core or truth, no matter who it is staged for and
whether they like it or not.[58] Authentic brands appear financially "disinterested" and in it "for themselves"—their ideals ranging from perfecting a craft
to changing the world and being driven by the un-swayed vision of the creator.[59] Inauthentic brands appear to exist just to make checkout registers ring
and it is that self-interest that advertisers forever endeavor to obfuscate.

"The profit motive must not taint the process," one marketing analysis concludes. "Rather, profit is the reward for authenticity."[60] Cash might rule everything around us, but never a heartfelt brand: "It really is about being genuine
and not looking to sell someone on something or trying to, you know, immediately get them to the store to go buy the product," says Hudson Sullivan, brand
partnership director at TikTok.[61]

A number of ideals and rules help maintain the "aura" that legitimizes a
brand.[62] These include: foregrounding "behind-the-scenes" production processes and virtuous moral motives; never focus-grouping innovations with
consumers (which would Goffmanian affirmation-seeking and "commercially
motivated compromise") when designers can go with their gut; and showing,

through attributes, rather than boasting explicitly in ad messages, about being real.[63]

The first rule of selling authenticity, it turns out, is that you don't talk about selling authenticity: "The fact that it's not advertised everywhere and whispers rather than shouts its benefits helps convey something meaningful and subtle," one cosmetics brand executive hypes.[64] Wine branding, in particular, emphasizes organic, traditional, or handcrafted methods; maintains fidelity to a unique, local terroir; and, again, appears above grubby marketplace motives.[65] "I do not make a wine for a consumer," one Bordeaux purveyor puffs, channeling his inner Rousseau about that raisin *d'etre*. "I make a wine that best expresses the vineyard and the vintage. I do not change it to suit a particular segment."[66]

Over the years, other such avowals abounded from a wide range of brands. During Snapple's ascendance in the '90s, it spun a populist self-mythology of profit-amoral amateurism against "big corporations and the overpaid elites who ran them [that] only gummed up the works" when it came to purity of purpose in tea and juice-making.[67] More recently, Patagonia ran an ad headlined, "Don't buy this jacket," on one Black Friday; its "director of philosophy" explains that, not being a publicly traded company (and therefore not facing the wrath of shareholders who prevaricate less when it comes to marketplace motives), it could pull off such a stunt, which—he claimed, with a straight face at least—aimed for no change in sales.[68]

In short, we judge the authenticity of a product based upon the perceived intentions of the producer or company that created it—avoiding, say, a restaurant that caters to tourists, assuming that it's (inauthentically) placating pedestrian palates to make money rather than pursuing a bolder vision and purer flavor, unadventurous eaters be damned.[69] Further, by downplaying commercial intent, a brand can help the consumer construct *themselves* with the purpose and meaning of identity furnished.[70] "[Clients] look at the world and they don't even call consumers 'consumers,'" explains Margaret Coles, an associate partner at a San Francisco ad firm. "They call them, you know, 'small car buyers' or 'printer targets.' Nobody ever woke up in the morning [and said], 'I am a home printer purchase intender.'"[71]

Moreover, any strategy aiming for commercial authenticity conceptualizes and targets an emotional rather than a rational consumer. Over the course of the twentieth century, ad copy trended away from "utility-oriented" claims in this way—a triumph of industry legend David Ogilvy's soft-sell school of thought that favored imbuing commercial goods, names, and logos with recognizable social and cultural identities (instead of enumerating product attributes) and encouraging buyers to see themselves in those product personalities.[72]

"Five percent of decisions—of all decisions—that we make in life are made rationally," estimates Meredith Chase, chief strategy officer at Swift. "90 to 95 percent of it is driven by emotion."[73] And, bonus, consumers evaluate those evocative narratives less skeptically than when they encounter persuasive arguments.[74] Thus, marketing scholar Douglas Holt proposes, brands must jockey in "myth markets" for identity as much as "product markets" for utility, which makes persuasion—in any kind of deliberative sense—irrelevant: "The product is simply a conduit through which customers can experience the stories that the brand tells."[75] More beneficial still, identity myths need not be circumscribed by truth-in-advertising restrictions.

"Brands must sell something else other than the products," Anselmo Ramos, a chief creative officer, summarizes. "Apple sells creativity. Volvo sells safety. Nike sells confidence. Dove sells self-esteem. The best brands sell an emotion."[76] That Ramos named the firm he co-founded, Gut, bespeaks that ideal of being driven by an inner core of instinct. And in a social media landscape, he adds, emotion is currency more than ever: "People will only like, comment, or share a piece of content if they feel something. The new KPIs [key performance indicators] are the heart emoji, the LOL emoji, the fire emoji, and phrases like 'OMG' or 'I can't believe this!' Those are the most challenging KPIs to get."

Craft Imperfections

The theory of the "rough cut"—that authenticity has a particular aesthetic bias—maps onto commercial strategy, just as it did in an earlier chapter on tech culture. Consumers allegedly associate authenticity with what seems natural: "organic ingredients, simple products, unpolished processes, [and] untamed places."[77] Though that might sound highly specific to, say, the packaging at a Whole Foods, it's emblematic, metaphorically, of all products: foregrounding "flaws" and demonstrating "realistic imperfection" in response to the presumed cynicism about most brands' "perfectly polished, highly aspirational" imagery.[78]

If you smooth over coarse edges and sanitize the brand narrative and aesthetic, so goes this industry thinking, it drains anthropomorphized corporate entities of the "humanity" otherwise indexed by imperfection.[79] One study of Los Angeles restaurants, for example, found that consumers cared less about violations of the city's hygiene code if a hole-in-the-wall was seen as sufficiently "authentic"—irrationally prioritizing foodie status over digestive safety.[80]

The authenticity ideal is artisanal craft, romantically conjuring premodern labor that is "self-directed and untainted by the massive machineries of industrialism"—a worker unfettered by marketplace motives and an output unfettered by technological uniformity.[81] "Handmade" acts as antidote to McWorld homogeneity; "small-batch" inoculates against any cash-grab suspicions (i.e., being scarce rather than standardized, curated rather than commercialized).[82]

But in order to sell craft products at a premium, as they often are, the brand must explain why cheaper, mass-produced alternatives wouldn't suffice just as well and narratives of authenticity articulate the answer.[83] "You have aspirational positioning from every brand out there to want to make their offering feel bespoke and handcrafted and unique," Ryan Schram, a marketing COO, quips. "The fact of the matter is that that there's tens of thousands of others of [that product] pumping out every single week."[84]

One of the methods of proving that authenticity can be found in the methods themselves: foregrounding, rather than obfuscating or outsourcing, the production process and showing, backstage, how the sausage gets made.[85] Hence, say, the open-kitchen concept at an In-N-Out burger joint—still a factory line, certainly, but one that makes visible the (typically behind-the-scenes) performance of operations in terms of procedural craft and material freshness.[86] This is meant to soothe the psychological distance between where and how stuff usually gets made—somewhere far off, even on the other side of the world, by labor bureaucratically subcontracted and often exploited—and where and how it gets consumed.[87] Methodologically, authenticity upholds those earlier principles of amateurism: unpaid, untrained, unsavvy at business dynamics, and unencumbered by professional obligation.[88]

Here, as everywhere throughout the book, social media's ascent influenced aesthetic calculations. "When brands started engaging in social media, there was a very intentional attempt, approach, philosophy about not looking too polished, right?" Meredith Chase, chief strategy officer at Swift, recalls. " 'Cause you wanted to fit in with the rest of the content—you wanted your brand's content to look like what other people were posting, which was being done by amateurs, by regular people. And, so, there was an intentionality of rawness and low-fi and low production quality."[89] Consumers are, indeed, two-thirds more likely to trust and one-third more likely to buy products (especially beauty and apparel) in images authentically uploaded by "real people" rather than the "stiff, expensive photoshoots" that a company can afford.[90]

The approach is not particularly new, even if many of today's platforms and formats are: In 2006, a mere year after YouTube debuted, Doritos inaugurated its annual "Crash the Super Bowl" contest, offering fans the chance to craft a homemade ad that, following public vote, could air during the big game.[91] More recently, Buffalo Wild Wings, Fanta, and Wayfair all invited user-generated photo and video submissions to their social media pages.[92] Domino's re-posted "real people's photos" on its official social feeds, with all the (authentic) imperfections of cheese stuck to the top of the delivery box and asymmetrical toppings distribution, rather than "the sort of highly stylized, perfect-looking, appetizing pizzas" common to competitors.[93]

"Anything that's trying to be an ad, they tune it out," says Evan Horowitz, CEO of an agency that specializes in TikTok campaigns. "[But] they love brands that engage with them in a way that feels authentic to the way that they actually talk to their friends."[94] This, he adds, translates to a more freewheeling, raw aesthetic. Casting real people in ads is also seen as selling authenticity, as both clients and creatives opt for non–Screen Actors Guild talent.[95] In other instances, retailers like American Eagle banned digital retouching in their #AerieREAL campaign, reportedly spiking sales.[96] As one interviewee summarizes, this quest within advertising often boils down to the pursuit of a human rough cut: "It's no longer the pretty face on TV—it's a real person and [audiences] think that's authentic."[97]

Against McWorld

In advertising, as in other contexts explored in the book, origins authenticate. Tap water flows free, but if you evoke some special source where it's bottled, you can sell at a premium.[98] Brands thus ought to maintain consistency and fidelity to their roots, be those geographic spirit, founding legacy, or any other expressions of tradition.[99]

Take beer branding, for example, which—like wine earlier—formulates authenticity as antithetical to marketplace motives and technological standardization:

> [It] stems more or less directly from nature, without much technological interference (naturalness), whereas the human labour involved in the brewing process is decidedly of a non-alienated variety (craftsmanship). Authentic beers are moreover not produced in anonymous breweries that may be found

anywhere on the globe (location), but are parts of historically grown traditions: they have quenched thirst since times immemorial (historical rootedness). They do as such not satisfy an artificially incited pseudo-need, invented to quench capitalism's thirst for profits, but a long-lasting, time-proven and genuine human need that is part and parcel of a locally rooted tradition.[100]

Whether it be the sepia-toned 30-spot imagery that anchors Coors in the frontier-era Rockies or a Trappist brand signaling place and means of production via cloaked monks and old-timey fonts on bottles, brewers emphasize an "unbroken commitment" to origins as the guarantor of authenticity.[101] Similarly, tasked with stemming Miller Genuine Draft's decades-long decline, one creative agency latched onto "humble authenticity" at the core of its "genuine" name, sought to "retain the important memory structures and respect the heritage" of the brand, and issued ad-slogans like "Scratch beneath the surface" and "Forge your own path."[102] By "traditionalizing" a product in this vein, a company evokes sacred purity and craftsmanship credibility.[103]

There's a whiff of nostalgic populism at play, too, for populism is partly defined by unevolved fidelity to core values over time (a focus of chapter 7); hence, the frequent stamp of company origin date as an index of authenticity via conviction of longevity.[104] *Ad Age* noted a late-decade swing toward vintage aesthetics—dozens of campaigns, slogans, and logos from yesteryear dusted off and trotted out, from Pizza Hut's "Red Roof" icon to Miller Lite's throwback font. "It's important for brands to have a story that goes beyond just that product," one youth marketing strategist commented of the quasi-garage myth trend. "Brands want to say, 'We're still that same company with humble roots,' so [they] reverse-engineer that value to an audience that may not be privy to a backstory."[105]

The marketplace necessitates those distinctions. "We have so many choices today for every single product and there is kind of the loss of meaning with such abundance. . . . It makes people feel better to know that if there's a story they're relating to, that's where they're putting their money. . . . It helps them feel like . . . 'I am part of that community,'" explains Yael Cesarkas, executive strategy director for R/GA. "It's not going to work for every single brand, right? Like, not everyone cares about the creation story of their conditioner."[106]

Yet if that creation story retains some "moral authenticity" of the creator, a brand ought to hype his or her credentials: artisanal love of craft and creativity (never money) and a distinctly "human component" rather than an "impersonal mass-produced" good.[107] Playing up the naïve, untrained professionalism of founders works well, because—unlike work—it inoculates against the taint of marketplace motives and frames any success there as golly-gee luck.[108]

For amateurs and artisans alike, even being considered a "brand" should elicit bashful reticence, as does any acknowledgment of "marketing," which undermines the sincerity of authenticity claims.[109] Hence, the dreamy arc of founder as creative genius: helming a once-struggling start-up, celebrating failures along the way (since it was just for fun anyhow), and driven to solve some problem with intuition and innovation rather than to rake in billions.[110] Research suggests that these tales of founding intent matter a great deal to consumers: If seen as "self-transcendent" (i.e., for societal or communal purpose) rather than "self-enhancement" (for wealth and status), the brand scans authentic.[111] Greed, for lack of a better word, isn't good, nor does it convey the creation process as genuine.

One chief strategy officer, Lesley Bielby, oversaw a case study of just this sort when her firm won the Chili's account and tried to rebrand the casual chain for consumers "hungry for authenticity." Disavowing Chili's as a "'concept' restaurant conceived in a boardroom"—an implied slight of contrast to other inauthentic office-park staples like Applebee's, TGI Fridays, and Ruby Tuesdays and the soul-deadening, ubiquitous homogeneity they represent—Bielby dug into their business lore and found a Ben and Jerry's–worthy origin story about a gang of rambling biker friends obsessed with chili who started the company out of a "little shack" in Texas.

The ensuing 30-spot campaign ("Chilin' Since '75") features the grainy montage of a shirtless hippie-slacker crew clowning around to Foghat's "Slow Ride" and opening said shack. But the *Dazed and Confused*–worthy footage is not actually "real"—it's faux-found, recreated by the agency to look authentic to the origins and heritage. Interviewing the founder, Bielby got chills of excitement about the semiotic potential she had unearthed: "I said, 'Do you know that anyone would kill for this story you're telling me right now?' . . . When you get bought by a holding company [as Chili's was] or a kind of parent company, I think a lot of that sort of goes away."[112] Indeed, said parent company, Brinker International (EAT on the NYSE, trading, at peak, at 77.77), gives off a much less scruffy—read here: authentic—vibe.

Bielby's instinct is not incorrect when it comes to resolving the tensions between an authentic mom-and-pop shop and a faceless corporate chain defined by marketplace motives and technological standardization. The humble origins and local identity of a business—being small-scale and aesthetically idiosyncratic, with a "down-home touch" relative to capitalist monoliths—sell consumers a soothing authenticity of stewardship rather than an icy, spreadsheet-based, bean-counter calculation in some far-off franchise headquarters.[113]

Management scholars confirm that consumers rate independent, family-run, or single-category restaurants as more authentic than those that are chain, corporate, or generalist.[114] And one interviewee notes that as conglomerates and private equity interests subsume smaller, craft outfits—like, say, coffee retailers—they often still want them "to feel like they're human and local and personal" and thus try to obscure the scale and size of said overlords.[115] When, for example, Colgate-Palmolive bought Tom's of Maine, it did so with "minimal fanfare" to avoid eroding the "grassroots," vegan-vibe of the founding ethos that represented no small share of its purchase value.[116]

Against this McWorld backdrop of cookie-cutter commercialism, place authenticates because it anchors. Rooting an offering as local rather than universal, and unique rather than standardized, makes a product more tangible and "real" in its identity and heritage.[117] As brand scholar Michael Beverland discerns: "At a time when consumers find that traditional markers of identity make less and less sense in a globalized, borderless, multicultural world, brands that allow them to connect to . . . regional place and traditions, industry, and cultural ideals and subcultures are critical."[118]

Ironically, as Irish pubs mushroomed worldwide and Guinness prepackaged a concept standardized for "reality engineers" franchising them via "authentic" décor and staff, bars in Dublin actually had to *redesign* to meet those simulacra expectations of tourists, for whom the native original wasn't real enough.[119] Place can also be embodied in an individual, as in Juan Valdez's casting to sell the authenticity of Colombian coffee: the symbolically humble handpicker of beans with a "convincingly rural" backstory.[120]

Speaking of coffee, longtime Starbucks CEO Howard Schultz has variously declared "the companies that are lasting are those that are authentic" and that "authenticity is what we stand for."[121] In an interview, Stanley Hainsworth, his former vice president of global creative, elaborates on how that informed aesthetic ambition in the "brand book" he designed: "The music that [customers] hear when they walk in to hearing their name being called out, you know, 'Your drink is ready,' the furniture, the whole environment—so it's all five senses. . . . Most useful were these five words—they were these filters that we applied," he says. " 'Handcrafted,' 'artistic,' 'sophisticated,' 'human,' and 'enduring.' And the trick was all five had to be present in anything we did or made from the brand."[122]

Theoretically, Starbucks was responding to those anxieties of profit and automation in the modern world: accentuating naturalism—earth hues, handmade wicker baskets, curvilinear motifs, stained woods, unfinished metals, and environmentalist greens—as ambience against the emptiness of prepackaged synthetics and staging nostalgic rituals of familiarity to compensate for a rudderless, fragmented society that otherwise abandons traditions.[123] Such philosophical strategy shows up in the tiny details that Hainsworth notes: the affirmation of an individual's handwritten name on a global product that's utterly ubiquitous; the customized music selection unique to locals' preferences and geolocated by Spotify playlist likes, within a space that looks the same around the world. "There is that human element that it might even be that if you live in New York City, let's say, and you go into a Starbucks, it might be the only time that anyone actually calls your name or smiles at you the whole day," he laments.

This "third place" experience—not home and not work, where "you just wanted to get out and be with other people even though they were strangers," where "all of a sudden you're part of something bigger"—drew Hainsworth to the job, even though Starbucks is technically grouped among other quick-service restaurant franchises. He wanted to cultivate "an environment where you wouldn't feel weird turning to a stranger and maybe even [saying], 'Hey, I see you're reading this book—you know, I heard that it's good.' You might not do that at McDonalds. . . . It created this environment where you're allowed to be more human."

Yet the challenge remains that Starbucks mass-markets a mass-produced version of that cute little neighborhood coffee shop.[124] Thus, more than a decade ago, a global brand redesign tried anchoring authenticity even more in the local and the rustic—rough cutting stores rendered "purposefully grainy" and "uneven" in their textures.[125] One of the most effective monolith-faking-modesty techniques, Hainsworth reports, was putting up a handwritten sign on the door when a store was closing rather than a printed, laminated one that might be expected from a giant brand: Call this a work of indie aura in an age of mechanical reproduction.

Hence, too, some garage mythmaking: that performative clinging to humble origins, even after becoming a multibillion-dollar trademark. In its corporate history, Schultz recounts discovering the "morning ritual and sense of community" cultivated in the Milanese espresso bars he visited in the 1980s that would serve as brand inspiration—a heritage of old-world habits and European café lifestyles.[126] Hainsworth recalls Schultz, at a shareholder meeting, showing off the key to the original Pike Place Market store that he always kept in his pocket (and would later bequeath, symbolically, to a successor CEO): "And he said, 'Sometimes I just go in there when no one's there and I just reflect on where this brand started and where it came from'"—a space that Hainsworth would also return to for aesthetic inspiration, from the wood texture pattern to the countertop style. Fittingly, Hainsworth's last project for the company was reviving the 1971 logo as the visuals for a "back-to-roots" theme—Big Coffee aiming for human scale.[127]

Brand Politics

Later in the book, we'll see how politicians are acting more and more like brands; conversely, in recent years, brands have also started acting like politicians. As one *Adweek* op-ed advocates, marketers must concern themselves with strategizing a "moral framework—some foundation of what a brand believes in and believes is worth fighting for."[128]

Such commodity activism—that is, performing politics through consumption habits—traces a decades-long history.[129] Yet as media scholar Sarah Banet-Weiser critiques, converting social movements into branded movements turns political activism goals from the communal and systemic to the individual and idiosyncratic.[130] It's not only unthreatening to capitalism; it's increasingly a prerequisite for its perseverance. Moreover, commodity politics tend to be uncontestable and mainstream; when you buy to save the world, you usually buy into a fundamentally status quo vision.[131] This "market for virtue" reaps revenue rewards.[132] As corporations partner with charities, advertising critic Mara Einstein discerns, they have historically favored noncontroversial issues popular among wealthy, young demographics.[133]

Hence, the announcement at decade's end by almost 200 leading chief executives that the purpose of a corporation should not be to *exclusively* pursue shareholder interest—as had been the ideal since the high priest of neoliberalism, Milton Friedman, foreswore profit as a business's foremost social responsibility. As the *New York Times* tartly reported, this group, which averages 250 times the salary of their median employee, "did not provide specifics on how it would carry out its newly stated ideals, offering more of a mission statement than a plan of action."[134]

Not long after, the *Times* interviewed Whole Foods libertarian founder John Mackey about his "preaching of the redemptive power of what he calls 'conscious capitalism'" and how, in his words, "having a higher purpose can result in higher profits, and having a stakeholder philosophy doesn't mean that the investors start making less money."[135] Do good and do well: Who says an anthropomorphized corporation can't have it all?

More than ever, then, brands have been posing as activists, however concep-
tually tangential: from Delta and Levi's pushing gun control to gay rights Oreo's
to one Burger King ad explaining and affirming the value of net neutrality internet regulations (e.g., "the Internet should be like the Whopper sandwich: the
same for everyone"—get it?).[136] By one count, politicized ads shown during the
Super Bowl—Madison Avenue's premier stage to reflect zeitgeist—quadrupled
in the past decade.[137] This crescendoed with 2017's "Super Bowl of sadness," as
one interviewee mocked it, when, post-Trump election and proposed Muslim
ban, "every single ad, like, literally every chewing gum brand was trying to say
something about immigration, because you want to be relevant," which Coca-
Cola, Budweiser, Airbnb, and 84 Lumber indeed attempted.[138]

The traditional brand attribute framework might have been based upon features and benefits: "If I'm going to buy paper towels, are they useful? Are they
inexpensive?" says Catherine Reynolds, senior vice president at a global PR and
marketing agency. "Now, societal issues have become brand attributes. . . . Now
they're becoming attributes in terms of product purchases."[139] With "purpose"
as more of a buzzword that my interviewees are hearing from clients and consumers alike—the industry's pandering "new religion," one *Ad Age* columnist
grumbles—the question becomes: How woke are my paper towels?[140]

Plenty of survey data testifies to the demand for this. An *Adweek* article
claims that nearly three-quarters of Americans want corporations to "stand
up for what they believe politically" and more than a third of Americans—
neologized, inelegantly, as "corpsumers"—care about those positions as much
as the products themselves.[141] Another study found almost two-thirds of Americans would switch from a brand because of its perceived politics.[142] And no
demographic gets hyped more for this than youth: millennials and their suc-
cessors, Generation Z, more than half of whom prioritize buying brands that
"enhance their spirit and soul."[143] Ironically, seeming like your company stands
for more than just marketplace motives appears to have real marketplace value:
Brands perceived as retaining a strong "purpose" doubled their value and
growth relative to competitors with "weaker" virtue signaling.[144]

The simultaneous politicization and fragmentation of, well, everything
surely tendered fertile conditions for this opportunism. Trump was, of course,
a huge factor in the Great Awokening of brands, but so, too, is social media's
call-out culture, as well as the massive protest movement sparked in the wake
of George Floyd's murder.[145] (Ad-land being staffed by young, ticked-off libs in
coastal urban enclaves surely also explains the tilt.[146])

"Brands cannot expect to play Switzerland as the rest of the world picks a side," one *Adweek* author admonishes.[147] Not when—as Edelman's CEO echoes—"consumers are not just voting in elections, they are voting at the stores by choosing brands aligned with their values."[148] For example, despite Levi's and Wrangler originating among cowboys and railroad workers, they now represent a stark partisan divide among voters, the latter far more likely to be worn by Republicans, the former by Democrats (perhaps owing to the pro-immigration, anti-gun stances that earned Levi's CEO death threats).

Industry wisdom now holds that brands need to have a "clear point of view about life and current events," especially one that resonates powerfully with a particular, walled-off tribe, rather than blandly and limply trying to woo all of them.[149] Niche-oriented start-ups, rather than, say, legacy companies, can afford to be "edgier," given that they're not trying to be diplomatic people-pleasers— really just to sell far and wide—in that inauthentic, two-faced, marketplace-motivated fashion.[150]

To be clear, too, advertising professionals inured to insularity don't always consider this brand activism as being expressly "political" or "partisan"— framing it instead as "purpose," "humanity," or "social justice"–oriented and seeing any issues around race, sexuality, immigration, or climate as not plausibly having two sides.[151] (Moreover, not all causes are created equal: When the Supreme Court overturned *Roe v. Wade*, you heard nary a peep from most corporations.[152])

All of this seems indicative of brands trying to fill the vacuum of institutional decline in American life. More than a quarter of Americans do not affiliate with any religious tradition and confidence in political representatives slides ever-downward; we are, in short, living through an era where belief in faith and government is in free-fall.[153] And even though businesses themselves also tend to do poorly on those barometers of trust (see, for example: banks, 2008), brands still want to pitch in as a means of helping source and shape identity, the way that those declining institutions might have once furnished.[154]

"[Consumers] are laying more at the feet of brands," speculates Meredith Chase, chief strategy officer at Swift. "They think and believe and expect brands to be able to make the change in the world that the government institutions cannot."[155] Whether that's ridiculous or not, it's an ideology that informs a wide array of campaign strategies and examples of late. According to one emblematically titled textbook on the subject, *The Culting of Brands*, corporations need to offer a solution for the human condition: the urge "to belong, make meaning, feel secure, have order within chaos, and create identity."[156] Values that once derived from where you prayed now arrive from where you shop, as retailers pose as "arbiters of public morality" on a variety of current issues they never wanted to touch before.[157]

One of the earliest and most prominent brands that pursued authenticity through politics was Ben & Jerry's, pioneering the concept of corporate social responsibility.[158] At a conference put on by the Association of National Advertisers' Center for Brand Purpose, the company's "head of global activism" retells the brand's origin story, with details and vintage photos disavowing marketplace motives: Flashback to two ambling hippies who worked up an ice cream shop in a dilapidated gas station "because they didn't know what else to do" and just "so that they could eat and hang out with each other" and—well, golly, would you look at that?[159] Sold to Unilever for $300 million a couple decades later.[160] The executive adds that they had almost sold off sooner, disillusioned with the brand's go-go growth in the early '80s that demanded more hiring, firing, sourcing, and distributing yet afforded less time for just "hanging out" as they could in those humble origin days.

Simultaneously from the start and relentlessly in the years since, Ben & Jerry's defined itself with aww-shucks earnestness as a "social justice company that happens to make ice cream," as the executive puts it, with fourteen "activism managers" worldwide who come from civil society and advocacy backgrounds rather than soulless MBAs.[161] As environmentalism became "*the* political brand slogan" of this century—and indispensable to any business plan—the ice cream maker staked its identity most to that cause.[162] And although the executive says they "embrace the idea that it's better to be intensely loved by some than inoffensive to everyone"—posturing antithetical to the two-faced self—he also cautions "we have always been non-partisan, we don't endorse candidates, nor do we endorse parties." (This seemed dubious after the eponymous Ben served as national co-chair of Bernie Sanders' presidential campaign and rolled out a "Bernie's Yearning" mint chocolate flavor.[163]) By 2021 the ice cream maker inserted itself into that most fraught of geopolitical conflicts when it ceased sales in the Israeli-occupied territories—irking Prime Minister Benjamin Netanyahu ("Now we Israelis known which ice cream NOT to buy").[164]

Another key corporate forerunner here is Dove, whose "Real Beauty" campaign fronted both feminist politics and authenticity earnest, as media scholar Sarah Banet-Weiser tallies; indeed, several interviewees pointed to it as an originating influence for their later work.[165] Joah Santos, a chief "human-centric strategist," helped hatch the concept in the early 2000s, which advocated repositioning the brand away from product utility (because "like, how interesting can you make the soap?") and toward societal reform by empowering female self-confidence and affirming the natural, preexisting splendor of product users. To this, Unilever replied, dryly, "So you want to tell women that they're already beautiful while we're trying to sell beauty products?"[166]

The campaign, which *Ad Age* heralded as the single-best of the century and nearly doubled sales to $4 billion while earning scores of free media hype, included interactive billboards, viral videos, and supposedly "real" women in commercial imagery (i.e., not the typically emaciated models)—all trying to battle the unrealistic, inauthentic standards of female beauty that have persisted in Western culture and mass advertising.[167] One spot—viewed more than 20 million times on YouTube—pulled the curtain back to deconstruct the Photoshop machinations that disfigure a model toward idealized ends and finishes with a "Dove Self-Esteem Fund" appeal rather than a sales pitch, meant to distance the brand from any grubby marketplace motives: "It almost seemed like Dove was creating a charity," notes Santos, rather slinging soap.

But Dove didn't want *too* much authenticity, as some wrinkles, blemishes, and hairs were still retouched in postproduction: "a challenge, to keep everyone's skin and faces showing the mileage but not looking unattractive," the photo-fixer later admitted.[168] Santos adds, "Our guidance was just to use real women. . . . It was polished, but they were real people"—by which I assume he means nonprofessional models—"whereas, today, I feel like people are making it unpolished to make it feel authentic," evoking the rough cut ideal.

As explained by the chief creative officer for Dove's "Sketches" viral hit, where women react, tenderly, to portrait renderings suggested by others: "Authenticity was the core of the production and execution of the idea. We had real women meeting real strangers. They reacted to real sketches done by an actual FBI sketch artist. All the reactions were authentic. Everything was 100% genuine and non-scripted."[169]

In the wake of Real Beauty, other brands suddenly felt the need to chase a cause of some sort; one recent example also engaging gender issues is Gillette, which, in 2019, targeted toxic masculinity with the online release of an ad, "The Best Men Can Be." #MeToo predators like Harvey Weinstein loomed large in headlines, but so, too, did wider anxieties about masculine value and identity.[170] With men's suicide rates, cosmetics use, and share of household chores increasing—and testosterone levels down—masculinity is up for debate (and for brands, up for grabs) more than ever.[171]

Against that backdrop, Gillette tried to start a Very Important National Conversation. "This group of consumers expects brands to stand for more than the delivery of their functional benefit," a CEO at the parent company, Procter &

Gamble, testified.[172] The campaign theme played against Gillette's classic slogan, "The Best a Man Can Get," and the '80s-era, alpha male, *Wall Street* yuppie–type its advertising earlier idealized. The 2019 update, which opens with a character literally bursting through a screening of the old ad, quite self-consciously sought to redress that dated vision: to redefine and retire the "boys will be boys" cop-out that has historically excused inexcusable male behavior.

The ad montages images, tableaus, and news reports of masculine toxicity—slimy harassment, school bullying, workplace mansplaining, and crude objectification—before segueing into the performance of more chivalrous interventions. It even abides by "rough cut" aesthetics, according to Pankaj Bhalla, the in-house executive who oversaw the campaign, and aimed for "real footage, real people as much as possible," including minimalist production values for lighting and camerawork.[173] In an interview, Bhalla elaborates: "[Authenticity] was repeatedly mentioned in our brief. It was repeatedly mentioned in our meetings. It was repeatedly mentioned when we were editing the film," he says. "I wasn't trying to be popular. I was just trying to be authentic, because I know that if I'm authentic consistently on values that are right for the way the world is evolving and reflect how my brand is made, over time, we will win."

The campaign, alas, quickly became one of the most disliked videos in You-Tube history, inflamed Twitter and cable news, and triggered calls to boycott Gillette, especially from reactionary conservatives, "men's rights" types, and however one categorizes Piers Morgan these days.[174] One social media sentiment analysis inferred 7-to-1 negative-to-positive reactions; surprisingly, Gillette weathered the backlash with its YouTube channel comments kept on.[175]

Despite that polarizing response, Bhalla claims the ad helped brand equity and purchase intent, to say nothing of buzz: "Never in the last thirty years has a razor ever made it to a dinner conversation in an American household. And it did." That much is undeniable. He quotes the inner-directed, anti-two-faced-self philosophy of a fellow Gillette executive near the end of our interview: "The future belongs to brands that are loved by an overwhelming majority deeply, but not necessarily by everyone equally."

In 2017 Pepsi managed to annoy the entirety of the internet with its quasi–Black Lives Matter spot described in the opening pages of this chapter—dunked on by everyone from Martin Luther King's daughter ("If only Daddy would've known about the power of #Pepsi") to activist DeRay Mckesson ("If I had carried Pepsi I guess I never would've gotten arrested").[176] Several ad industry leaders called it the worst of all time, surely savoring the schadenfreude of Pepsi's in-house studio creation, all of whom on the production team were reportedly

White.[177] Starbucks similarly flopped mid-decade when it unveiled its "Race Together" initiative that encouraged baristas to scribble the phrase on coffee cups and strike up conversations in response to the police-exonerated killings of Black men. Within days, following a torrent of Twitter sarcasm, Starbucks ceased the initiative.[178]

By contrast, when Nike made blackballed NFLer Colin Kaepernick the face of its "Dream Crazy" campaign—with billboards tag-lined, "Believe in something. Even if it means sacrificing everything," an meta-epigram for the self-pretense of brand politics—the company won industry awards, courted young buzz (along with conservative backlash), and netted an estimated $6 billon in brand value.[179] One marketing pundit framed it as Rousseauian triumph: "Nike is supporting the idea of authenticity and being truthful to yourself."[180] Unlike the diplomatic insincerity a two-faced self might otherwise demand, the brand didn't flinch when "a whole bunch of white guys burned their Nikes and Trump was like, 'Nike's just fucking killed their stock price,'" Jason Lonsdale, Ogilvy brand strategy head, notes. "They knew who their audience was. . . . It's about knowing who you are."[181]

That Trump invocation is pertinent here. Throughout his years of campaigning and presidency, brands and consumer culture became the terrain for political expression like never before. This is no doubt partly owing to Trump himself being so obsessed with and motivated by brand logic as a businessman and politician.[182]

A #GrabYourWallet movement (riffing against Trump's crude *Access Hollywood* comments) listed companies with links to the president deserving of economic boycott like Home Depot, Nordstrom, and L.L. Bean.[183] Still others capitalized on the market potential of conservative consumers alienated by this "new liberal corporate consensus" in their branding: from Chic-fil-A to Hobby Lobby to the Black Rifle Coffee Company's anti-Starbucks ambition to become "a cool, kind of irreverent, pro–Second Amendment, pro-America brand in the MAGA era," as its co-founder mused.[184]

All these brand politics, whether arising from left or right, attempt to provide the authenticity of moral authority within consumerism, fill the vacuum of lost faith in other societal institutions, and respond to newly politicized cultural domains in hyper-polarized times. This is quite the departure from playing commercial "Switzerland," selling to partisans alike, and keeping out of the fray.

It's also not actually selling the *product*, materially. To be sure, brands have long receded utility and practicality behind imagery and lifestyle invocations—

being cool, athletic, or beautiful as the identity, rather than commodity, purchased. Now those lifestyle invocations have become politically righteous as well—aiding "self-actualization and transcendence to support higher-order beliefs about ourselves," even as those marketplace politics fail to substitute for traditional civic engagement like voting, protesting, and local community participation.[185]

As emblematic denouement to a tumultuous era, an array of brands—from Coca-Cola to Chevron to Verizon—took the unprecedented step of denouncing January 6 violence and urging the acceptance of electoral outcome, a governmental foundation previously unthinkable in its fortitude.[186] "We'd rather be lonely than with that mob," Axe announced on Twitter. "We believe in the democratic process and the peaceful transition of power." Amidst a looming constitutional crisis, citizens could take comfort in those noble sentiments—and that the sober wisdom of a humanized body spray might indeed prevail.

If only Kendall Jenner had been there on the steps of the Capitol to broker the peace.

FIVE

xxxxxx

The Rise of Influencers

Corporatizing the Human

I know how to market a product and I know how to do it in a way
that people don't feel like they're being sold to, which I think is
huge. That's the reason why these companies are paying me.

—KRISTIN QUINN, parenting influencer[1]

Now, it's like everyone has a side hustle; everyone is trying to be
an entrepreneur; everyone's trying to make it. . . . "Selling out"
previously was like, "Hey, you're not being true to your craft." Now
it's more, "Hey, you're working with a brand [that's] super lame."

—MAE KARWOWSKI, influencer firm CEO[2]

The wildest, swankiest party of the twenty-first century only and ever existed
on social media.

Fyre Festival co-founders Billy McFarland and Ja Rule conjured a dreamy
vision optimized for and implemented through the Instagram influencers they
enlisted to hype it: sun-kissed supermodels bathing in bright Bahamian sun-
shine beside pool-water-blue ocean; hip headlining acts vaulting dance-floor-
jammed bacchanalia through the night and into the dawn; a private island once
owned by Pablo Escobar, wink-wink hinting that the cocaine would flow freely;
lush villas and gourmet meals; private jets and jet-ski clowning; white-glove
treatment and VIP exclusivity—a lifestyle paradise with a price tag touching
six-figures for those who wanted to flex fanciest in their postings.[3]

Rather than fantasy come true, Fyre Festival attendees were treated to a car-
crash pileup of insufficient planning and bad decisions: soggy beds in disaster-

relief tents; sad cheese sandos in foam containers; decidedly uncool school-bus transportation; unpaid artists bailing with last-minute cancellations; all of which was livestreamed via "status" updates from enraged, defrauded millennials.

How on earth could Fyre Festival have mounted such a scam? The shortest answer: influencers.[4]

A Brief History of Buzz

In a way, influencer strategy is more than a century old.

During World War I, the US government's propaganda division conscripted community leaders to rally support by delivering hawkish talking points at movie theaters, restaurants, and town meetings.[5] Around the same time, Edward Bernays, public relations pioneer, got hired by a bacon company and coaxed thousands of physicians into recommending it to patients as part of a healthy breakfast. Befitting the feminized heritage of influencing, Avon and Tupperware sold through local women's networks, leveraging their friendships and get-togethers.[6]

None of this, of course, was meant to *feel* like advertising, because it was delivered from a trustworthy third-party rather than the benefitting entity. By midcentury, communication studies established the "two-step flow" theory of influence, whereby media persuasion trickles down, secondhand, through opinion leaders to most of the population.[7] Seventy years on, this basic premise underpins one of the fastest-growing segments of the marketing industry.[8]

Influencing also traces lineage to celebrity endorsements, a practice now nearly a century old.[9] Recently, celebrities themselves—albeit of the D-list variety—have been stooping to influencer gigs: Via the app, Cameo, businesses of modest size can hire the (modestly) renowned for quick, personalized testimonials; this is how the rapper-actor Ice-T was tapped to do spokesman work for one Colorado real estate agent.[10] Another start-up affords low-price bids to coax celebrities to simply interact with fans' social media accounts.[11]

Influencer strategy has also been central to music promotion, as noted in chapter 3, with Steve Rifkind, manager for the Wu-Tang Clan, enlisting cool kids on "street teams" to seed hype and hand out swag.[12] Some of this influencer work—known until the late 2000s as "word-of-mouth" or "buzz" marketing—had a shadowy, secretive sheen: General Mills named its influencer unit "Pssst" and another firm called itself "Girls Intelligence Agency."[13] One executive, who hatched a campaign for street team actors to pose and play with a newly released phone in public settings, explained, "If you put them in a Sony Ericsson shirt, then people are going to be less likely to listen to them."[14]

The internet supercharged influencer potential: It rendered explicitly visible (and invidiously quantifiable) friendship networks; made public all that natural opinion-sharing about goods, services, and entertainment; and enabled efficient platforms to harness socializing on behalf of brands.[15] Chat rooms, message boards, ratings sites, and above all, social media suddenly presented a massive trove of untapped advertiser inventory. Ted Murphy is credited with starting the first influencer network when he roped in a few thousand tastemaker bloggers and MySpace users in the mid-aughts to sprinkle #spon-con in their online output in exchange for gift cards and promo codes to places like Red Lobster and Burger King.[16]

As influencer scholar Emily Hund chronicles, this combination of social media ascendance, metrics tools like Klout, and cultural trends of microcelebrity and self-branding all exploded industry growth in the early 2010s, as agencies sprang up to shepherd creators and play brand matchmaker.[17] PR firms—long having orchestrated grassroots perception and earned media seeding—also jumped into the influencer space.[18] At annual confabs like VidCon, a "land grab" for talent ensued, with brands, platforms, and agencies like CAA and WME wooing those with massive digital followings.[19] Collaborative content collectives popped up across Los Angeles, full of late teens chronicling the minutiae of their daily lives to unfathomably large audiences— TikTok's Hype House had 100 million views just one month into its existence.[20]

What began as one-off brand insertions and fleeting namechecks from creators shifted toward longer-term, co-creative, ambassador-style partnerships, partly to fortify the believability and, hence, authenticity of endorsements; for example, TikTok supernova Charli D'Amelio hooked up with Dunkin' for a signature merchandise line.[21] Influencing often skews youthful, sometimes astonishingly so: A ten-year-old Texas boy with 18 million YouTube subscribers who watch him unbox and review toys launched a line of his own ("Ryan's World") and earns an estimated $25 million annually thanks to deals with Nickelodeon, Sketchers, and others.[22]

Still, it's not all prepubescent shilling; companies ranging from Master-Card to Macy's to Amazon started drafting employees to post on their behalf. GameStop encouraged its workforce to upload clips of themselves dancing, while at work, to a TikTok hashtag challenge; winners (if that's the right term) would receive the chance to schedule extra store hours on Black Friday.[23] One survey found that 90 percent of brands were conscripting or contemplating such employee advocacy, seeing it as "more real" and credible than their official statements.[24] As the head of one such program at United Airlines explains, "It's about having them be their authentic selves and finding ways to give them more access and a bigger platform."[25]

By the Numbers

Authenticity is, of course, the basis for value—both cultural and financial—within this booming industry. Spending rocketed from $500 million in 2015 to $8 billion in 2019 and was anticipated to grow to $15 billion by 2022.[26] One advertising trade group found that three-quarters of its membership had run influencer campaigns and nearly half planned to spend more on them in the future.[27] Instagram, more than any platform, reaped this bounty, netting $5 billion in influencer revenues by decade's end, as sponsored posts grew sixfold.[28]

For campaigns, industry average runs about $10-per-thousand audience members.[29] Thus, a microcelebrity with a mere 10,000 followers can grab $100 for a posting, while megastars like Kylie Jenner command $500,000 or even $1 million for similar product placement.[30] Child influencers do even better—one estimate holds that a kid can pull ten times the rate of an adult counterpart.[31] (Companies can also pay influencers to hate on a rival by dropping negative reviews.[32]) And all these marketing dollars sloshing around explains the odd phenomena of not-quite-famous-enough users *falsifying* influencer status within their feeds: captioning a post #sponsored that's actually not, to impress followers or the companies they hope to work with.[33]

For their part, brands, platforms, and agencies tout a slew of metrics affirming the effectiveness of influencer strategy (these, of course, being self-interested, though not necessarily invalid). One study claims influencer content pulls 50 percent more engagement than conventional advertising; on YouTube, for example, influencer #spon-con holds seven seconds of eyeball attention compared to just two for traditional commercials.[34] About half of all Americans follow influencers on social media and half have bought something based upon their recommendations.[35] Gen Z, which watches an average of seventy YouTube videos per day, is considered an especially receptive demographic target: Nearly half have actually *shared* sponsored content.[36]

The production process unfolds like this: An aspiring influencer signs up with a clearinghouse brokerage for brands seeking digital talent.[37] From those sites, corporations browse keywords (e.g., location, interests, demographics, prior sponsorship) to pinpoint influencers who seem relatable to the product or campaign, as well as their metrics showing return-on-investment. Not unlike traditional advertising, these suitors then put out for bid a particular opportunity and see who bites.

In other cases, agencies or brands might reach out directly to creators seeking collaborative deals or managerial representation (e.g., this is the spammy "DM me!" sometimes seen in comment threads). Some influencer firms augment these tactics with natural-language machine learning and AI data analysis to identify and pair especially relevant talent with clients. Mazda, for example, was chasing flamboyant extroverts for a new compact SUV and screened for those with five-figure followings who post a lot of emojis and exclamation point–capped captions.[38]

Categorically, fashion and beauty have long dominated the influencer space, though consumer-packaged goods and quick-service restaurants saw uptick toward decade's end; one interviewee noted, however, that you'd find many more "really authentic" cosmetics influencers, given their daily devotion to makeup tutorials, whereas #spon-con for fast-food or grocery stores comes off comparatively "transactional" and reeking of "phony" marketplace motives.[39] Certain categories tend to map onto particular sites: DIY types congregating on Pinterest and conventional blogs; fashionistas and wanderlusts on Instagram; and parenting and housebound lifestyles on Facebook.[40]

Individual creators internalize these patterns and nuance their output accordingly, a different genre of brand-self for each platform. For example, one mommy influencer explains how she'll allocate her picturesque poses to Instagram; her down-to-earth misadventures to Facebook; and her recipe procedurals to TikTok.[41] Some interviewees also think strategically about timing: avoiding posting on weekends and holidays and optimizing for commute hours or after children's bedtimes.[42]

All this is driven by an obsession with statistical effectiveness—above and beyond mere reach or page views. Even likes have become, as one interviewee puts it, an empty-calorie "vanity metric."[43] Because commercialism craves not just our undivided attention but our active participation in its capital schemes, "engagement" became the umbrella ideal for measuring impact: video duration and image linger time; comments and friend tags; saves and shares and sign-ups.[44] Mae Karwowski, CEO of Obviously, notes that her influencer firm even mines sentiment analysis on those comments to sponsored posts, searching for thematically groupable reactions from particular user demographics.[45] Another interviewee's company data-analyzes to calculate a numerical tally, between 1 and 100, that ranks a given influencer based upon both quantity of followers and quality of their engagement—a more sophisticated metric-descendent of Klout scoring from years past when social popularity first won retail perks.[46]

Such demands can feel relentless and exhausting—and, given ever-changing algorithmic conditions, capricious—for those trying to eke out a profession as an influencer, much less a "living." One estimate noted those who had "made it" in the business spent anywhere from two to eight hours every day populating their accounts with content.[47] Instagram itself was apparently advising select influencers, on the down-low, that they could improve follower counts and engagement levels if they dropped 3 in-feed posts, 8–10 stories, and 4–7 reels each week.[48]

A lifestyle influencer I interviewed illustrated a variety of tricks she relies on to boost her numbers: reciprocal shout-outs (i.e., tagging and recommending others to follow) and link-ups (posting on a coordinated topic); larding captions with no "hashtag shame" to optimize searchability (including all 30 #'s allowed); trolling for responses, and thus engagement, with open-ended questions ("which of these breakfast sandos would you have ordered?"); and aiming to publish about once or twice a day, with thematic routines ("quotes on Mondays, food on Fridays," etc.).[49]

One *New York Times* column tallies these "burnout-inducing" expectations: "spot trends, experiment relentlessly with new formats and platforms, build an authentic connection with an audience, pay close attention to their channel analytics, and figure out how to distinguish themselves in a crowded media environment."[50] These are basically the same marching orders a global media conglomerate faces, but heaped upon what is usually a one-woman band.

An assortment of feminist scholars criticize the dynamics of this arrangement. Sarah Banet-Weiser observes that this kind of digital labor—affective, relational, immaterial—is not often recognized (and rewarded) as work by "conventional capitalist exchange."[51] Angela McRobbie points out that the repertoires on display in these social media spaces condition young women to internalize femininity as a "finely tuned instrument of social calibration" with a neoliberal pressure on measurement and objectives.[52] Kyla Schuller adds that such self-optimization has become the gospel of postfeminism: disciplining and perfecting the performance of a life in a fashion that conforms to capitalist imperatives.[53] And as women shouldered that burden of selling through their intensely curated selves, corporations had to teach themselves to offload the responsibility rather than micromanage it.

Authenticity Off-Script

Back in 2006, the CEO of Procter & Gamble, a corporation that routinely spends more globally on advertising than any other, issued a cryptic proclamation in his opening address to the annual trade meeting of US advertisers: "We now have a greater opportunity to move beyond transactions to relationships than ever before, but to do so requires that we strike the right balance between being in control and being in touch," he proposed. "Ironically, the more in control we are, the more out of touch we become. But the more we're willing to let go, the more we're able to get in touch with consumers."[54]

This premise—that brands must relinquish the iron fist they've historically wielded over the promotion process—is central to the influencer space. The premise often gets idealized in democratic, populist terms—the byproduct, surely, of a landscape of social media that is itself often mistaken for democratic and populist.[55] Within the ad industry, few refrains are more clichéd by now than rhapsodizing about "dialogue": that a company needs to talk *with* rather than *at* consumers. During the 2010s, the influencer became the chief vehicle for those pretensions.

"[If] you don't want to sell out, how do you make sure that you're not creating a campaign that looks like you're just pushing products?" asks Hudson Sullivan, TikTok's brand partnership director. "Just talking really personally and in a real fashion about the experience you've had with the product. . . . It makes it feel more relatable and makes it feel less like you've been given this script and reading off the script."[56] The slogan for his team's creative ethos denies the very act of commercialism they oversee: "Don't make ads; make TikToks."[57]

Likewise, Lena Young, director of communications at Klear, explains that her firm will pass along a brief to talent that offers some general guidelines and suggested hashtags, delineates forbidden settings or props (e.g., alcohol, cigarettes), and establishes the requisite volume of content, but otherwise leaves creative license entirely in the influencer's hands: "That's what makes it not feel like a real ad," she adds.[58]

This aversion to overtly scripting the sales pitch—and accommodating supposedly authentic reflections about the product—defined word-of-mouth marketing practices well before "influencer" came into vogue.[59] When IZEA's Ted Murphy pioneered sponsored tweets over a decade ago, less got him more: By allowing a tailored, seemingly natural message, it performed and engaged much better than pre-stocked #spon-con simply copy-and-pasted into someone's stream.[60] That ad message also benefits from countless unique, creative slants about the product afforded by influencer freedom—each relevant to different niche followings—rather than one standardized, repetitious, dumbed-down hard sell.[61]

Influencers themselves get this. Brittany DiCapua, a foodie, explains her approach to simulating a *mise-en-scene* of lived fun:

> Let's say I'm working with an alcohol brand. I'm not just going to post a picture of a liquor bottle on my cabinet or my counter and say, "Yummy—get this liquor!" You have to work your content into your daily lifestyle. So, instead of just posting a bottle of liquor, I'm going to create a scene that other people might find enticing and want to recreate themselves. I'm going to make a beautiful cocktail, be sitting with my friends on my couch, watching football games to showcase that brand. So, creating real-life authentic situations and incorporating the brand into that is best. . . . I need to create a scenario that, you know, John could see themselves in or Andy can see themselves doing and being natural with it and aligning it to things I already talk about or things people already trust me for.[62]

Similarly, Lisa Santangelo, a parenting influencer, strives "to represent a brand in the most authentic way," by not just, say, posing with a food product but instead weaving it into a recipe demo; still, she acknowledges, "You can't really make it look totally natural when you have #ad at the beginning of your caption—they're gonna know you're working with a brand."[63]

Perhaps unsurprisingly, lower-tier influencers tend to be more malleable and willing to accede to heavy-handed brand demands compared to those approaching actual celebrity status, who can scoff at corporations impinging upon their autonomy.[64] Luxury and fashion brands also tend to expect the most creative control when enlisting influencers, with multiple rounds of edits and approvals as the norm.[65]

Still, treating the influencer space like any other media buy—no different from a billboard—not only risks campaign failure but backlash against the influencer for selling out their authenticity.[66] In the worst-case scenario you get mishaps, like one reality TV star who accidentally copy-and-pasted the agency instructions into his sponsored post (i.e., "Here you go, at 4pm, write the below [caption]").[67] As sociologist Erving Goffman observed, you have to keep that stuff backstage.

Ordinary Aspirations

"It's not about, 'I wanna be like Mike'—Michael Jordan. It's about, '[I wanna be] like Steve'—and Steve's the kid around the corner. Because they have a hell of a lot more credibility. And you can get 10,000 Steve's for the price of one Mike," the CEO of an influencer agency tells me. "It's about getting someone who's authentic in my peer group that will endorse the product. And that's what 'real life product placement' was about—it was about getting *real* people to use *real* products in *real* ways."[68]

Indeed, as the years wore on, the stars of social media no longer sufficed. In pursuit of that "real" authenticity—scare-quoted here for apposite irony—the influencer industry needed to slip its promotional tentacles ever deeper into average folks' lives and networks. Hence, one of the biggest trends in the business aimed for those with the tiniest footprint: a downward drift away from Kardashian-level ambassadors and toward those with more modest, targeted, and engaged followings that allow for "really small bets" on return-on-investment to be placed.[69] Ten thousand followers was once table stakes in the influencer game; now, "micro-" and, subsequently, "nano-influencers," with as few as a thousand, became fair play.[70]

This began squeezing out that middle tier of influencer, and one interviewee advises against using them, having seen their engagement numbers plummet and their authenticity become a washed-up commodity: "People are sniffing that lack of credibility [from] influencers that are selling out or jumping around from brand to brand."[71] By contrast, nano-influencers serve as cheap test pilots for campaigns before scaling up strategy to more popular nodes with lessons learned—filtering the message through dozens or even hundreds of those trackable nanos and then reverse A/B testing to see what nuances of stylistic and substantive detail performed most powerfully with the sought-after demographic.[72] Johnson & Johnson, for example, tapped teenagers on Instagram with a mere 500 followers to hype a new line of cleansers and creams, claiming these acned nanos were "doing things that other kids responded to authentically."[73]

One firm scrapes and catalogs the years of organic and paid content from its stable of creators to pin down, say, "Is there a Bernie Sanders sticker on someone's Subaru?" to filter out during the virtual casting call within its database.[74] Another interviewee's website touts their targeting talents to extreme ends: "If you need someone who skateboards only pools in LA, we can help you find that person. Or if you wanted to find someone who paraglides in the Midwest and has an affinity for veganism, we can help you find that."[75]

The appeal of tapping these nano-influencer unknowns is that they don't (yet) seem corrupted like higher-profile counterparts.[76] "If you can really stay authentic to who you are and what you'd actually use and recommend, people will stick with you," argues Kristin Quinn, a parenting influencer. "I always say to people that are like, 'Well, you know, you don't have 20 million followers' or whatever—it's, like, yeah, but the 10,000 followers I do have on my blog will buy what I'm saying."[77] One study claims, in fact, such nano-influencers have seven times more engagement on Instagram than those with massive followings.[78] And smaller audiences don't even necessarily hurt, because they frequently come with valuable consistency for brands seeking to drill down to a particular niche; for that reason, one parenting influencer quite deliberately tries to curate for and cultivate "people that are like me," because she knows brands desire those more homogenous distillations.[79]

As shown throughout the book, familiarity fuels credibility and authenticity: You are but a distant fan of mega-influencers with their million-plus followers, but you might actually, really, *know* that nano with three- or four-digit audience counts—and, vice versa, that nano can keep track of and cater to you as well, leveraging what a less commercialized era might have called a "relationship."[80] "Their lack of fame is one of the qualities that makes them approachable," according to a *New York Times* diagnosis of the nano trend. "When they recommend a shampoo or a lotion or a furniture brand on Instagram, their word seems as genuine as advice from a friend."[81]

Not only are these folks cheaper to work with—even doing it for free, since they usually have a day job—they're often more pliable in the process: willing to enthuse and emote and contort to keep corporate patrons pleased.[82] Indeed, an influencer's willingness to shill for samples alone used to be, for one agency CEO, "our authenticity test," but even many of those players have gotten wise to the game, calculating their value, and demanding market rates in actual cash.[83] (Alas, with budget cutbacks and fears of a recession swirling in 2022, the "barter economy" resurfaced for nanos who "can't really say no to proposals from cash-strapped marketers" offering services or goods in lieu of money.[84])

As noted, an influencer cultivates and maintains their value by way of authenticity, an authenticity translated further here, like reality TV, as *ordinariness*. To establish a parasocial bond with followers, they must reject any pretense of status and come across as "genuine" and proximate to those in their audience—ideals afforded by social media architecture and everyday lives publicly lived.[85]

"[Followers] can see what's going on, on a day-to-day basis. And they know if someone broke up with someone and someone's, like, dieting; if someone's sick," explains Krishna Subramanian, co-founder of Captiv8, an influencer firm. "[That's] why digital influencers are more powerful on social than celebrities."[86] Indeed, unlike a traditional celebrity, harboring some entertainment skill, an influencer's fame and value is entirely identity-based and often platform-circumscribed: "Just good-looking guys and girls that have yet to figure out if they have any talents," as one interviewee quips.[87]

Yet talent would beget status and status would invalidate that proximate familiarity. As digital anthropologist Crystal Abidin finds, creators need to seem "ordinary, everyday, and mundane" and their main "anchor material," especially in the family influencer category, tends to be banal, household activities, maintaining the same ethic and aesthetic of amateurism that vaulted them to fame in the first place.[88] In other words, one's "quotidian" and "private" life is the very commodity that's exchanged on social for clicks and, therefore, revenues.[89] When food influencer Brittany DiCapua noticed that photos and videos including her tended to outperform cuisine shots alone—even prosaic selfies just slurping coffee in traffic—it dawned on her: "People want connection—they want to know who they're looking at and who they're getting these recommendations from. They want to know your life."[90]

Thus, influencers realized that they needed to give away more and more of what Goffman would call that "backstage self" if they wanted to sufficiently monetize themselves—exchanging exposure for exposure, in a sense, and stripping away not garments but any pretense of perfection.[91] One estimate holds that vignettes from family life and personal trials do 50 percent better than other postings.[92] A happy home, demanded of women since time immemorial, now becomes a staged enterprise to optimize for maximum "return on investment."[93]

Jasmine Star, who runs a consultancy for influencers, advises based upon that pattern: "Female small business owners, they say, 'Do I have to share pictures of my children to get that engagement?'. . . . If you really want to drive engagement, post a picture of your puppy or your baby and you're just winning."[94] Sharing about births and deaths can also juice metrics, she adds, because such universal rites of joy and grief are #relatable.

For example, one mommy influencer, Kristin Quinn, posted a photo of her cute, dimpled son dunking a cookie into a glass next to a posed carton of milk with the poignant caption, "Transitions remind us that time is fleeting. I like to think they help us stay in the present that way. The end of an era with diapers, ditching the crib, the 1st day of kindergarten. . . . I specifically remember the day we transitioned from formula to cow's milk. . . . #ad #HoodMilk #Because itMatters."

Quinn admits that she's sometimes gotten asked—with implied judgment— if she has any trepidation about using her kids in her #spon-con, but counters that others routinely fill their feeds with her children and "the only difference here is that I'm more professional about it and, obviously, I have a lot more followers." Moreover, she adds, her kids have shown increasing enthusiasm to shill themselves as they've gotten older: "They'll be, like, 'Mommy, can we help promote, you know, Legos or Beyblades' or whatever. . . . Companies that work with me and that have followed me just kind of know that's what they're gonna get: the authenticity of my kids."[95]

Children and pets "play" well in the influencer space, because their intrinsic innocence helps obfuscate the commercial machinations at work in the background: They appear to lack a "puppeteer," whereas the influencer herself might come across as tethered, and they can't help but exude authenticity because, per Jean-Jacques Rousseau's philosophizing, societal convention has not yet drained them of those instincts. They appear as an oasis of "real" in a landscape parched from fakery and pretense and calculation—offsetting the marketplace motives that have conscripted their parents. After all, the first commandment of influencing, according to Star, remains: "Social media should do one thing: It should be social. It should not be selling."[96]

Bringing people backstage along the journey, she adds—even if the view there isn't always pretty—offers vulnerability, which secures credibility and authenticity. Being "real," for influencers, then, means being consistent, both online and off, and proving there's no two-faced-self lurking behind the scenes.[97] Beauty vloggers literally prove what you see is what you get by embedding products within a "mundane morning grooming routine," recording the transition from bare-faced starting point, and peppering in intimate tales of their relationship to the branded good.[98] This unstaged, rough cut self is the most authentic self and, ironically, a great vehicle for selling: a selfie, sans makeup, shows there's only one—trustworthy—face on-screen.

Some of these ideals emerged in response to influencers producing overly planned and thus standardized content, particularly Instagram imagery: amateurs, ironically, adopting the very same habits of the highly professionalized advertising industry that influencing originally served as an authentic antidote to.[99] Thus, a countertrend surfaced toward "intimate moments," more "candor," and fewer "posey" photos.[100] Star, who once advised creator clients to curate their accounts "like a museum," reversed her sensibilities as she watched everyone copycat from the same perfectly manicured template playbook and now favors a less finely coifed presentation of self: "What I'm saying is show up and be real. . . . Everyday life doesn't look that [perfect] way."[101]

By decade's end, as previewed in chapter 2, TikTok's ascendance both animated and was animated by these cultural yearnings. One meme found TikTokkers posting influencer parodies explicitly mocking their superficial, hyper-polished tropes.[102] Mae Karwowski, an influencer firm CEO, detects a nascent generational shift, almost *anti*-aspirational in nature: "There are a lot of influencers [now] who have actually, like, kind of pretty ugly content, especially younger influencers."[103]

Instagram, of course, responded with its disappearing Stories feature: "to keep it, like, super low-tech, low-key, to maintain engagement" by "showing a behind-the-scenes look at your day," explains Lena Young, director of communications at Klear, adding that a third of Instagram's sponsored posts are now Stories. "[It] offers really the most authentic look at someone's life and they can be lying in bed talking to you and people really feel like they're looking at their friend talking to them."[104] As befitting the rough cut archetype, unfiltered spontaneity is prized: natural light, unedited postproduction, self-deprecating moments of frankness—pretty much any form of presentation that can seem authentically unstaged.[105]

Influencers' divulsions of discontent can also (usefully) stand in sharp contrast to the smiley perfection that usually surrounds them.[106] Such is the unfiltered substance analogous to the unfiltered style of presentation: "letting you into perhaps the not-so-shiny life that is shown on social media" normally, as one interviewee puts it.[107] One trend that swept across YouTube found influencers in front of their cameras spilling intense secrets they'd kept hidden to "level with their audiences a little bit and say, hey, like, 'This is the real me.' "[108]

Feminist theorists Rosalind Gill and Akane Kanai term this "emotional capitalism"—fostering and monetizing affective, intimate modes of being, from previously private spaces, that play well on social media's self-monitoring and *depend* on "performative insecurity," as women rough cut themselves down from showing too much confidence or unrelatable perfection.[109] Sheryl Sandberg, *Leaner*-in-chief, exemplifies this tension and balance: rich, powerful, and obviously optimized but also showing "visibly flawed" "emotion and vulnerability"—regaling us with anecdotes of, say, throwing up and likeably masking success with confessional shortcomings that prove "capitalism can have a heart."[110] Such traits and performances power the social media market-place: a good cry becomes an advantageous asset.[111]

Another interviewee, a family influencer, explicitly touts that raw, messy content as a badge of trustworthiness in her materials for sponsors: "We have a unique advantage that we think is extremely useful to our readers in that we write from the perspective of a regular old family with 2 crazy kids. This is as real as you can get and our readers love that!"[112] Moreover, the pandemic disruption increased the market for mundane, vulnerable content of precisely that sort: Influencers could produce remotely (and cost effectively) in-home amidst lockdowns and, tonally, seem to have their finger on the pulse of a nation utterly incapable of pretense while confined to couches, clad in sweatpants, and doom-scrolling for hours on end.[113] Who needed aspirational? Christmas 2020 saw a 25 percent rise in influencer bids.[114]

All of this, of course, remains highly gendered. *Adweek* tallies 95 percent of influencers identifying as female (with three-quarters in their late twenties or early thirties) and one agency's annual report declares, "Women rule the influencer kingdom."[115] Yet this highly feminized creative workforce is also quite precarious; one interviewee told me that male influencers, few as they are, tend to garner $100 more per post than female counterparts.[116] Many female creators initially came out of the DIY mommy blogging space, a genre of branded-self that can be difficult to maintain as babies age out.[117]

Significantly, too, the biggest categories of brand patrons tend to derive from historically feminized consumer goods, with beauty and fashion spending more on these strategies than almost any other.[118] The nature of these practices demands and rewards affective, eager-to-socialize self-presentations, which explains the almost oppressively chipper, exclamation point–peppered packaging of many influencers' experiences.[119] In the 1950s, Tupperware made a similar plea of its quasi-laborers: Lady-sellers were "dissuaded from adopting a corporate image" and encouraged to socialize a sales setting into a "positive party date."[120]

Today that peppy, commercialized vacuity shows up in caption examples from interviewees' feeds: "It's Monday night and you know what that means: Aperol Spritz timeeee [orange emoji, stars emoji]." Mae Karwowski, an influencer firm CEO, laments, "Women are used to being objectified in a way and being in, like, acting and performing and they're used to that from a younger age than men. And, so, it's a really easy fit with social media."[121] Thus, scholars have argued that social media, as a "self-surveillance technology," helps reproduce the male gaze in this complicit fashion: women "empowered" to post pictures of themselves that seem to invite that desire.[122] As a bombshell whistleblower's report on Instagram reveals, this has deeply destructive impact on the mental health, self-esteem, and body image of young women.[123]

How to Sell Friends and Influence People

"It's not that things are necessarily any more authentic than they ever were," one interviewee tells me. "It's that the perception of authenticity is what's selling right now more than ever."[124] Nowhere is that perception more vital to the market—because it seems *distanced* from it—than in the influencer space. When scouring for talent, the chief technology officer for a digital agency links this explicitly: "We're looking into the people that have a very authentic following," he says. "Not because they do it because they want to make money with it."[125]

Authenticity—whether specifically referenced or an unspoken ideal—is ubiquitous here: on websites, at industry events, pouring forth from the lips of interviewees. Scholars have coined a spate of seemingly contradictory terms to capture this strategic labor: "calibrated amateurism," "curated imperfection," and "aspirational ordinariness."[126] Authenticity balances the tensions of being "true" to one's self, one's audience, and one's patron and choreographs "a strategic form of self-presentation" in that process.[127] It defines monetization potential and, once exploited, influencers must cling to it even more.[128] In other words, getting paid—ostensibly, a sign of success—simultaneously corrupts the reason that got you paid in the first place.[129]

Once upon a time, as in pop music, the scarlet letter was "sellout." Ostensibly, this remains a "huge danger in the space," an influencer executive tells me, because his talent is "living and dying" by their follower counts.[130] One food influencer admits, "Money matters, but you never want to look like you're doing it for that, because then your word is going to be less valued and, with less value, you're not really an influencer anymore"—diminishing metric effectiveness and getting dropped by brands anyhow.[131]

Part of the problem is blurring where the influencer "self" ends and the brand begins, aesthetically and rhetorically: a boundary so weathered and faint, you could be forgiven for doubting its very existence.[132] One lifestyle influencer, Grace Atwood, formally apologized on her feed for a deluge of #spon-con that would inundate her fans the following week: "I realize this may be annoying for some of you."[133]

How, then, to insulate authenticity amidst its long-standing antithesis, commerce? A number of tactics can safeguard against the optics of selling out:

concealing advertising disclosure; openly wrestling with the presence of sponsorship; integrating the brand into the signature organic output; or leveraging it to provide even more backstage intimacy.[134] In some cases, influencers double-down on the pretense of "passion" as a prophylactic for the product placement (i.e., emphasizing prior love for the brands featured).[135]

Equally critical is the nature of the patronage: Local mom-and-pop shops typically exude more authenticity (as the last chapter argued, being nonstandardized) and thus are better for maintaining an influencer's authenticity as compared to multinational chains. "I do get some hate when I post McDonald's [ads]," admits food influencer Brittany DiCapua. "But, also, you can't live your life with what other people are saying online. Like, this is my job and a lot of times the larger brands pay the money."[136] DiCapua even acknowledged that ambivalence in a blog posting about an invite-only McDonald's event—showcasing its new "signature-crafted menu concepts" (read: artisanal authentic)—when she admitted her preference to work with independently owned alternatives.

Elsewhere, she has a 1,900-plus-liked "Mood. #quarantine"-captioned shot of her enjoying a bubble bath, mud mask, and bowl of Oreo O's cereal (with Hershey's chocolate syrup and Nutella perched precariously at tub's edge)—a tableau so over-the-top with commercialism, the fact that DiCapua's mouth is closed surely indicates that it's tongue-in-cheek. Still, when she posted a similarly unsubtle shot with a stack of eleven Domino's pizza boxes atop her bed and two pepperoni slices dribbling from her maw—intended as a joke—"[people] were like mad, they were like, 'Ewww, sell out.'" But since smaller businesses often don't have as much dough as conglomerates—this, again, is why they have the authenticity—interviewees will sometimes treat those as pro bono cases.[137]

Chelsea Marrs, a lifestyle influencer, shrugs:

If it's working with bigger corporations to make money in order to keep giving your audience the content that they're loving, I am okay with it. . . . Would you tell a painter, "Why would [you] sell out to a museum?" He has to get paid. Like, he wants to continue doing the art that he loves. And I think a lot of people look at influencers like it's not art; it's not real business; they're not authentic enough. But they're just trying to do what they love, like anyone else, and also be able to pay their bills.[138]

Best-case scenario is when an influencer hooks up with a brand that they've already hyped in-feed. In her influencer consultancy, Marrs often recommends that clients reach out to companies they already adore, organically, to pitch them on making a formal deal: "That way it is authentic already—you don't have to try and only accept things that feel true to you."

One fashion micro-influencer admits that she name-dropped Rent the Runway, an e-commerce apparel platform, no fewer than fifty-eight times prior to becoming an official ambassador for them: faking it—persistently, relentlessly, weirdly—till she made it.[139] Another Instagrammer tagged Dunkin' almost daily and wore orange-and-magenta branded outfits with longing captions like, "Unfortunately, not a @dunkin ad," before eventually snagging a product placement deal.[140]

Long-standing, pre-deal enthusiasm also gives the *patron* rhetorical cover for what is, ultimately, payout for affection, as seen with sponsored musicians in chapter 3. When the NFL rolled out its influencer program, it tried to make it seem more than transactional: "We just call them new friendships," the league's vice president of influencer marketing mused, torturing the meaning of the word "friendship."[141] Even "influencer" itself was being phased out as a phrase among influencers and platforms, in favor of the more artistically inclined "creator," which supposedly connotes being less driven by marketplace motives to push product: more Spielberg than Saatchi, more Picasso than Publicis. Influencer "almost feels like you're being used in some capacity," the chief strategy officer at an influencer agency (correctly) notes.[142]

Perhaps most pivotal for maintaining authenticity is restraining the ratio of organic-to-sponsored content within one's feed: "You can get to a point in your career where you're just diluting everything you're talking about, because you're saying yes to every [deal]. That, to me, is selling out as an influencer and it seems desperate," says Kristin Quinn, a parenting influencer.[143] Because this oversaturation annoys followers (and saps authenticity), my interviewees try to limit ads to about one of every three-to-five posts.[144] The temptation to shill more, though, forever tantalizes: "I feel kind of like an infomercial, and I'm generally uncomfortable pushing things on people," laments one nano-influencer spin-class instructor. "But I've seen a return on that, albeit small."[145]

Seemingly Real

What is true, then, for the latest sponsored TikTokker was true for World War I propagandists a century ago: a persuasive message coming from a reliable third-party works best because it doesn't seem like an ad.[146] "By human nature, we trust people rather than corporations," says one influencer firm CEO—and this is precisely why corporations have been colonizing people's lives.[147]

Management scholars have found that consumers with a heightened yearning for authenticity also place greater faith in influencer endorsements relative to conventional advertising featuring experts; another study claimed that nearly half of teens felt their favorite YouTube creator "understands them better" than their IRL friends.[148]

When Clorox started an advisory board of content creators, its goal was to ensure that the brand's social media output came across "more human, more authentic, and less obvious in our approach to driving demand."[149] These imperatives become more urgent in a landscape where consumers simultaneously grow accustomed to ad-free contexts and also tire of encountering commercial clutter in other media spaces: Frustrated and rebuffed with attempts to interrupt content, the market responds by trying to make capitalism the content.[150]

Creators themselves seem to get that their #spon-con is most effective if it blends, indistinguishably, with organic output. "If you're doing a good job with the ads, people probably won't notice," says foodie influencer Brittany Di-Capua, who notes that keeping herself as the center of focus—rather than the product placed—both minimizes the obtrusiveness of the sponsored interruption and pulls better engagement numbers. "I can place myself as the main element and people might not even realize that I have hashtag #ad at the bottom of my caption. . . . As much as you can try to really work it in and make it kind of a hidden notion, that's best."[151]

In general, advertising seems to be more effective when audiences don't recognize it as such.[152] This underpins the premise of guerrilla marketing: commercial content that seeps into noncommercial forms, slides under the radar of audiences, and self-effaces its own persuasive intent.[153] Tellingly, the umbrella category for influencer marketing—"native" advertising, which also shows up in branded journalism initiatives—bespeaks a guerrilla pretense of blending in, rather than sticking out, in the effort to reach targets.[154]

This made regulation a tricky task over the years. In 2009 the US Federal Trade Commission updated endorsement guidelines for the first time in decades to reaffirm that this new generation of bloggers and word-of-mouth marketers "must disclose" if they're on the take.[155] Mid-decade, as influencers swelled, the FTC suggested "clear and conspicuous" #ad or #sponsored language in postings (and other regulators abroad in Europe, Asia, and Australia maintain similar requirements).[156] Hundreds of influencers, including celebrities like Jennifer Lopez and Sean Combs, got letters warning they hadn't properly disclosed paid relationships and a few prominent YouTube game vloggers and a department store paid out for violations.[157]

Still, enforcement remains fairly rare and generally toothless; practically, monitoring a zillion individual influencer accounts is not plausible, least of all when certain #spon-con disappears within, say, twenty-four hours of an Instagram Story being posted.[158] And because audiences have a "visceral reaction" to #ad or #spon caveats and bloggers say engagement for those posts track lower, a survey of influencers found one in three had been explicitly asked *not* to disclose.[159]

Finally, for all its obsessions with authenticity—if not transparency—influencer marketing is increasingly beset by formal fakery. As the *New York Times* exposed, a whole subterranean specialty of fraudulence festers, where companies make millions selling the appearance of audiences and engagement to celebrities, businesses, and creators; one such firm, Devumi, peddled more than 200 million Twitter followers from its stock of 3.5 million bots and 55,000 quasi-real humans built from thieved data.[160]

For a couple hundred bucks a month, an aspiring influencer can acquire a steady stream of sham likes and retweets.[161] Buying these bogus metrics pays off in various lines of work where social status converts to actual currency and can cue a virtuous (albeit duplicitous) cycle of *seeming* big-time to help *make* you big-time.[162] One estimate holds as many as three-quarters of influencers' audiences for big-brand campaigns might be phony—totaling over a billion dollars of wasted outlay.[163]

A digital detective counter-industry thus sprang up to sell brands and marketers the machine-learning tools to ferret out such chicanery—drawing upon account country-of-origin and rate of interactivity and selling authenticity in a more literal sense.[164] But this only triggers a "cat-and-mouse game" on the part of fake social media activity providers, who tinker and tweak their pace of mass-populating accounts and hype the "authentic-enough" appearance of that output to black-market buyers (including sham DMs between bot handles to make them seem real).[165] In response, corporate backers ranging from Unilever to Procter & Gamble stopped paying influencers based upon easily fakeable followers and instead calculate on engagements—which, as seen, can also be dubiously verifiable.[166]

As the founder of one cybersecurity company cautions, "Social media is a virtual world that is filled with half bots, half real people. You can't take any tweet at face value. And not everything is what it seems."[167] He could be summarizing the story of the influencer era.

Always Be Closing

Media scholar Brooke Duffy uses the term "aspirational labor" to describe the ambition that entices influencers with the (too-often illusory) prospect of actually making a living to go along with making a lifestyle; sure, some do effectively combine personal relatability with community building with entrepreneurial logic, but more seek than succeed at this line of work.[168] Ironically, the initial absence of apparent marketplace motives affirms the authenticity needed to eventually exploit that opportunism; thus, every influencer's personal and professional narrative seems animated by an overriding mandate to "Do What You Love," above all.[169]

And there's that "garage myth" ethos again, echoed from chapter 2, showing up in the aww-shucks tales my interviewees told of gaining popularity and then deciding to try to make a financial go of it. What had been an innocent hobby gives way to colder calculations in an arc like this: A naturally inclined recommender-type, with a flair for writing or photography, starts a blog just for fun, to entertain friends, or slake a creative thirst; dabbles in a few other platforms as they arise; and—by golly!—suddenly finds hundreds have begat thousands among their eager audience. As patrons offer free samples, she realizes maybe, just maybe, she could even demand actual compensation: pins down personal valuation; polishes a media kit; lands higher-profile patrons; quits her day job; and perhaps starts a consultancy dedicated to helping others follow this yellow-brick road. That's the dream, at least, as sketched by those supposedly living it.

Yet from that early unsophistication about one's output to "self-professionalization," her thinking is transformed: She internalizes market logic; commodifies her communities; obsesses over optimizing metrics; and embraces instrumentality instead of the initial innocence.[170] In short, capitalism becomes her.

Some scholars suggest that social media intrinsically imprints this entrepreneurial, self-promotional, marketing mentality on *all* users—influencers and ordinaries alike—by encouraging the pursuit of attention and visibility in platforms' architectural design.[171] The American Influencer Council, a trade group that coalesced by decade's end, sought to cultivate the perception that "to be an influencer means essentially running a small business where the product is oneself," and 50 million people worldwide now consider themselves creators of this sort, reportedly the fastest-growing type of small business.[172]

As media scholar Sarah Banet-Weiser points out, such a striver is ideal for neoliberal capitalism—people pursuing their dreams, independent of state or corporate safety net—as well as postfeminism—whereby women are assumed unshackled from historic oppression and empowered toward their corporate ambitions.[173] Aspirational labor, however, means straight hustle: It's enterprising, temporary, precarious, and always-on.[174] It's often immaterial, the individual flexibly shouldering financial risk—befitting an increasingly project-based work culture rather than long-term commitments being offered.[175] It's emblematic of a gig economy that finds one-third of the US workforce now employed in some freelance capacity—and with 94 percent of new jobs created being contract-based, it's a designation increasingly creeping into once-dependable white-collar professions like law and information technology. And it is *exhausting*, as one freelancer tallies:

> Everyone I know has some kind of hustle, whether job, hobby, or side or vanity project. Share my blog post, buy my book, click on my link, follow me on Instagram, visit my Etsy shop, donate to my Kickstarter, crowdfund my heart surgery. It's as though we are all working in Walmart on an endless Black Friday of the soul. Being sold to can be socially awkward, for sure, but when it comes to corrosive self-doubt, being the seller is a thousand times worse. . . . Like many modern workers, I find that only a small percentage of my job is now actually doing my job. The rest is performing a million acts of unpaid micro-labor that can easily add up to a full-time job in itself. Tweeting and sharing and schmoozing and blogging. . . . In the cutthroat human marketplace, we are worth only as much as the sum of our metrics.[176]

Self-branding helps one imagine "influencer" as a possible human endeavor and also buttress its instability within the labor market.[177] Business consultant Tom Peters' manifesto is credited with making this an imperative for creative-class aspirants back in the late '90s.[178] "Today, in the Age of the Individual . . . we are CEOs of our own companies: Me Inc. To be in business today, our most important job is to be the head marketer for the brand called You," he writes. "You don't 'belong to' any company for life."[179] Advanced capitalism sells this as a liberating narrative, but freedom is just another way of saying you're all alone with no institutions to depend upon for material survival.

Technological empowerment, relative to elite media gatekeeping, dovetailed with and informed this self-ideology; Peters himself linked his faith that "everyone has a chance to stand out" with "what the Web says: Anyone can have a Web site," at a time when you still needed complex coding rather than simplified interfaces to project yourself, digitally, to the world. In the years since, self-branding got taken up by increasingly "ordinary" people fronting like microcelebrities, thanks to that combination of social media affordances and individualistic neoliberalism.[180] (Generations being weaned on reality TV perhaps also factors in.) "People are much more public; brands are trying to humanize themselves," concludes Pierre-Loic Assayag, an influencer firm CEO. "As a result, it creates more of a gray zone between the two."[181]

The dystopian extremes of this ideology have already manifest. More than a decade ago, one Canadian blogger attempted to live an "entirely sponsored life" for a whole year.[182] By 2021 a "human stock market" app start-up allowed paying fans to vote on the everyday decisions of an influencer-participant (e.g., what to wear, activities, etc.) to "live out their wishes"—pretty much a *Black Mirror* episode begging to be written.[183] "Creators are burning out, but their fans want more and more," one expert observes. "By monetizing each aspect of their life, they can extract value from everyday interactions." Such is the "ad-creep" inertia imposing itself everywhere: reconfiguring not just the spaces in which we live but the means by which our identities form.[184]

Even so, dystopian is a judgment that only makes sense if "selling out" is still a way to throw shade. As in the chapter on pop music, it was not clear from my interviews that such a phrase has much cachet anymore. As Mae Karwowski's epigraph that opened this chapter indicates, selling out is "really around who you're doing the [brand] partnerships with and less that you are doing brand partnerships;" because participation in the system and a culture of uninhibited shilling is a given, best to hook up with, say, Urban Outfitters ("what a boss, like, you're the best") rather than Clorox bleach ("or, like, a seriously unsexy brand").[185]

Again, as with pop music, executives in the advertising and influencer world discern a generational shift in this regard: "In some senses, selling out has become a success," says Chris Cummings, chief strategy officer for BSSP. "If you can sell out, you are now successful."[186] Other interviewees echo that, while selling out might have warranted more caution when strategizing older cohorts, their millennial and Gen Z counterparts—we children of an utterly unrestrained commercial landscape—don't recoil in the same way from capital intrusion.[187] Insulating our lives and dreams, even just a little bit, from the marketplace? Okay, Boomer.

"We live in a world where capitalism in general has seeped into every aspect of everything we do. And, so, the idea of, like, monetizing your personality isn't that weird—which is, like, it should be weirder," acknowledges Karwowski, the influencer firm CEO. "Part of that comes with the fact that every single person has a video camera in their pocket at all times and they can just set up a free account and potentially become famous."[188] Indeed, if social capital was philosopher Pierre Bourdieu's term for the sum value of your network of acquaintances, the influencer industry heralds the full deployment of "social capitalism" in extracting those riches. Or, if not "riches," Red Lobster gift certificates at least.

Influencing blurs, indecipherably, the boundary of personal lives and professional commerce; it forces you calculate the value of your friends and leverage those relationships for a quick buck; and it keeps you forever "on the job," because when work finances the performance of play, play suddenly becomes the calculation of work.[189] This is not to blame the influencer: A hustler's mindset amidst tough times necessitates the hollowness of these interactions as a hedge against economic insecurity.[190] "When you are constantly selling yourself, it becomes less disconcerting to sell for others," advertising scholar Mark Bartholomew puts it. "It becomes more and more difficult to determine who is being genuine, who is trying to sell to us, and where the difference lies."[191]

PART III

ELECTORAL CAMPAIGNS *and* POLITICAL CULTURE

SIX

xxxxxx

Performative Politics

Unscripting the Identity Show

There are many ways to succeed in American politics,
but most of them involve authenticity.

—MICHAEL GERSON, *Washington Post* columnist[1]

The two areas of human enterprise most concerned with sincerity
as opposed to the truth—namely, politics and advertising—
are also the two areas most steeped in bullshit.

—ANDREW POTTER, cultural critic[2]

Some 423 days before the 2020 presidential election, in a raucous New Hampshire arena wallpapered with political poster platitudes and thick with down-ballot bit players, more than a dozen Democratic headliners hoping to unseat Donald Trump are flexing their authenticity bona fides.

Julian Castro, former San Antonio mayor, takes the microphone and righteously avers, "I'm the proud product of public schools," while his supporters on the convention floor shake generic "People First" signs aloft. South Bend mayor Pete Buttigieg telegraphs informality with his first name–basis branding and sleeves-rolled-up, blue-collar fashion feint. Congressman Beto O'Rourke—sans tie, as usual, to similar aesthetic ends—gripes to reporters backstage about the state of politics ("this shit does not work"), salty language penchant for salt-of-the-earth affect.

Back onstage, hedge fund manager Tom Steyer disavows his inauthentic press framing: "When I read stories about myself, I sometimes think my first name is billionaire." Despite that net worth, he reminds the crowd that he was neither born with, nor should be defined by, marketplace motives: the son of a public-school teacher who's battled corporate power all his life. He, too, has sleeves rolled up in case there is some dirty work that $1.4 billion cannot pay someone else to do. Bernie bros thunder the senator's first name, while Sanders, at the podium, stakes his authenticity on a consistency of message, some four decades of economic populism in the making: No two-faced self here.

But the candidate who rattles the rafters most—earning a two-minute-long standing ovation—is Senator Elizabeth Warren. With scratchy vocal-cord fervor, she delivers the authenticity goods: on ideal origins ("I grew up in a paycheck-to-paycheck family"); autonomy of purpose ("I don't go behind closed doors to fancy fundraisers—instead, I spend time with you"); and, throwing her arms wide open, accessibility—namely, the social media kind ("the real measure of democracy—more than 50,000 selfies!").

Authenticity, scholars argue, has become vital to contemporary Western politics: a "currency by which politicians purchase the affection of the masses"; the index of a "sense of conviction, a hidden force that orients their political pursuits."[3] This chapter examines how intimacy, ordinariness, and spontaneity, inherited from the environmental conditioning of reality TV and social media culture, impress themselves upon campaign strategy.

Those countervailing pressures, introduced in the introductory chapter, forever threaten to compromise political authenticity: both the two-faced candidate self, torn between base purity and centrist accommodation in polarized times, and the marketplace motives of backroom billionaires unbridled by *Citizens United*. To offset, consultants deploy a variety of authenticating tactics, from ad cliches to press access to identity origins; these might make candidates seem more "real," but they don't make our politics any better.

The Political Is Personal

A brief tour through the history of American political authenticity could start with the first maestro of mass media, Franklin Roosevelt, whose radio oratory scanned as authentic thanks to folksy language, impromptu asides, and addressing the listener as though a friend. Yet these famous "fireside chats" were not actually recorded adjacent a crackling hearth but rather in an office—the projected illusion of cozy intimacy—and Roosevelt himself seemed to understand the performative nature of gig, once confiding to Orson Welles, "You and I are the best actors in the country."[4]

Before midcentury, however, authenticity was less of a political preoccupation, until television increased both strategic staging and audience suspicion of that staging. Politics embraced more colloquial self-disclosure and informality as TV shrank the distance from (and thus awe of) leaders.[5] Dwight Eisenhower's media advisor coached him to act natural in proto-authenticity terms: "Viewers would respond to the real . . . not the manufactured."[6] In the 1970s, authenticity became a more ubiquitous feature of political ambition and voter judgment, variously based upon personal sincerity, Americana clichés, emotional affectation, and outsider posturing.[7] "Confessional, sentimental, and intimate" types of casual talk overtook formality and reserve, as public-private boundaries eroded.[8]

By the 1990s, it would not break decorum for an audience of teens to ask a presidential candidate in an MTV town hall if he wore boxers or briefs. Candidates increasingly took advantage of such softball questions from late-night comedians and daytime talk shows to better "humanize" their appearance and likeability.[9] At century's end, when voters supposedly would rather share a beer with folksy George W. Bush than leaden Al Gore, authenticity had ascended to the "single most dominant theme in campaign discourse," according to political historian Erica Seifert.[10]

Simultaneously, political figures (especially conservatives) began appearing on reality TV shows: Trump's *The Apprentice*, most conspicuously, but also Texas governor Rick Perry, House majority leader Tom DeLay, and Trump spokesman Sean Spicer on *Dancing with the Stars* as well as Sarah Palin's eponymous *Alaska* TLC show and a surreal *Masked Singer* appearance rapping to Sir Mix-a-Lot's "Baby Got Back" in a fuzzy neon bear costume.[11]

This supply of authenticity (or, at least, authenticity framing by campaigns and journalists) matched an apparent demand-side pull. Studies suggest American voters crave it, especially against the backdrop of scandals like Watergate and the presumption that politicians remain a "self-serving" class of connivers.[12] One poll from the mid-2010s found that authenticity is now prized more than policies themselves, particularly among Trump supporters.[13] An assortment of consultants I interviewed echoed this: "Authenticity is literally [in] half of our current PowerPoint presentations when we go pitch," claimed one; it's "everything—it was the first, second, and third thing you thought of," enthused another.[14]

Like Gore and John Kerry before them, inauthenticity was seen as costing Mitt Romney and Hillary Clinton the Oval Office, despite wide variance about what the term actually means.[15] Jim Margolis, a senior media advisor to Barack Obama, outlines for me the key themes of authenticity as being impromptu rather than standardized, and belying any two-faced self: "Voters smell in-authenticity when politicians are feeding them one stock line after another—robotically giving talking points that feel straight out of a poll. . . . Or [the politician's] really looking at this race and campaign from the perspective of what they need to say rather than what they really feel or believe. . . . Ideally, that [authenticity] has some emotional content as well, where people go, 'Okay, they've had some of those experiences or they understand what it is I'm facing every single day.' "[16]

As forecast by philosopher Jean-Jacques Rousseau in the opening chapter—and alluded to by Margolis here—a key aspect of political authenticity might be framed as the inner "outered"; that is, "a pure external reflection of some internal truth of selfhood."[17] In turn, voters and journalists demand more access to politicians' private lives, because those become central to electoral evaluations.[18] Following sociologist Erving Goffman, if authenticity represents "minimal difference between the frontstage persona presented to the public and the backstage persona presented to intimates," then "the search for the 'real' candidate is an effort to drag the backstage persona to the front."[19]

Consistent performance often defines political authenticity (to the point that, ideally, it doesn't seem like performance): The candidate says the same thing no matter when or where they find themselves.[20] Alas, because of the manipulative presumptions within politics—the "canned" messaging and phony façades—audiences who desire the pre-strategic backstage can be fed a staged version of it.[21]

Thus, the consultant strategizes, paradoxically and self-effacingly, to help politicians seem "as non-strategic and non-performative as possible," as political communication scholar Simon Luebke observes.[22] "The best quality that I'm trying to convey is that they're real people," the vice president of one digital agency declares. "But I want it coming out of their mouth in a way that's natural for them."[23]

Compromising Authenticity

The polarized conditions in today's American politics—fragmented media, gerrymandered districts, loony conspiracy subcultures—also bear upon the dynamics of authenticity, as do consumer choices and lifestyles that have been politicized toward culture war "signaling" ends.[24] This helps cast political struggle in good-versus-evil terms, whereby one's own side is sacred and must be defended against cunning, corrupt counterparts across the aisle.[25] How, indeed, could you ever morally justify deal-making with a cabal of cannibalistic, Satan-worshipping pedophiles, as QAnon subscribers purport?

This Manichean framing infects the logic of politics not just across parties but within them: the rock-ribbed base—and those who truly represent it—are authentic, holding firm to the same interests, undeterred, no matter what the stage, while the center—with its squishy, two-faced political selves—is untrustworthy. At the "extremes," at the margins, where—the introductory chapter noted—authenticity tends to be most fertile, you find politicians who never waver from their principles.[26] In a primary, solidifying ideological bona fides, such authenticity reigns; in the general, tacking cautious and selling out, inauthenticity haunts two-faced selves.[27]

Indeed, during primary season, "electability" is arguably as much liability as benefit—at least, relative to a purity of purpose in which attaining power is not seen as the endgame in and of itself.[28] The very skills that make a politician electable—"smooth with words, knows how to please disparate audiences, and who tries to be all things . . . to a spectrum of constituents," as political scientist Timur Kuran summarizes—and are fundamentally necessary for democratic governance and coalition-building toward collective action are also the font of perceived inauthenticity, because it means spinning, dissembling, and conciliating.[29]

Much better to be Rousseauian to the core: ride-or-die on issues near and dear to the heart of the base. "I can't recall any candidate—Republican or Democrat—ever running to say, 'I'm going to go to Washington to compromise for you,'" quips one congressional deputy chief of staff.[30] Compromise, after all, is inauthentic and flip-flopping—as John Kerry was flayed for in 2004—is anathema.

The flood of unrestrained money into politics, post–*Citizens United*, is equally relevant here as a threat to authenticity. Just two years after the ruling that deregulated campaign finance, independent groups were already spending nearly a billion dollars more than the parties themselves and 2020's election price tag ran up a frothy $14 billion.[31] Moreover, *Citizens United* empowered rogue megadonors to singularly finance primary long-shots, exasperating establishment expectations and bypassing backroom brokers; gradually, the term "establishment . . . became code for inauthentic: [it] became code for party machines thwarting the will of the people," one strategic communications consultant translates.[32]

To be clear, big bucks don't vouchsafe victory (as testified by Michael Bloomberg's $1 billion that bought him just fifty-eight delegates in 2020).[33] But money *does* buy "symbolic power" (i.e., the communication advantage of a well-funded megaphone), which attracts attention and gets one a shot at votes or, cyclically and cynically, more money for the campaign.[34] "But you don't see people run TV commercials in their own districts saying, 'I raised $4 million to make sure I could represent you,'" cracks Chuck Rocha, a senior advisor on Bernie Sanders 2020 run.[35]

Hence, once more, the inauthenticity of marketplace motives: a politician's internal autonomy of purpose (what they believe, what they stand for) being corrupted by the external venality of funding. Candidates have to front like the money doesn't matter to their ambitions, even as they canvass slavishly for it; being cause-driven, not dollar- or even vote-driven, necessarily, power is but the means, never remotely the ends, in this pose.[36] Even Trump tried this well-worn "outsider" tack in some 2016 messaging, castigating his opponents as "controlled fully by the lobbyists, by the donors, and by the special interests."[37]

Because politicians wield such power—and because that power is mediated by money—authenticity has the thankless task of wallpapering over that reality: "under-communicat[ing] the real power relations between politicians and voters," as media scholar Gunn Enli discerns.[38] Small donations can offset this problem as grassroots ratification.

Managing Howard Dean's 2004 Democratic primary bid, Joe Trippi pioneered these techniques and their framing: "There's a lot of power in the argument that we're being funded by people who give $10 and $15 and $20—not, you know, people who are lobbyists," he tells me, and that modest buy-in vaulted Dean's candidacy from long-shot to fleeting frontrunner.[39] Bernie Sanders sang from this same hymnal a decade later, hyping, David-style, the $27 average-giver amount against Clinton's 2016 Goliath operation (one also attacked for lucrative Goldman Sachs speech-giving and, it was implied, access peddling).[40]

An emblematic example of these tensions boiled over in the 2020 Democratic primary when Buttigieg was taken to task for his big donor liability: Instagram snaps had caught "Wall Street Pete" with lucrative bundlers and celebrity glitterati in Manhattan and at a Napa Valley wine cave fundraiser beneath crystal chandeliers. The wealth-taxing Warren peddled popular "Billionaire Tears" coffee mugs as a righteous declaration of her independence (and thus authenticity) from financial strings attached, also making a show of her refusal to accept donations from PACs, corporate executives, lobbyists, and high-dollar dinner events.[41]

"We made the decision . . . that rich people in smoke-filled rooms would not pick the next president," she beamed during one televised debate. "According to *Forbes* magazine," Buttigieg icily shot back, "I am literally the only person on this stage that is not a millionaire or a billionaire." Neither would earn the nomination, of course, but authenticity was the "real" winner, yet again.

Stages, Sets, Props

"The first thing is—give the appearance that there is no strategy, right? The minute you give the appearance there's no strategy, then people automatically think you're authentic. People have a sense—the camera has a sense for it when you are trying to fake authenticity. . . . Trump is a type of guy that he would tell you it's great to be sincere, but it's even better if you can fake sincerity. 'Cause then you can turn the switch on at any time."[42]

Can you even *fake* political authenticity? That, obviously, is the crux of this chapter, with the job of the consultant to channel the authenticity of clients, whether "real" or staged. Yet more than one interviewee scoffed at that premise—including, above, Anthony Scaramucci, Trump's evanescent communication director.

On the other hand, Harry Gantz—who, fittingly, transitioned from producing reality TV (*Taxicab Confessions*, as detailed in chapter 1) to political media consulting—touts this service specifically on his website: "Harry can help a candidate with their presentation and messaging to bring out their most authentic self," specifically *because* of his "years uncovering the authentic personal stories" of "real people" on the HBO show.[43]

An abiding challenge to creating political authenticity is how much audiences are assumed to have become aware of and cynical about the mediation machine behind those efforts—the authenticity industries, if you will. Thus, the more that strategists, speechwriters, and ad-makers try to make politicians seem real, and the more that the media covers that meta-effort ("the campaign behind the campaign," as one calls it), and the more that politicians become self-aware of all that scheming, the phonier the whole enterprise comes across.[44]

Still, such is the purview and handiwork of some 7,000 schemers in a $6 billion political consulting field.[45] And because spontaneity (now a stand-in for trustworthiness) has to be "carefully worked out and rehearsed" under the watchful eye of these image-makers, media scholar Tamar Liebes notes, it "contradicts the very nature of the quality one is attempting to imitate, as to be 'genuine' is to be 'left in its natural state, not worked over and complicated by reflection.'"[46] That's the Rousseauian ideal, at least.

"Politics is signifying, but if is appears to *be* symbolic action, it is bound to fail," cultural sociologist Jeffrey Alexander diagnoses, echoing Scaramucci's point above. "Because political performance succeeds only when it seems natural, it must not betray its own construction."[47] Power, in other words, and the attempt at power, must always self-efface its own machinations—otherwise it seems inauthentic and illegitimate.

In that quest, a consultant can stage a client in a wide variety of contexts and media formats, but "there's a tension between what we think about in terms of sort of polish and brand cohesion on the one hand and authenticity on the other," Matt Compton, deputy digital director for Clinton 2016, explains to me—a diagnosis that lends itself to the rough cut concept developed earlier. And political advertising, especially, is rife with shorthand clichés of authenticity.[48] Familiar visual tropes tend to get trotted out over and over again: "You could watch 100 ads and you're going to see the 'diner shot' a lot; you're going to see the 'walking through the factory shot' a lot; you're going to see the 'walking down Main Street shot,'" the president of a media consulting firm tallies.[49]

Such spaces and symbols offer lingering proxies of integrity and nostalgia amidst widespread political cynicism, even as their cynical use might evacuate them of the trustworthiness sought. Backgrounds anchor and humanize, so advance scouts chase down photogenic tableaus: "A great, seemingly spontaneous scene where [the candidate] goes out for ice cream in a town or goes into a sports bar to watch football with the guys," says one US senate press secretary, "you're always looking for . . . moments like that."[50] The B-roll visual helps define and project an authenticity of identity.

This depends upon a profoundly superficial level of news consumption assumed, as intimated by the communications director for a leading House representative:

I wouldn't say [my boss] is, like, a very attractive man, but for a member of Congress, he has really good hair—so, like, what are the visuals that we can use to build his brand? . . . And, so, even if he's on TV and the volume is off—it's not that I don't care what he's saying, but . . . the people that are on the treadmill at the gym, that may not be listening to what he's saying, see him and think, "You know what? That guy looks like a real nice guy."[51]

Regular folks are, moreover, vital props for staging political authenticity—literally when casting faces of endorsement behind a speaker's podium shot.[52] One ad-maker likes to "stack" the campaign message by scripting it in a succession of a half-dozen "normal people's mouths" as opposed to just the candidate, who might show up, interlaced in the monologue, maybe 22 seconds into the 30-spot;

that's effective, he claims, "because in large measure these are not TV-attractive folks. You know, I'm not going to go out and seek ugly people, but they're not what you ordinarily expect to see on television talking about politics."[53] More nefarious, astroturfing tactics hire out "real people" to pose as protestors; one investigation found a dozen actors brought in to disrupt a city council hearing and ventriloquize special-interest talking points to the local crowd.[54]

A *Campaigns & Elections* advice column adds that such folks—a diner owner, a longshoreman, a tattoo artist—are "worth their weight in gold" and "provide a visceral jolt that hits a little harder with their audience, because, well, they represent their audience," serving as an "intermediary" for relatability when a voter won't ever get to know a candidate personally.[55] (This echoes the logic and production of authentic identification strategized throughout the book—from reality TV casts to social media influencers.) Plus, filming in their natural setting means they supply the authentic props from their lives.

These are, then, *human* proxies for authenticity, serving the same purpose as a neighborhood diner or factory floor—set pieces to fasten the politician's identity to something specific, local, familiar, believable, and therefore "real"— their unpolished quality valuable for precisely that in the overcalculated spectacle that is politics.[56] Mike Murphy, senior GOP campaign advisor from McCain 2000 to Bush 2016, elaborates on how he tries to capture this:

> The subtext of the visual—a construction site, an auto plant when people were worried about auto layoffs, a bunch of nurses in an ER when there's no hospital funding—[we'd] go where the problem is in real life and have the candidate talk to four or five people, while [I'm] creeping around like a person watching [and filming].... Now, when it's too stagey, it doesn't work... which is why you don't just drop them in. While the crew sets up, you have the candidate hang out with the people and bond a little. So, while they're having that conversation, like, a *cinema verité* documentary crew can manage and catch the real.... It could be for a very authentic moment.[57]

Beyond advertising, other authenticity platforms and formats beckon. Some interviewees regard town halls as an effective way to illustrate the— somewhat oxymoronic—performance of listening.[58] On the other hand, what's gained with the spontaneity of a town hall is lost with the control and message discipline of a 30-spot—a truism of authenticity being inversely correlated with prepackaged polish that defined influencer experiences in the last chapter.[59]

Similarly, the get-out-the-vote, ground-game efforts of a field office can lend an authentic vibe: being hand-crafted, individualized outreach by way of door-knocking and phone-banking rather than assembly-line, technologically standardized, mass broadcast messaging.[60] And softballs from friendly press help a candidate hit authenticity home runs, one congressional communications director notes: "Before I put my boss on TV, I have an extended conversation with the producer of the show about what we will and will not consent to be discussing. . . . There are some shows that are very friendly—generally, you put them on Fox News, if you're a Republican politician, I can send them our talking points in advance and some suggested questions for the host to ask and that's exactly how the interview will go down."[61]

Other journalists see themselves as "authenticating agents," judging the credibility of political performances—a posture of instinctive cynicism, assuming "duplicity" in the selling of authenticity and deputizing themselves as "unmaskers of the hypocrisy" by trying to access and reveal the backstage self.[62] This is especially true of biographical features—the reporter endeavoring to pierce the façade, "contesting the public image or unraveling the private mysteries."[63]

To subsidize the hunger for those types of stories, consultants feed journalists behind-the-scenes access, who then conflate that with actual authenticity rather than yet-another-performance. Sometimes the scheming wins results: George W. Bush's backstage charm offensive with the press pack ("convinc[ing] them first that they had access to the 'real' person," one no different than his "frontstage persona") might have won him friendlier ink than his counterpart Al Gore's frosty reserve.[64] Lis Smith became a consultant rock star for campaign managing Pete Buttigieg from small-town mayor to 2020 primary headliner, giving journalists "what they wanted: not just a good quote but a good character" who could banter, informally, with the cultural sophistication they loved to indulge.[65]

Perhaps most emblematically, on his "Straight Talk Express" bus tour in 2000, John McCain would regale reporters with funny, seemingly off-the-cuff tales, demonstrating he was an unpredictable "maverick," in the mythologized framing: "He'd be like, 'Oh, I want to take questions from the press' . . . to show he was authentic, right?" recalls his communications director. "We always played this game where [we], the press staff, would be like, 'We're done. We're done' [to reporters]. He's like, 'No, no—I wanna take questions.' It's kind of like an Al Green concert, like, 'No, no, no—I want to do more. You can't stop me.'"[66] And, like an Al Green concert, this show of authenticity convincingly charmed the crowd.

The Authenticity of Spontaneity

Well before an *Apprentice* star ascended to the Oval Office, politics had become a reality TV culture industry, whereby personality and style are foregrounded as a substitute for (and, sometimes, obfuscation of) actual ideology—dating back to, arguably, the first political consultants, Clem Whitaker and Leone Baxter, who refined dumbed-down simplification and fired-up emotion as their aspirational output.[67]

As Mark McKinnon, who served as chief media advisor for George W. Bush, emphasizes to me: "[Voters] have this antenna and this internal thing that says, 'Oh, here's a political ad—highly unlikely anything they're telling me is true.'"[68] McKinnon, however, had the good fortune of Bush seeming "very real" and "very down to earth," even if "he didn't read a teleprompter well—I mean, whenever we wrote a script for him, it looked like he was reading a script," which voters picked up on as inauthentic anyhow.

Thus, McKinnon decided early on that he'd never script an ad for Bush, instead opting for "stuff that was just spontaneous"—his informal, backslapping, freewheeling self out on the campaign trail—or interview him to "get those natural responses and pull pieces out of that." For the Republican convention biofilm that would precede Bush's marquee speech, McKinnon drew upon footage collected while tagging along in a truck at Bush's Crawford ranch and even left in a flubbed take (where "he just completely mangled what he's trying to say" with self-deprecating laughter) rather than the eventual polished version of the point being made:

> There was a time in politics where people believe you can have these perfect, ideal candidates. People don't believe that anymore. . . . So, if you can show them some humanity. . . . Even an ounce of vulnerability, if you're willing to kind of let down the guard and say, "You know what, guys? [He's] not perfect. But he's kind of like you—you know, he's human. He's got a human side. And, by the way, he's funny and he's real and it's not some bullshit, you know, made-up, one-dimensional, plastic-cardboard thing that's going to get up and read talking points." . . . And let's be honest, folks—let's just admit that we don't have the best orator in this race and let's go ahead and lower the bar of expectations now.

Hence, the myth was built of Dubya being the candidate to crack a beer with.

Again, this is surely not about political honesty (i.e., "speaking the truth and avoiding lies") but about political *authenticity* ("the performer seems as though he or she is true to his or her inner self"), as media scholar Gunn Enli nuances.[69] Voters, this presumption holds, privilege politicians who seem to be true to that self rather than campaign strategy or teleprompter speech, and yearn for spaces and moments that enable them to "see 'inside' candidates"; consistency (in appearance, manner of speech, and issue positions) is one primary way to communicate that authentic self, contra flip-floppers' lack of an iron core.[70] More important—and paradoxical—is the necessity to open up about that private self, but "never to try to have someone talk about something that seems like someone told him to talk about it," as fellow Bush campaign veteran Stuart Stevens prescribes.[71]

Achieving political authenticity depends on overcoming citizens' suspicion of the two-faced self that Goffman identified, but manifest here as messaging that is diplomatic, cautious, focus-grouped, over-repeated, and thus fundamentally insincere. "Politics is even more in an image-bind than almost any other profession, because they're trying to appeal to everybody and to do that, they feel like they can only show a certain part of themselves and they have to compartmentalize their personalities," explains Harry Gantz, a progressive media consultant.

He'll thus offer clients advice before ad-making interviews that, not coincidentally, echoes much of what his former reality TV colleagues aimed for in chapter 1: "Don't work with your inner censor. . . . Allow the trust we have that together in post[production] we're going to censor the parts that maybe you don't like. . . . People will, in a sense, like you more and be more passionate about you if they know more about you—the, I hate to call it your 'dark side,' but you know, your 'real side.' "[72] (The difference, of course, with reality TV is that it usually *won't* censor out the excesses that a participant doesn't like.)

The suspicion of inauthenticity in political communication may well stem from the success its strategic polish achieved over decades of scripting. The Reagan administration, for example, maintained such a "Hollywood production ethos" and "rehearsed" message control (pivoting regardless of the actual question) that, while effective in winning the news cycle of the day, it might have poisoned the long-term well of political sincerity, one interviewee suggests: "Discipline became so ubiquitous that it just created a systemic sense of falseness and inauthenticity. . . . Voters began to rebel—they wanted fewer protected moments."[73]

Stereotypically, politicians are seen as saying what audiences want to hear rather than what they truly believe.[74] That's a trade-off between personal authenticity and "accommodating social pressures," for an ambitious politician knows that they can't *really* be themselves if they hope to ascend to the highest office.[75] One recourse, then, is to blow, conspicuously and unrepentantly, against the prevailing, politically popular wind. "If you put out something that sounds poll-tested, people see right through it and that's what they despise about so many politicians," Trump flak Sean Spicer tells me.[76]

Thus, acknowledging and even embracing a policy position that seems to go against public opinion represents "the most underrated campaign tactic," according to one interviewee: Because "voters smell bullshit when a candidate says only things that the voters agree with," they're "actually looking occasionally for people to disagree with them," which means that a candidate who aligns on eight or nine of ten issues gets more authenticity traction than one that lines up on all ten, who is "clearly just saying things to please me, as opposed to saying what they really believe."[77]

Campaign manager Joe Trippi touts Howard Dean's antiwar stance in 2004 as emblematic of such contrarian authenticity, coming at a time when the Iraq invasion still had broad national support and the effort there had not yet devolved into a bloody, unpopular quagmire; likewise on the left, Bernie Sanders drew plaudits from even conservative pundits for winning the "sincerity caucus" through not just an "utterly unpolished speaking style" but an unshakable, decades-old commitment to socialist substance.[78] Authenticity is, moreover, forever in the eye of the beholder: a more moderate candidate playing to the base in the primaries can come across as insincere, just as a more extreme candidate tacking center in the general.[79]

A second authenticity option on this front is to strategize more spontaneity, contradictory as that may sound. Because political discourse tends to be so staged, unscripted talk carries the sheen of authenticity, being in-the-moment rather than premeditated.[80] But this, too, has long been gamed.

President Dwight Eisenhower would dramatically toss out prepared speeches and pretend to can his speechwriters.[81] Al Gore aggressively kissing his wife, Tipper, at the 2000 Democratic national convention may have caught observers (and Tipper, perhaps) by surprise, but it smacked of an authenticity gambit, not unlike the profoundly stupid attention paid to his earth-tone clothing choices.[82] By contrast, Obama's apparent teleprompter dependency became, for a time, a GOP gripe about his inauthenticity.[83] An authentic politician can, in short, fake it well.

And a third strategy to offset the inherent scheming of a two-faced self is to open up and parade around more backstage life and the intimate personal details buried within "non-public contexts."[84] Hence, congresswoman Alexandria Ocasio-Cortez livestreaming her cooking and Ikea furniture assembly.[85] Hence, Sanders being nudged by aides to talk about his 2019 heart attack as a means of making Medicare-for-all more personal and empathetic, even choking up "ever-so-slightly" in his video introspection rather than delivering the usual "laundry list of statistics."[86]

Again, though, all this can be cynically schemed and staged, as betrayed by an anecdote about McCain 2000 from his consultant Mike Murphy: "You could never script John—it was who he was. . . . McCain hated debate prep—he was just ready to go be authentic, but the problem is you had certain performance tricks that help in the debate. . . . In New Hampshire, we opened our debate prep to some reporters where it was a lot of [him going], 'I'm not going to read your 3-by-5 card, you guys! Murphy, you're out of line!' You know, we made a show out of it. And then we'd have real debate prep after [reporters] left and we'd practice the fucking card."[87]

Leaders of the Free World—They're Just Like Us!

Judging an appearance of authenticity means judging character: the biography, geography, and demography that defines a politician as well as the lifestyle choices that contribute to that identity.[88] Above all, this narrative should emphasize an anti-elitist, "down-to-earth similarity" to voters—"a feeling of 'this guy's like me'"—not least because they're competing to occupy a position of power so incredibly far removed from those plebians that the campaign must, in a sense, protest too much about that eventual, sought-after reality of status.[89]

Departing from this pretense—that politicians aren't "real Americans," as one congressional communications director summarizes—many successful DC rookies hadn't run for office before and were heralded and rewarded for that lack of experience: "They were pizza shop owners; they were car salesman; they were other things. And I think people think: 'Oh, I'm sending regular Joe to Congress—regular Joe understands my needs.'"[90]

Biography authenticates, especially through ideal origin stories of struggle that consultants and campaigns peddle for identification purposes: "If you were raised by a single mom, if you had to work in a factory, if you were a waitress [like] AOC, then you become authentic because you are perceived as one of us," notes Chuck Rocha.[91] He served as a senior advisor to the Sanders 2020 team, which notably tweaked its authenticity strategy from 2016 to emphasize more of the senator's personal story—an impoverished childhood in a rent-controlled Brooklyn apartment and a father's flight from European antisemitism: "I know where I came from!" Sanders barked at the first rally, an epigram of authenticity.[92]

Sanders, Rocha notes, didn't really want to go the US Weekly personality cult route, but the news environment and political culture demanded it: "The press is going to want something new," he explains. "The new thing was— let's talk more about your vulnerabilities, about your real story. That connects you directly to people more intimately than just the policy. . . . That's—as a strategist—what had to be said and done to make it different so that the press and other people wouldn't say, 'This is just the same shit we've always heard.'" Backstage, however, Sanders would be asking (once again?) to talk more about the issues: "I don't ever want to see a picture of my food or a cat on our social media," he reportedly demanded of his staff.[93]

There is, of course, a long tradition within American political culture of accentuating "working-class tastes," even if they're fabricated.[94] Blue-collar roots are the best kind of roots to showcase, for as the introductory chapter foregrounded, authenticity derives from socioeconomic margins. One interviewee recalls always namechecking a client as "the son of a saw-mill worker, so, in two seconds, you've already gotten an idea of who he is."[95]

Similarly, Boston mayor Marty Walsh liked to tote his union book around with him—"it signals his coming from the working class . . . the people who hump drywall," an aide boasts.[96] By contrast, someone with a gilded professional life like Michael Bloomberg couldn't compete in this performative arena, his press secretary explains: "Politics, [Bloomberg] would often say privately, is a debate about whose mother washed more floors for less money—like, we all have to cry poverty, right?"[97]

Geography also authenticates: What is local is real, while DC is Othered. The more granular the geographic claim—right down to the neighborhood block level—the stronger the authenticity lure: "Instead of doing the, you know, so-and-so's from Cook County or from the south side of Chicago, it's talking about the high school they went to and the first job they had and the friends that are still in the neighborhoods," explains one Democratic chief strategist. "Not just name the place, but you want to find some connective tissue that actually routes you in some emotional part of your life."[98]

Befitting a long-standing bias within American culture, small and rural packs maximum authenticity. "I took a shot of [one US senate candidate] standing in front of the water tower in the little town where he grew up and that shot . . . became a very iconographic image. . . . Everybody in [that state] knows what a water tower with a town name on it means—it means . . . 'This is your hometown,'" the president of a media consulting firm explains, sounding like a John Mellencamp lyric. "By standing him in front of that water tower, it said to people . . . 'Well, okay, he's a Democrat, but he's really a small-town guy and he shares your values and he's not going to be a crazy liberal like the rest of them.'"[99] The premise of small town as "real America" tends to redound to conservative advantage among red states in the South, Midwest, and Mountain West, as opposed to supposedly duplicitous coastal cosmopolises.[100] It is its own elitist form of anti-elitism that looks down on those who fly over as inauthentic.

A prominent example of geographic authentication that came out of my interviews is, again, George W. Bush. In 1978, after he lost a bid for a congressional seat in the Lone Star State's nineteenth district by being "attacked for being kind of a Yale-educated, Ivy League son of a senator," he decided he'd never be out-Texaned in terms of identity.[101]

Strategist and advisor Stuart Stevens' film for the Republican convention thus emphasized he had a "very American childhood in Midland, Texas," a baseball-obsessed boy who went on to marry a librarian: "It was just a way to sell the normality of his life."[102] Another aide, Mark McKinnon, who worked on that iconography, adds, "Even though he'd gone to Yale and came from this sort of dynastic family, it was really important to show that he had sort of authentic roots," which meant lots of footage of riding around together in a truck at the Crawford ranch, "clearing brush and stuff. He genuinely loved to do that, he loved to go out there and break a sweat."[103]

In that way, appearance telegraphs geographic identity. The president of a political ad agency recalls crafting a 30-spot very attentive to particular sartorial nuances for a Hawaii governor hopeful who donned a traditional shirt "wearing a unique pattern that has something to do with plantation life" that older audiences would pick up on, thus "authenticating him to the local culture" in distinctively hard-working ways.[104] On the flip side, another advertising consultant likes to cast an opponent as a "Washington insider" by featuring familiar imagery cliches, "always in the suit-and-tie with the Capitol in the background," unlike his more casually dressed protagonist: evoking a tension of tribal familiarity versus conspiring outsider.[105]

Manner of speech also anchors geography and, thus, authenticity. Sarah Palin's "g-droppin' vernacular" stylistically signaled the substance of her anti-establishment critique.[106] Ironically, the opponent that she infamously accused of "pallin' around with terrorists," Barack Obama, indulged some of the same inflections, often dropping his g's in front of African American audiences.[107] At one *Campaigns & Elections* webinar ("The Art of Authenticity in Voiceover"), a panelist notes that her firm's site can filter citizen testimonial offerings by regional accents, depending on what is needed to convince of local upbringing in ads.[108]

To that end, demography authenticates: Who can speak on behalf of whom in what credible fashion and in front of which audiences is, in some ways, the central interrogation of identity politics. For candidates of color—most prominently, Barack Obama and Kamala Harris—this can be a narrow bind of authenticity to have to thread, both representing (literally) a historically marginalized people while also needing to not appear like that's the exclusive constituency they'll serve: "A Black man has to be careful not to scare white people, right?" one interviewee explains. "But at the same time be Black enough to be perceived as authentic."[109]

Often this necessitates the kind of linguistic code-switching (a Goffmanian tactic) that, vexingly, can "look like you're trying to play both sides."[110] Rob Shepardson, a senior advisor to Obama's media team, notes that they leaned into "his own anecdotes of being raised by a White family, White grandparents, and being comfortable in a VFW Hall in Southern Illinois with a lot of old White guys who were veterans. He could go in there and say, 'Look, you're like my grandfather. I get it.'"[111] (Gendered authenticity in politics, which could occupy a book-length treatment of its own, will be examined in the next chapter's focus on Hillary Clinton.)

Finally, offstage lifestyle choices authenticate, helping connect to followers' everyday lives rather the actual "qualities" of a candidate—a shift away from ideological affinities and party-driven agendas and toward "personality-bound forms of political recognition and engagement" that prioritize aesthetic.[112] One might frame this as identity politics by way of hobbies and who has "better leisure pursuits."[113]

Such symbolic scheming attends to the identity project inherent to all branding: furnishing signs that can help a voter discover themselves. The Lincoln Project, a band of Never Trump Republican apostates working to get Biden elected, reverse-strategized this in their advertising:

> We wanted that educated, suburban, college-educated voter to see [our] ad
> with the 300-pound white guy carrying the Confederate flag in one hand and
> an AR-15 in the other, we wanted her to think, "Oh, God, if I vote for Trump,

I'm with him. If I vote for Trump, that's me." . . . Where you're saying to people, you're not just making a political decision, you're buying into to a whole lifestyle. Is your lifestyle the Alt-Right and the screamers and the crazies and the QAnon and the Confederate flag and the Charlottesville boys?[114]

Context poses work better for identity than issue stances: "I'm an Obama person" a smoother form of social differentiation than, say, "I'm a 39.6 percent highest marginal tax rate person," to take one arcane (but important!) policy example.[115] The goal of authentic political communication is, therefore, not to persuade voters of what a candidate will actually *do*, but to create a candidate "who most reminds voters of themselves."[116] Moreover, when certain political leaders are mocked for their appearance or affect, it triggers, helpfully, "every cultural slight" that their *supporters* have faced over the years, securing loyalty evermore.[117]

This might feel superficial, even to the authenticity industry workers pursuing it, but it's assumed effective, notes Lindsay Holst, director of digital strategy for Vice President Biden:

> We used to get a lot of shit at the White House for doing what people would call, "empty calorie content." You think about all the hard-hitting proposals that cross our desks on a given day that we should talk about—tax cuts and loopholes and trips the president's taking in diplomacy and we would be like, "Well, we want to do this video of the president's dog running around the south lawn. . . . And isn't [Obama] like us?" . . . [*Later in the interview, she adds,*] With every piece of content like the dog content, we are adding an additional layer of texture to this idea of Barack Obama as a human that people can like and relate to . . . and the more willing they'll be to listen when he delivers what otherwise might have been a pretty dry policy proposal. And maybe the more convinced they are that he actually gets them.[118]

Other examples of these tactics abound. Sport helps: Feigning fandom to strike a chord with bleacher creatures as seen throughout the century, from William Taft inaugurating the Opening Day first pitch to Richard Nixon releasing bowling photos to Obama's annual March Madness bracket.[119] For one presidential candidate's press secretary, seeing George W. Bush appear on a fishing show—having already made an October 2002 cover of *Runner's World*—epitomized this trend: "Everyone thought it would be beneath him—previously it would be like, 'You're the president of the United States, what are you doing on a fucking bass show?' Well, they realized that, like, if you're running for president and the idea or best question is, 'Would you like to have a beer with them?' then it's not too far a stretch to go . . . to, '[I want to] see them on the shows that I actually watch.'"[120]

Food—particularly junk food—is another way to authenticate lifestyle. When pressed by a BBC interviewer about how (celebrity, billionaire) Donald Trump could plausibly pose as anti-elitist, his communication director Anthony Scaramucci shot back, "How about the cheeseburgers? How about the pizza?"—the implication being a dreadful, drive-thru diet gives you salt-of-the-earth cred (and intake).[121] It's ironic, of course, that fast food would endear audiences to candidates posing like common folk, being "synthetically mass-produced and designed to be impersonal and familiar"—the kind of technological standardization that's normally antithetical to authenticity, yet retains an "unassuming," "democratic" lack of "pretense," probably on account of cost and availability.[122]

In other cases, food and drink fails have betrayed the *inauthenticity* of a politician: George H. W. Bush famously, if apocryphally, marveled at a supermarket scanner, suggesting that he couldn't relate to everyday folks who have to queue up to check out at grocery stores.[123] Elizabeth Warren's Instagram livestream wherein she went to "get me" a beer from her kitchen scanned awkwardly inauthentic, inviting immediate mockery (even if her native Okie roots should have technically authenticated the syntactical tactic of the Harvard professor).[124] Recall, too, John Kerry trying to order swiss, rather than the apposite "whiz wit," on his cheesesteak in South Philly or Gerald Ford mouthing an unshucked tamale as revealing a lack of local savvy.[125]

Vacations represent another timeless ritual for Americans to signal their class-based tastes and interviewees used these alternately as fodder for authenticity or its absence. Working on behalf of Chris Christie, one interviewee tarred his opponent for helicoptering to the Hamptons rather than battling Turnpike traffic en route to the Shore: "Like—what's the matter with the Jersey Shore? Isn't that good enough for you?" This, he adds, became a stand-in for being "rich and out of touch" with the "blue-collar working class" on substantive Great Recession issues like the economy and jobs.[126]

Another veteran GOP consultant recalls a gubernatorial campaign where they made hay of an incumbent's use of the state helicopter to fly him on vacations compared to his own candidate's righteous declaration he'd only take roadies in the Oldsmobile: "That thing became a symbol for our authenticity. . . . If you were an accountant, you'd say [the helicopter's] not a material factor in the state budget, but it was a symbol. People don't understand budget tables. They understand jet helicopters flying the governor around on vacation."[127]

Irrational Exuberance

"The best commercials are similar to Rorschach patterns. They do not tell the viewer anything. They surface his feelings and provide a context for him to express those feelings." So advised Tony Schwartz, creator of the most infamous political ad in history, "Daisy," in which a young girl plucking flower petals is interrupted by the countdown to a nuclear mushroom cloud.[128] The quote and the 60-spot may be decades old, but the underlying principle—that political communication should stress symbolism over substance—continues to inform the authenticity stratagems showcased throughout this chapter.

For as cultural sociologist Jeffrey Alexander argues, political struggle is fundamentally theatrical: a battle of performance, in which campaigns try to align to their candidates with sacred moral symbols rather than courting "the objective interests of citizens."[129] More than ever, this means emphasizing experiences of *identity* over experiences of *ability*, much less issue stances.[130]

"The hardest advice to give [Bernie Sanders] . . . is that people don't really vote for people because for their policy positions," acknowledges Chuck Rocha, a senior advisor on that presidential campaign.[131] Even when issues *are* engaged—in, say, a crowded presidential primary—they're done so according to the logic of brand differentiation, as a contender vying for party nomination can only become a successful symbolic representation to the degree that he or she carves out an identity-space not yet colonized by opponents: e.g., the Bible Thumper, the War Monger, the Politically Incorrect Uncle, the Ayn Rand Acolyte, to name a few of the widest lanes in recent GOP races.[132]

Partly, too, there is the challenge of the immateriality of the consumer decision in the voting booth: Unlike commercial goods, one interviewee notes, "With politics, you're not selling them a product by which you can say, 'It does all these things'—they can go to the store and buy it and they can come home and have that immediate satisfaction."[133] Despite the undeniable power that political choice grants to real-life outcomes (taxes, wars, etc.), it exists, first—and increasingly foremost—as identity badge. Hence, the superficiality of campaign output to cater to that: "People don't read—if we put up a 20-page white paper, nobody would read that," laments one congressional communications director.[134]

By contrast, Alexandria Ocasio-Cortez's internet-breaking Met Gala dress ("tax the rich") is emblematic of *stunts* schemed to grab attention. On the other side of the aisle, the GOP's deputy communications director sent a man in a dolphin suit to shadow John Kerry at events during the 2004 Bush campaign: "If I have a person in a dolphin suit waving and holding a sign that says, 'I'm a flip-flopper, too,' the chance of a television station putting that on air are quite a bit higher than if we were to say, 'Come by the state party headquarters and interview our chairman.'"[135]

Another interviewee summarized the conventional wisdom here: "If I could choose my opponent in a political debate, I would pick someone that's talking policy and statistics, while I'm delivering a message that has an emotional appeal. . . . There's a reason that works, like, neuro-physically. When you activate higher order reasoning—like, math, things like that—you're actually going to deactivate the emotional centers of the brain. . . . So, if you're talking statistics, you're no longer talking emotions . . . and if the other guy's talking emotion, they're going to win."[136]

Emotions are authentic, politically and otherwise, because they are assumed to be immune from calculation, whereas rationality is deliberate (and, hence, the ideal for political *deliberation*); emotions are "hard to fake" and "make politicians appear . . . human."[137] Authenticity is, indeed, both the *process* of filtering experience through deepest emotion and the *product* of a culture of unreason, where feelings, above all else, express the self-discovery of identity.[138]

This underpinned the satirical brilliance of Stephen Colbert's "truthiness"—a synonym for political authenticity that prioritizes "emotional truth and personal perception" rather than objective facts and shared reality, and it's reflected in the chapter-opening epigraph's "bullshit" distinction between sincerity and truth in politics and advertising.[139] The triumph of political aesthetic and performance—"spectacle, style, emotion, and the cult of personality"— over "rationalist logic" is one of Romanticism trouncing Enlightenment ideals: a Rousseauian rejection of "I think, therefore I am" with "I *feel*, therefore I am [with that tribe]."[140]

After all, says the chief creative officer at one political consulting firm, "I know of no household that holds big meetings where they all do opposition research and sit down and spend four hours going through an issue matrix to decide who they're going to vote for. It's done on a much more visceral level."[141] Neuroscience advances confirm that the "political brain" as dispassionate calculator might be theoretical folly.[142]

Any rationality, argues one Republican media advisor, is just the after-the-fact legitimation of some gut vibe, consciousness *priori*: "We are intuitive and then our reasoning mind rationalizes why we feel some way . . . 'There's something about [the candidate]—I like her. She's got a good sense of humor. Seems like real people . . . I like her family or kids are cute.' . . . And then, later on, they're like, 'You know, the reason I like her is she's going to hold the line on spending.' 'She's definitely going to cut government.' . . . So, emotion and tapping into that is absolutely critical from beginning, middle, and end."[143]

Authenticating Ourselves to Death?

Add up all these authenticity industry machinations and you total a political communication environment streamlined for superficiality.[144]

"Policy matters in politics, but less so," explains the president of a political ad agency. "I mean, you can vote for someone you admire and like and respect but disagree with—comfortably. It's harder to vote for someone with whom you agree on policy but whom you don't care for."[145] That supposition might be objectively testable, but—and it feels obvious to state this aloud—in no sober democratic universe should citizens be voting for policies they disagree with (or those who represent them). Yet an American politics obsessed with authenticity hinges on easily manipulable obsessions with representing identity over issues.

The utility of democracy is, theoretically, to be found in quality self-governance, not actualized self-discovery. As shown in chapter 4, commercial branding decouples the material dimension of the marketplace exchange in favor of dreamy, mythic facades. The consultants' work on display here seems to evince the same ambition: receding considerations of policy and material reality behind invocations of image and identification. The people who write speeches, cut ads, and connive journalists are less interested in making you, the voter, *think*—especially if feelings can be conjured first to short-circuit rational, deliberative calculations.[146]

On balance—and though they wouldn't openly admit to it—interviewees conceptualize the audiences they target as somewhat childish: apathetic toward public affairs, incapable of handling complexity, and easily titillated by flashy visual and emotional devices. It is a political strategy that presumes, first and foremost, that the public couldn't care less about political debate.[147] In turn, they work toward reducing that public sphere to the shallow simplicity of cheeseburgers and dolphin suits and small-town water towers. The more that politicians recognize the advantage of a family photo posted to Instagram or the lure of a jokey late-night interview, the less they'll be willing to subject themselves to traditional journalistic scrutiny (and, behind the scenes, strategists have already made these trade-offs).[148]

To be certain, this is a dated lament. Suspicion of political performance earned Greek philosophical handwringing; the demagogic force of feeling conceived as distinct from, lesser than, and intruding upon the sober wisdom of reason.[149] Millennia later, cultural critic Neil Postman named these anxieties crisply in his fear that we were *Amusing Ourselves to Death*: "knowing" (superficially) politics through television imagery.[150] Today, as TV morphs toward—if not yet fully into—social media as the dominant environmental conditioning, one might say we run the risk of *authenticating* ourselves to death.

This "public performance of politics," rather than being secondary to governance, is now primary: a simulacra cart jumping the horse. One freshman congressman boasted to Republican colleagues he'd built his staff "'around comms rather than legislation' . . . [and that] his office planned to focus its energies not on lawmaking but on getting [him] on TV to fire up the base."[151]

This is, in Marxist terms, indicative of the sign-value of a politician—what they represent as a personality-accessory for voters—eclipsing the use-value of a politician—what they'll actually *do* in office. Voting values derive from the appearance of political style (e.g., the aforementioned water tower as authenticating scrim) rather than the nuances of policy substance (e.g., how, concretely, that candidate might help the fortunes of that small town).[152] The silly spectacle of culture war, in particular—forever prioritizing identity and style over substance and outcomes—peaked mid-pandemic when a great moral panic got ginned up about Dr. Suess books being "cancelled" from and thereby unavailable at schools—many of which had not even *reopened* for in-person learning.[153]

Just as corporations, seduced by branding ideals, seek to make themselves organizationally "weightless"—that is, detached from the manufacture of goods on balance sheets in favor of a less tangible, but more profitable ownership of brand meaning—so, too, do politicians, in pursuit of authenticity, try to detach themselves from the manufacture of policies in favor of more advantageous cultural meaning.[154]

"American politics has become more aesthetically sophisticated even as it grows frustrated by its inability to identify shared values or solve collective problems," one observer mourns. "There are historical precedents for what happens to a democracy when it gets more invested in its own mythology and less patient with its own political process, and those precedents are not good."[155]

SEVEN

xxxxxx

Populist Politics

Technologies of Informality

Rule number one [on social media] is to be authentic; to be yourself and don't try to be anyone you're not. So don't try to talk like a young kid if you're not a young kid; don't post a meme if you don't know what a meme is. . . . [And] don't talk like the Founding Fathers on Twitter.

—ALEXANDRIA OCASIO-CORTEZ, Democratic congresswoman[1]

There is no other Donald Trump. What you see is what you get.

—HILLARY CLINTON, presidential nominee[2]

In 2016, with a divisive US election looming, a brigade of government-affiliated trolls in St. Petersburg made memes and mischief that altered history an ocean away.

Russia's Internet Research Agency faked thousands of individual accounts and seeded social media with disinformation to boost Donald Trump's chances; his campaign affiliates and even Trump himself engaged and amplified the sham handles.[3] IRA-generated Facebook groups like "United Muslims of America" and "Secured Borders" swelled to six-figure followings; they also bought $100,000 worth of targeted ads and posed as real citizens or entities, demonizing Hillary Clinton.

More spectacular, the foreign propagandists attempted to dupe and sometimes did dupe actual people into attending actual rallies, exacerbating cultural and political fissures in US society via phony activist pretenses: initiating Black Lives Matter protests; pro- and anti-Muslim events; and gay rights' rallies. After initially poo-pooing the prospect that it had unwittingly served as a vessel for

176

these dirty tricks, Facebook owned up to the reality that 125 million users may have been exposed to the content. Seeking, in particular, to suppress key Democratic constituencies of color, the Russian trolls "take how we speak and manipulate it, allowing their messaging to sound authentic," one Black activist lamented.[4]

All this chicanery built upon the architecture and, moreover, ethos of social media, which, as we've seen from chapter 2 onward, drives and is driven by populist undercurrents. And in the mischief unleashed, we find themes and lessons that epitomized Trump's eventual electoral victory: an eroded faith in establishment authorities; a perception that grassroots flows of communication and organizing are more trustworthy than top-down tactics; and an impetus toward more content—and more emotionally charged content—to best carry the message online.

This chapter disentangles how we got there.

An Anarchy of Authority

Populism is a slippery term, often used interchangeably as both substance and style. As ideology, it encompasses anti-elitism and in-group purity; as communication strategy, it bespeaks bluntness and social media savvy.[5] As policy, it champions nationalism, both cultural and economic; as rhetoric, it affects skepticism of institutions and authorities.[6]

The means of communicating populist ideas often mesh neatly with the ideas themselves (and the authenticity of amateurism, chapter 2's ideal, corresponds to political invocations of restoring power to "the people").[7] It plays well digitally, because the internet theoretically democratizes information hierarchies, allows leaders to directly address supporters, and cocoons those followers within "filter bubbles and echo chambers" where outside mindsets are algorithmically Othered, in favor of simple, searing emotion.[8]

In the 2010s, a populist turn swept the globe on both left and right: from Andrés Manuel López Obrador in Mexico to Jair Bolsonaro in Brazil, from Boris Johnson in Britain to Viktor Orban in Hungary, from Narendra Modi in India to Rodrigo Duterte in the Philippines.[9] The populist typically emerges from the far ends of the political spectrum and performs—in both senses of the term—better as challenger than incumbent.[10] Nonetheless, "right-wing populism tends to define the people as *nation*, left-wing populism rather conceives it as *class*," with the former inveighing against immigration, crime, "supranational institutions, the mass media and the courts," and the latter denouncing capitalism, neoliberal policies, and "economic and religious elites."[11]

Tribal invocations populistically stitch together an identity message of us-versus-them: a "morally superior, homogenous, and monolithic entity" set against "problematic minorities, self-serving elites, [and] scapegoats presented as threats" to the heartland, thereby necessitating ostracism.[12] Still, it bears repeating that when populist politicians rhapsodize on behalf of "the people," they don't actually mean *all* of the people—leaving out either the ethnically different or economically privileged.[13]

Without question, populism traces a long history in American politics, notably escalating in the 1960s with Richard Nixon's campaign talk of "forgotten Americans" in "middle America" and his attack on the "nattering nabobs" in the elite media who impeded his connection to that "silent majority."[14] Still, certain more recent factors swelled the populist tide. First, echoing Nixon, a deep insecurity among groups once assumed favored and stable in both economic and cultural terms; in the United States, such "threats" appeared as both demographic diversity and the hollowing out of the middle class.[15]

Party power—or its increasing lack of it—matters, too. For several decades, traditional parties in the Western world have earned skepticism for being "self-serving" and unresponsive to public need; simultaneously, outsider candidates could skirt orderly leadership monopolies, unencumbered by campaign finance regulations and fueled by charismatic wattage.[16] The rising number of registered political independents indicates that parties don't feel authentic to their citizens.[17] More sharply, the US alt-right stakes out its identity as a more "authentic" conservatism than that which RINOs—"Republicans in name only," as they are sneeringly dismissed—have forever promised but underdelivered to the base, keeping them unsatisfied and angry.

This "paranoid" streak about conspiratorial power fueled anti-establishment politics in American public life for generations, especially amidst downturns and crises.[18] Closely related is a decades-long decline in faith in all manner of large social institutions: Congress, public schools, corporations, organized religion.[19] In early 2020, Edelman's "Trust Barometer" found that no such institution was seen as ethical and competent.[20] That compels people to search for authenticity within *themselves*, because they can't trust that external structures and forces will provide it—much less trusting news from outside of tribal nodes that now deliver it digitally.

"We call it the 'anarchy of authority' right now—it's just crazy," sighs Rob Shepardson, a senior media advisor to the Obama campaigns.[21] A decade ago, in the wreckage of the Bush presidency, the Tea Party rebranded the GOP by channeling suspicion among a base that doesn't "defer to experts and . . .

[scorns] educated people who try to devise plans for regular citizens," as political scientists Theda Skocpol and Vanessa Williamson summarize.[22]

As coronavirus hospitalizations and deaths peaked, this became especially dire for amateurs emboldened to masquerade as infectious disease specialists, having "done the research" themselves on masks, vaccines, and horse de-wormers (via their algorithmically tailored, filter-bubbled social graph). The Trump administration was propelled into the Oval Office by this ethos, as we'll see, and it informed their anti–"Deep State" staffing principles biased, at great risk, against experience and expertise.[23] Weirdly, politics remains that rare profession—versus, say, neurosurgery—where applicants are rewarded for proudly boasting, "I've never done this before!"

This is because an overly polished politician, slick with focus group–approved soundbites, appears ripe for duplicity—not being true to themselves on account of either the cynical calculations of social decorum or the marketplace motives of backroom financiers.[24] To be an outsider to politics, then, is to fulfill that amateur ideal of authenticity, implying one is "uncorrupted" by any prior exercise of power, unlike elites tainted by those long-standing associations.[25]

Increasingly, some evidence suggests this works: Despite the long-standing political science truism that experience outperforms—thanks to durable donors and name recognition—recent research documented an uptick in electoral victories by novices, especially in late 2010s cycles, when about half of congressional and US Senate freshmen had no governing background.[26] A viral video from an unknown can strike a fertile ideological chord and raise millions overnight from outside a district.

Yet that populism is posed as much as proven—a communicative style and orientation to the world, not simply (or ever, necessarily) a set of policy positions. Its messaging is plain-spoken, emotional, dramatic, negative, vulgar, and Othering.[27] And though scholarship has long examined populism as *content*, it has less often been treated as *production*—especially in the wake of technological transformation, as illuminated here.[28]

Netroots Mythologies

Throughout history, advances in communication technology prefigured transformations in both campaign practice and the substance of political communication.[29] In the twenty-first century, as once-authoritative information gatekeepers lost their monopoly over the news agenda, information abundance, rather than scarcity, animated the conditions and challenges of that fragmentation.[30] The dynamics of authenticity have, in turn, defined and been defined by these new digital platforms, as chapter 2 underscored.

"[Social media] is like a steroid tool to amplify authenticity," declares George W. Bush's chief media advisor, Mark McKinnon. "But for people who use it well, they don't just sort of use talking points from their latest policy proposal; they show, you know, Jill or Joe at the barbeque interacting with supporters."[31] A slew of scholarship echoes this claim: that politicians seem more authentic and populist on social media than via traditional journalism, thanks to the platforms' texture of amateur production and heterarchical circulation.[32]

To be sure, the platforms themselves like to upsell their "humanizing" potential, affording and encouraging that personal disclosure by public figures: "This is something we drum into [candidates] every time we talk to them: Be authentic, be authentic," explains Katie Harbath, former director of political outreach at Facebook, where employees reportedly worried that their site's design had a bias toward populists (given its effective, affective deployment by Trump, Modi, Duterte, and others).[33]

A grassroots theory hence took hold: that social media politics represent the righteous, organic, spontaneous movements that rise *up* from the people rather than being imposed *upon* them by entrenched interests.[34] Yet those social media politics can also serve power *because* they seem to operate furthest from the appearance of it.

This conventional wisdom emerged alongside the first presidential campaign to enthusiastically employ digital tools and frame their use through populist rationale: Howard Dean's 2004 Democratic primary bid.[35] Campaign manager Joe Trippi had long experimented with new technologies—from early computer-based strategizing to the use of an 800 phone number to solicit supporter input, "wrestling with how do you . . . connect somebody like [client] Jerry Brown, an authentic guy, with people," he recalls. "'Cause you're never gonna meet enough people at their door to do that—and TV is too constraining."[36]

While Dean failed to secure the nomination, he pioneered the "netroots" model of meet-up mobilization, blog interactivity, and small-dollar fundraising techniques. "There was a hunger, I think, after years of sort of 30-second spots and polished pols with blow-dried hair and carefully worded speeches— there was suddenly this authentic, real campaign and candidate," says Trippi, whose subsequent memoir title, *The Revolution Will Not Be Televised*, encapsulates the fusion of populist themes and digital means.

By definition, *social* media accommodates dialogue, and the willingness to take risks of spontaneity there also, allegedly, communicates authenticity; politicians can pose like they care about ordinary folks when connecting with them in those spaces.[37] Indeed, one study confirmed that candidates interacting with constituents in informal settings were perceived as more transparent and relatable.[38]

The founding partner of Bully Pulpit Interactive, an influential firm of Obama veterans, articulates the ideology here—echoing a notion from the introductory chapter that mass broadcast, because of its inherent messaging standardization, feels comparatively inauthentic:

> It used to be you're reaching people through their TV screen, which used to be the most intimate way that you could do that. But over time, people realize everybody is seeing this message—it is extremely canned. It has, like, been poll-tested [with] focus groups. So, there's a level of mistrust with the super, uber, glossy advertising that you see [there]. . . . They want to feel they know you [the candidate], right? They want to feel like they know what you're about; what your family is about. . . . Authenticity is the most important thing that you have to get across.[39]

The "playing field" for political content thus widened dramatically relative to previous decades, in that more venues are available for that messaging; a consultant might start by planting items on blogs, social media, or targeted ads until traditional news outlets pick them up, marginalizing journalistic arbiters by seeding "around" them.

"If I wanted to break a story [before], we had to sell it to a reporter. Now I can sell it to someone local or in the blogosphere who's much more likely to be on my side," an opposition research specialist explains. "[Then] I can go and say to reporters, 'Hey, look what's on site X,' and, 'This is getting some traction—you may want to cover it.'"[40] Populist politicians can also plot and pose antagonistically on social media toward intermediary journalists who—they accuse—impede that one-to-one connection with their community of supporters.[41]

An oft-cited cliché here is that, as one interviewee told me they advise clients, "everybody's a media brand" and, in some cases, a politician may actually have a bigger following on social than the media outlets that tail them, so there's no need to wait for a cable news appearance when an immediate Instagram story via iPhone will suffice (and since cable might well run that raw footage anyhow).[42] According to one leader at the Democratic National Committee, in 2022 midterms, there was an "insane" increase to two-dozen staff members whose roles were to, effectively, run "a publishing and media company in-house in the name of their candidate or their committee"—not unlike a "newsroom" churning daily output on digital.[43]

"Content is king. The answer to almost any situation is more content, not less," Rubio 2016 campaign manager Terry Sullivan explains to me. "Before, you'd try to, like, starve the media from being able to cover something: release one statement, don't say anything more, and they can't cover."[44] In an era of information abundance, you instead flood the zone.

This quicker turnaround and more steady stream of political fodder online lowers expectations and debases norms of decorum ("If it gets so much attention that it creates controversy, it's, like, a good problem," one interviewee shrugs); being more "raw," aesthetically and substantively, it also signals authenticity.[45] Intense, speedy output beats carefully tested material in a media environment where caution and prudence is actually a liability for leaders: "The more instinctive politicians will do well," notes Mike DuHaime, Rudy Giuliani 2008 campaign manager, echoing the Rousseauian premise that reflex and feeling is more authentic than calculation and calibration. "If it's a politician who needs to, you know, get the tweet approved by 17 layers of bureaucracy, they're going to fail."[46]

Consultant elites now also see, in everyday citizens, a way of embedding and ventriloquizing political messages.[47] Like Howard Dean before him, Barack Obama in 2008 tried to crowdsource his campaign narrative through the personal experiences of supporters on the official blog—filtering the top-down message through bottom-up amateur interlocutors: "Telling their specific stories about why they decided to get involved," recalls the chief blogger. "People who [were], in a sense, becoming their own micro [versions of Obama]."[48]

Their words resonated more than anything campaign head David Plouffe could have scripted in the war room—an influencer innovation years before that catchphrase even had meaning. Worming into word-of-mouth maximizes authenticity, because, as the chief creative officer at a political media consultancy explains, "I can never do an ad that is more effective than one friend telling another friend something," he says. "What we try to do is think a lot less like a political candidate and much more like somebody who is just having a conversation with a neighbor or a friend."[49]

These tactics of crowdsourcing political authenticity grew more ubiquitous and refined with each passing campaign cycle, especially as paid political ad bans cascaded across leading social networks. In the 2020 Democratic primary, for example, Mayor Pete Buttigieg ran ads in Iowa featuring direct address cellphone testimonials from supporters specifically targeting those supporters' communities.[50] Senator Elizabeth Warren scaled out this "illusion of intimacy" by posing for endless snaps with fans and Instagramming videos of her shout-out calls to small donors, with hopes that the content might be shared with *their* social media contacts.[51] And billionaire Michael Bloomberg bought himself a slew of #spon-con via meme postings and text messages from hundreds of on-the-take influencers.[52]

In a campaign postmortem, President Joe Biden's digital director emphasized the importance of this "micro-influencer engagement," including outreach to Instagrammers with as few as 5,000 follows.[53] The Biden campaign also developed apps accessing cellphone contacts to map friendships and "leverage established rapport," through campaign-crafted scripts that could be tweaked for more authentic nuance.[54] On Facebook, it played upon lookalike targeted audiences whose attitudes were swayed by earlier experimental A/B content and peddled to moms, who "spend a lot of time sharing cute and uplifting content," million-plus-viewed clips such as Biden encouraging a boy who suffered from a stutter like he once did.[55]

Such content travels quickly and effectively because emotion—being authentic, as opposed to abstract, calculated rationality—is incentivized there.[56] Anger, in particular, spreads far and fast on social, as the algorithms prioritize engagement and nothing engages quite like being pissed off.[57] All this information architecture caters well to a certain class of politician at the expense of civil, constructive public discourse: "The more direct, unmediated, outrageous, polarizing, shocking, and emotional the message is, the more chances of becoming viral and populistically effective," one study by digital politics scholars concludes.[58]

Context for consumption also determines production ethics. A 30-spot that could only air in the family living room had to abide by certain (inauthentic, two-faced) norms of decorum that more provocative, outlandish digital ads do not have to obey when they land in personalized feeds on individualized screens: "There's less limitations," notes one interviewee. "You would do things online that you might not do on television. . . . There's more of an openness or sort of a Wild West quality."[59]

The Rough Cut Candidate

Social media generates political authenticity primarily because it appears to offer backstage access to private lives: breaching that two-faced self that Erving Goffman diagnosed of our social interactions. Campaigns thus use these platforms to offer a glimpse of the ordinary and unrehearsed, the intimate and informal—staging "illusions of authenticity . . . by performing spontaneity," which, they believe, connect emotionally and, thus, have the best shot at going viral.[60]

This is due, in no small part, to the frontstage of politics seeming so predictable and formulaic, so preplanned by spin doctors even as those clichés explored in the last chapter are meant to *overcome* that feeling of inauthenticity.[61] "It's sort of like, how do we create the space for this human to be human in public?" Lindsay Holst, director of digital strategy for Biden's vice presidency, explains to me.[62]

Indeed, driven by social, there seems to be an assumption that politicians *must* disclose previously hidden, unfiltered inner lives, because that's what the medium demands, whether that be Alexandria Ocasio-Cortez gardening or Beto O'Rourke skateboarding.[63] "Being yourself"—as performance, of course—includes indulging outspokenness, writing in a casual manner, and dropping revealing details about lifestyle habits.[64] The minutiae on display in Ocasio-Cortez's Instagram feed—displaying "intentional vulnerability," as feminist scholar Kyla Schuller observes—helps "break down barriers between government and the people" and foregrounds her imperfections.[65]

One study found that, on Facebook, candidates who posed only in formal situations came across as less sincere to citizens; thus, candid snaps communicate relatability and trustworthiness, for nonpolitical diversions authenticate political machinations.[66] Another study by digital media scholar Delia Dumitrica found that those who were willing to display such private traits—"signaling that the politician was 'one of them'"—elicited, from citizens, the perception that they genuinely cared about their problems, which could be converted into policy goals.[67] (And those policy goals, of course, need not be tethered to the *actual* problems that citizens experience.)

Channeling Marshall McLuhan's adage here, the medium is the message: The context for and affordances of social media contribute to the bias and logic of how it's supposed to be used, whether by plebeian or president alike (or president fronting as plebeian). These are vehicles expressly built for sharing and disclosure and they're sold to the public (as shown in chapter 2) as revealing that "'real' self" along the way—an environment qualitatively distinct from prior alternatives like, say, journalism or broadcasting, with their historic formality of aesthetic and substance.[68] On social media platforms, there is a gravity of personalization and informality, one might say, that weighs down stiff pretense: "You can let your hair a little bit more" in those spaces, notes one interviewee.[69] You must, in fact.

And yet, as has been true throughout the book, authenticity is being industrially schemed in these spaces: "The challenge is to try to do it in a way that actually feels real rather than a whole campaign team, you know, worked to try to make it feel real," quips Jim Margolis, senior media advisor to the Obama and Clinton presidential campaigns.[70] For one thing, social accounts—despite the façade of direct access to leaders—are almost always carefully managed by staffers (Trump, of course, being an exception that proves how authenticity rules).[71]

Aesthetically, the "rough cut" remains ideal here: simple, even shoddy, production values convey amateurism that conveys authenticity. The ascendance of the camera phone as a means of producing and distributing content has been essential to these norms and clichés. Some interviewees like to lurk with such lightweight recording devices at town halls, rallies, and local fundraisers to give "a little voyeur" quality to the recording, *cinema verité* style, without the heavy apparatus of a film crew dousing the spontaneity with obvious, clunky mediation—ideally capturing "unscripted moments" as though "you're hearing actually what this candidate really thinks."[72] (Barack Obama, Mitt Romney, and Hillary Clinton discovered this, bitterly, when secret recordings at big-dollar fundraising events revealed them griping, respectively, about gun-and-religion-clingers, the "47 percent" of untaxed moochers, and "deplorables."[73])

One *Campaigns & Elections* article touts that lower-production-value, "organic" seeming clips get skipped less than fancier formal ads, "signal[ing] to your audience that they're seeing something unvarnished and unscripted."[74] Emphasizing that studied extemporaneity, the article advocates, "People know canned lines when they hear them. A little stammering actually makes it more authentic."

The roughness of the aesthetic implicitly affirms its trustworthiness: "Production value is no longer king, authenticity is, and the new bar is emotional transparency that we've all been trained to expect in our online universe," hypes one interviewee who tries to harness amateur volunteers into "video strike force teams."[75] Another interviewee confirms a trend in recent cycles whereby candidates who scrapped fancy fundraising footage in favor of vertically oriented, direct address asks hit their goals more frequently.[76] Emblematically, Bernie Sanders' media team quit in a huff when the senator panned their fast-paced, "sleek" 2020 campaign announcement in favor of a "no-frills," single-shot, eleven-minute lecture he wrote himself, which feels almost too on-the-nose.[77]

In another telling example of this, Republican Voters Against Trump, an election group headed by neoconservative Bill Kristol, compiled hundreds of selfie videos of voters who had bailed on the president between 2016 and 2020—many being poorly lit, "bare-bones," grainy-pixelated testimonials like that of Josh, a shirtless, Marlboro-sucking, North Carolina pest exterminator, slouching on his back deck in the middle of the night and confessing a rambling conversion story.[78] It rang up more than a million views. And in Josh's "third-party authentication," the Never Trumpers hoped, other apostates might see their own identity suitably reflected in a way that, say, the patrician Kristol could never conceivably pull off.

This approach is benefited—and perhaps necessitated by—the accelerated velocity of political communication in today's media environment. "Crappier quality may come across as more authentic. . . . When people post to social media, we're typically shooting from our phones, so that is what fits with the medium. Also because of commercials, I think we're hard-wired to be immediately wary of anything that looks produced," notes one interviewee.[79] Speed makes for sloppiness, which is not actually a liability in these aesthetic confines, since professionalized content looks elitist and therefore insincere.

Memes, for example, are crude but democratic in their slapdash participatory design: splice image macro, append Impact-font commentary, publish, go![80] What matters more is keeping up with the real-time, emotional flow of mediated culture, messy as might be required. A rough cut aesthetic substantiates a purity and integrity of purpose and, in turn, affirms the paradoxical ambition to construct media that appears to lack any construction at all—manufacturing a political image devoid of apparent artifice. Walter Ludwig, who runs a political media agency, elaborates:

> Facebook and Instagram allow you to put up a shit-ton more content at essentially no incremental costs. And that's helpful because it allows you to show more moments in a campaign, more moments in a candidate's life, more moments in a candidate's point of view without having to go out and rustle up a crew and buy time and budget for that. . . . It has [also] accultured people to seeing much less-produced content. . . . One of the ideas that's floating around the business right now is that you're almost better off doing a phone video on Facebook than a produced piece of content because people will pay attention to it. It's like what their friends put out.[81]

Anecdotally, such claims abound. The Biden 2020 campaign pointed to internal testing that showed "impromptu, behind-the-scenes footage and ads," including average voters recording selfie videos declaring their support, were far more effective than "professionally produced, slick-looking" 30-spots. They thus commissioned those "lo-fi" ads and teamed up with "'small-batch creators'—lesser known producers . . . [who] had little experience making political ads" and could generate something that didn't look inauthentically mass-standardized.[82] "People don't want to feel like they're being sold something," adds Lindsay Holst, who worked digital strategy for Biden. "The whole point is to sort of translate this person into a platform and provide as little stagecraft as possible."[83]

This evolution in strategy was already in motion before pandemic necessity wreaked havoc on production plans during the 2020 cycle, what with its lockdowns and social distancing. Work-from-home arrangements brought colleagues in all domains into each other's "backstages" like never before—obliterating previously public-private distinctions in favor of more transparent honesty—and candidates followed suit, equipped with remote film kits that consultants provided to capture living room and kitchen scenes.[84] With citizens supposedly desperate for that "touch of authenticity" and "human connection," notes Kim Alfano, head of a GOP media firm, "people accepted a grittier product" sent back from those spaces, and the lack of flash, in some ways, mirrored a collective year being sedentary in sweatpants—it spoke, visually, to the housebound realities and anxieties of the electorate.[85]

The pandemic thus amped up "natural authenticity," political ad-makers told *Campaigns & Elections*—the aesthetic textures of the rough cut more acceptable than ever and "old family photos" of the candidate substituting for posh shots captured out on the trail. The vulnerability that could be shown there—not just in performing a nonperformance but also in the very medium itself conveying crisis conditions—elicited advantageous empathy and identification with voters.[86]

"This has been a great thing to sort of demystify candidates and give you the Trump aura without the Trump personality," jokes Alfano.[87] Indeed, that Trump-Clinton battle represented a turning point in the history of political authenticity.

Donald Trump Didn't Come Here to Make Friends

In 2016, conventional wisdom held that authenticity "defined and perhaps even decided" the US presidential campaign, permeating "every aspect" of the contest; authenticity was, in the lamenting estimation of one Democratic strategist, the "big takeaway" and real "winner."[88]

As foreshadowed by the philosophical musings of Jean Jacques-Rousseau and the tactics of compelling reality TV, coming across as a jerk is a pretty good way to convince people of your authenticity. I suspect that even Trump supporters might grant that as crude compliment rather than outright insult, for Trump's willful disregard for political correctness and apparent inability to formulate different selves for different stages (as Erving Goffman held that we naturally do) are simultaneously badges of honor and also the external manifestation of someone who has zero fucks left to give.

This scans as authentic given the phoniness of the environment it stands in contrast to, as Terry Sullivan, campaign manager for competitor Marco Rubio, riffs: "People don't care about issues. They're going to claim they care about issues. . . . We're in a situation now where people don't trust anything or anyone and what they want is some sense of authenticity. It doesn't matter what you believe; it matters that you believe it. And they saw that with Trump because, in their mind, no one would say crap that crazy, because [others seemed] poll-tested."[89] Indeed, as Sullivan conducted focus groups during Trump's primary season ascent, to his own client's unsolvable detriment, he told me he often heard invocations of policy nihilism and indiscriminate disgust for the establishment status quo: "I don't agree with all the crazy stuff that guy says; I just liked the fact that he's got the balls to say it."[90]

Trump purchased his authenticity with communicative style rather than ideological substance. His coarse manner-of-speech juxtaposed the PR-caution and refined output of Clinton especially (not to mention most politicians, at most levels, in most cycles, in most places): speaking in repetitive, monosyllabic, "staccato bursts" so inartful—and apparently allergic to alliteration—at third- or fourth-grade reading levels, that they register as genuine and peddling simplistic solutions to complicated problems ("build a wall!") where other politicians dally in dissembling nuance.[91]

Trump convinced "by being politically incorrect, by driving through all the guard rails, baiting his opponents, wearing his bigotry and racism on his sleeve, where his base feels like he will say things that no one else will," observes one veteran Democratic media advisor. "And his incivility and assault on political correctness is true evidence of him being straight, real, and unfiltered and—wait for it—authentic."[92]

This "Archie Bunker" act populistically tickled an audience, because, in the words of his former communication director Anthony Scaramucci: "[He] speaks to them in a way that lacks the formality that you would typically see in the political class. . . . [It's], 'I'm at the bar with you; I'm your uncle complaining about things that you always complain about.'"[93] Such plainspokenness projects him as someone who rejects the "whole charade" of tact and nuance—and dissembling (an impressive feat for someone who lied 30,573 times during his presidency).[94]

The more garish the vulgarity, the more evidence that Trump was a "straight shooter."[95] Hence, Mexican "rapists," American prisoner-of-war disses, and "shithole" African nations were not gaffes or liabilities, as staid political communication principles would hold (and as no consultant in their right mind would script), but rather accomplishments of authenticity—evidence that he *wouldn't* say just anything to get elected (in a decorous sense), even as he was saying *exactly* the sort of things that he needed to say in order to get elected (in an indecorous sense).[96] That off-the-cuff stridency and boorishness could be decoded, in its violation of platitudinal norms and good taste, as somehow legitimizing any pursuit of power, as these are the sorts of howlers that would surely doom any other campaign.[97]

It is also the mark of a megalomaniacal narcissist whose brain has been soaked in seventy years of fame-chasing media logic: If Trump sensed that the red lights on the TV cameras at rallies might go dim, indicating he was no longer live on cable news channels, "I would say something new to keep the red light on."[98] These shockers deprived competitors of press oxygen: In 2016, barely spending on political ads, Trump nonetheless scored $6 billion in free media coverage.[99] The TV camera red lights could not pull away from the spectacle, like political onlookers rubbernecking past a car crash of a campaign.

Style was, in fact, the actual *substance*: for Trump, and for his followers, political incorrectness not merely a prick's tic—secondary to policy seriousness—but an issue position itself. In other words, conveniently, being anti-PC wasn't a problem to fix but a "solution" to a problem: in his view, and that of his base, the societal suffocation of free speech.[100] A majority, in fact, agreed: On the eve of Trump's election, Pew found that nearly three in five Americans felt "too many people are easily offended these days" over language seen as inappropriate.[101]

For loudmouths, political correctness is, in fact, inauthentic: "hostile to the truth of the self," in Rousseauian terms.[102] And so Trump's anti-PC indulgences license and cultivate tribal identification with his followers, who hear a version of themselves in him and feel the same slights heaped upon him by tasteful elites policing politeness.[103] "Trump has given them permission to express views that were not socially acceptable," laments Bush and Romney advisor (and anti-Trumper) Stuart Stevens. "We all have moments of road rage out there and Trump tells you, like, 'That's your best self. . . . That's who you ought to be.' "[104]

A seeming consistency of performance—no matter who the audience—further offsets that two-faced self. Most politicians adeptly adapt and adopt the right tone, inauthentically, depending on the crowd; Trump, for the most part, sounds pretty much the same across Twitter, rally speeches, news interviews, and debate stages.[105] This is why, when Hillary Clinton thought she was dissing him in this chapter's epigraph ("There is no other Donald Trump. What you see is what you get."), it actually serves as a *compliment* given the dynamics of political authenticity in general, and her liabilities in particular.

Fittingly, Trump's tropes of authenticity track back to themes established in chapter 1: The most compelling reality TV characters seem to act as though the cameras aren't rolling (or, at least, can't contain their emotional outbursts despite them) and act consistently, if obnoxiously, across settings rather than contorting themselves to please.[106] They did not, as the cliché holds, come here to make friends, which tends to require affable accommodation; no one ever accused Trump of this, either.

If you ever got the feeling, watching Donald Trump over the years—or, emblematically, in his unhinged first debate against Joe Biden—that he somehow simply couldn't "help himself," then you were witnessing authenticity in its rawest form. The ad-libs, the rambles—the careening, free-jazz, where-is-this-going extemporaneity of thought—all of it scans as from the heart (or, at least, an addled brain), just as his scripted appearances like the State of the Union sound so hostage-forced bizarre.[107]

"The fact that he's unfiltered, it creates the sense that you're seeing the real thing, whether or not you are," notes one CEO of a political consulting firm. "His mistakes and his verbal gaffes and inconsistencies . . . are there for everybody to see."[108] Another Democratic consultant summarizes thus, "He's not trying to be all things to all people."[109] Jean-Jacques Rousseau would presumably salute that autonomy of social purpose; Erving Goffman (or, at least, his theory) might cringe.

"With Trump, either the whole thing's an act or nothing's an act—I've been in private rooms with him where he's exactly the same as he is from the podium at the White House," confirms Mike DuHaime, veteran Republican campaign manager.[110] Other insiders, even closer to the former president, tell me a similar tale—and not necessarily in flattering self-interest: "With Trump, you see an *Access Hollywood* tape, you see all these other things about how he talks when no one's listening, right? And then you match that to the rhetoric that you sometimes hear, and you go, 'Oh, it's actually not that different,'" notes Sean Spicer, his first press secretary.[111]

"Nobody advises President Trump," adds his (very brief) communication director Anthony Scaramucci. "There's only one way to get to him—and that is through the prism of his brain where every light that goes into that prism shines the word 'Trump' on the wall. And, so, if you want to advise him or try to get him to do something, you have to explain it in the context of why and how it is good for him."[112]

This is, again, the Rousseauian ideal of authenticity (and also the behavior of a petulant child): totally committed to prioritizing the inner self, despite efforts of outside courtiers to steer and frame that self toward the opinions of others. This performance of nonperformance sold, at least among supporters: Amidst the 2016 primary battle, three-quarters of GOP voters believed that Trump "says he what he believes" as opposed to "what people want to hear."[113] His freewheeling, seemingly impromptu campaign announcement speech—a total desecration of the principles of deliberation and precision within that genre—telegraphed this, for instinct authenticates, contra the same "practiced, polished speech" every candidate gives.[114]

And yet, the lies. The lies! President Trump committed mendacity at a rate that most people breathe.

He supercharged journalistic operations committed solely to fact-checking. A lie from day one—overstating the size of his inauguration crowds—set the tone for so many "alternative facts" that would snowball in years to follow. That lying metastasized, exponentially: from six falsehoods a day in 2017 to thirty-nine a day in reelection year.[115] The lies ranged from wonkish (the US previously had a half-trillion-dollar trade deficit with China) to clownish (a Sharpie-amended hurricane projection map) to corrosive (he won reelection) to catastrophic (coronavirus is "totally under control" and "disappearing").[116]

How on earth could such flagrant deceitfulness possibly square with the pretense of authenticity? In an interview, Scaramucci, his communications director, elaborates:

When you're talking about authenticity, he's got one thing that is an amazing piece of his authenticity, right? He's the most authentic liar that you could ever find because the typical politician will haze something; they'll use semantics; they'll create a turn of phrase and stuff like that. He will get to the camera, and he will deliver bald-faced lies with total aplomb and with a lack of any regard for the ethics or the integrity of that. And so that is a very effective device. Being an authentic liar is one of the most manipulative things that you can do in a civilization. . . . Trump is a pure, like, a hundred-proof pure distillation of crystal-clear lying. And, so, there's a level of authenticity to that—you know, it's on the spectrum of the macabre, it's on the spectrum of the nasty. But make no mistake, that is part of his operating skill set.[117]

For supporters, all that dishonesty and exaggeration didn't seem to trouble: "[Trump] was trustworthy not because he told the truth, but because he lived a truth," and an undercurrent of authenticity ("a deeper, personal consistency") buoyed, keeping his head above water when one big fat fib after another threatened to sink him.[118]

His mentor, Roy Cohn, apparently gleaned this tactical insight from Senator Joseph McCarthy prior to a congressional hearing: "People aren't going to remember the things we say on the issues here, our logic, our common sense, our facts. They're only going to remember the impressions."[119] Emotion always trumps fact, as does authenticity over rationality.

A deliciously phrased, oft-cited aphorism from an *Atlantic* think-piece late in the 2016 campaign offers clues here: "The press takes him literally, but not seriously; his supporters take him seriously, but not literally."[120] And that mainstream media—to Trump supporters, at least—isn't authentic anyhow, having been smeared for decades as illegitimate (due to liberal bias, cultural elitism, etc.), so who cares if a bunch of liars call your identity avatar a liar?

Over five years of campaign debates and president-press skirmishes, the signature retort to critiques was to defame the accuser for either corruption or ineptitude themselves (e.g., snapping back and talking over Clinton on the debate stage: "you're the puppet").[121] Counterattack against rivals and reporters alike, with broadsides about *their* inauthenticity—evading, distracting, and evoking shadowy conspiracies with populist rhetorical flourish.[122]

Social media also obviously aided Trump's ascent and authenticity—not least in its contrast with his 2016 opponent. While the Clinton campaign stayed, digitally, well within the norms of caution and professionalization, Trump's output was unrepentantly amateurish in aesthetic. One study, for example, found that a third of Trump tweets had markers of authenticity (e.g., exuding passion, sharing the backstage self, violating decorum, being politically incorrect, and using capital letters to "emphasize one's sincerity [and] spontaneity") compared to just 5 percent of Clinton tweets.[123]

This rough cut amateurism flew in the face of otherwise posh, official online political content, signaling an outsider, "anti-elite disposition" in its off-script sloppiness.[124] Trump's social feeds often featured pixelated photos with shoddy lighting and odd cropping; little consistency in visual branding around type-face and color; unedited videos with shaky camerawork; and at least twenty-five different font choices during the campaign season.[125]

It looked, in short, like that which your less technologically adept aunt or uncle might post to Facebook. And Trump might well have retweeted *them*—elevating ordinary, obscure Twitter users to his 88-million-follower stage, as he did more than a hundred times during his campaign season and then well onward into his presidency.[126]

One clever analysis of the texture and metadata of Trump's tweets further explains the achievement of authenticity: Typographically, the misspellings (covfefe!), scattershot punctuations, and grammatical torture communicated spontaneity and lack of emotional restraint.[127] Yet the timestamp, too, indexed instinct, for tweets sent at all hours of the night could not be possibly have been vetted (and, therefore, "inauthenticized") by his comms team, and offered proof of the *absence* of political strategy; those posts between midnight and 6 a.m. were, perhaps not coincidentally, often the most commented upon.[128] In sum, his tweets offered direct traces of "frenetic thumbs, impulsive personality, nocturnal restlessness, unrefined passion, insistence on using his personal phone, and independence from his campaign team," as disinformation scholar Tommy Shane tallies.[129]

Thus, "Twitter is the authentic Trump, the one not lawyered up and filtered down," in the apt phrasing of *Washington Post* blogger Chris Cillizza.[130] He speaks internet: the platform having "liberated our voices, training us to expect people to speak for and as themselves, with all their idiosyncrasies and imperfections," including the unfiltered and undignified (i.e., authentic)—a markedly different tone from traditional media, which presented selves as calm, poised, neutral, and impersonal (i.e., phony).[131]

"Even the typos end up working in his favor," defends Scott Adams, Dilbert creator and Trump champion, "because you know he wrote it. That makes it feel personal and you feel connected to your leader in a way that we never have before."[132] Amusingly, Trump staffers apparently peppered social media output with errors so that the content scanned as "authentic" to him.[133] And the fact that Clinton would tweet—via her campaign team, of course—*during* debates when she was still onstage, signaled that the messaging was not "really" her, literally or in terms of authenticity ideals.

The Many Selves of Hillary Clinton

If, in political and technological culture, the private backstage is where the "real self" resides, then Hillary Rodham Clinton has been dogged on that front throughout her career perhaps more than any: as first lady, US senator, secretary of state, and presidential aspirant.[134]

"I think a lot of women out there love that Hillary is kind of reserved and not always on Instagram," Adrienne Elrod, press spokeswoman for her 2016 run, defends. "She just doesn't think that she needs to have her life out there 24/7. She believes some things should remain private. And I think that's even more difficult to reconcile in today's social media-driven environment."[135] Difficult—if not impossible.

Indeed, the press corps breathlessly seized upon a moment of "human ordinariness" from Clinton in January 2008, in the aftermath of an Iowa primary loss, when she responded to an audience member's question with a "never-before-heard," voice-cracking, character-softening tone: "This is very personal for me. It's not just political; it's not just public."[136] Tears were not shed (at least based on the available video footage), but collective memory seems to have recorded it as so. And when she went on to win New Hampshire days later, emotional correlation, of course, became political causation. "Down double-digits, and she had this completely authentic, documentary moment where she kind of teared up, showed a vulnerable side and boom! She wins the [New Hampshire] election," one interviewee recalls. "That's what people want to see."[137]

Inconsistent appearances forever bedeviled Clinton, seemingly masking "her true self" in order to achieve calculating goals, as Shawn Parry-Giles, a political rhetoric scholar, argues in a book-length treatment; repeatedly, she cycled through a pattern of "authentic outspokenness and overexposure . . . followed by an inauthenticating image makeover."[138]

That double bind was established as first lady: If she played the role of ambitious political activist, haters lamented her feminist break from the stay-at-home, doting spouse mold, smiling and speechless on the ceremonial stage; however, if she dialed that back and played coy to expected form, then she was "chastised as an imposter" for the part.[139] Ultimately, Clinton got caught in an "authenticity doom loop"—incapable of evolving the self while remaining true to a core—and burned by one-makeover-too-many to overcome the framing of her true motives, political marriage, and geographic anchoring as ever-inauthentic.[140]

Unquestionably, authenticity in politics operates atop a legacy of sexism. Political communication scholars suggest that personalization redounds to the benefit of men more than women on the campaign trail.[141] The problem, in a context historically biased toward masculine values, is to project toughness without, as more than one interviewee put it, looking "bitchy."[142] That bias of the press, complains veteran Democratic consultant Bob Shrum, is "to think that what makes a man [look] strong can make a woman shrill."[143]

The irony, of course, is that technology has arguably "feminized" political culture, in all of the ways detailed in this chapter and the last: rewarding the "most emotionally available and personally authentic contender," while Clinton, in both 2008 and 2016, delivered instead a serious, knowledgeable, *impersonal* performance.[144] She came prepared, had done the homework, when instinct and spontaneity evinced authenticity; she prioritized rationality and projected sobriety when unrestrained sentiment carried the day. Clinton's big, televised addresses could seem "robotic and awkward—filled with strange pauses and painfully delivered jokes"—a rehearsed-ness which contributed to that legacy of inauthenticity.[145]

In one quintessential entry in the Hillary Makeover genre, the *New York Times* charted (yet another) authenticity reboot by the 2016 campaign: "no rope lines to wall off crowds, which added to an impression of aloofness"; "new efforts to bring spontaneity to a candidacy that sometimes seem wooden and overly cautious"; aides promising "the public would see sides of Mrs. Clinton that are often obscured"; bookings on nontraditional shows like *Ellen* and *Jimmy Fallon*; and highlighting her favorite TV shows (*The Good Wife*!) that showed up in those infamous State Department emails.[146]

In an interview, Jim Margolis, a senior media advisor, explains how they tried to navigate these frustrations within the campaign, and it's worth quoting him at length here:

> Sometimes people who are tagged as inauthentic are just not as comfortable in their interactions with people or don't publicly exude warmth. They kind of have a defective charisma gene. . . . [At one debate prep], she was getting frustrated about, you know, how we were talking about the importance of emotional connection and . . . the things that had affected her in her own

life that help to make those connections with people. And, at one point, she said, "Look, I am not my husband. I am not Barack Obama. It does not mean I don't feel at least as strongly as either one of them and the problems that we face or the things that people experience in their everyday lives, but I'm never going to be that person that they are in how I come across." . . . [*Later in the interview, he adds,*] She had deep, deep policy knowledge and was always ready to go right to the solution. So, if you're in a town hall and someone gets up and says, "Last year, I lost my job; I lost my health care. I have three kids. Now I'm standing for two hours in a community clinic line because they aren't covered. . . . What am I going to do?" Often, Hillary would—because she knows so much—go right to the solution. You know: "Let me tell you— there are things we need to do in this country and it's one, two, three, four, and this is what I intend to do as president of the United States." And what we would often encourage her to do was, yes, you want to get to that solution, but you might want to take a little bit of time at the front asking that woman the kinds of things that she's experiencing and what are the costs? How do you feel about what was just expressed? . . . [It's] the ability to carry that forward and make sure that, to a certain extent, people recognize how you as a candidate are being touched by those same experiences.[147]

The aforementioned "doom loop" analogy is apt here, another Democratic strategist concedes: With consultants and advisors whispering in Clinton's ear for decades—"talk a certain way, dress a certain way, play up the story, don't play up that story . . . I mean, God, how hard to be who you are," which, as we saw in the introductory chapter, is the first commandment of authenticity.[148]

Because one of her best assets is as a listener, claims Matt Compton, her deputy digital director, the strongest performing campaign videos would often feature imagery from those one-on-one moments "where she is, like, hearing directly from a person and then responding to it in a way that shows that she internalized the thing they were telling her." Another strategy, he adds, was to find podcast interview opportunities that offered an "intimacy to those conversations that made people hear her and think about her in a new way," not talking day-to-day campaign tactics—for those betray an inauthenticity of calculating toward power—but instead "the formative experiences of her career, the reason why she wanted to run" (i.e., that allegedly inner self, unencumbered by externally oriented motives).[149]

While most of Clinton's boring social media output lacked the unscripted, error-addled quality of Trump's—and, thus, its authenticity—she did hit one home run that seemed human when she tweeted @RealDonaldTrump, "Delete your account."[150] This was, for her, an exception that proved the rule of informality on social media.

She would not—perhaps could not—manage to do that often enough.

Let Them Eat Cheeseburgers

Whether one took Donald J. Trump literally or seriously, his campaign and presidency offered an unprecedented performance of populist authenticity. Most consequential, of all the paradoxes and contradictions and ironies that accompanied his surreal ascent (looking at you, especially, evangelical "values" voters), this was perhaps most baffling: The working class—a socioeconomic strata the most laid-off and furthest left behind by the cruel forces of globalization, technology, and inequality—somehow got seduced by a billionaire born with a silver spoon whose signature tagline is, "You're fired."

How? In his boorish, anti-PC manner of speaking, Trump voiced solidarity—stylistically, if not substantively—with those proletarian audiences who look down upon the cosmopolitan elitism of those perceived as "above" them in status.

In his love of, say, fast food—serving it on *silver platters* in White House settings, grinning on social media hunched over McDonald's or KFC on his *private plane*—Trump showed off his populist diet, a punch in the gut to those who can pronounce (much less want to eat) quinoa. As noted earlier, one of my interviewees, Anthony Scaramucci, author of the non sequitur paean, *Trump, The Blue-Collar President*, defended the president's anti-elitist credentials to a BBC reporter by citing, first and apparently foremost, his affection for cheeseburgers and pizza.[151]

At other times, Trump went beyond indulging the appetites and vulgarity of his followers and outright faked their relationship with the means of production: clambering into an eighteen-wheeler and tooting the horn like a trucker; donning a construction hardhat and flexing his biceps at a rally for coal industry deregulation.[152] Call it blue-collar cosplay, from someone who, as a child, was chauffeured along his paper route during bad weather.[153]

The central question of the Trump era, attended to by journalists and scholars alike, was what *sort* of populism animated his supporters: "economic deprivation" or "cultural anxieties"?[154] Was it, for the base, that the jobs were disappearing or the neighborhood was getting browner? What *New York Times* TV critic James Poniewozik cleverly discerns is that, like other alt-righters,

Trump viewed culture *as* politics, and probably the primary part: "More than policy, people see culture as an extension of themselves, their ancestors, and the people they love. No one dances to a budget amendment, gathers with their family to watch healthcare legislation, or wakes their excited kids on Tax Day morning."[155]

In the early 2010s, attempting to capitalize on the financial discontent of the Great Recession, the Tea Party converted that resentment into cultural terms, while Occupy Wall Street targeted the neoliberal economics that produced and exacerbated it.[156] Trump and Bernie Sanders got conflated in similar ways mid-decade—their "authenticity" felt by followers who chafed at either cosmopolitan disdain or capitalist inequity.[157]

Yet to what end was Trump's blue-collar cosplay put? The major, signature legislative accomplishment of his presidency was a tax cut overwhelmingly tilted toward corporations and the wealthy. This should not surprise. When *identity* is the definition of political authenticity, policy becomes just another fill-in-the-blanks afterthought.

Two decades ago, cultural critic Thomas Frank asked *What's the Matter with Kansas?*, a shrewd Gramscian critique of the heartland's persistent, irrational abdication of material self-interest, as Republicans fed voters a steady diet of culture-war issues (i.e., guns, gays, and God).[158] Trump updated and filtered this populist authenticity through his performance of Archie Bunker reruns: making American unashamed to be nativist again.

He stoked fear and loathing of vague sociocultural specters—a mediated performance of lifestyle politics meant to channel that sense of disenfranchisement—even as issues of pronounced wealth disparity, stagnant wages, and diminishing social mobility continued to fester. He putatively addressed the anxieties of those feeling marginalized without actually redressing the formal polices and structural patterns that gave rise to many of their concerns—redirecting pitchforks away from those with monetary capital and toward those with political and, more so, cultural capital.

Historically, populism found a base of support among blue-collar workers, but today it's just a way of winning power by posing like a trucker or a coal miner in how you talk and eat: "Class" means elitist expertise and taste (i.e., education, lifestyle) as opposed to financial status. Yet as enormous sums of money flow into political coffers, everyday citizens lack the access and influence of major donors and special interests; simultaneously, and not coincidentally, economic gains are accrued by those at the top. Trump's messaging spoke to those anxieties; it did not, however, offer a course of action to change the lived conditions.[159] It didn't need to.

"The secret to politics [is] trying to control a segment of people without those people recognizing you're trying to control [them]," one Machiavellian GOP strategist tells me.[160] As the past two chapters have shown, there is perhaps no better performance to achieve that power than authenticity—in part, because, if successful, it never seems like a performance at all.

CONCLUSION

xxxxxx

The Business of Keeping It "Real"

> The first duty in life is to be as artificial as possible. What
> the second duty is no one has as yet discovered.
>
> —OSCAR WILDE, poet and playwright

The question of authenticity might be nothing less than the question of what drives us, fundamentally, as human beings: Do desires and actions stem from inner emanation or external pressures?

In that struggle for meaning, authenticity positions itself as the language and mechanisms of self-actualization: being who we believe we're supposed to be, without interference, and expressing that without "editing," as philosopher Jean-Jacques Rousseau romanticized and as authenticity industry professionals scheme to stage or stress.[1] Hence, the clear-your-conscience conceit of *Taxicab Confessions*, spilling secrets to strangers; rock musicians' unrestrained pursuit of some artistic muse, norms and friendships be damned; and Donald Trump's plowing through the guardrails of political correctness, indulging indecorous id.

Authenticity, ideally, doesn't *try*: It's effortless, natural, uncontrived. It seems innate, but often that's because it's been cleverly *orchestrated* to seem innate.

As projects go, this makes for some of the most challenging, self-effacing forms of media work: to produce content for a client—a reality TV show, a #spon-con tableau, a presidential candidate—that appears unmediated. Throughout the litany of examples appraised here, an assumption pervades that sociologist Erving Goffman first articulated: The true self is calculating backstage.

Hence, the effort of authenticity industry labor, throughout, to *frontstage* that backstage: Alexandria Ocasio-Cortez livestreaming her Ikea furniture assembly on the floor; the metrics-juicing inclusion of children and pets by nano-influencers; and the TikTokkers of Hype House, gyrating in their bathroom-mirror selfie videos.

The development and now-ubiquity of social media afforded powerful tools for executing that ambition—although, chicken-or-egg, one could also ponder if they necessitated it. Of the countless ways of studying social media's impact on society, culture, and politics, the book has tried to illuminate one acute angle: the ascendance and amplification of authenticity as the overriding norm and virtue in our contemporary world. These chapters have catalogued the devices, the textures, the synonyms with which to convey authenticity, many building upon the foundational insights of media scholar Gunn Enli: self-disclosure, amateurism, going off-script, informality, handcrafting, and ordinariness.[2]

Yet authenticity is defined just as much by conspicuous *absence*—specifically, the absence of those key theoretical dimensions reiterated throughout: No two-faced self; no marketplace motives; no technological standardization. Authenticity yearns for autonomy from social pressures, commercial necessity, and homogenized landscapes, and the professionals interviewed here endeavor to furnish those pretenses on behalf of their clients.

Those professionals came from a pretty wide array of backgrounds: some surveyed for reality TV talent; others hatched ad campaigns for big consumer-goods corporations; still others tangled with reporters on behalf of elected leaders—not to mention a bunch of gigs and domains in between. Yet no matter who I asked, they all venerated authenticity with equal enthusiasm, albeit inflected in different ways.

For reality television, authenticity means uninhibited self-revelation; for social media, dilettante identity rather than professional pressures and perfected production practices; for musicians, chasing creativity no matter what the cost; for brands, a higher moral calling than venal profit; for influencers, autonomy in executing endorsements; and for politicians, being driven by convictions rather than donors or focus groups.

These interviewees operated under the assumption that the audiences for their work (e.g., fans, shoppers, voters, and so on) yearned for authenticity, but—to state the obvious—I didn't confirm that yearning with those targets. Strictly, and contentedly, production-side oriented, this was a study of *encoding* authenticity: the principles and practices of casting shows, designing websites, promoting bands, making ads, positioning candidates, and so on.

Still, though, it's worth pondering, in these closing pages, *why* the obsession with authenticity? What anxieties or longings did producers believe they were attempting to quell or slake?

Extending the ideas introduced in the opening chapter, the speculation here orients authenticity as nostalgically responsive; that is, the more staged, manipulated, and *un*real that mediated culture becomes, especially technologically—the more "virtual" our everyday experience, the more "post-human" lives merge with machines—the greater the hope that authenticity might quench some thirst for what's been lost, recovering what's human after all.

To be certain, claims of being surrounded by the "unreal" are both hopelessly subjective and naïvely ahistorical; mediated culture surely felt just as unreal as in 1981 when philosopher Jean Baudrillard tried to red-pill us out of the matrix simulacra as it did in 1967 when his fellow Frenchman Guy Debord warned of the stupefying spectacle of images as it did in 1896 when, myth apocryphally holds, early cinema audiences fled, panicked, at the sight of a train bearing down upon them, on-screen.[3]

Thus, this is not—again, stating the obvious—any sort of untenable claim that early twenty-first-century populations living in advanced techno-capitalist societies experience reality as any less "real" than their predecessors. It *has* been a 100,000-word argument that a set of authenticity industries are more committed than ever to selling them the pretense of clients as real against that backdrop of enduring, alienating anxiety.

Equally true, and relevant here, is the fact that we *are* spending more time than ever with, on, and through our screens. (Also equally true, if I may hazard a bet, is that a decade or two from now, today's screen-time numbers will pale in comparison to our future immersion.) With ever greater hours left to our own digital devices comes the disquieting suspicion of inauthentic communication coursing through them—from friends and famous alike. Hence, authenticity's nostalgic pull surges to the forefront *most* when times feel like they're rapidly changing.

Thanks to social networking sites, audiences consume (and co-produce) more media content made by amateurs as opposed to professionals than ever before. This renders palpably explicit, via digital entrails, what Goffman long ago diagnosed as more interpersonally ephemeral: the performance of the self as a construction and projection.

Certainly, it's always been a construction and projection, but it hasn't always been so *traceable* as such—as Instagram and TikTok accounts now make abundantly clear. If *our* selves sometimes feel phony on those stages, aren't we just as dubious of *others'* selves as performed there, too? Hence, the content imperative for more and more backstaged lives, as though this could repudiate the reality of calculated performance (and isn't just another meta-level calculation of performance itself).

The erosion of once-private selves into public spaces well predates Friendster and MySpace, but this, nonetheless, remains what social media does best, architecturally speaking. Mundane details and vulnerable revelations conveyed there authenticate the user. Reality TV long pursued this same self-disclosure, but social media carried the ambition forward in spirit and design to anyone who wanted to sign up.

To construct a self that appears uncontrived often involves downplaying or naturalizing the media production apparatus, ideally, to the point of invisibility: reality's omniscient 24/7 taping such that cameras become forgettable "wallpaper"; the live- and acoustic-bias of rock music sound recording; and political consultants' lurking for the *cinema verité* B-roll of candidates for ads. Coaxing that "realness" out of clients—be they pop artists, commercial brands, or campaigning politicians—is the foremost task of media professionals within the authenticity industries and, paradoxically, it means making it look like no labor of staging has been done at all.

Because social media is purportedly of "the people"—that is, amateurs, historically, mostly animating it—it offers vectors of authenticity, seeming less instrumentally inclined toward power or money as might motivate celebrities, politicians, and corporations (excepting, of course, the billion-dollar social media corporations themselves). It's easier, therefore, to pose populistically within those spaces; to astroturf that which appears grassroots. Even celebrity itself has been democratically fragmented thanks to the proliferation of social media, reorienting the logic and work of the authenticity industries both within and without entertainment confines.

Aesthetically, this might not have birthed the rough cut ideal—mediated culture has been slouching toward informality for some time now in public appearance and speech—but it placed ever more of a premium on imperfection.

We saw this in the sloppy slapstick of YouTube's Emma Chamberlain; the anti-glam ascendance of TikTok; Dove pledging "real" beauty on behalf of models who didn't look emaciated; and George W. Bush's handlers leaving in a flubbed line-read for his RNC biofilm. We saw this, peak-pandemic, in the work-from-home, Zoom-screen arrangements that spilled backstage backgrounds into public (or at least professional) purview.

Aesthetically, too, authenticity has been meant to counter the stultifying sameness that machines, historically, tended to generate—those landscapes of life, work, and play drained of the unique, the handcrafted, the local. To the machines, any such nuance of "imperfection" is irrational inefficiency; to the human, it signals something recalcitrantly natural in a silicon-cage world. Hence, Starbucks' indie coffee shop imitations and affectations; craft beer's foregrounding of artisanal production methods; and, even more metaphorically, corporations and politicians embedding their persuasive message in non-standardized crowdsources (which is to say, "influencers").

Yet it's not just the tentacles of technology infiltrating and imprinting themselves on any and all human spaces that authenticity positions itself to buffer against and contrast; it is also, equally, arm-wrestling the marketplace. In this, authenticity seeks to resolve the tensions of capitalism between commerce and culture, allaying anxieties about the financial motivations of (hit-chasing) musicians, (revenue-maximizing) corporations, (partnership-pursuing) influencers, and (donation-seeking) politicians alike.

On one hand, the decades-old dread about "selling out" sounds dated, maybe even irrelevant in this landscape—the vestige of a Gen X gripe that's aged about as well as '90s fashion. It asks us to imagine interactions and experiences external to commercialism—a "purity" that maybe has been snuffed out by ideological forces of varying coordination.

Influencer culture, particularly as brands have conscripted smaller and smaller nodes of human popularity, represents peak weirdness that we take for granted at our social peril. When friends see our spaces for sharing as inventory for shilling, it can't help but raise the question of what friendship is for in the first place.

Yet even that mild provocation invites an "okay, Boomer" eyeroll—toward this elder millennial, no less—as interviewees regularly ruminated on their perception of a Gen Z acceptance of rampant commercialism (a perception that, perhaps, gives them moral license to rampantly commercialize). As music industry professionals testify, reluctance to "sell out" is something of a luxury—one stripped down by practicality when a revenue model implodes. It is revealing that hip-hop, an art form and subculture born of material deprivation and racial oppression, was the genre of pop culture that most destigmatized making "money moves," as Cardi B alliterated. In the decades that followed an alleged "end of history"—the era under study here—neoliberal capitalism proved victorious in extending market logic into any and all cultural sensibilities it could find.

On the other hand, if selling out is no big deal, why the frequent need to elide or offset commercial appearance in these authenticity practices, presentations, and performances? Why would marketplace motives still be a specter that interviewees needed to scheme against? Why couldn't neoliberal capitalism simply spike the football and celebrate its own success?

Quite the opposite, it seems: The more that ads show up in contexts they hadn't before—social media feeds, activist stances, your network of contacts— the more the ads must contort themselves, guerrilla marketing–style, toward blending in with whatever the native (i.e., uncommercialized) vessel existed for in the first place.[4]

Because brands have colonized so much, of course they would aim for our art, our friendships, and our politics. Anywhere that hasn't already been instrumentalized for a sale is the most authentic place to seed an ad message. Anywhere that has been used is useless. Just ask those macro-influencers who "corrupted" their credibility with followers by cutting one too many deals.

Moreover, few of these authenticity industries' efforts at persuasion are inclined toward rational petition. Rather—following Rousseau, who felt that *feelings* were real and could be excavated only external to civilization's dulling deliberative ways—social media platforms, brand advertising, and political campaigns target and leverage our emotions first and foremost.

Thinking calculates and calculation is inauthentic. The *utility* of a choice— what features a product can offer, what policies a candidate will implement— matters less than what that choice *symbolizes* about ourselves in making it. Identity therefore trades in authenticity, which makes it uniquely well-suited for this era. Conservative media provocateur Andrew Breitbart's alleged mantra—"politics is downstream of culture"—rightly, if cynically, captures the primacy of identity in forging ideological battles.

Some of the work of the authenticity industries explored here is about furnishing content that helps with the discovery of that identity, drafting off the power of relatability as a contemporary virtue. This enables audiences to see themselves in reality show characters; in musical artistry and lyrics that reflect die-hard followers; in political statements issued by commercial brands; and in shared lifestyles and fandoms with electoral leaders.

The ongoing decline of trust in traditional institutions and the rejection of their authority and expertise—much of which might have furnished that identity in the past but has withered in credibility—contributes to the vacuum that authenticity seeks to fill. This also tenders fertile soil, culturally, for conspiracies to take root—because irrational dot-connecting "feels right" in the absence of metanarratives that might have explained otherwise. QAnon might be crazy, but it offers authentic answers if *identity*—rather than factual demonstrability—is the question posed: Who are you? Who are they?

This market for identity also explains the steady supply of genealogical authenticity my interviewees sought to stage. Geography authenticates, ideally, and ancestry even more so, particularly when these professionals, again, believe audiences need to see themselves reflected in some mediated form—a reality TV setting, a trademarked logo, a political aspirant.

Humble roots are authentic, especially if you can show (or fake) that a client has stayed true to them: Observe Hewlett-Packard's ramshackle garage birthplace; the Wisconsin-shaped tattoo on the breastplate of Bon Iver's Justin Vernon; Chili's hippie-slacker biker friends founding the chain in a little roadside shack; and George W. Bush's brush-clearing on his "native" Texas ranch.

According to this misguided thinking, squalor authenticates: Those of lower socioeconomic origins have more authenticity because they surely haven't been as complicit with and corrupted by marketplace motives over the years. This, too, reaffirms authenticity's antimodern biases, whether they be agrarian simplicity or proletarian credibility, where disadvantage is prestige; blight is hip; and graffiti marks out what'll make a cute brunch spot one day.

Gentrification plays out this inversion in urban development form, but those colonized edge-worlds are just the spatial manifestation of a trend-spotting process across multiple dimensions of marginalization. The "street," historically in hip-hop, ideally originates: the authentic space you don't sell out from, even within a genre totally cool with getting paid for art.

And, ultimately, my interviewees were the ones getting paid for all this scheming. Theirs is a business of keeping it real and it is a *booming* business.

The book has been a study of how authenticity is engineered—the thinking that informs the strategies that inform the content produced in reality TV, social media, pop music, commercial advertising, and electoral politics. It has been intended as a panoramic tour—pulling back the curtain on the ways that the curtain is being pulled back for audiences to see how backstage contexts and selves are increasingly foregrounded for public view. And because, one last time, authenticity is a project of creating something that seems *unmediated*, there's no shortage of irony in examining that mediation process.

In the end, authenticity is presumed powerful—if not, why else would all this money and effort be expended in trying to achieve it? It's also a moving target, as seen from reality TV's restless search for auditionees who don't perform impressions of previous participants to marketing's restless search for influencers who don't give off an already-commercialized vibe. Thus, these professionals' clients that seem authentic today—and, more so, their tactics and contexts of making them seem that way—will probably not last much beyond publication of this book, even as business remains booming.

The authenticity industries are real enough. Their product isn't always.

Acknowledgments

The older I get, the more I find that humility-plus-gratitude has become a mantra equation of instinctive incantation: the only plausible response to a series of "if not for" counterfactuals that remind of the fragility of fate. Which makes a space like this impossibly insufficient. But, hey, here goes my best shot.

First off, to the many brilliant scholars, reporters, and writers long trail-blazing this space whose names line the hundreds of endnotes at the back of the book: Sarah Banet-Weiser and Gunn Enli, chiefly, but also, alphabetically speaking, Hugh Barker, Michael Beverland, David Boyle, David Craig, Stuart Cunningham, Brooke Duffy, Delia Dumitrica, Mara Einstein, Thomas Frank, Erving Goffman, David Grazian, Laura Grindstaff, Charles Guignon, David Hesmondhalgh, Douglas Holt, Mathew Humphrey, Emily Hund, Bethany Klein, Daniel Kreiss, Charles Lindholm, Taylor Lorenz, Farhad Manjoo, Alice Marwick, Vicki Mayer, Leslie Meier, Jack Neff, Richard Peterson, Jefferson Pooley, Andrew Potter, Devon Powers, Jean-Jacques Rousseau, Erica Seifert, Charles Taylor, Yuval Taylor, Sarah Thornton, Lionel Trilling, Graeme Turner, Maiken Umbach, and Jason Zengerle.

Some of y'all I know well already; others only distantly by the page; all I hope to buy a drink of thanks someday for the inspiration of precedence. (This, I understand, will be somewhat difficult with Rousseau.) And several rounds more are due to the anonymous reviewers of this manuscript; please know how appreciative I am of your time, wisdom, and feedback.

Much as the book could not have been conceptualized without the afore-mentioned bibliographic sources, so, too, could it not have been reported out without the dozens of interviewee sources, listed in the appendix, generously carving time from busy schedules to offer their professional insights and expe-riences. I remain forever sheepish about what people think about what I write of them (one of the reasons I exited daily journalism), but I hope this captures your hard work as accurately and objectively as possible.

Alas, cited scholars and interviewee quotes make for but a Word file on my laptop; for this to have landed in readers' hands, I have effusive gratitude to Stanford University Press to ladle out. Thanks especially to Erica Wetter for her immediate interest and devoted oversight of the project and also to Kate Wahl, Caroline McKusick, Paul Tyler, and other SUP staff who assisted—you've all been so generous, helpful, and attentive in bringing this to publication life.

If not for my teachers and mentors over the years, and the institutions that afforded space to learn and grow, there's no way I'd be capable of writing books in the first place: Catalina Foothills High School, University of San Francisco, Sophia University, Columbia University, the *Houston Press*, the University of Pennsylvania's Annenberg School for Communication, and Fairfield Univer-sity; and Barbie Zelizer, Katherine Sender, Joseph Turow, Joseph Jones, Amy Schuff, Bryan Whaley, Bernadette Barker-Plummer, Michael Robertson, Rick Roberts, Thierry Robouam, S.J., Stephen Isaacs, Margaret Downing, and David Gudelunas, among many others—you remain in my head and my heart.

Somehow, too, I hit the jackpot, career-wise, and landed the good fortune of a gig at a place whose mission I believe in deeply, to the marrow of my bones: Boston College. Thanks to everyone there for making the Heights an inspiring and joyful place to clock in every day—from dedicated leadership (including President William Leahy, S.J., Dean Gregory Kalscheur, S.J., and Chair Matt Sienkiewicz) to warm-hearted department colleagues to the energetic under-graduates who enliven our classroom conversations together. If they bury me in my office one day, it will mean I led a very lucky professional life.

And, finally, there are those who I love the most: Lucy, Jules, Mom, Dad, friends, fam. If not for you, nothing means anything, because y'all are my ev-erything. You bring meaning to my world till my heart overflows: Home is wherever I'm with you.

The ultimate "if not for" counterfactual is, finally, reserved for the grace of God. I did nothing to deserve it; owe more than can ever be repaid because of it; and remain, till the end, most grateful for it. I pray that it continues to shine—on your lives as mine.

Appendix
Interview Details

KEVIN ALLOCCA
Head of culture & trends—YouTube
18 September 2020; 55 minutes

PIERRE-LOIC ASSAYAG and
EVY WILKINS
CEO and VP marketing—Traackr
26 September 2019; 58 minutes

DAVID BASON
A & R manager and label executive—The
Strokes, etc.
1 May 2020; 63 minutes

PANKAJ BHALLA
VP of shave care—Procter & Gamble
1 July 2020; 49 minutes

LESLEY BIELBY
Chief strategy officer—Hill Holiday
7 January 2020; 59 minutes

ERIKA BRYANT
Producer and showrunner—*Real
Housewives of Atlanta, Extreme
Makeover*, etc.
20 October 2020; 41 minutes

JEFF CASTELAZ
Former president and artist
management—Elektra Records and
Dropkick Murphys, etc.
5 May 20; 46 minutes

YAEL CESARKAS
Executive strategy director—R/GA
21 February 2020; 48 minutes

MEREDITH CHASE
Chief strategy officer—Swift
20 December 2019; 47 minutes

MARGARET COLES
Associate partner for research data &
analytics—Goodby Silverstein &
Partners
11 November 2019; 47 minutes

MATT COMPTON
Deputy digital director—Clinton 2016
29 July 2019; 63 minutes

SHEILA CONLIN
Casting, development, and producer—
Nanny 911, Hell's Kitchen, etc.
14 September 2020; 52 minutes

211

JAMES CRUZ
President of artist management and head
of creative enterprises—Combs
Enterprises
8 June 2020; 39 minutes

CHRIS CUMMINGS
Chief strategy officer—BSSP
9 January 2020; 53 minutes

COLIN DELANY
Editor and consultant—Epolitics.com
23 July 2019; 65 minutes

DANNY DIAZ
Campaign manager—Bush 2016
13 December 2019; 31 minutes

BRITTANY DICAPUA
Social media influencer (food)
24 September 2020; 35 minutes

KELLY DIETRICH
Founder—National Democratic Training
Committee
24 July 2019; 39 minutes

ICARO DORIA
Chief creative officer—Arnold
10 December 2019; 51 minutes

MIKE DUHAIME
Campaign manager—Giuliani 2008
21 December 2020; 44 minutes

ADRIENNE ELROD
Press spokeswoman—Clinton 2016
4 October 2019; 27 minutes

KYLE FRENETTE [joint interview with
Josh Sundquist]
Management team—Bon Iver
29 April 20; 48 minutes

HARRY GANTZ
Creator and producer—*Taxicab
Confessions*
15 May 20; 56 minutes

DANIELLE GERVAIS
Casting director—*Queer Eye, Pawn
Stars, Housewives of New Jersey,* etc.
8 October 2020; 46 minutes

STANLEY HAINSWORTH
Former VP global creative—Starbucks
28 February 2020; 54 minutes

MARTIN HAMBURGER
President—Hamburger Gibson Creative
advertising agency
7 August 2019; 40 minutes

LINDSAY HOLST
Director of digital strategy—Vice
President Biden
6 September 2019; 64 minutes

BRIAN JONES
Communication director and strategist—
McCain 2008 and Christie 2016
25 October 2019; 45 minutes

MAE KARWOWSKI
Founder and CEO—Obviously
23 October 2019; 54 minutes

LUCAS KELLER
President—Milk & Honey Management
7 June 2020; 48 minutes

TIM KENDALL
Director of monetization—Facebook
20 January 2020; 36 minutes

JON LANDAU
Manager—Bruce Springsteen
2 June 2020; Email exchange

JACOB LANE
Co-executive producer and editor—
Bunim-Murray (*Real World*,
Kardashians, etc.)
8 September 2020; 46 minutes

JOYCE LINEHAN
A & R director—Sub Pop
29 July 2020; 54 minutes

STU LOESER
Press secretary—Mayor Bloomberg
7 August 2019; 53 minutes

JASON LONSDALE
Head of brand strategy and planning—
Ogilvy
11 September 2019; 55 minutes

WALTER LUDWIG
Managing partner and senior creative—
Indigo Strategies
16 September 2019; 55 minutes

LIZ MAIR
Online communications director—RNC
2008
16 December 2019; 68 minutes

JIM MARGOLIS
Senior media advisor—Clinton 2016 and
Obama 2008, 2012
6 March 2020; 28 minutes

CHELSEA MARRS
Social media influencer (travel, fashion)
16 October 2020; 38 minutes

LADD MARTIN
Head of home print marketing—HP
2 December 2019; 43 minutes

SHANNON MCCARTY
Casting director—*Real World*, *Biggest
Loser*, *Apprentice*, *Circle*, etc.
3 August 2020; 60 minutes

MARK MCKINNON
Chief media advisor—Bush 2000
and 2004
8 August 2019; 43 minutes

PETER MENSCH
Manager—AC/DC, Red Hot Chili
Peppers, Metallica, etc.
18 June 2020; 48 minutes

MIKE MURPHY
Senior advisor—McCain 2000 and
Bush 2016
29 July 2020; 26 minutes

DORON OFIR
Casting director—*Jersey Shore*, *Drag
Race*, *Amazing Race*, etc.
6 August 2020; 64 minutes

JULIE PIZZI
President of entertainment and
development—Bunim-Murray (*Real
World*, *Kardashians*, etc.)
24 August 2020; 37 minutes

KRISTIN QUINN
Social media influencer (parenting)
24 February 2020; 35 minutes

ANSELMO RAMOS
Co-founder and chief creative officer—
Gut
10 September 2020; Email exchange

ADAM REIDER
Producer and development consultant—
Survivor, etc.
10 September 2020; 48 minutes

CATHERINE REYNOLDS
Senior vice president and partner—
FleishmanHilard TRUE Global
Intelligence
21 August 2020; 43 minutes

JANET BILLIG RICH
A & R manager and label executive—
Nirvana, Smashing Pumpkins, Jewel, etc.
30 May 2020; 49 minutes

BAILEY RICHARDSON
Community curator—Instagram
12 November 2020; 59 minutes

STEVE RIFKIND
Founder and CEO—Loud Records (Wu
Tang Clan, etc.)
19 May 2020; 26 minutes

MATT RINGEL
Managing partner—New Era Media and
Marketing
29 May 2020; 43 minutes

CHUCK ROCHA
Senior advisor—Sanders 2020
24 July 2019; 44 minutes

ALEX ROETTER
Senior vice president of engineering—
Twitter
30 November 2020; 48 minutes

LISA SANTANGELO
Social media influencer (family, food,
travel)
16 October 2020; 27 minutes

JOAH SANTOS
Chief human-centric strategist—Nylon
(also Dove Real Beauty)
14 February 2020; 47 minutes

ANTHONY SCARAMUCCI
Communication director—President
Trump
1 April 2020; 24 minutes

RYAN SCHRAM
COO—Izea
23 September 2019; 55 minutes

ROB SHEPARDSON
Senior paid media advisor—Obama
2008, 2012
20 August 2019; 40 minutes

BOB SHRUM
Senior advisor—Gore 2000 and Kerry
2004
13 August 2019; 30 minutes

RICH SILVERSTEIN
Co-chair and creative director—Goodby
Silverstein & Partners
4 November 2019; 47 minutes

MARK SKIDMORE
Founding partner and former chief
strategist—Bully Pulpit Interactive
25 July 2019; 62 minutes

SEAN SPICER
Press secretary—President Trump
25 November 2020; 22 minutes

JASMINE STAR
Social media business strategist
28 February 2020; 42 minutes

STUART STEVENS
Senior strategist and media advisor—
Bush 2004 and Romney 2012
29 January 2020; 39 minutes

KRISHNA SUBRAMANIAN
Co-founder—Capitv8
25 September 2019; 35 minutes

JOSH SUNDQUIST [joint interview with
Kyle Frenette]
Management team—Bon Iver
29 April 20; 48 minutes

HUDSON SULLIVAN
Brand partnership director—TikTok
22 October 2020; 67 minutes

TERRY SULLIVAN
Campaign manager—Rubio 2016
30 July 2019; 52 minutes

JOE TRIPPI
Campaign manager—Dean 2004
29 January 2020; 53 minutes

CRAIG VAROGA
President and founder—Varoga and
Associates
28 August 2019; 54 minutes

BARRY WACKSMAN
Global chief strategy officer—RG/A
17 January 2020; 41 minutes

BOB WICKERS
Media advisor—Huckabee 2008 and
Romney 2012
3 October 2019; 44 minutes

SAM YAGAN
Co-founder—OkCupid
25 November 2020; 42 minutes

LENA YOUNG
Director of communications—Klear
28 October 2019; 48 minutes

Notes

Introduction: Our Enduring Quest for Authenticity

1. David Boyle, *Authenticity* (London: Harper Perennial, 2004), 56.

2. Guy Debord, *The Society of the Spectacle* (New York: Zone Books, 1967).

3. Daniel J. Boorstin, *The Image* (New York: Vintage, 1961).

4. John Cloud, "Synthetic Authenticity," *Time*, March 13, 2008, http://content.time
.com/time/specials/2007/article/0,28804,1720049_1720050_1722070,00.html.

5. Scott Nover, "The Circle's Joey Sasso Preaches the Gospel of Being Real Online,"
Adweek, 2020, https://www.adweek.com/convergent-tv/qa-the-circles-joey-sasso
-preaches-the-gospel-of-being-real-online/.

6. Scott Cacciola, "LeBron James Is [Three Fire Emoji] Online," *New York Times*,
December 17, 2019, https://www.nytimes.com/2019/12/17/sports/basketball/lebron
-james-instagram-emojis.html.

7. Lisa Granatstein, "Why JLo's Star Won't Stop Rising," *Adweek*, September 19,
2021, https://www.adweek.com/brand-marketing/why-jlos-star-wont-stop-rising/.

8. Erin Vanderhoof, "How the Royal Family Is Stepping Up Its Social Media during
Quarantine," *Vanity Fair*, May 5, 2020, https://www.vanityfair.com/style/2020/05/royal
-family-social-media-during-quarantine.

9. Sarah Todd, "Quartzy: The Aspirational Realness Edition," *Quartz*, November 15,
2019, https://qz.com/emails/quartzy/1749080/.

10. Trey Williams, "Vice Media CEO Nancy Dubuc Lays Out New Executive Team
as Refinery29 Deal Closes," *The Wrap*, November 4, 2019, https://www.thewrap.com/
vice-media-ceo-nancy-dubuc-lays-out-new-executive-team-as-refinery29-deal-closes
/; Jeremy Barr, "The New CNN Is More Opinionated and Emotional: Can It Still Be 'The
Most Trusted Name in News'?," *Washington Post*, May 12, 2021, https://www.washing

217

tonpost.com/lifestyle/media/cnn-opinionated-emotional-zucker/2021/05/11/5f32eb38
-7f92-11eb-81db-b02f0398f49a_story.html.

11. Garrett Sloane, "Tacos for $187,336 and Digital Basketballs for $69,000 . . . the
Crypto-Bubble Comes to Marketing," *Advertising Age*, March 16, 2021, https://adage.
com/article/media/tacos-187336-and-digital-basketballs-69000-crypto-bubble-comes
-marketing/2321851; Taylor Lorenz, "Are Disposables the Future of Photo Sharing?,"
New York Times, February 25, 2021, https://www.nytimes.com/2021/02/25/style/dispo
-david-dobrik-disposable-camera-app.html.

12. Kimeko McCoy, "Surging Photo-Sharing App BeReal Has Brands like Chipotle,
e.l.f. Cosmetics Rushing to Understand Platform's Appeal with Gen Z," *Digiday*, October 5, 2022, https://digiday.com/marketing/surging-photo-sharing-app-bereal-has--
brands-like-chipotle-e-l-f-cosmetics-rushing-to-understand-platforms-appeal-with
-gen-z/.

13. David W. Lehman et al., "Authenticity," *Academy of Management Annals* 13, no.
1 (2019): 1; Joshua Benton, "An Incomplete History of Forbes.Com as a Platform for
Scams, Grift, and Bad Journalism," *NiemanLab*, February 9, 2022, https://www.nieman
lab.org/2022/02/an-incomplete-history-of-forbes-com-as-a-platform-for-scams-grift
-and-bad-journalism/.

14. Andrew Brodsky, "Communicating Authentically in a Virtual World," *Harvard
Business Review*, January 20, 2022, https://hbr.org/2022/01/communicating-authenti
cally-in-a-virtual-world.

15. Pope Benedict, "Truth, Proclamation and Authenticity of Life in the Digital
Age," June 5, 2011, https://www.vatican.va/content/benedict-xvi/en/messages/communi
cations/documents/hf_ben-xvi_mes_20110124_45th-world-communications-day.
html.

16. Eliza Berman, "A Comprehensive Guide to the *Ghost in the Shell* Controversy,"
Time, March 29, 2017, https://time.com/4714367/ghost-in-the-shell-controversy-scarlett
-johanson/; Oberlin College and Conservatory, "Colleges Are Losing Control of Their
Story: The Banh-Mi Affair at Oberlin Shows How," November 13, 2019, https://www
.oberlin.edu/news/colleges-are-losing-control-their-story-banh-mi-affair-oberlin
-shows-how; Daniel Hernandez, "'American Dirt' Was Supposed to Be a Publishing
Triumph: What Went Wrong?," *Los Angeles Times*, January 26, 2020, https://www.la
times.com/entertainment-arts/story/2020-01-26/american-dirt-publishing-latino-rep
resentation.

17. Sarah C. Haan, "Bad Actors: Authenticity, Inauthenticity, Speech, and Capitalism," 22 *University of Pennsylvania Journal of Constitutional Law* 619 (2020): 621.

18. Priyanjana Bengani, "As Election Looms, a Network of Mysterious 'Pink Slime'
Local News Outlets Nearly Triples in Size," *Columbia Journalism Review*, August 4,
2020, https://www.cjr.org/analysis/as-election-looms-a-network-of-mysterious-pink
-slime-local-news-outlets-nearly-triples-in-size.php.

19. Jay Owens, "The Age of Post-Authenticity and the Ironic Truths of Meme Culture," *Medium*, April 11, 2018, https://medium.com/s/story/post-authenticity-and-the
-real-truths-of-meme-culture-f98b24d645a0.

20. AI Foundation, "Reality Defender 2020, Concerted Effort by the AI Foundation Nonprofit, Kicks Off to Protect US Elections from Deep Fakes and Media Manipulation," *Business Wire*, November 5, 2019, https://www.businesswire.com/news/home/20 191105005834/en/Reality-Defender-2020-Concerted-Effort-AI-Foundation.

21. Gunn Enli, "'Trust Me, I Am Authentic!'," in *The Routledge Companion to Social Media and Politics*, ed. Axel Bruns et al. (New York: Routledge, 2016), 122.

22. Silverstein. [Note: Last names without page references refer to interviews; see appendix.]

23. Alexander Stern, "Authenticity Is a Sham," *Aeon*, April 27, 2021, https://aeon.co/ essays/a-history-of-authenticity-from-jesus-to-self-help-and-beyond?utm_source= pocket-newtab.

24. Lionel Trilling, *Sincerity and Authenticity* (Cambridge, MA: Harvard University Press, 1971), 93.

25. Theo Van Leeuwen, "What Is Authenticity?," *Discourse Studies* 3, no. 4 (2001): 392, 393; Kent Grayson and Radan Martinec, "Consumer Perceptions of Iconicity and Indexicality and Their Influence on Assessments of Authentic Market Offerings," *Journal of Consumer Research* 31, no. 2 (2004): 298.

26. George E. Newman and Rosanna K. Smith, "Kinds of Authenticity," *Philosophy Compass* 11, no. 10 (2016): 611; Michael Beverland, *Building Brand Authenticity* (New York: Palgrave Macmillan, 2009), 27.

27. Maiken Umbach and Mathew Humphrey, *Authenticity* (Cham, Switz.: Palgrave Macmillan, 2018), 2.

28. Annette Hill, "Reality TV," in *A Companion to Television*, ed. Janet Wasko (Malden, MA: Blackwell, 2005), 462.

29. Trilling, *Sincerity and Authenticity*, 2; Meredith Salisbury and Jefferson Pooley, "The #nofilter Self," *Social Sciences* 6, no. 10 (2017): 6.

30. Alice Audrezet, Gwarlann de Kerviler, and Julie Guidry Moulard, "Authenticity under Threat," *Journal of Business Research*, 2018, 3; Clayton Fordahl, "Authenticity," *American Sociologist* 49, no. 2 (2018): 301.

31. Charles Guignon, *On Being Authentic* (London: Routledge, 2004), 81–82.

32. Rebecca J. Erickson, "The Importance of Authenticity for Self and Society," *Symbolic Interaction* 18, no. 2 (1995): 132; Newman and Smith, "Kinds of Authenticity," 613.

33. Newman and Smith, "Kinds of Authenticity," 609; Paul Frosh, "To Thine Own Self Be True," *Communication Review* 4 (2001): 542.

34. Umbach and Humphrey, *Authenticity*, 95, 124.

35. Andrew Potter, *The Authenticity Hoax* (Toronto: McClelland & Stewart, 2010), 133.

36. Salisbury and Pooley, "The #nofilter Self," 2, 3; Michael Pickering, "The Dogma of Authenticity in the Experience of Popular Music," in *The Art of Listening*, ed. Graham McGregor and R. S. White (London: Croom Helm, 1986), 213.

37. Jenny L. Davis, "Accomplishing Authenticity in a Labor-Exposing Space," *Computers in Human Behavior* 28, no. 5 (2012): 2.

38. Guignon, *On Being Authentic*, 18, 19.

39. Charles Taylor, *The Ethics of Authenticity* (Cambridge, MA: Harvard University Press, 1991), 25.

40. Taylor, *The Ethics of Authenticity*, 2, 26; Trilling, *Sincerity and Authenticity*, 24.

41. Russell Belk, "Brands and the Self," in *The Routledge Companion to Contemporary Brand Management*, ed. Francesca Dall'Olmo, Jaywant Singh, and Charles Blankson (New York: Routledge, 2016), 70; Trilling, *Sincerity and Authenticity*, 24–25.

42. Philip Lewin and J. Patrick Williams, "The Ideology and Practice of Authenticity in Punk Subculture," in *Authenticity in Culture, Self, and Society*, ed. Phillip Vannini and J. Patrick Williams (Burlington, VT: Ashgate, 2009), 66; Lehman et al., "Authenticity," 7; Taylor, *The Ethics of Authenticity*, 46.

43. Guignon, *On Being Authentic*, 59.

44. Fordahl, "Authenticity," 302; Charles Lindholm, *Culture and Authenticity* (Malden, MA: Blackwell, 2008), 8.

45. Taylor, *The Ethics of Authenticity*, 27; Guignon, *On Being Authentic*, 151.

46. Owens, "The Age of Post-Authenticity."

47. Potter, *The Authenticity Hoax*, 72.

48. Robert Wokler, *Rousseau* (Oxford: Oxford University Press, 2001), 23–24, 26.

49. Guignon, *On Being Authentic*, 56.

50. Trilling, *Sincerity and Authenticity*, 62.

51. Salisbury and Pooley, "The #nofilter Self," 5.

52. Hanno Hardt, "Authenticity, Communication, and Critical Theory," *Critical Studies in Mass Communication* 10 (March 1993): 52.

53. Erickson, "The Importance of Authenticity," 121, 122; Guignon, *On Being Authentic*, 51.

54. Fordahl, "Authenticity," 304.

55. Wokler, *Rousseau*, 64.

56. Wokler, *Rousseau*, 47, 64.

57. Lindholm, *Culture and Authenticity*, 3.

58. Martin Montgomery, "The Uses of Authenticity," *Communication Review* 4, no. 4 (2009): 460.

59. Guignon, *On Being Authentic*, 34.

60. Trilling, *Sincerity and Authenticity*, 66.

61. Stern, "Authenticity Is a Sham."

62. Erving Goffman, *The Presentation of Self in Everyday Life* (New York: Anchor, 1959), 15, 16, 107.

63. Goffman, *The Presentation of Self*, 112; David Grazian, "Demystifying Authenticity in the Sociology of Culture," in *Handbook of Cultural Sociology*, ed. John R. Hall, Laura Grindstaff, and Ming-Cheng Lo (New York: Routledge, 2010), 194.

64. Goffman, *The Presentation of Self*, 133.

65. Goffman, *The Presentation of Self*, 132; Allan Louden and Kirsten McCauliff, "The 'Authentic Candidate,'" in *Presidential Candidate Images*, ed. Kenneth Hacker (Oxford: Rowman & Littlefield, 2004), 93.

66. Michael Hughes, "Country Music as Impression Management," *Poetics* 28, no. 2/3 (2000): 185, 187.

67. Davis, "Accomplishing Authenticity in a Labor-Exposing Space," 7.

68. Mariah L. Wellman et al., "Ethics of Authenticity," *Journal of Media Ethics: Exploring Questions of Media Morality* 35, no. 2 (2020): 71.

69. Gilad Edelman, "Authenticity Just Means Faking It Well," *The Atlantic*, April 25, 2019, https://www.theatlantic.com/ideas/archive/2019/04/what-makes-candidate-authentic/587857/.

70. Guignon, *On Being Authentic*, 74, 75.

71. Kembrew McLeod, "Authenticity within Hip-Hop and Other Cultures Threatened with Assimilation," *Journal of Communication* 49, no. 4 (1999): 140.

72. James H. Gilmore and B. Joseph Pine, *Authenticity: What Consumers Really Want* (Boston: Harvard Business School Press, 2007), ix.

73. Hardt, "Authenticity, Communication, and Critical Theory," 54.

74. Potter, *The Authenticity Hoax*, 45; Trilling, *Sincerity and Authenticity*, 123; E. Doyle McCarthy, "Emotional Performances as Dramas of Authenticity," in *Authenticity in Culture, Self, and Society*, ed. Phillip Vannini and J. Patrick Williams (Burlington, VT: Ashgate, 2009), 243.

75. Guignon, *On Being Authentic*, 2; Lindholm, *Culture and Authenticity*, 6.

76. John Durham Peters, "The Subtlety of Horkheimer and Adorno,'" in *Canonic Texts in Media Research*, ed. Elihu Katz et al. (Cambridge: Polity, 2003), 63.

77. Gunn Enli, *Mediated Authenticity* (New York: Peter Lang, 2014), 7.

78. Jefferson Pooley, "The Consuming Self: From Flappers to Facebook," in *Blowing Up the Brand*, ed. Melissa Aronczyk and Devon Powers (New York: Peter Lang, 2010), 74.

79. Lindholm, *Culture and Authenticity*, 53.

80. Joseph Heath and Andrew Potter, *Nation of Rebels* (New York: HarperBusiness, 2004), 128.

81. Robert Goldman and Stephen Papson, *Sign Wars* (New York: Guilford Press, 1996), 142; Jacqueline Botterill, "Cowboys, Outlaws and Artists," *Journal of Consumer Culture* 7, no. 1 (2007): 109.

82. Bethany Klein, *Selling Out* (New York: Bloomsbury, 2020), 62.

83. Sarah Banet-Weiser, *Authentic* (New York: NYU Press, 2012), 118.

84. Brooke Erin Duffy, *(Not) Getting Paid to Do What You Love* (New Haven, CT: Yale University Press, 2017), 7.

85. Banet-Weiser, *Authentic*, 99; Potter, *The Authenticity Hoax*, 114.

86. Frosh, "To Thine Own Self Be True," 542; Trilling, *Sincerity and Authenticity*, 99–100; David Hesmondhalgh, *The Cultural Industries*, 4th ed. (Los Angeles: Sage, 2019).

87. Gary Alan Fine, "Crafting Authenticity," *Theory and Society* 32, no. 2 (2003): 165–66.

88. Klein, *Selling Out*, 9–10.

89. Klein, *Selling Out*, 1, 42.

90. Klein, *Selling Out*, 61.

91. Potter, *The Authenticity Hoax*, 75.

92. Banet-Weiser, *Authentic*, 220; Heath and Potter, *Nation of Rebels*.

93. Mark Bartholomew, *Adcreep* (Palo Alto, CA: Stanford University Press, 2017), 38; Klein, *Selling Out*, 158.

94. Guignon, *On Being Authentic*, 31; Salisbury and Pooley, "The #nofilter Self," 5.

95. Guignon, *On Being Authentic*, 78; Taylor, *The Ethics of Authenticity*, 5.

96. Stjepan G. Meštrović, *Postemotional Society (London: Sage, 1997)*, 73.

97. Taylor, *The Ethics of Authenticity*, 94.

98. Juan-Carlos Molleda, "Authenticity and the Construct's Dimensions in Public Relations and Communication Research," *Journal of Communication Management* 14, no. 3 (2010): 226; Gilmore and Pine, *Authenticity: What Consumers Really Want*, 160.

99. Lindholm, *Culture and Authenticity*, 13; Walter Benjamin, "The Work of Art in the Age of Mechanical Reproduction," in *Media and Cultural Studies*, ed. Meenakshi Gigi Durham and Douglas Kellner (Malden, MA: Blackwell, 2001), 48–70; Fine, "Crafting Authenticity," 155.

100. Paddy Scannell, "Benjamin Contextualized,'" in *Canonic Texts in Media Research*, ed. Elihu Katz et al. (Cambridge: Polity, 2003), 74–89.

101. Boyle, *Authenticity*, 8, 11.

102. Balázs Kovács, Glenn R. Carroll, and David W. Lehman, "Authenticity and Consumer Value Ratings," *Organization Science* 25, no. 2 (2013): 5; Heath and Potter, *Nation of Rebels*, 238.

103. Roland Marchand, *Creating the Corporate Soul* (Berkeley: University of California Press, 1998); Eric Guthey and Brad Jackson, "CEO Portraits and the Authenticity Paradox," *Journal of Management Studies* 42, no. 5 (2005): 1066.

104. Greg Dickinson, "Joe's Rhetoric," *Rhetoric Society Quarterly* 32, no. 4 (2002): 7–8.

105. Andreas Reckwitz, *The Society of Singularities* (Cambridge: Polity, 2020).

106. Eric J. Arnould and Linda L. Price, "Authenticating Acts and Authoritative Performances," in *The Why of Consumption*, ed. S. Ratneshwar, David Glen Mick, and Cynthia Huffman (New York: Routledge, 2000), 142; Richard Peterson, "In Search of Authenticity," *Journal of Management Studies* 42, no. 5 (2005): 1084.

107. Tom van Nuenen, "Here I Am," *Tourist Studies* 16, no. 2 (2016): 8–9.

108. Djavlonbek Kadirov, Richard J. Varey, and Ben Wooliscroft, "Authenticity," *Journal of Macromarketing* 34, no. 1 (2014): 75.

109. Banet-Weiser, *Authentic*, 69.

110. Potter, *The Authenticity Hoax*, 7; Boyle, *Authenticity*, 181, 201.

111. Farhad Manjoo, "The Next Decade Will Be Just as Bad," *New York Times*, November 20, 2019, https://www.nytimes.com/2019/11/20/opinion/grifter-decade-trump-theranos.html.

112. Thomas Thurnell-Read, "A Thirst for the Authentic," *British Journal of Sociology* 70, no. 4 (2019): 1452.

113. Heath and Potter, *Nation of Rebels*, 269.

114. Beverland, *Building Brand Authenticity*, 69, 70; Amanda Koontz, "Constructing Authenticity: A Review of Trends and Influences in the Process of Authentication in Consumption," *Sociology Compass* 4, no. 11 (2010): 982.

115. Potter, *The Authenticity Hoax*, 133.

116. David Lewis and Darren Bridger, *The Soul of the New Consumer* (London: Nicholas Brealey, 2001), 14, 15.

117. David Grazian, *Blue Chicago* (Chicago: University of Chicago Press, 2003), 6–7; Umbach and Humphrey, *Authenticity*, 96.

118. Lindholm, *Culture and Authenticity*, 58–59; Richard A. Peterson, *Creating Country Music* (Chicago: University of Chicago Press, 1997), 211.

119. Umbach and Humphrey, *Authenticity*, 96.

120. Gilmore and Pine, *Authenticity: What Consumers Really Want*, 12, 13, 65.

121. Michael B. Beverland, "Crafting Brand Authenticity: The Case of Luxury Wines," *Journal of Management Studies* 42, no. 5 (2005): 1008.

122. Gilmore and Pine, *Authenticity: What Consumers Really Want*, 88.

123. Umbach and Humphrey, *Authenticity*, 126.

124. Potter, *The Authenticity Hoax*, 11.

125. David R. Shumway, "Authenticity," *Modernism/Modernity* 14, no. 3 (2007): 528.

126. Dickinson, "Joe's Rhetoric," 10; Peterson, *Creating Country Music*, 67.

127. Grazian, "Demystifying Authenticity in the Sociology of Culture," 191.

128. Trilling, *Sincerity and Authenticity*, 127–28.

129. Lindholm, *Culture and Authenticity*, 73; Jennifer Rauch, *Slow Media* (Oxford: Oxford University Press, 2018), 13, 17.

130. Marwan Kraidy, "Reality Television, Gender, and Authenticity in Saudi Arabia," *Journal of Communication* 59, no. 2 (2009): 359, 360; Potter, *The Authenticity Hoax*, 255.

131. Robert V. Kozinets, "Can Consumers Escape the Market? Emancipatory Illuminations from Burning Man," *Journal of Consumer Research* 29, no. 1 (2002): 20, 21, 24.

132. Sarah Thornton, *Club Cultures* (Hanover, NH: Wesleyan University Press, 1996), 6.

133. Koontz, "Constructing Authenticity," 978.

134. Grazian, "Demystifying Authenticity in the Sociology of Culture," 192; Botterill, "Cowboys, Outlaws and Artists," 117.

135. Heath and Potter, *Nation of Rebels*, 226; Potter, *The Authenticity Hoax*, 220.

136. Sharon Zukin, "Consuming Authenticity," *Cultural Studies* 22, no. 5 (2008): 724, 725, 729.

137. Zukin, "Consuming Authenticity," 732.

138. Devon Powers, *On Trend* (Urbana: University of Illinois Press, 2019), 65.

139. Lindholm, *Culture and Authenticity*, 30, 35.

140. McLeod, "Authenticity within Hip-Hop," 142–43.

141. McLeod, "Authenticity within Hip-Hop," 143.

142. Koontz, "Constructing Authenticity," 980.

143. Banet-Weiser, *Authentic*, 122; Michael Serazio, *Your Ad Here* (New York: NYU Press, 2013), 62.

144. Powers, *On Trend*, 51, 64, 75.

145. Potter, *The Authenticity Hoax*, 124; Malcolm Gladwell, "The Coolhunt," *New Yorker*, March 17, 1997, http://www.gladwell.com/1997/1997_03_17_a_cool.htm.

146. Salisbury and Pooley, "The #nofilter Self," 6; Potter, *The Authenticity Hoax*, 82.

147. Lindholm, *Culture and Authenticity*, 61.

148. Thurnell-Read, "A Thirst for the Authentic," 9, 10; Koontz, "Constructing Authenticity," 981.

149. Koontz, "Constructing Authenticity," 978, 981.

150. Eric Hobsbawm, "Introduction," in *The Invention of Tradition*, ed. Eric Hobsbawm and Terence Ranger (Cambridge: Cambridge University Press, 1983), 2, 9.

151. Stefanie Duguay, "Dressing Up Tinderella," *Information Communication and Society* 20, no. 3 (2017): 351, 353.

152. Fine, "Crafting Authenticity," 163; Lindholm, *Culture and Authenticity*, 21.

153. Umbach and Humphrey, *Authenticity*, 87, 88; Peterson, *Creating Country Music*, 218.

154. Courtney Idasetima, "Industry Panel Suggests Ways to Better Represent Muslims in Film and TV," *Hollywood Reporter*, December 11, 2017, https://www.hollywoodreporter.com/news/general-news/industry-panel-suggests-ways-better-represent-muslims-film-tv-1064478/; Chris Eyre, Joely Proudfit, and Heather Rae, "Authentic Stories about Native Americans Need Hollywood's Attention," *Variety*, February 24, 2017, https://variety.com/2017/voices/columns/native-americans-hollywood-1201993362/.

155. Alexandra del Rosario, "'Glee,' 'One Day a Time' Writers Talk Authenticity and Representation with Amnesty International," *Hollywood Reporter*, April 12, 2019, https://www.hollywoodreporter.com/tv/tv-news/panel-tv-film-writers-producers-discuss-authenticity-representation-film-television-amnesty-internat-1201636/.

156. Lindholm, *Culture and Authenticity*, 33.

157. E. Patrick Johnson, *Appropriating Blackness* (Durham, NC: Duke University Press, 2003), 3.

158. Peterson, "In Search of Authenticity," 1086, 1087; Potter, *The Authenticity Hoax*, 80.

159. Carlos Lozada, *What Were We Thinking: A Brief Intellectual History of the Trump Era* (New York: Simon & Schuster, 2020), 124.

160. Paul Freathy and Iris Thomas, "Marketplace Metaphors," *Consumption Markets and Culture* 18, no. 2 (2015): 180.

161. Edward L. Bernays, *Propaganda* (New York: Horace Liveright, 1928).

162. Phillip Vannini and J. Patrick Williams, "Authenticity in Culture, Self, and Society," in *Authenticity in Culture, Self, and Society*, ed. Phillip Vannini and J. Patrick Williams (Burlington, VT: Ashgate, 2009), 6; Fiona Kennedy and Darl G. Kolb, "The Alchemy of Authenticity," *Organizational Dynamics* 45, no. 4 (2016): 317.

163. Fordahl, "Authenticity," 305; Taylor, *The Ethics of Authenticity*, 23; Guignon, *On Being Authentic*, xi.

164. Potter, *The Authenticity Hoax*, 12.

165. Banet-Weiser, *Authentic*, 5.

166. Boyle, *Authenticity*, 282–85.

167. Potter, *The Authenticity Hoax*, 5.

168. Guthey and Jackson, "CEO Portraits and the Authenticity Paradox," 1058.

169. I am grateful to an anonymous manuscript reviewer for this point.

170. Banet-Weiser, *Authentic*, 112.

171. Giorgia Aiello and Greg Dickinson, "Beyond Authenticity," *Visual Communication* 13, no. 3 (2014): 316.

172. Stephen K. Medvic, *Political Consultants in U.S. Congressional Elections* (Columbus: Ohio State University Press, 2001), 43, 47.

173. Klein, *Selling Out*, 23.

174. Hesmondhalgh, *The Cultural Industries*, 14.

175. I am grateful to an anonymous manuscript reviewer for this point.

176. Vannini and Williams, "Authenticity in Culture, Self, and Society," 2.

177. Grazian, "Demystifying Authenticity in the Sociology of Culture," 192.

178. Pooley, "The Consuming Self," 78; Salisbury and Pooley, "The #nofilter Self," 4.

179. Georgia Gaden and Delia Dumitrica, "The 'Real Deal'," *First Monday* 20, no. 1 (2015), https://journals.uic.edu/ojs/index.php/fm/article/view/4985/4197.

180. Peterson, *Creating Country Music*, 5.

181. Brooke Erin Duffy, "The Romance of Work," *International Journal of Cultural Studies* 19, no. 4 (2016): 443; David Hesmondhalgh, *The Cultural Industries*, 2nd ed. (Los Angeles: Sage, 2007), 4, 37.

182. Vicki Mayer, Miranda J. Banks, and John T. Caldwell, "Introduction," in *Production Studies: Cultural Studies of Media Industries*, ed. Vicki Mayer, Miranda J. Banks, and John Thornton Caldwell (New York: Routledge, 2009), 4; Vicki Mayer, "Bringing the Social Back In: Studies of Production Cultures and Social Theory," in *Production Studies*, ed. Vicki Mayer, Miranda J. Banks, and John T. Caldwell (New York: Routledge, 2009), 15.

183. Mayer, "Bringing the Social Back In," 19.

184. David Grazian, "The Production of Popular Music as a Confidence Game," *Qualitative Sociology* 27, no. 2 (2004): 138; Grazian, "Demystifying Authenticity in the Sociology of Culture," 192; Hughes, "Country Music as Impression Management," 190.

185. Gilmore and Pine, *Authenticity: What Consumers Really Want*, 43.

186. Frosh, "To Thine Own Self Be True," 542; Brooke Erin Duffy, "Manufacturing Authenticity," *Communication Review* 16, no. 3 (2013): 137.

187. Banet-Weiser, *Authentic*, 47, 48, 215.

188. Enli, *Mediated Authenticity*, 137.

189. Enli, *Mediated Authenticity*, 17.

190. Enli, *Mediated Authenticity*, 137.

191. Candace Jones, N. Anand, and Josè Luis Alvarez, "Manufactured Authenticity and Creative Voice in Cultural Industries," *Journal of Management Studies* 42, no. 5 (2005): 894.

192. Daniel Herbert, Amanda D. Lotz, and Aswin Punathambekar, *Media Industry Studies* (Cambridge, UK: Polity, 2020), 125.

193. Enli, "'Trust Me, I Am Authentic!'," 134.

194. Lehman et al., "Authenticity," 11.

195. Martyn Hammersley and Paul Atkinson, *Ethnography*, 3rd ed. (London: Routledge, 2007); Barney G. Glaser and Anselm Leonard Strauss, *The Discovery of Grounded Theory* (Chicago: Aldine, 1967).

Chapter 1: Casting Reality Television

1. Laura Grindstaff, "Just Be Yourself—Only More So," in *The Politics of Reality Television*, ed. Marwan M. Kraidy and Katherine Sender (London: Routledge, 2011), 44.

2. Harriet Ryan and Yvonne Villarreal, "Casting About for Reality TV Hopefuls," *Los Angeles Times*, January 24, 2011, https://www.latimes.com/entertainment/la-xpm-2011-jan-24-la-et-reality-casting-20110125-story.html.

3. Elizabeth Currid-Halkett, *Starstruck* (New York: Farrar, Straus and Giroux, 2010), 194.

4. Portions of this section were featured in a *Communication, Culture & Critique* article on celebrity culture, social media, and school shootings. Michael Serazio, "Shooting for Fame," *Communication, Culture & Critique* 3, no. 3 (2010): 416–34.

5. Leo Braudy, *The Frenzy of Renown* (New York: Oxford University Press, 1986), 6.

6. P. David Marshall, *Celebrity and Power* (Minneapolis: University of Minnesota Press, 1997), ix; Graeme Turner, *Understanding Celebrity* (London: Sage, 2004), 62.

7. Braudy, *The Frenzy of Renown*, 27.

8. Currid-Halkett, *Starstruck*, 10; Mingyi Hou, "Social Media Celebrity and the Institutionalization of YouTube," *Convergence*," 25, no. 3 (2018), 536.

9. Currid-Halkett, *Starstruck*, 11.

10. Graeme Turner, *Ordinary People and the Media* (Los Angeles: Sage, 2010).

11. Laura Grindstaff and Vicki Mayer, "The Importance of Being Ordinary," in *Brokerage and Production in the American and French Entertainment Industries*, ed. Violaine Roussel and Denise Bielby (Lanham, MD: Lexington Books, 2015), 131; Laura Grindstaff and Susan Murray, "Reality Celebrity," *Public Culture* 27, no. 1 (2015): 109.

12. Theresa M. Senft, "Microcelebrity and the Branded Self," in *A Companion to New Media Dynamics*, ed. John Harley, Jean Burgess, and Axel Bruns (Malden, MA: Blackwell, 2013), 346.

13. Alice E. Marwick, "You May Know Me from YouTube," in *A Companion to Celebrity*, ed. P. David Marshall and Sean Redmond (Malden, MA: John Wiley & Sons, 2015), 334, 338; Alice E. Marwick, *Status Update* (New Haven, CT: Yale University Press, 2013), 114.

14. Marwick, "You May Know Me from YouTube," 333.

15. Currid-Halkett, *Starstruck*, 71, 78, 79.

16. Grindstaff, "Just Be Yourself—Only More So," 53; Grindstaff and Mayer, "The Importance of Being Ordinary," 134; Marwick, "You May Know Me from YouTube," 335.

17. Joshua Gamson, "The Unwatched Life Is Not Worth Living," *PMLA* 126, no. 4 (2011): 1062, 1063; Tyler Cowen, *What Price Fame?* (Cambridge, MA: Harvard University Press, 2000), 101.

18. Enli, *Mediated Authenticity*, 73.

19. Turner, *Ordinary People and the Media*, 37; Jon Caramanica, "Hollywood's First Family, Putting It Out There," *New York Times*, February 10, 2022, https://www.nytimes.com/2022/02/10/arts/music/will-jada-willow-jaden-smith.html.

20. Grindstaff and Mayer, "The Importance of Being Ordinary," 134, 135.

21. Scott Collins, "'American Idol' Finale Is Least Watched since '02," *Los Angeles Times*, May 21, 2009, https://latimesblogs.latimes.com/showtracker/2009/05/american-idol-finale-draws-277-million.html; Laura Grindstaff, "Self Serve Celebrity," in *Production Studies: Cultural Studies of Media Industries*, ed. Vicki Mayer, Miranda J. Banks, and John Thornton Caldwell (New York: Routledge, 2009), 73.

22. Elizabeth Weil, "What Do Teens Learn Online Today? That Identity Is a Work in Progress," *New York Times Magazine*, November 13, 2019, https://www.nytimes.com/interactive/2019/11/13/magazine/internet-teens.html.

23. Ilyse Liffreing, "Top Influencers Reach Twice as Many Gen Zers on Social as Do Top Broadcasters," *Ad Age,* April 28, 2021, https://adage.com/article/media/top-influencers-reach-twice-many-gen-zers-social-do-top-broadcasters/2330956.

24. Paul Taylor and Scott Keeter, "A Portrait of 'Generation Next'" (Washington, DC, January 9, 2007), https://www.pewresearch.org/politics/2007/01/09/a-portrait-of-generation-next/; Lakshmi Chaudhry, "Mirror, Mirror on the Web," *The Nation*, January 11, 2007.

25. Jean M. Twenge, *Generation Me* (New York: Free Press, 2007), 69, 82.

26. Turner, *Ordinary People and the Media*, 14, 19; Hou, "Social Media Celebrity," 535.

27. Matthew Stahl, "Authentic Boy Bands on TV?," *Popular Music* 21, no. 3 (2002): 309.

28. Hill, "Reality TV," 449, 451.

29. Enli, *Mediated Authenticity*, 66, 71.

30. Jane Shattuc, "The Shifting Terrain of American Talk Shows," in *A Companion to Television*, ed. Janet Wasko (Malden, MA: Blackwell, 2005), 324–36.

31. Grindstaff and Mayer, "The Importance of Being Ordinary," 132; Grindstaff, "Self-Serve Celebrity," 73.

32. Laura Grindstaff, "Reality TV and the Production of 'Ordinary Celebrity,'" *Berkeley Journal of Sociology* 56 (2012): 36; Grindstaff and Mayer, "The Importance of Being Ordinary," 133, 138; Stahl, "Authentic Boy Bands on TV?," 312.

33. Enli, *Mediated Authenticity*, 65, 71; Chad Raphael, "The Political-Economic Origins of Reali-TV," in *Reality TV*, ed. Susan Murray and Laurie Ouellette (New York: NYU Press, 2008), 127, 128, 132, 137; Grindstaff, "Self-Serve Celebrity"; Vicki Mayer, "Cast-Aways," in *A Companion to Reality Television*, ed. Laurie Ouellette (Malden, MA: John Wiley & Sons, 2014), 60.

34. Enli, *Mediated Authenticity*, 65.

35. Gamson, "The Unwatched Life Is Not Worth Living," 1064; Stahl, "Authentic Boy Bands on TV?," 308.

36. David Carr, "Casting Reality TV, No Longer a Hunch, Becomes a Science," *The New York Times*, March 28, 2004, https://www.nytimes.com/2004/03/28/business/casting-reality-tv-no-longer-a-hunch-becomes-a-science.html.

37. Gervais.

38. Conlin; Lauren Horwitch, "The Art of Getting Real," *Backstage*, August 25, 2008, https://www.backstage.com/magazine/article/art-getting-real-20358/.

39. Conlin.

40. Conlin.

41. Gervais.

42. Ryan and Villarreal, "Casting About for Reality TV Hopefuls."

43. Rupert Russell, "The Bouncer Who Runs Reality Television," *Salon*, December 25, 2012, https://www.salon.com/2012/12/25/the_bouncer_who_runs_reality_television /.

44. Ofir.

45. Jelle Mast, "Negotiating the 'Real' in 'Reality Shows,'" *Media, Culture and Society* 38, no. 6 (2016): 908.

46. McCarty.

47. Molly Mulshine, "Bravo Casting Director Finds Next Season's Reality Stars on Instagram," *Observer*, March 19, 2014, https://observer.com/2014/03/notheretomake friends-casting-director-finds-next-seasons-reality-stars-on-instagram/.

48. Amber Dowling, "The Challenges of Reality Casting Post #MeToo," *Variety*, August 16, 2018, https://variety.com/2018/tv/features/reality-tv-casting-me-too-bache lor-big-brother-1202905049/.

49. Calum Marsh, "Reality Show Casting Joins Social-Media Age but Human Judgment's Still Key," *Variety*, June 13, 2018, https://variety.com/2018/artisans/production/ reality-show-casting-1202843563/.

50. Gervais.

51. Ofir.

52. Russell, "The Bouncer Who Runs Reality Television."

53. Enli, *Mediated Authenticity*, 79.

54. Pizzi.

55. Currid-Halkett, *Starstruck*, 197.

56. Grindstaff, "Self-Serve Celebrity," 72, 76.

57. Morgan Baila, "15 Seconds of Fame: The Future of Reality TV Is on Our Phones," *Refinery29*, July 21, 2020, https://www.refinery29.com/en-us/2020/07/9914977/reality-tv -shows-social-media-instagram; Dana Vachon, "Poof!," *Slate*, July 28, 2010, https://slate .com/culture/2010/07/why-the-hills-defined-the-boom-and-jersey-shore-defined-the -bust.html.

58. Mayer, "Cast-Aways," 61, 62; Grindstaff, "Reality TV and the Production of 'Ordinary Celebrity,'" 31; Grindstaff and Murray, "Reality Celebrity," 130.

59. Stahl, "Authentic Boy Bands on TV?" 309.

60. Rachel E. Dubrofsky, "Surveillance on Reality Television and Facebook," *Communication Theory* 21, no. 2 (May 2011): 117, 119, 124.

61. Rosalind Gill and Akane Kanai, "Mediating Neoliberal Capitalism," *Journal of Communication* 68, no. 2 (April 1, 2018): 320.

62. Reider.

63. Pizzi; Lane.

64. Lane.

65. Bryant.

66. Grindstaff, "Just Be Yourself—Only More So," 49.

67. Enli, *Mediated Authenticity*, 71; Mast, "Negotiating the 'Real' in 'Reality Shows,'" 910; Kraidy, "Reality Television, Gender, and Authenticity," 360.

68. Emily Yahr, "The Unsung Heroes of Reality Television," *The Guardian*, March 11, 2014, https://www.theguardian.com/tv-and-radio/2014/mar/11/reality-tv-casting-amer ican-idol.

69. Lane.

70. Grindstaff and Mayer, "The Importance of Being Ordinary," 132.

71. McCarty.

72. Laura Rosenfeld, "Now We Know What Denise Richards Meant by 'Bravo, Bravo, F—King Bravo' in the RBOBH Season 10 Premiere," *The Daily Dish*, April 16, 2020, https://www.bravotv.com/the-daily-dish/denise-richards-bravo-fight-explained.

73. Pizzi.

74. Reider.

75. C. Brian Smith, "An Oral History of 'Taxicab Confessions,'" *Mel Magazine*, 2019, https://melmagazine.com/en-us/story/an-oral-history-of-taxicab-confessions.

76. Smith, "An Oral History of 'Taxicab Confessions.'"

77. Gantz; Dan Neilan, "Taxicab Confessions Was Initially More about Heart than Salaciousness," *A.V. Club*, November 14, 2018, https://www.avclub.com/taxicab-confes sions-was-initially-more-about-heart-than-1830440635.

78. Grindstaff and Murray, "Reality Celebrity," 125, 127; Grindstaff, "Just Be Yourself—Only More So," 46; Grindstaff and Mayer, "The Importance of Being Ordinary," 142, 146, 147.

79. Grindstaff, "Self-Serve Celebrity," 75, 77; Vicki Mayer, *Below the Line* (Durham, NC: Duke University Press, 2011), 132, 133; Mayer, "Cast-Aways," 67; Grindstaff and Murray, "Reality Celebrity," 131.

80. Banet-Weiser, *Authentic*, 60.

81. Lindholm, *Culture and Authenticity*, 8.

82. Banet-Weiser, *Authentic*, 60.

83. Guignon, *On Being Authentic*, 81.

84. Kim Allen and Heather Mendick, "Keeping It Real? Social Class, Young People and 'Authenticity' in Reality TV," *Sociology* 47, no. 3 (2013): 461, 465.

85. McCarty.

86. Enli, *Mediated Authenticity*, 2, 10, 85.

87. Smith, "An Oral History of 'Taxicab Confessions.'"

88. Bryant.

89. Gervais.

90. Ofir.

91. Reider; Pizzi.

92. McCarty.

93. Gantz.

94. Minna Aslama and Mervi Pantti, "Talking Alone," *European Journal of Cultural Studies* 9, no. 2 (2006): 167.

95. Reider; Pizzi.

96. Lane.

97. Mary Sollosi, "'Wives Gone Wild: The All-Stars of Real Housewives Ultimate Girls Trip Dish on the New Series," *Entertainment Weekly*, October 12, 2021, https://ew.com/tv/real-housewives-ultimate-girls-trip-zoom-roundtable/.

98. Reider.

99. Conlin.

100. Bryant.

101. Grindstaff and Murray, "Reality Celebrity," 114; Mayer, "Cast-Aways," 69.

102. Laura Grindstaff, *The Money Shot* (Chicago: University of Chicago Press, 2002).

103. Grindstaff and Mayer, "The Importance of Being Ordinary," 135.

104. Grindstaff and Mayer, "The Importance of Being Ordinary," 136.

105. McCarty.

106. Grindstaff and Murray, "Reality Celebrity," 112; Grindstaff and Mayer, "The Importance of Being Ordinary," 141.

107. Aslama and Pantti, "Talking Alone," 175, 178.

108. Lane.

109. Lane.

110. Conlin.

111. Sarah McRae, "'Get Off My Internets,'" *Persona Studies* 3, no. 1 (2017): 16.

112. Alison Hearn and Stephanie Schoenhoff, "From Celebrity to Influencer," in *A Companion to Celebrity*, ed. P. David Marshall and Sean Redmond (Malden, MA: John Wiley & Sons, 2015), 199–200.

113. Mayer, *Below the Line*, 104, 121; Mayer, "Cast-Aways," 62.

114. Gervais.

115. Mast, "Negotiating the 'Real' in 'Reality Shows,'" 908; Enli, *Mediated Authenticity*, 85.

116. Grindstaff, "Reality TV and the Production of 'Ordinary Celebrity,'" 26.

117. Tanja M. Laden, "Doron Ofir: The King of Reality TV Casting," *LA Weekly*, May 15, 2013, https://www.laweekly.com/doron-ofir-the-king-of-reality-tv-casting/.

118. Russell, "The Bouncer Who Runs Reality Television."

119. Pizzi.

120. Enli, *Mediated Authenticity*, 75.

121. Guthey and Jackson, "CEO Portraits and the Authenticity Paradox," 1057.

122. Enli, *Mediated Authenticity*, 68.

123. Grindstaff and Mayer, "The Importance of Being Ordinary," 143.

124. Pizzi; Reider.

125. Pizzi.

126. Gervais.

127. McCarty.

128. Pizzi; Reider.

129. Lane.

130. Gervais.

131. Lane.

132. Ryan and Villarreal, "Casting About for Reality TV Hopefuls"; Grindstaff and Mayer, "The Importance of Being Ordinary," 143.

133. Grindstaff and Murray, "Reality Celebrity," 122–23.

134. Ofir.

135. Taylor Lorenz, "It Looks like a Reality Show: Why Not Just Make It One?," *New York Times*, July 9, 2020, https://www.nytimes.com/2020/07/09/style/tik-tok-drama-taylor-lorenz.html.

136. Conlin.

137. Gervais.

138. Lorenz, "It Looks like a Reality Show"; Pizzi.

139. McCarty.

140. Reider; Baila, "15 Seconds of Fame."

141. Pizzi.

142. Gervais; Conlin.

143. McCarty.

144. Ofir.

145. Grindstaff and Murray, "Reality Celebrity," 131; Mayer, *Below the Line*, 103, 105, 123, 129; Mayer, "Cast-Aways," 61.

Chapter 2: Social Media Designs

1. Tommy Shane, "The Semiotics of Authenticity," *Social Media + Society* 4, no. 3 (2018): 3.

2. Tiffany Hsu, "These Influencers Aren't Flesh and Blood, yet Millions Follow Them," *New York Times*, June 17, 2019, https://www.nytimes.com/2019/06/17/business/media/miquela-virtual-influencer.html.

3. Caroline Hamilton, "Symbolic Amateurs," *Cultural Studies Review* 19, no. 1 (2013): 179.

4. Enli, "'Trust Me, I Am Authentic!'" 125.

5. Christina Spurgeon, *Advertising and New Media* (London: Routledge, 2008).

6. Andrew Tolson, "A New Authenticity?" in *Self-Mediation*, ed. Lilie Chouliaraki (London: Routledge, 2012), 87.

7. Enli, *Mediated Authenticity*, 87, 95.

8. Gaden and Dumitrica, "The 'Real Deal.'"

9. van Nuenen, "Here I Am," 6; Duffy, *(Not) Getting Paid to Do What You Love*, 99.

10. Kevin Allocca, *Videocracy* (New York: Bloomsbury, 2018), 20–22.

11. Allocca, *Videocracy*, 226–27; Enli, *Mediated Authenticity*, 87.

12. Allocca, *Videocracy*, xi, xii.

13. Kimberly Ann Hall, "The Authenticity of Social-Media Performance," *Women and Performance* 25, no. 2 (2015): 133.

14. Hamilton, "Symbolic Amateurs," 179.

15. Serazio, *Your Ad Here*, 123.

16. Hamilton, "Symbolic Amateurs," 183.

17. Hamilton, "Symbolic Amateurs," 177.

18. Salisbury and Pooley, "The #nofilter Self," 1.

19. Arielle Pardes, "All the Social Media Giants Are Becoming the Same," *Wired*, November 30, 2020, https://www.wired.com/story/social-media-giants-look-the-same-tiktok-twitter-instagram/.

20. Catherine Price, *How to Break Up with Your Phone* (New York: Crown, 2018).

21. Roger McNamee, *Zucked* (New York: Penguin, 2019).

22. Rachel Lerman, "Social Media Influencers Are Balancing 'Authentic' Messaging during Protests and the Pandemic," *Washington Post*, June 12, 2020, https://www.washingtonpost.com/technology/2020/06/12/influencers-social-media-pandemic/.

23. José van Dijck, "'You Have One Identity,'" *Media, Culture and Society* 35, no. 2 (2013): 211, 213.

24. Marwick, "You May Know Me from YouTube," 343.

25. Avery Hartmans, "Instagram Is Celebrating Its 10th Birthday: A Decade after Launch, Here's Where Its Original 13 Employees Have Ended Up," *Business Insider*, October 6, 2020, https://www.businessinsider.com/instagram-first-13-employees-full-list-2020-4; "5 Questions with Bailey Richardson," *New York Times*, December 4, 2019, https://open.nytimes.com/5-questions-with-bailey-richardson-e533e9f9d5e0; Elizabeth Dwoskin, "Quitting Instagram: She's One of the Millions Disillusioned with Social Media—But She Also Helped Create It," *Washington Post*, November 13, 2018, https://www.washingtonpost.com/technology/2018/11/14/quitting-instagram-shes-one-millions-disillusioned-with-social-media-she-also-helped-create-it/.

26. Richardson.

27. H. Sullivan.

28. Hamilton, "Symbolic Amateurs," 178.

29. Stuart Cunningham and David Craig, *Social Media Entertainment* (New York: NYU Press, 2019), 155.

30. Allocca.

31. Turner, *Ordinary People and the Media*, 128.

32. Silverstein.

33. Cesarkas.

34. Coles.

35. Cummings.

36. Hall, "The Authenticity of Social-Media Performance," 140.

37. Arienne Ferchaud et al., "Parasocial Attributes and YouTube Personalities," *Computers in Human Behavior* 80 (2018): 93.

38. McRae, "'Get Off My Internets,'" 19; Brooke Erin Duffy and Emily Hund, "Gendered Visibility on Social Media," *International Journal of Communication* 13 (2019): 4984.

39. Rachel E. Dubrofsky and Megan M. Wood, "Posting Racism and Sexism," *Communication and Critical/Cultural Studies* 11, no. 3 (2014): 284.

40. Allocca, *Videocracy*, 284, 285.

41. Salisbury and Pooley, "The #nofilter Self," 3.

42. Crystal Abidin, "#Familygoals: Family Influencers, Calibrated Amateurism, and Justifying Young Digital Labor," *Social Media + Society* 3, no. 2 (2017): 4, 7, 8.

43. Hou, "Social Media Celebrity and the Institutionalization of YouTube," 542.

44. Taylor Lorenz, "Hype House and the Los Angeles TikTok Mansion Gold Rush," *New York Times*, January 3, 2020, https://www.nytimes.com/2020/01/03/style/hype-house-los-angeles-tik-tok.html.

45. Taylor Lorenz, "We're All in the Bathroom Filming Ourselves," *New York Times*, January 23, 2020, https://www.nytimes.com/2020/01/23/style/tik-tok-bathrooms.html.

46. Ferchaud et al., "Parasocial Attributes and YouTube Personalities," 93; Cunningham and Craig, *Social Media Entertainment*, 13.

47. Alice Marwick and Danah Boyd, "To See and Be Seen," *Convergence* 17, no. 2 (2011): 139, 147.

48. Marwick and Boyd, "To See and Be Seen," 151, 155–56.

49. Caitlin Dewey, "Beme Wants to Be the App for Social Media 'Authenticity': Too Bad There's No Such Thing," *Washington Post*, July 28, 2015, https://www.washingtonpost.com/news/the-intersect/wp/2015/07/28/beme-wants-to-be-the-app-for-social-media-authenticity-too-bad-theres-no-such-thing/.

50. Davis, "Accomplishing Authenticity in a Labor-Exposing Space," 1, 4.

51. Pooley, "The Consuming Self," 83.

52. Gaden and Dumitrica, "The 'Real Deal.'"

53. Roetter; Salisbury and Pooley, "The #nofilter Self," 8, 10.

54. Alice E. Marwick and Danah Boyd, "I Tweet Honestly, I Tweet Passionately," *New Media and Society* 13, no. 1 (2011): 124.

55. Jennifer M. Whitmer, "You Are Your Brand," *Sociology Compass* 13, no. 3 (2019): 4.

56. Salisbury and Pooley, "The #nofilter Self," 9, 10.

57. Kendall.

58. Sheera Frenkel and Cecilia Kang, *An Ugly Truth* (New York: HarperCollins, 2021), 61.

59. Kendall.

60. Emily A. Vogels, "10 Facts about Americans and Online Dating," February 6, 2020, https://www.pewresearch.org/fact-tank/2020/02/06/10-facts-about-americans-and-online-dating/.

61. Yagan.

62. Duguay, "Dressing Up Tinderella," 351, 358.

63. Enli, *Mediated Authenticity*, 90.

64. Enli, *Mediated Authenticity*, 1, 17.

65. Hall, "The Authenticity of Social-Media Performance," 131; Rose and Wood, "Paradox and the Consumption of Authenticity," 292.

66. Salisbury and Pooley, "The #nofilter Self," 2, 3.

67. Dewey, "Beme Wants to Be the App for Social Media 'Authenticity'".

68. Sadhbh O'Sullivan, "Why Bother with Authenticity?," *Refinery29*, August 25,

2022, https://www.refinery29.com/en-gb/bereal-authenticity-performance-online -instagram; Will Oremus, "BeReal Is Hotter than TikTok: So TikTok Is Copying It," *Washington Post*, September 17, 2022, https://www.washingtonpost.com/technology /2022/09/17/bereal-copy-tiktok-instagram-snapchat/.

69. Marwick and Boyd, "To See and Be Seen," 149; Enli, *Mediated Authenticity*, 91.

70. Allocca.

71. Shane, "The Semiotics of Authenticity," 4; Abidin, "#Familygoals," 8.

72. Salisbury and Pooley, "The #nofilter Self," 3; Tolson, "A New Authenticity?," 88; Jean Burgess and Joshua Green, *YouTube* (Cambridge: Polity, 2009), 54.

73. Taylor Lorenz, "The Instagram Aesthetic Is Over," *The Atlantic*, April 23, 2019, https://www.theatlantic.com/technology/archive/2019/04/influencers-are-abandoning -instagram-look/587803/.

74. Isabelle Truman, "How Embracing Your Toxicity Became the Latest Internet Trend," *Vice*, November 18, 2021, https://i-d.vice.com/en_uk/article/z3nxz4/tiktok -toxic-traits.

75. Cate Matthews, "The 25 Most Influential People on the Internet," *Time*, July 16, 2019, https://time.com/5626827/the-25-most-influential-people-on-the-internet/.

76. Rebecca Alter, "In the Messy Land of Internet Video, the Editor Is King," *New York*, May 10, 2021, https://www.vulture.com/article/online-video-editing.html; Madison Malone Kircher, "25 Edits That Define the Modern Internet Video," *New York*, May 10, 2021, https://www.vulture.com/2021/05/best-online-videos-tiktok-youtube-vine. html.

77. Jonah Engel Bromwich, "The Evolution of Emma Chamberlain," *New York Times*, July 9, 2019, https://www.nytimes.com/2019/07/09/style/emma-chamberlain -youtube.html.

78. Alter, "In the Messy Land of Internet Video."

79. Allocca.

80. Richardson.

81. Duffy and Hund, "Gendered Visibility on Social Media," 4988.

82. Katharina Lobinger and Cornelia Brantner, "In the Eye of the Beholder," *International Journal of Communication* 9, no. 1 (2015): 1849.

83. Salisbury and Pooley, "The #nofilter Self," 12.

84. Rex Woodbury, "The Rejection of Internet Perfection," *Substack*, February 24, 2021, https://digitalnative.substack.com/p/the-rejection-of-internet-perfection?s=r.

85. Sheila Marikar, "You Won't Find Your Self Worth on Instagram," *New York Times*, November 2, 2019, https://www.nytimes.com/2019/11/02/opinion/sunday/insta gram-social-media.html.

86. Matthew Dalton, "For Olivier Rousteing, the Designer behind a Social Media 'Army,' Instagram Looks Stale," *Wall Street Journal*, March 2, 2018, https://www.wsj. com/articles/for-olivier-rousteing-the-designer-behind-a-social-media-army -instagram-looks-stale-1520001880.

87. Michael Andor Brodeur, "Snapchat, Instagram, and the Rise of the Social-Media

Story," *Boston Globe*, August 7, 2016, https://www.bostonglobe.com/lifestyle/2016/08/07 /snapchat-instagram-and-rise-social-media-story/msTHnpZfsiSHrNkGCiEUrJ/story. html.

88. Salisbury and Pooley, "The #nofilter Self," 13.

89. O'Sullivan, "Why Bother with Authenticity?"

90. Juan De Anda, "6 Trends to Keep Advancing This Year," *MediaPost*, January 28, 2020, https://www.mediapost.com/publications/article/346326/6-trends-to-keep-ad vancing-this-year.html.

91. Sarah Roach, "TikTok Is Now More Popular than Google," *Protocol*, December 22, 2021, https://www.protocol.com/bulletins/tiktok-google-ranking; Ilyse Liffreing, "TikTok Marketers Can Now Directly Sponsor Trending Creator Posts," *Advertising Age*, July 20, 2021, https://adage.com/article/digital-marketing-ad-tech-news/tiktok -marketers-can-now-directly-sponsor-trending-creator-posts/2351561.

92. H. Sullivan.

93. Andrew Hutchinson, "TikTok Shares New Insights into Why People Use the App, and How It Celebrates Authenticity," *Social Media Today*, October 20, 2021, https: //www.socialmediatoday.com/news/tiktok-shares-new-insights-into-why-people-use -the-app-and-how-it-celebrat/608617/.

94. Lorenz, "Are Disposables the Future of Photo Sharing?"

95. Allocca.

96. Rachel Monroe, "98 Million TikTok Followers Can't Be Wrong," *The Atlantic*, December 2020, https://www.theatlantic.com/magazine/archive/2020/12/charli-dame lio-tiktok-teens/616929/.

97. Lorenz, "Hype House and the Los Angeles TikTok Mansion."

98. Cunningham and Craig, *Social Media Entertainment*, 150.

99. Enli, *Mediated Authenticity*, 52; Tolson, "A New Authenticity?" 86.

100. Valerie Gannon and Andrea Prothero, "Beauty Blogger Selfies as Authenticat- ing Practices," *European Journal of Marketing* 50, no. 9–10 (2016): 1861, 1867.

101. Hou, "Social Media Celebrity and the Institutionalization of YouTube," 548.

102. Allocca, *Videocracy*, 292.

103. Ferchaud et al., "Parasocial Attributes and YouTube Personalities," 88.

104. Cunningham and Craig, *Social Media Entertainment*, 92, 155; Abidin, "#Fami- lygoals," 8.

105. Allocca.

106. Sam Leith, "What Memes like Maru the Cat and Star Wars Kid Say about Us," *Slate*, October 15, 2011.

107. Allocca, *Videocracy*, 234, 236; Ilyse Liffreing, "How Brands Can Make the Most of TikTok," *Advertising Age*, January 14, 2020, https://adage.com/article/cmo-strategy/ how-brands-can-make-most-tiktok/2221676; Ben Smith, "How TikTok Reads Your Mind," *New York Times*, December 5, 2021, https://www.nytimes.com/2021/12/05/busi ness/media/tiktok-algorithm.html?referringSource=articleShare; Alter, "In the Messy Land of Internet Video."

108. Allocca, *Videocracy*, 42.

109. Allocca, *Videocracy*, 10.

110. Kevin Roose, "The Making of a YouTube Radical," *New York Times*, June 8, 2019, https://www.nytimes.com/interactive/2019/06/08/technology/youtube-radical.html.

111. Matthew Lynley, "An Interview with Alex Roetter, Twitter's Head of Engineering," *TechCrunch*, July 9, 2015, https://techcrunch.com/2015/07/09/an-interview-with-alex-roetter-twitters-head-of-engineering/?guccounter=1.

112. Roetter.

113. Garrett Sloane, "Can TikTok Prove the Effectiveness of Influencer Marketing?," *Advertising Age*, January 28, 2020, https://adage.com/article/cmo-strategy/can-tiktok-prove-effectiveness-influencer-marketing/2230771; Smith, "How TikTok Reads Your Mind."

114. H. Sullivan.

115. Salisbury and Pooley, "The #nofilter Self," 7.

116. Steven Levitt, "Sam Yagan," *Time*, April 18, 2013, https://time100.time.com/2013/04/18/time-100/slide/sam-yagan/.

117. Yagan.

118. van Dijck, "'You Have One Identity,'" 200, 202.

119. Shoshana Zuboff, "Big Other," *Journal of Information Technology* 30, no. 1 (March 15, 2015): 75; Kyla Schuller, *The Trouble with White Women* (New York: Bold Type Books, 2021), 237.

120. Zuboff, "Big Other," 77; Norma Möllers, David Murakami Wood, and David Lyon, "Surveillance Capitalism," *Surveillance & Society* 17, no. 1/2 (2019): 260.

121. Zuboff, "Big Other," 77, 79.

122. Haan, "Bad Actors," 643, 661.

123. Sarah C. Haan, "The Authenticity Trap," *Slate*, October 21, 2019, https://slate.com/technology/2019/10/mark-zuckerberg-facebook-georgetown-speech-authentic.html.

124. Haan, "Bad Actors, 627.

125. Stuart Cunningham and David Craig, "Being 'Really Real' on YouTube," *Media International Australia* 164, no. 1 (2017): 71; Cunningham and Craig, *Social Media Entertainment*, 11, 12.

126. Kevin Roose, "Don't Scoff at Influencers: They're Taking over the World," *New York Times*, July 16, 2019, https://www.nytimes.com/2019/07/16/technology/vidcon-social-media-influencers.html; Rebecca Jennings, "A Celebrity Endorsement, for $500," *Vox*, July 17, 2020, https:/ https://www.vox.com/the-goods/2020/7/17/21328582/cameo-promotional-influencer-marketing.

127. Cunningham and Craig, *Social Media Entertainment*, 4, 5.

128. Cunningham and Craig, *Social Media Entertainment*, 11, 80, 82, 83.

129. Hou, "Social Media Celebrity," 535.

130. Tim Peterson, "Future of TV Briefing: How Hollywood Is Overcoming Its Resistance to Embracing Creators," *Digiday*, April 28, 2021, https://digiday.com/future-of

-tv/future-of-tv-briefing-how-hollywood-is-overcoming-its-resistance-to-embracing
-creators/.

131. Allocca, *Videocracy*, 47; Jin Kim, "The Institutionalization of Youtube," *Media, Culture and Society* 34, no. 1 (2012): 54, 55.

132. Sarah Roach, "The Creator Economy Competition Is Just Beginning," *Protocol*, November 12, 2021, https://www.protocol.com/bulletins/creator-economy-instagram.

133. Serazio, *Your Ad Here*, 124.

134. Hamilton, "Symbolic Amateurs," 180.

135. Greg Goodfried, personal communication, November 19, 2009.

136. Allocca, *Videocracy*, 30, 31.

137. Hall, "The Authenticity of Social-Media Performance," 129, 131.

138. Abidin, "#Familygoals," 7.

139. Hamilton, "Symbolic Amateurs," 182, 183.

140. Cunningham and Craig, *Social Media Entertainment*, 86–87.

141. Richardson.

142. Allocca, *Videocracy*, 36.

143. Duffy, *(Not) Getting Paid to Do What You Love*, 137.

144. Wacksman.

145. Cunningham and Craig, *Social Media Entertainment*, 156.

146. Cunningham and Craig, *Social Media Entertainment*, 162.

147. Allocca, *Videocracy*, 286.

148. Cunningham and Craig, *Social Media Entertainment*, 168, 169.

149. Serazio, *Your Ad Here*.

150. Kendall; Connie Loizos, "Former Facebook and Pinterest Exec Tim Kendall Traces 'Extractive Business Models' to VCs," *TechCrunch*, October 26, 2020, https://techcrunch.com/2020/10/26/timkendall/.

151. Richardson.

152. Elizabeth Dwoskin, "Quitting Instagram: She's One of the Millions Disillusioned with Social Media—But She Also Helped Create It," *Washington Post*, November 13, 2018, https://www.washingtonpost.com/technology/2018/11/14/quitting-instagram-shes-one-millions-disillusioned-with-social-media-she-also-helped-create-it/.

153. Richardson.

154. Georgia Wells and Jeff Horwitz, "Instagram's Content Factories Are Huge—and That's a Problem for Facebook," *Wall Street Journal*, September 26, 2019, https://www.wsj.com/articles/instagrams-content-factories-are-hugeand-a-growing-problem-for-facebook-11569510271.

155. Carina Chocano, "The Coast of Utopia," *Vanity Fair*, July 2, 2019, https://www.vanityfair.com/style/2019/07/the-coast-of-utopia-surfer-moms-instagram-influencers; Wells and Horwitz, "Instagram's Content Factories Are Huge."

156. Roetter.

157. H. Sullivan.

158. Garrett Sloane, "Marketers of the Year No. 1: TikTok," *Advertising Age*, Decem-

ber 7, 2020, https://adage.com/article/special-report-marketers-year/marketers-year
-no-1-tiktok/2297606.

159. Garrett Sloane, "Leaked TikTok Email Reveals Hashtag Challenge Changes and
Big Brand Media Incentives," *Advertising Age*, June 14, 2022, https://adage.com/article/
digital-marketing-ad-tech-news/tiktok-reveals-hashtag-challenge-changes-and-big
-brand-media-incentives-leaked-email/2420216.

160. Kimeko McCoy, "The Woman behind Making TikTok Tick for Creative Agencies," *Digiday*, November 1, 2022, https://digiday.com/marketing/how-an-industry-vet
eran-is-teaching-creatives-what-makes-tiktok-tick/.

161. Allocca, *Videocracy*, 49.

162. Shane, "The Semiotics of Authenticity," 3.

163. McRae, " 'Get Off My Internets,' " 18.

164. Jordyn Tilchen, "Chase Hudson, TikTok's Tongue-out Heartthrob, Wants to
Keep It 'Authentic,' " *MTV News*, May 7, 2020, https://www.mtv.com/news/fcoj1f/chase
-hudson-lil-huddy-interview.

Chapter 3: Pop Music's Sponsorship Play

1. Hugh Barker and Yuval Taylor, *Faking It* (New York: W.W. Norton, 2007), 24.

2. Landau.

3. Hans Weisethaunet and Ulf Lindberg, "Authenticity Revisited," *Popular Music
and Society* 33, no. 4 (2010): 466; Enli, *Mediated Authenticity*, 12.

4. Barker and Taylor, *Faking It*, ix.

5. Peterson, *Creating Country Music*, 3.

6. Sundquist.

7. Rich.

8. Allan Moore, "Authenticity as Authentication," *Popular Music* 21, no. 2 (2002): 209.

9. Julyssa Lopez, " 'Truth Hurts' Was a Viral Hit, but Lizzo's Stardom Is No Acci-
dent," *Billboard*, September 19, 2019, https://www.billboard.com/music/music-news/
lizzo-billboard-cover-story-interview-8530113/.

10. Chris Martins, "2017 No. 1s: Cardi B on Her Rise to Hot 100 History," *Billboard*,
December 21, 2017, https://www.billboard.com/pro/cardi-b-hot-100-history-interview
-no-1s-2017/.

11. Mickey Rapkin, "Demi Lovato on Touring with DJ Khaled, Avoiding 'Fake'
People and the Need for Brutal Honesty," *Billboard*, March 8, 2018, https://www.bill
board.com/music/features/demi-lovato-interview-billboard-cover-story-2018-8235911/;
Molly Lambert, "Billboard Women in Music 'Rule Breaker' Kehlani on Emerging from
Personal Crisis," *Billboard*, November 30, 2017, https://www.billboard.com/music/
awards/kehlani-billboard-women-in-music-rule-breaker-interview-8053738/.

12. Kerri Mason, "The Mau5 That Roared," *Billboard*, December 4, 2010, https://
www.billboard.com/music/music-news/deadmau5-to-resuscitate-dance-scene-with--
4x412–950052/; Rob Tannenbaum, "Robin Thicke on His Next Chapter and Why
'Regret Is Boring' after 'Blurred Lines,' " *Billboard*, April 11, 2019, https://www.billboard
.com/music/pop/robin-thicke-next-chapter-new-album-interview-8506616/.

13. Steven J. Horowitz, "Lana Del Rey: The Billboard Cover Story," *Billboard*, January 13, 2012, https://www.billboard.com/music/music-news/lana-del-rey-the-billboard-cover-story-512467/; Meaghan Garvey, "Lana Del Rey on Finding Her Voice and Following Her Muse: 'I Have Never Taken a Shortcut,'" *Billboard*, August 22, 2019, https://www.billboard.com/music/pop/lana-del-rey-billboard-cover-story-2019-8527901/.

14. Lizzy Goodman, "5SOS' Teenage Wasteland," *Billboard*, October 3, 2015, https://www.billboard.com/music/music-news/5-seconds of summer-sounds-good-feels-good-one-direction-good-charlotte-fall-out-boy-6707203; Garvey, "Lana Del Rey on Finding Her Voice"; Christina Lee, "Pierre 'Pee' Thomas and Kevin 'Coach K' Lee on Quality Control's Takeover of Hip-Hop," *Billboard*, September 27, 2018, https://www.billboard.com/music/rb-hip-hop/pierre-thomas-kevin-lee-quality-control-hip-hop-executives-of-the-year-2018-8477087/; Shumway, "Authenticity," 529.

15. Gail Mitchell, "Mike Posner: No College Dropout," *Billboard*, July 3, 2010, https://www.billboard.com/music/music-news/duke-grad-mike-posner-heats-up-the-charts-957614/.

16. Taylor, *The Ethics of Authenticity*, 62–65.

17. Botterill, "Cowboys, Outlaws and Artists," 112.

18. Julie Guidry Moulard, Randle D. Raggio, and Judith Anne Garretson Folse, "Brand Authenticity," *Psychology & Marketing* 33, no. 6 (2016): 422, 423.

19. Landau.

20. Barker and Taylor, *Faking It*, 246.

21. Keith Negus, "Where the Mystical Meets the Market," *Sociological Review* 43, no. 1 (1995): 328.

22. Grazian, *Blue Chicago*, 237.

23. Weisethaunet and Lindberg, "Authenticity Revisited," 471; Lindholm, *Culture and Authenticity*, 37.

24. Wokler, *Rousseau*, 7, 136.

25. Enli, *Mediated Authenticity*, 12, 13.

26. Barker and Taylor, *Faking It*, 2, 191, 194.

27. Peterson, "In Search of Authenticity," 1090; Lindholm, *Culture and Authenticity*, 38; Barker and Taylor, *Faking It*, 105, 130.

28. Negus, "Where the Mystical Meets the Market," 336; Shumway, "Authenticity," 531.

29. Castelaz.

30. Weisethaunet and Lindberg, "Authenticity Revisited," 469, 472.

31. Barker and Taylor, *Faking It*, 61, 63.

32. Michael Coyle and Jon Dolan, "Modeling Authenitcity, Authenticating Commercial Models," in *Reading Rock and Roll*, ed. Kevin J. H. Dettmar and William Richey (New York: Columbia University Press, 1999), 27, 28.

33. Grazian, "The Production of Popular Music," 138; Klein, *Selling Out*, 20; Pickering, "The Dogma of Authenticity," 205.

34. Pickering, "The Dogma of Authenticity," 214; J. Patrick Williams, "Authentic Identities," *Journal of Contemporary Ethnography* 35, no. 2 (2006): 174.

35. Coyle and Dolan, "Modeling Authenitcity, Authenticating Commercial Models," 23; Goffman, *The Presentation of Self in Everyday Life*, 49, 50.

36. Cruz.

37. Castelaz.

38. Leslie M. Meier, *Popular Music as Promotion* (Cambridge: Polity, 2017), 18, 20, 22.

39. Pickering, "The Dogma of Authenticity," 201, 214.

40. Coyle and Dolan, "Modeling Authenitcity, Authenticating Commercial Models," 23.

41. Thornton, *Club Cultures*, 6.

42. Serazio, *Your Ad Here*, 101.

43. Roy Shuker, *Popular Music* (New York: Routledge, 2017), 15, 16.

44. Keller.

45. Shuker, *Popular Music*, 24; Potter, *The Authenticity Hoax*, 122.

46. Doria.

47. David Hesmondhalgh and Leslie M. Meier, "Popular Music, Independence and the Concept of the Alternative in Contemporary Capitalism," in *Media Independence*, ed. James Bennett and Niki Strange (New York: Routledge, 2015), 94, 95.

48. Shuker, *Popular Music*, 24, 186, 187.

49. Keller.

50. Klein, *Selling Out*, 65, 66, 76; Hesmondhalgh and Meier, "Popular Music, Independence," 94.

51. Keith Negus, *Music Genres and Corporate Cultures* (New York: Routledge, 1999), 91, 92.

52. Coyle and Dolan, "Modeling Authenticity, Authenticating Commercial Models," 19, 20.

53. Rich.

54. Klein, *Selling Out*, 46, 47.

55. Klein, *Selling Out*, 4.

56. Bethany Klein, Leslie M. Meier, and Devon Powers, "Selling Out," *Popular Music and Society* 40, no. 2 (2017): 223; Coyle and Dolan, "Modeling Authenticity, Authenticating Commercial Models," 22; Klein, *Selling Out*, 4.

57. Castelaz.

58. Bason.

59. Barker and Taylor, *Faking It*, 160; John Gunders, "Electronic Dance Music, the Rock Myth, and Authenticity," *Perfect Beat* 13, no. 2 (2012): 147.

60. Gunders, "Electronic Dance Music," 148, 149; Stahl, "Authentic Boy Bands on TV?," 320.

61. Moore, "Authenticity as Authentication," 212; Shuker, *Popular Music*, 24.

62. Gunders, "Electronic Dance Music," 149; Coyle and Dolan, "Modeling Authenitcity, Authenticating Commercial Models," 17.

63. Klein, *Selling Out*, 50, 51, 53, 58; Hesmondhalgh and Meier, "Popular Music, Independence," 97, 98; Moore, "Authenticity as Authentication," 213; Enli, *Mediated Au-*

thenticity, 13; Michael Serazio, "The Irreverent Life and Uncompromising Death of Deadspin," *Journalism* 23, no. 2 (2022): 463, 471.

64. Serazio, "The Irreverent Life," 463; Barker and Taylor, *Faking It*, 20, 289.

65. Nicholas Carah, *Pop Brands* (New York: Peter Lang, 2010), 26.

66. Linehan.

67. Barker and Taylor, *Faking It*, 5, 23.

68. Gunders, "Electronic Dance Music," 149.

69. Gunders, "Electronic Dance Music," 150, 152, 153, 155.

70. Derek Thompson, "The Dark Science of Pop Music," *The Atlantic*, November 17, 2014, https://www.theatlantic.com/magazine/archive/2014/12/the-shazam-effect/382237.

71. Barker and Taylor, *Faking It*, 236, 252.

72. Gunders, "Electronic Dance Music," 147; Grazian, *Blue Chicago*, 237.

73. Moore, "Authenticity as Authentication," 210; Leslie M. Meier, "Promotional Ubiquitous Musics: Recording Artists, Brands, and Rendering Authenticity," *Popular Music and Society* 34, no. 4 (2011): 411.

74. Grazian, "The Production of Popular Music."

75. Grazian, "The Production of Popular Music," 155.

76. Barker and Taylor, *Faking It*, xi, xii.

77. Shuker, *Popular Music*, 44; Peterson, "In Search of Authenticity," 1085.

78. Peterson, "In Search of Authenticity," 1091.

79. Jones, Anand, and Alvarez, "Manufactured Authenticity and Creative Voice," 893; Peterson, *Creating Country Music*, 10.

80. Hughes, "Country Music as Impression Management," 194; Peterson, *Creating Country Music*, 67, 68, 69, 83.

81. Peterson, *Creating Country Music*, 218, 219, 225, 226; Lindholm, *Culture and Authenticity*, 35, 36; Hughes, "Country Music as Impression Management," 194, 196.

82. Hughes, "Country Music as Impression Management," 187.

83. Nick Reilly, "Charli XCX 'Stormed Out' of Meeting with Label Bosses after 'Authenticity' Argument," *NME*, April 9, 2021, https://www.nme.com/news/music/charli-xcx-stormed-out-of-meeting-with-label-bosses-after-authenticity-argument-2930319.

84. Rich.

85. Landau.

86. Ringel.

87. Keller.

88. Rifkind.

89. "Billboard's 2017 Branding Power Players List Revealed, Led by Citi's Jennifer Breithaupt," *Billboard*, June 9, 2017, https://www.billboard.com/pro/2017-branding-power-players-list-revealed/.

90. Jon Caramanica, "Who, What and Where Is Bon Iver?," *New York Times*, June 3, 2011, https://www.nytimes.com/2011/06/05/magazine/who-what-and-where-is-bon-iver.html; Chris Whibbs, "Bon Iver's Good Winter," *Exclaim*, March 2008, https://web.archive.org/web/20091005051227/http://exclaim.ca/articles/multiarticlesub.aspx.

91. Frenette.

92. Sundquist.

93. Caramanica, "Who, What and Where Is Bon Iver?"

94. Barker and Taylor, *Faking It*, 183.

95. Peterson, "In Search of Authenticity," 1088; Grazian, *Blue Chicago*, 13, 52, 59.

96. Weisethaunet and Lindberg, "Authenticity Revisited," 469; Grazian, *Blue Chicago*, 14.

97. Grazian, *Blue Chicago*, 36.

98. Grazian, *Blue Chicago*, 236; Mickey Hess, "Hip-Hop Realness and the White Performer," *Critical Studies in Media Communication* 22, no. 5 (2005): 374.

99. Banet-Weiser, *Authentic*, 105.

100. McLeod, "Authenticity within Hip-Hop," 145.

101. McLeod, "Authenticity within Hip-Hop," 137, 139, 140; Klein, *Selling Out*, 30.

102. Anthony Kwame Harrison, "Racial Authenticity in Rap Music and Hip Hop," *Sociology Compass* 2, no. 6 (2008): 1787; Hess, "Hip-Hop Realness and the White Performer," 375; Tricia Rose, *Black Noise* (Wesleyan, CT: Wesleyan University Press, 1994), 99.

103. Alan Light, "About a Salary or Reality?," in *That's the Joint!*, ed. Murray Foreman and Mark Anthony Neal (New York: Routledge, 2004), 144.

104. Klein, *Selling Out*, 2; McLeod, "Authenticity within Hip-Hop," 141.

105. Hess, "Hip-Hop Realness and the White Performer," 375, 376, 379; Reebee Garofalo, "Culture versus Commerce," *Public Culture* 7, no. 1 (1994): 277, 283.

106. McLeod, "Authenticity within Hip-Hop," 143, 144.

107. Harrison, "Racial Authenticity in Rap Music and Hip Hop," 1786.

108. Cruz; Enli, *Mediated Authenticity*, 12; Barker and Taylor, *Faking It*, 244.

109. Eithne Quinn, *Nuthin' but a "G" Thang: The Culture and Commerce of Gangsta Rap* (New York: Columbia University Press, 2005), 20, 53; Light, "About a Salary or Reality?," 142.

110. Martins, "2017 No. 1s: Cardi B"; Quinn, *Nuthin' but a "G" Thang*, 70, 72, 77.

111. Light, "About a Salary or Reality?," 139.

112. Hess, "Hip-Hop Realness and the White Performer," 372, 374, 382, 385.

113. Rifkind; Negus, *Music Genres and Corporate Cultures*, 96–99; Insanul Ahmed, "Drop a Gem on 'Em: How Steve Rifkind Became One of the Greatest Rap Execs Ever," *Complex*, March 19, 2015, https://www.complex.com/music/2015/03/steve-rifkind-is-one-of-the-greatest-rap-execs-ever.

114. Cruz.

115. Klein, *Selling Out*, 93, 98, 103.

116. Quinn, *Nuthin' but a "G" Thang*, 5; Kamau High, "6 Questions with James Cruz," *Billboard*, July 19, 2008.

117. Klein, *Selling Out*, 86.

118. Cruz; High, "6 Questions with James Cruz."

119. Quinn, *Nuthin' but a "G" Thang*, 5, 7, 15.

120. Mensch.

121. Bason.

122. Meier, *Popular Music as Promotion*, 3, 4.

123. Klein, Meier, and Powers, "Selling Out," 225.

124. Meier, *Popular Music as Promotion*, 38.

125. Shuker, *Popular Music*, 4.

126. Meier, *Popular Music as Promotion*, 90.

127. Meier, *Popular Music as Promotion*, 93.

128. Meier, "Promotional Ubiquitous Musics," 402; Klein, *Selling Out*, 146; Hesmondhalgh and Meier, "Popular Music, Independence," 107.

129. Cruz; "Revealed: Billboard's 2018 Top Branding Power Players," *Billboard*, June 18, 2018, https://www.billboard.com/music/music-news/billboard-top-branding-power-players-2018-list-8460771/.

130. Meier, *Popular Music as Promotion*, 87, 90, 99; Klein, Meier, and Powers, "Selling Out," 234.

131. Carah, *Pop Brands*, 3, 4.

132. Meier, *Popular Music as Promotion*, 6, 8; Meier, "Promotional Ubiquitous Musics," 399, 400; Carah, *Pop Brands*, 74, 81.

133. Max Freedman, "The WORLDZ Interview: Red Light EVP and New Era Managing Partner Matt Ringel," *Flood Magazine*, September 9, 2019, https://floodmagazine.com/67771/the-worldz-interview-red-light-evp-and-new-era-managing-partner-matt-ringel/.

134. "Revealed: Billboard's 2018 Top Branding Power Players."

135. Andrew Hampp, "Why Converse, Scion, Intel, PepsiCo, Others Are Spending Big on Underground Music," *Billboard*, November 29, 2011, https://www.billboard.com/music/music-news/why-converse-scion-intel-pepsico-others-are-spending-big-on-1159618/.

136. "Revealed: Billboard's 2018 Top Branding Power Players."

137. Jessica Wohl, "How to Promote Your Brand at a Music Festival," *Advertising Age*, July 29, 2019, https://adage.com/article/cmo-strategy/how-promote-your-brand-music-festival/2186251; Freedman, "The WORLDZ Interview."

138. Freedman; Klein, Meier, and Powers, "Selling Out: Musicians, Autonomy," 225; Carah, *Pop Brands*, 70.

139. Ringel; Carah, *Pop Brands*, 65.

140. Freedman, "The WORLDZ Interview."

141. Freedman, "The WORLDZ Interview."

142. Ringel.

143. "Revealed: Billboard's 2018 Top Branding Power Players."

144. Meier, *Popular Music as Promotion*, 102, 104; Serazio, *Your Ad Here*.

145. Hampp, "Why Converse, Scion, Intel, PepsiCo, Others."

146. Carah, *Pop Brands*, 2, 3, 65, 67, 78.

147. Hampp, "Why Converse, Scion, Intel, PepsiCo, Others."

148. Hampp, "Why Converse, Scion, Intel, PepsiCo, Others."

149. Meier, *Popular Music as Promotion*, 106, 107.

150. H. Sullivan.

151. H. Sullivan.

152. H. Sullivan; Amos Barshad, "Can Mountain Dew Save the Music Industry?," *New York*, August 12, 2011, https://www.vulture.com/2011/08/can_mountain_dew_save _the_musi.html; "New Talent: Hudson Sullivan," Little Black Book, April 29, 2015, https://www.lbbonline.com/news/new-talent-hudson-sullivan.

153. Klein, *Selling Out*, 131; Klein, Meier, and Powers, "Selling Out: Musicians, Autonomy," 229.

154. Ben Sisario, "Musicians Say Streaming Doesn't Pay: Can the Industry Change?," *New York Times*, May 7, 2021, https://www.nytimes.com/2021/05/07/arts/music/ streaming-music-payments.html.

155. Leslie M. Meier, "Popular Music Making and Promotional Work inside the 'New' Music Industry," in *The Routledge Companion to the Cultural Industries*, ed. Kate Oakley and Justin O'Connor (New York: Routledge, 2015), 404, 405.

156. Bason.

157. Ringel.

158. Cruz.

159. Meier, "Popular Music Making," 403, 408; Klein, Meier, and Powers, "Selling Out: Musicians, Autonomy," 228, 229; Charlie Harding, "The Pop Star versus the Playlist," *Vox*, June 29, 2021, https://www.vox.com/the-highlight/22538526/playlists-spotify -music-pop-stars-charts.

160. Ringel; Karen Allen, "Five Things Melissa Etheridge's Livestreamed Concerts Get Exactly Right," *Variety*, August 13, 2020, https://variety.com/2020/music/news/mel issa-etheridge-tv-livestreams-1234734440/.

161. Keller.

162. Cruz.

163. Carah, *Pop Brands*, 74; Negus, *Music Genres and Corporate Cultures*, 3; Hesmondhalgh and Meier, "Popular Music, Independence," 94.

164. Bason; Kozinets, "Can Consumers Escape the Market?," 34.

165. Klein, Meier, and Powers, "Selling Out: Musicians, Autonomy," 224.

166. Barker and Taylor, *Faking It*, 4.

167. Hesmondhalgh and Meier, "Popular Music, Independence," 106–7.

168. Klein, *Selling Out*, 14, 56, 57.

169. Mensch.

170. Castelaz.

171. Bason.

172. Klein, Meier, and Powers, "Selling Out: Musicians, Autonomy," 223; Meier, "Promotional Ubiquitous Musics," 402.

173. Hesmondhalgh and Meier, "Popular Music, Independence," 108.

174. Klein, Meier, and Powers, "Selling Out: Musicians, Autonomy," 224; Klein, *Selling Out*, 111, 113, 128.

175. Klein, Meier, and Powers, "Selling Out: Musicians, Autonomy," 225, 231.

176. Meier, *Popular Music as Promotion*, 2.

177. Brian Braiker, "Wyclef Jean on Cannes, Brands and Gary Vee," *Advertising Age*, January 6, 2020, https://adage.com/article/podcast-ad-lib/wyclef-jean-cannes-brands -and-gary-vee/2224516.

178. Klein, *Selling Out*, 1.

179. Ringel.

180. Shuker, *Popular Music*, 68; Moore, "Authenticity as Authentication," 211; Lewin and Williams, "The Ideology and Practice of Authenticity," 67; Grazian, *Blue Chicago*, 234; Peterson, *Creating Country Music*, 206.

181. Carah, *Pop Brands*, 70.

182. Klein, Meier, and Powers, "Selling Out: Musicians, Autonomy," 231; Carah, *Pop Brands*, 67.

183. Chris Constantine, "Linkin Park and Mercedes Partner to Celebrate AMG's Heritage," *The Drive*, June 14, 2017, https://www.thedrive.com/article/11542/linkin-park -and-mercedes-partner-to-celebrate-amgs-heritage.

184. E. J. Schultz, "Watch Bruce Springsteen in Jeep's Super Bowl Ad That Calls for the 'Reunited States of America,'" *Advertising Age*, February 7, 2021, https://adage.com /article/special-report-super-bowl/how-jeep-got-bruce-springsteen-its-reunited-states -america-super-bowl-ad/2312151.

185. Cruz.

186. Keller.

187. H. Sullivan.

Chapter 4: The Commercial Brand Sell

1. Gilmore and Pine, *Authenticity: What Consumers Really Want*, 174.

2. Lonsdale.

3. Daniel Dayan and Elihu Katz, *Media Events* (Cambridge, MA: Harvard University Press, 1992).

4. Michael Serazio, "How News Went Guerrilla Marketing," *Media, Culture and Society* 43, no. 1 (2021): 122.

5. Wacksman.

6. Wacksman.

7. Lesley Bielby, "Adland's Year of Natural Selection: Only the Fittest Will Survive," *MediaPost*, April 9, 2019, https://www.mediapost.com/publications/article/334298/ad lands-year-of-natural-selection-only-the-fitte.html; Lindsay Rittenhouse, "Blurred Lines," *Advertising Age*, October 28, 2019, https://adage.com/article/news/pr-agencies -invade-adland/2210016.

8. Gilmore and Pine, *Authenticity: What Consumers Really Want*, 148.

9. H. Sullivan.

10. Meredith Chase, "Brands That Score on Social with Gen Z Will Win Wall Street, Too," *Medium*, March 21, 2018, https://medium.com/possible-pov/brands-that-score -on-social-with-gen-z-will-win-wall-street-too-2e1e370a0656.

11. Michael Serazio, "Selling (Digital) Millennials," *Television and New Media* 16, no. 7 (2015): 599–615.

12. Jill Kipnis, "The Wonder Years," *Billboard*, November 6, 2004.

13. Boyle, *Authenticity*, 109, 114.

14. Doria.

15. Powers, *On Trend*, 3, 7.

16. Powers, *On Trend*, 63, 64.

17. Boyle, *Authenticity*, 119.

18. Powers, *On Trend*, 84, 87.

19. Douglas B. Holt, *How Brands Become Icons* (Boston: Harvard Business School Press, 2004) , 210, 214.

20. Martin.

21. Coles; Cummings; Powers, *On Trend*, 92, 97.

22. Lonsdale.

23. Chase.

24. Serazio, *Your Ad Here*, 141; Powers, *On Trend*, 26.

25. Wacksman.

26. Garrett Sloane, "Facebook Lets Brands Dive into People's Posts," *Advertising Age*, October 16, 2017, https://adage.com/article/digital/facebook/310888.

27. Bielby.

28. Lewis and Bridger, *The Soul of the New Consumer*, 200.

29. Boyle, *Authenticity*, 59.

30. Michael Beverland and Michael Ewing, "Slowing the Adoption and Diffusion Process to Enhance Brand Repositioning," *Business Horizons* 48, no. 5 (2005): 385, 389.

31. Thomas W. Leigh, Cara Peters, and Jeremy Shelton, "The Consumer Quest for Authenticity," *Journal of the Academy of Marketing Science* 34, no. 4 (2006): 491; Janna Michael, "It's Really Not Hip to Be a Hipster," *Journal of Consumer Culture* 15, no. 2 (2015): 176.

32. Potter, *The Authenticity Hoax*, 103; Michael B. Beverland, Adam Lindgreen, and Michiel W. Vink, "Projecting Authenticity through Advertising: Consumer Judgments of Advertisers' Claims," *Journal of Advertising* 37, no. 1 (2008): 5.

33. Chase.

34. Cesarkas.

35. James H. Wittebols, "Crisis and Contradiction: Promotional Authenticity in the Digital World," in *Explorations in Critical Studies of Advertising*, ed. James F. Hamilton, Robert Bodle, and Ezequiel Korin (New York: Routledge, 2017), 55.

36. Tony Pec, "The Importance of Building an Authentic Brand," *Forbes*, January 18, 2020, https://www.forbes.com/sites/forbesagencycouncil/2020/06/18/the-importance-of-building-an-authentic-brand/.

37. Anne Hamby, David Brinberg, and Kim Daniloski, "It's about Our Values," *Psychology and Marketing* 36, no. 11 (2019): 1015; Steve Ellwanger, "Brand Authenticity, Transparency Outweigh Sustainability," *MediaPost*, November 26, 2019, https://www.mediapost.com/publications/article/343863/brand-authenticity-transparency-outweigh-sustaina.html.

38. Botterill, "Cowboys, Outlaws and Artists," 110; Gilmore and Pine, *Authenticity: What Consumers Really Want*, 3.

39. Serazio, *Your Ad Here*, 93.

40. Lindholm, *Culture and Authenticity*, 52.

41. Enli, *Mediated Authenticity*, 6; Lindholm, *Culture and Authenticity*, 55–56.

42. Lewis and Bridger, *The Soul of the New Consumer*, 28; Whitmer, "You Are Your Brand," 3; Michael B. Beverland and Francis J. Farrelly, "The Quest for Authenticity in Consumption," *Journal of Consumer Research* 36 (2010): 839.

43. Boyle, *Authenticity*, 40.

44. Umbach and Humphrey, *Authenticity*, 115; Botterill, "Cowboys, Outlaws and Artists," 105.

45. Holt, *How Brands Become Icons*, 1.

46. Beverland, *Building Brand Authenticity*, 16, 20.

47. Bielby.

48. Umbach and Humphrey, *Authenticity*, 95.

49. Beverland, *Building Brand Authenticity*, 26.

50. Beverland, *Building Brand Authenticity*, 7, 8; Julie Napoli et al., "Measuring Consumer-Based Brand Authenticity," *Journal of Business Research* 67, no. 6 (2014): 1091.

51. Silverstein.

52. Marchand, *Creating the Corporate Soul*.

53. Banet-Weiser, *Authentic*, 7.

54. Banet-Weiser, *Authentic*, 4, 7.

55. Sivan Portal, Russell Abratt, and Michael Bendixen, "The Role of Brand Authenticity in Developing Brand Trust," *Journal of Strategic Marketing* 27, no. 8 (2019): 725.

56. Chuck Kapelke, "Adding a Little of That Human Touch," *ANA Magazine*, January 25, 2019, https://www.ana.net/magazines/show/id/ana-2019-01-humanizing-the-brand.

57. Kapelke.

58. Moulard, Raggio, and Folse, "Brand Authenticity," 421–23.

59. Audrezet, de Kerviler, and Guidry Moulard, "Authenticity under Threat," 3; Douglas B. Holt, "Why Do Brands Cause Trouble?," *Journal of Consumer Research* 29, no. 1 (2002): 83; Hamby, Brinberg, and Daniloski, "It's about Our Values."

60. Kadirov, Varey, and Wooliscroft, "Authenticity," 75.

61. H. Sullivan.

62. Beverland, "Crafting Brand Authenticity," 1004; Beverland, *Building Brand Authenticity*, 2.

63. Michael Beverland, "Brand Management and the Challenge of Authenticity," *Journal of Product and Brand Management* 14, no. 7 (2005): 460, 461; Beverland and Farrelly, "The Quest for Authenticity in Consumption," 846, 847; Beverland, *Building Brand Authenticity*, 123, 124, 132, 139, 178.

64. Beverland and Ewing, "Slowing the Adoption and Diffusion Process," 386.

65. Beverland, "Crafting Brand Authenticity," 1003, 1012; Beverland, *Building Brand Authenticity*, 16–17.

66. Beverland, "Crafting Brand Authenticity," 1023.

67. Holt, *How Brands Become Icons*, 33.

68. Vincent Stanley, "Don't Buy This Jacket, Part 2: What's Next for Patagonia" (ANA Center for Brand Purpose, 2021), https://www.ana.net/membersconference/show/id/MOC-APR21E.

69. Robert Kreuzbauer and Joshua Keller, "The Authenticity of Cultural Products," *Current Directions in Psychological Science* 26, no. 5 (2017): 419.

70. Beverland and Ewing, "Slowing the Adoption and Diffusion Process," 389.

71. Coles.

72. William Leiss et al., *Social Communication in Advertising*, 3rd ed. (New York: Routledge, 2005), 22; Mara Einstein, *Advertising* (Oxford: Oxford University Press, 2017); Liz Moor, *The Rise of Brands* (Oxford: Berg, 2007); Adam Arvidsson, *Brands* (London: Routledge, 2006).

73. Chase.

74. Hamby, Brinberg, and Daniloski, "It's about Our Values," 1015.

75. Holt, *How Brands Become Icons*, 2004, 36, 39.

76. Ramos.

77. Gilmore and Pine, *Authenticity: What Consumers Really Want*, 52.

78. Michael Serazio, "Ethos Groceries and Countercultural Appetites," *Journal of Popular Culture* 44, no. 1 (2011): 158–77; Duffy, "Manufacturing Authenticity," 151; "Gen Z & Millennials Are Getting Real: Here's How Brands Are Keeping Up," *PSFK Research*, November 15, 2019, https://www.psfk.com/2019/11/millennials-gen-z-getting-real-social-media-brands-impact.html.

79. Beverland, *Building Brand Authenticity*, 32, 46.

80. Glenn R. Carroll, "Authenticity," in *Emerging Tends in the Social and Behavioral Sciences*, ed. Robert A. Scott and Stephen M. Kosslyn (Hoboken, NJ: John Wiley & Sons, 2015), 6–7.

81. Carly O'Neill, Dick Houtman, and Stef Aupers, "Advertising Real Beer," *European Journal of Cultural Studies* 17, no. 5 (2014): 589.

82. Thurnell-Read, "A Thirst for the Authentic," 1; Moulard, Raggio, and Folse, "Brand Authenticity," 425.

83. Thurnell-Read, "A Thirst for the Authentic," 5, 6.

84. Schram.

85. Thurnell-Read, "A Thirst for the Authentic," 7, 8.

86. Beverland, *Building Brand Authenticity*, 106, 109, 110.

87. Beverland, *Building Brand Authenticity*, 120.

88. Beverland, *Building Brand Authenticity*, 65–67.

89. Chase.

90. Jake Loechner, "Peer-to-Peer Endorsements Powerful Authenticator," *MediaPost*, July 19, 2016, https://www.mediapost.com/publications/article/280494/peer-to-peer-endorsements-powerful-authenticator.html.

91. Serazio, *Your Ad Here*, 141.

92. "Effective UGC Campaigns Hint at a New Wave of Digital Marketing," *DMS Insights*, July 23, 2020, https://insights.digitalmediasolutions.com/articles/effective-ugc-campaigns.

93. Cummings.

94. Alex Vuocolo, "Gen Z Looks for Authenticity in TikTok Viral Marketing, Says Creative Agency CEO," *Cheddar News*, December 28, 2020, https://cheddar.com/media/gen-z-looks-for-authenticity-in-tiktok-viral-marketing-says-creative-agency-ceo.

95. Bielby.

96. Kaitlyn Tiffany, "Why the New Instagram It Girl Spends All Her Time Alone," *The Atlantic*, October 16, 2019, https://www.theatlantic.com/technology/archive/2019/10/instagram-lonely-gender-authenticity-natasha-stagg-sleeveless/600085/.

97. Santos.

98. Lewis and Bridger, *The Soul of the New Consumer*, 40.

99. Beverland, *Building Brand Authenticity*, 87, 89; Nicholas Alexander, "Brand Authentication: Creating and Maintaining Brand Auras," *European Journal of Marketing* 43, no. 3/4 (2009): 551.

100. O'Neill, Houtman, and Aupers, "Advertising Real Beer," 593.

101. O'Neill, Houtman, and Aupers, "Advertising Real Beer," 590; Beverland, Lindgreen, and Vink, "Projecting Authenticity through Advertising," 7, 9.

102. Ethan Jakob Craft, "Miller Genuine Draft Makes 'Genuine' the Keyword in New U.S. Rebrand," *Advertising Age*, February 17, 2021, https://adage.com/article/cmo-strategy/miller-genuine-draft-makes-genuine-keyword-new-us-rebrand/2314666.

103. Koontz, "Constructing Authenticity," 977; Shuling Liao and Yu-yi Ma, "Conceptualizing Consumer Need for Product Authenticity," *International Journal of Business and Information* 4, no. 1 (2009): 89; Navdeep Athwal and Lloyd C. Harris, "Examining How Brand Authenticity Is Established and Maintained," *Journal of Marketing Management* 34, no. 3–4 (2018): 347.

104. Holt, *How Brands Become Icons*, 110; Gilmore and Pine, *Authenticity: What Consumers Really Want*, 58–59; Moulard, Raggio, and Folse, "Brand Authenticity," 425.

105. Ethan Jakob Craft, "Why All Things Nostalgic Are Making a Big Splash in the Ad World," *Advertising Age*, July 15, 2019, https://adage.com/article/cmo-strategy/why-all-things-nostalgic-are-making-big-splash-ad-world/2183331.

106. Cesarkas.

107. Beverland, Lindgreen, and Vink, "Projecting Authenticity through Advertising," 12.

108. Beverland, *Building Brand Authenticity*, 7, 73, 75.

109. Beverland, *Building Brand Authenticity*, 72, 73.

110. Beverland, *Building Brand Authenticity*, 40, 48, 49, 50.

111. Hamby, Brinberg, and Daniloski, "It's about Our Values," 1014, 1016.

112. Bielby.

113. Kovács, Carroll, and Lehman, "Authenticity and Consumer Value Ratings," 5; Beverland, *Building Brand Authenticity*, 42.

114. Kovács, Carroll, and Lehman, "Authenticity and Consumer Value Ratings," 1.

115. Cummings.

116. Hamby, Brinberg, and Daniloski, "It's about Our Values," 1024.

117. O'Neill, Houtman, and Aupers, "Advertising Real Beer," 591–92.

118. Beverland, *Building Brand Authenticity*, 157.

119. Caroline L. Munoz, Natalie T. Wood, and Michael R. Solomon, "Real or Blarney?," *Journal of Consumer Behaviour* 5 (2006): 224, 232.

120. Juan-Carlos Molleda and Marilyn Roberts, "The Value of 'Authenticity' in 'Glocal' Strategic Communication," *International Journal of Strategic Communication* 2, no. 3 (2008): 165, 166, 169.

121. Lewis and Bridger, *The Soul of the New Consumer*, 22; Gilmore and Pine, *Authenticity: What Consumers Really Want*, 127.

122. Hainsworth.

123. Dickinson, "Joe's Rhetoric," 5, 10, 11, 14, 19, 21; Lindholm, *Culture and Authenticity*, 63.

124. Lewis and Bridger, *The Soul of the New Consumer*, 23.

125. Aiello and Dickinson, "Beyond Authenticity," 303, 309.

126. Heidi Peiper, "Howard Schultz and Starbucks: 25 Moments to Remember," *Starbucks Stories & News*, June 25, 2018, https://stories.starbucks.com/stories/2018/howard-schultz-and-starbucks-25-moments-to-remember/; Dickinson, "Joe's Rhetoric," 17.

127. Emily Bryson York, "How 'Mr. Starbucks' Became Mr. Tether," *Advertising Age*, May 5, 2008, https://adage.com/article/news/mr-starbucks-mr-tether/126826.

128. Molly DeWolf Swenson, "Why It's Critical Brands Take a Stand on Tough Social Issues," *Adweek*, November 26, 2017, https://www.adweek.com/brand-marketing/why-its-so-important-for-brands-to-take-a-stand-on-tough-social-issues/.

129. Banet-Weiser, *Authentic*, 16, 18.

130. Banet-Weiser, *Authentic*, 137, 138.

131. Banet-Weiser, *Authentic*, 148.

132. Banet-Weiser, *Authentic*, 144, 145.

133. Mara Einstein, *Compassion, Inc.* (Berkeley: University of California Press, 2012), xii, 92.

134. David Gelles and David Yaffe-Bellany, "Shareholder Value Is No Longer Everything, Top C.E.O.s Say," *New York Times*, August 19, 2019, https://www.nytimes.com/2019/08/19/business/business-roundtable-ceos-corporations.html.

135. David Gelles, "Whole Foods Founder: 'The Whole World Is Getting Fat,'" *New York Times*, September 24, 2020, https://www.nytimes.com/2020/09/24/business/john-mackey-corner-office-whole-foods.html.

136. Kate Reilly, "Allow Burger King's New Ad to Explain Net Neutrality to You," *Time*, January 24, 2018, https://time.com/5117628/burger-king-whopper-net-neutrality-ad/.

137. Erik Oster, "Why Brands Spend $5 Million (or More) on a Super Bowl Ad to Support a Cause," *Adweek*, January 28, 2019, https://www.adweek.com/brand-marketing/why-cause-related-super-bowl-ads-are-here-to-stay/.

138. Cesarkas.

139. Reynolds.

140. Bielby; Cummings; M. T. Fletcher, "How to Keep Your 'Purpose-Led Marketing' from Turning into Pointless Advertising," *Advertising Age*, September 27, 2021, https://adage.com/article/fletcher-marketing/how-keep-your-purpose-led-marketing-turning-pointless-pandering/2365916.

141. Erik Wander, "Infographic: What Consumers Expect of Brands When It Comes to Issues They Care About," *Adweek*, April 15, 2018, https://www.adweek.com/brand-marketing/infographic-what-consumers-expect-of-brands-when-it-comes-to-issues-they-care-about/; Kristina Monllos, "In 2019, We'll See More Brands Stand for Something," *Adweek*, December 3, 2018, https://www.adweek.com/brand-marketing/in-2019-well-see-more-brands-stand-for-something/.

142. Suzanne Kapner and Dante Chinni, "Are Your Jeans Red or Blue? Shopping America's Partisan Divide," *Wall Street Journal*, November 19, 2019, https://www.wsj.com/articles/are-your-jeans-red-or-blue-shopping-americas-partisan-divide-11574185777.

143. Tara Isabella Burton, "America's Civil Religion Is Capitalism: Trump's Coronavirus Response Proves It," *Washington Post*, March 26, 2020, https://www.washingtonpost.com/outlook/2020/03/26/fox-news-trump-dan-patrick-coronavirus/.

144. Julie Liesse, "Brand Purpose," *Advertising Age*, September 20, 2021, https://s3-prod.adage.com/s3fs-public/2021-09/kantar_aa_brandpurpose_wp2021.pdf.

145. Lindsay Stein, "Delta Learns the Hard Way There's No Such Thing as Neutral," *Advertising Age*, March 19, 2018, https://adage.com/article/cmo-strategy/delta-no-such-thing-neutral/312773.

146. Cesarkas.

147. Swenson, "Why It's Critical Brands Take a Stand."

148. Kapner and Chinni, "Are Your Jeans Red or Blue?"

149. Ramos; Assayag.

150. Stein, "Delta Learns the Hard Way"; Jessica Wohl, "How to Be Topical in an Election Year without Getting Burned," *Advertising Age*, February 25, 2020, https://adage.com/article/brand-playbook/how-be-topical-election-year-without-getting-burned/2238756.

151. Lonsdale; Bielby; T. L. Stanley, "How Brands like Hyatt and Orbitz Are Promoting U.S. Tourism in the Shadow of Trump's Travel Bans," *Adweek*, May 22, 2017, https://www.adweek.com/brand-marketing/how-brands-like-hyatt-and-orbitz-are-promoting-u-s-tourism-in-the-shadow-of-trumps-travel-bans/; Patrick Coffee, "How Agencies Are Channeling Their Pre-Election Passions into Trump-Era Political Activism," *Adweek*, April 23, 2017, https://www.adweek.com/agencies/how-agencies-are-channeling-their-pre-election-passions-into-trump-era-political-activism/.

152. Emma Goldberg and Lora Kelly, "Companies Are More Vocal Than Ever on Social Issues: Not on Abortion," *New York Times*, June 24, 2020, https://www.nytimes.com/2022/06/24/business/abortion-roe-wade-companies.html.

153. "In U.S., Decline of Christianity Continues at Rapid Pace," 2019, https://www.

pewforum.org/2019/10/17/in-u-s-decline-of-christianity-continues-at-rapid-pace/; "Confidence in Institutions," 2021, https://news.gallup.com/poll/1597/confidence-insti tutions.aspx.

154. Beverland, *Building Brand Authenticity*, 21, 23; Gilmore and Pine, *Authenticity: What Consumers Really Want*, 28.

155. Chase.

156. Douglas Atkin, *The Culting of Brands* (New York: Portfolio, 2004), xiii.

157. Burton, "America's Civil Religion Is Capitalism."

158. David Marchese, "Ben & Jerry's Radical Ice Cream Dreams," *New York Times Magazine*, July 27, 2020, https://www.nytimes.com/interactive/2020/07/27/magazine/ben-jerry-interview.html.

159. Chris Miller, "Ben & Jerry's: Where Social Justice Is a Key Ingredient" (ANA Center for Brand Purpose, 2021), https://www.ana.net/membersconference/show/id/MOC-APR21E.

160. Shelly Branch and Ernest Beck, "Unilever Buy Ben & Jerry's, SlimFast for Over $2.5 Billion," *Wall Street Journal*, April 13, 2000, https://www.wsj.com/articles/SB955522 850788928066.

161. Wohl, "How to Be Topical in an Election Year"; Miller, "Ben & Jerry's."

162. Banet-Weiser, *Authentic*, 151, 152.

163. Miller, "Ben & Jerry's"; Wohl, "How to Be Topical in an Election Year."

164. Eric Nagourney, "Ben & Jerry's to Stop Selling Ice Cream in Israeli-Occupied Territories," *New York Times*, July 19, 2021, https://www.nytimes.com/2021/07/19/world /middleeast/israel-ben-jerrys-ice-cream.html.

165. Banet-Weiser, *Authentic*, 19, 39; Cesarkas; Bielby.

166. Santos.

167. Jack Neff, "Top Ad Campaigns of the 21st Century," *Advertising Age*, January 12, 2015, https://adage.com/article/agency-news/top-15-ad-campaigns-21st-century/21629 16#realbeauty.

168. Lauren Collins, "Pixel Perfect," *New Yorker*, May 5, 2008, https://www.newyor ker.com/magazine/2008/05/12/pixel-perfect.

169. Ramos.

170. Emily Dreyfuss, "Gillette's Ad Proves the Definition of a Good Man Has Changed," *Wired*, January 16, 2019, https://www.wired.com/story/gillette-we-believe -ad-men-backlash/.

171. Kristina Monllos, "Futurist Faith Popcorn Explains Why Marketers Should Care about the Future of Masculinity," *Adweek*, June 11, 2018, https://www.adweek.com /brand-marketing/what-faith-popcorns-cant-miss-zine-tells-us-about-the-future-of -masculinity/.

172. Jack Neff, "Gillette's 'The Best Men Can Be' and the War on Toxic Masculinity," *Advertising Age*, September 30, 2019, https://c101.hongtaoh.com/files/14-week/gillette. pdf/.

173. Bhalla.

174. Dreyfuss, "Gillette's Ad Proves the Definition."

175. Neff, "Gillette's 'The Best Men Can Be'."

176. Angela Watercutter, "Pepsi's Kendall Jenner Ad Was So Awful It Did the Impossible: It United the Internet," *Wired*, April 5, 2017, https://www.wired.com/2017/04/pepsi-ad-internet-response/; Daniel Victor, "Pepsi Pulls Ad Accused of Trivializing Black Lives Matter," *New York Times*, April 5, 2017, https://www.nytimes.com/2017/04/05/business/kendall-jenner-pepsi-ad.html.

177. Steve Robson, "Team behind Controversial Pepsi Ad Accused of 'Lack of Diversity' as It Emerges 'ALL Those Credited Are White,'" *The Mirror*, April 6, 2017, https://www.mirror.co.uk/news/world-news/team-behind-controversial-pepsi-ad-10169148; E. J. Schultz and Ann-Christine Diaz, "Pepsi Is Pulling Its Widely Mocked Kendall Jenner Ad," *Advertising Age*, April 5, 2017, https://adage.com/article/cmo-strategy/pepsi-pulling-widely-mocked-kendall-jenner-ad/308575.

178. Austin Carr, "The Inside Story of Starbucks's Race Together Campaign, No Foam," *Fast Company*, June 15, 2015, https://www.fastcompany.com/3046890/the-inside-story-of-starbuckss-race-together-campaign-no-foam.

179. Alex Abad-Santos, "Nike's Colin Kaepernick Ad Sparked a Boycott—and Earned $6 Billion for Nike," *Vox*, September 24, 2018, https://www.vox.com/2018/9/24/17895704/nike-colin-kaepernick-boycott-6-billion.

180. Nadra Nittle, "Companies Used to Stay Quiet about Politics: In 2018, Social Causes Became Integral to Their Branding," *Vox*, December 17, 2018, https://www.vox.com/the-goods/2018/12/17/18139699/companies-nike-patagonia-dicks-politics-kaepernick-trump-ads.

181. Lonsdale.

182. James Poniewozik, *Audience of One* (New York: W.W. Norton, 2019); Naomi Klein, *No Is Not Enough* (Chicago: Haymarket Books, 2017).

183. Stephie Grob Plante, "Shopping Has Become a Political Act: Here's How It Happened," *Vox*, October 7, 2019, https://www.vox.com/the-goods/2019/10/7/20894134/consumer-activism-conscious-consumerism-explained; Lindsay Stein, "How and When Brands Should Jump into Trump-Charged Issues," *Advertising Age*, February 7, 2017, https://adage.com/article/print-edition/brands-jump-trump-charged-issues/307851.

184. Jason Zengerle, "Can the Black Rifle Coffee Company Become the Starbucks of the Right?," *New York Times Magazine*, July 14, 2021, https://www.nytimes.com/2021/07/14/magazine/black-rifle-coffee-company.html.

185. Einstein, *Compassion, Inc.*, 26, 105.

186. Ilyse Liffreing, "Ben & Jerry's Calls to 'Impeach' Trump as Brands like Coca-Cola and Chevron Break Their Silence on the Capitol Insurrection," *Advertising Age*, January 7, 2021, https://adage.com/article/media/ben-jerrys-calls-impeach-trump-brands-coca-cola-and-chevron-break-their-silence-capitol-insurrection/2304111.

Chapter 5: The Rise of Influencers

1. Quinn.

2. Karwowski.

3. Joe Coscarelli and Melissa Ryzik, "Fyre Festival, a Luxury Music Weekend, Crumbles in the Bahamas," *New York Times*, April 28, 2017, https://www.nytimes.com /2017/04/28/arts/music/fyre-festival-ja-rule-bahamas.html; Abby Ohlheiser, "The Complete Disaster of Fyre Festival Played Out on Social Media for All to See; 'NOT MY FAULT' Says Organizer Ja Rule," *Washington Post*, April 28, 2017, https://www.wash ingtonpost.com/news/the-intersect/wp/2017/04/28/the-complete-and-utter-disaster -that-was-fyre-festival-played-out-on-social-media-for-all-to-see; Gabrielle Bluestone, "Fyre Festival's 25-Year-Old Organizer: 'This Is the Worst Day of My Life,'" *Vice*, April 28, 2017, https://www.vice.com/en/article/qvz5m3/fyre-festivals-25-year-old-organizer -this-is-the-worst-day-of-my-life.

4. Jennifer Furst and Julia Willoughby Nason, dirs., *Fyre Fraud* (Hulu, 2017).

5. Serazio, *Your Ad Here*, 97.

6. Serazio, *Your Ad Here*, 98.

7. Elihu Katz and Paul Felix Lazarsfeld, *Personal Influence*, 2nd ed. (New Brunswick, NJ: Transaction, 2006).

8. Emily Hund, "The Influencer Industry: Constructing and Commodifying Authenticity on Social Media" (PhD diss., University of Pennsylvania, 2019), 12.

9. Hearn and Schoenhoff, "From Celebrity to Influencer," 198.

10. Jennings, "A Celebrity Endorsement, for $500."

11. Taylor Lorenz, "For Creators, Everything Is for Sale," *New York Times*, March 10, 2021, https://www.nytimes.com/2021/03/10/style/creators-selling-selves.html.

12. Rifkind; Carah, *Pop Brands*, xi; Serazio, *Your Ad Here*, 101–2.

13. Serazio, *Your Ad Here*, 118.

14. Serazio, *Your Ad Here*, 114.

15. Serazio, *Your Ad Here*, 104.

16. Paris Martineau, "The WIRED Guide to Influencers," *Wired*, December 6, 2019, https://www.wired.com/story/what-is-an-influencer/.

17. Hund, "The Influencer Industry," 21–23, 28, 75.

18. Jack Neff, "How to Succeed with Influencers: Brand Playbook," *Advertising Age*, January 23, 2019, https://adage.com/article/cmo-strategy/succeed-influencers/316313.

19. T. L. Stanley, "How Video Platforms and Brands Are Courting the Next Generation of Internet Stars," *Adweek*, July 24, 2017, https://www.adweek.com/convergent-tv/ how-video-platforms-and-brands-are-courting-the-next-generation-of-internet-stars/; Taylor Lorenz, "These Top Hollywood Agents Are Signing All the Influencers," *New York Times*, April 6, 2020, https://www.nytimes.com/2020/04/06/style/hollywood -agents-influencers.html.

20. Lorenz, "Hype House and the Los Angeles TikTok Mansion"; Taylor Lorenz, "Trying to Make It Big Online? Getting Signed Isn't Everything," *New York Times*, August 14, 2020, https://www.nytimes.com/2020/08/14/style/influences-tiktok-manage ment-brittany-broski.html.

21. Subramanian; Erika Wheless, "Dunkin' Donuts' Latest Merchandise Drop Builds on TikTok Popularity," *Digiday*, April 1, 2021, https://digiday.com/marketing/ dunkin-donuts-latest-merchandise-drop-builds-on-tiktok-popularity/.

22. Adrianne Pasquarelli and E. J. Schultz, "Move Over, Gen Z, Generation Alpha Is the One to Watch," *Advertising Age*, January 22, 2019, https://adage.com/article/cmo-stra tegy/move-gen-z-generation-alpha-watch/316314; Judann Pollack, "10 Influencers under 10," *Advertising Age*, January 22, 2019, https://adage.com/article/cmo-strategy/10-influen cers-10/316319; Jay Caspian Kang, "The Boy King of YouTube," *New York Times Magazine*, January 5, 2022, https://www.nytimes.com/2022/01/05/magazine/ryan-kaji-youtube.html.

23. Michael Waters, "Retailers Are Pushing Their Employees to Become TikTok Influencers," *Modern Retail*, November 11, 2020, https://www.modernretail.co/platforms /retailers-are-pushing-their-employees-become-tiktok-influencers/.

24. Christopher Heine, "Big Brands Are Enlisting Employees to Create an Army of Social Media Mavens," *Adweek*, October 24, 2016, https://www.adweek.com/perfor mance-marketing/big-brands-are-enlisting-employees-order-create-army-social -media-mavens-174152/.

25. Lauren Zumbach, "Are You Getting Paid for That Instagram Post? Companies Tap Employees to Spread More 'Authentic' Messages Online," *Chicago Tribune*, January 17, 2020, https://www.chicagotribune.com/business/ct-biz-employee-social-media-in fluencers-20200117-jv6zjtf5kndqbif65ca6dfj6ie-story.html.

26. Paris Martineau, "Inside the Weird, and Booming, Industry of Online Influence," *Wired*, April 22, 2019, https://www.wired.com/story/inside-the-industry-social -media-influence/; Lorenz, "These Top Hollywood Agents."

27. Sheila Marikar, "Instagram's Sneakiness Makes Super Bowl Ads Look Quaint," *New York Times*, February 2, 2019, https://www.nytimes.com/2019/02/02/opinion/sun day/super-bowl-commercials-instagram.html.

28. Martineau, "Inside the Weird, and Booming, Industry"; Sammy Nickalls, "Influencers Are Bigger Than Ever, and They're Just Getting Started," *Adweek*, June 3, 2018, https://www.adweek.com/brand-marketing/infographic-the-future-of-influencer-mar keting/; Lerman, "Social Media Influencers"; Traackr, "The State of Influencer Marketing 2021," 2021.

29. Chocano, "The Coast of Utopia."

30. Hadley Freeman, "Selfies, Influencers and a Twitter President: The Decade of the Social Media Celebrity," *The Guardian*, November 23, 2019, https://www.theguardian. com/culture/2019/nov/23/selfies-influencers-twitter-president-decade-of-social-media -celebrity-hadley-freeman; Suzanne Kapner and Sharon Terlep, "Online Influencers Tell You What to Buy, Advertisers Wonder Who's Listening," *Wall Street Journal*, October 20, 2019, https://www.wsj.com/articles/online-influencers-tell-you-what-to-buy-adver tisers-wonder-whos-listening-11571594003; Kimeko McCoy, "'Going Viral Is Not a Strategy': How Hotwire Is Leveraging Online Video and TikTok to Reach Its Younger Audience," *Digiday*, July 28, 2021, https://digiday.com/marketing/going-viral-is-not-a-strate gy-how-hotwire-is-leveraging-online-video-and-tiktok-to-reach-its-younger-audience/.

31. Pollack, "10 Influencers under 10."

32. Jack Neff, "Clean Break: Why J & J Is Enlisting Teens with Modest Followings as Influencers," *Advertising Age*, October 2, 2018, https://adage.com/article/cmo-strategy/ clean-break/315092; Martineau, "The WIRED Guide to Influencers."

33. Marikar, "Instagram's Sneakiness Makes Super Bowl Ads."

34. Jack Neff and Lindsay Stein, "Peer Pressure: Gen Z Shakes Up Influencer Ranks," *Advertising Age*, January 23, 2018, https://adage.com/article/digital/peer-pressure-gen-z-shakes-influencer-ranks/312021.

35. Sammy Nickalls, "Nearly Half of Americans Make Purchases Based on Influencer Recommendations," *Adweek*, May 5, 2019, https://www.adweek.com/brand-marketing/infographic-nearly-half-of-americans-make-purchases-based-on-influencer-recommendations/; Sammy Nickalls, "Influencers Are Getting Brands More Sales than Celebrities Are," *Adweek*, January 14, 2019, https://www.adweek.com/brand-marketing/infographic-influencers-are-getting-brands-more-sales-than-celebrities-are/.

36. Sammy Nickalls, "For Brands, Influencers Are More Powerful than Celebrities," *Adweek*, March 25, 2018, https://www.adweek.com/brand-marketing/infographic-for-brands-influencers-are-more-powerful-than-celebrities/; Neff and Stein, "Peer Pressure."

37. Hund, "The Influencer Industry," 45.

38. Kate Kaye, "Love Connection: How Brands Are Using AI to Find Influencer Matches," *Advertising Age*, May 12, 2017, https://adage.com/article/datadriven-marketing/love-connection-data-science-brand-influencer-coupling/309001.

39. Subramanian; Assayag.

40. Carrie Cummings, "How 'Microbloggers' Leverage Their Influence through Social Media Savvy," *Adweek*, September 5, 2016, https://www.adweek.com/performance-marketing/infographic-how-microbloggers-leverage-their-influence-through-social-media-savvy-173272/.

41. Santangelo.

42. Marrs; Quinn.

43. Marrs.

44. Quinn; Terry Lefton, "Brands Seek Social Influencers with Reach, Cachet," *SportsBusiness Journal*, June 4, 2018, https://www.sportsbusinessjournal.com/Journal/Issues/2018/06/04/In-Depth/Influencers.aspx.

45. Karwowski.

46. Klear, "The Klear Influence Score," n.d., https://klear.com/what-is-influence?source=whiteHeader; Alison Hearn, "Verified," *Popular Communication* 15, no. 2 (2017): 67.

47. Madalyn Amato, "Want to Be a Social Media Influencer? Here Are Some Tips for Getting Started," *Los Angeles Times*, August 31, 2021, https://www.latimes.com/entertainment-arts/business/story/2021-08-06/what-is-a-social-media-influencer-online-brand-guide.

48. Sydney Bradley, "Instagram Has Privately Advised Some Creators on How Often to Post, Offering a Rare Glimpse into How Its Mysterious Algorithm Works," *Business Insider*, January 4, 2021, https://www.businessinsider.com/instagram-gives-some-influencers-recommendations-on-how-much-to-post-2021-1.

49. Chelsea Marrs, "How to Grow Your Blog on Instagram," *Chowdown USA*, January 2015, https://www.chowdownusa.com/2015/01/how-to-grow-your-blog-on-instagram.html.

50. Roose, "Don't Scoff at Influencers."

51. Banet-Weiser, *Authentic*, 71.

52. Angela McRobbie, *Feminism and the Politics of Resilience* (New York: Polity, 2020), 2.

53. Schuller, *The Trouble with White Women*, 221, 222.

54. Serazio, *Your Ad Here*, 92; Bradley Johnson, "Procter & Gamble Set to Dethrone Amazon as the World's Biggest Advertiser," *Advertising Age*, August 12, 2021, https://ad age.com/article/datacenter-top-line-stats/were-calling-it-procter-gamble-dethrones -amazon-worlds-biggest-advertiser/2357166.

55. Serazio, *Your Ad Here*, 106.

56. H. Sullivan.

57. Beki Winchel, "KC Star Reports on Its Past Racist Coverage, Tropicana Apologizes for Mimosa-Themed Campaign, and TikTok's Top 2020 Campaigns," *PR Daily*, December 21, 2020, https://www.prdaily.com/kc-star-reports-on-its-past-racist-coverage-tropicana -apologizes-for-mimosa-themed-campaign-and-tiktoks-top-2020-campaigns/.

58. Young.

59. Serazio, *Your Ad Here*, 96.

60. Serazio, *Your Ad Here*, 136.

61. Serazio, *Your Ad Here*, 109.

62. DiCapua.

63. Santangelo.

64. Subramanian.

65. Karwowski.

66. Assayag; Karwowski.

67. Shane Barker, "5 Influencer Marketing Fails You Can Learn From," 2021, https:// shanebarker.com/blog/influencer-marketing-fails/#Influencer_Marketing_Fail_3_Ac cidentally_Copy-Pasting_Instructions.

68. Serazio, *Your Ad Here*, 92.

69. Karwowski; Sapna Maheshwari, "Are You Ready for the Nanoinfluencers?," *New York Times*, November 11, 2018, https://www.nytimes.com/2018/11/11/business/media/ nanoinfluencers-instagram-influencers.html.

70. Hund, "The Influencer Industry," 80; Maheshwari, "Are You Ready for the Nano- influencers?"

71. Cesarkas.

72. Karwowski; Jack Neff, "How Brands Can Still Do Influencer Marketing during the Pandemic," *Advertising Age*, May 13, 2020, https://adage.com/article/cmo-strategy/ how-brands-can-still-do-influencer-marketing-during-pandemic/2255116; Julie Liesse, "Influencers Deliver ROI as Marketers Embrace Them as Business Partners," *Advertis- ing Age*, June 9, 2021, https://adage.com/article/where-series/influencers-deliver-roi -marketers-embrace-them-business-partners/2341866.

73. Sheila Marikar, "Instagram's Sneakiness Makes Super Bowl Ads Look Quaint," *New York Times*, February 2, 2019, https://www.nytimes.com/2019/02/02/opinion/sun day/super-bowl-commercials-instagram.html.

74. Schram.

75. Captiv8, "Meet the Captiv8 Team," n.d., https://captiv8.io/about-us/.

76. Maheshwari, "Are You Ready for the Nanoinfluencers?"

77. Quinn.

78. IZEA, "Influencers," n.d., https://izea.com/influencers/.

79. Karwowski; Santangelo.

80. Schram; Marrs.

81. Maheshwari, "Are You Ready for the Nanoinfluencers?"

82. Karwowski.

83. Karwowski.

84. Seb Jospeh, "As Ad Budgets Are Slashed in the Absence of Cash, Marketers Are 'Bartering' Influencers," *Digiday*, September 12, 2022, https://digiday.com/marketing/as-ad-budgets-are-slashed-in-the-absence-of-cash-marketers-are-bartering-influencers/.

85. Loes van Driel and Delia Dumitrica, "Selling Brands While Staying 'Authentic,'" *Convergence*, 2020, 3, 4, 10.

86. Subramanian.

87. Keller; Martineau, "The WIRED Guide to Influencers."

88. Abidin, "#Familygoals," 4, 6.

89. Banet-Weiser, *Authentic*, 76, 78.

90. DiCapua.

91. Hund, "The Influencer Industry," 89, 97.

92. Duffy and Hund, "Gendered Visibility on Social Media," 4991.

93. McRobbie, *Feminism and the Politics of Resilience*, 5, 6.

94. Star.

95. Quinn.

96. Star.

97. Duffy and Hund, "Gendered Visibility on Social Media," 4991.

98. Hou, "Social Media Celebrity," 542; van Driel and Dumitrica, "Selling Brands While Staying 'Authentic,'" 4; Gannon and Prothero, "Beauty Blogger Selfies as Authenticating Practices," 1866.

99. van Driel and Dumitrica, "Selling Brands While Staying 'Authentic,'" 15.

100. Duffy and Hund, "Gendered Visibility on Social Media," 4989, 4991.

101. Star.

102. Abrar Al-Heeti, "Move Over, Instagram Influencers: The Magic of TikTok Is Authenticity," *CNET*, September 29, 2020, https://www.cnet.com/news/move-over-instagram-influencers-the-magic-of-tiktok-is-authenticity/.

103. Karwowski; Neff and Stein, "Peer Pressure."

104. Young.

105. Gannon and Prothero, "Beauty Blogger Selfies as Authenticating Practices," 1870.

106. van Driel and Dumitrica, "Selling Brands While Staying 'Authentic,'" 10, 11.

107. Star.

108. Karwowski.

109. Gill and Kanai, "Mediating Neoliberal Capitalism," 320, 322.

110. Schuller, *The Trouble with White Women*, 220, 230, 231.

111. Schuller, *The Trouble with White Women*, 236.

112. Santangelo; Lisa Santangelo, "About Us," Food, Family, and Chaos!, n.d.

113. Diana Pearl, "No, Coronavirus Isn't the End of Influencer Marketing: But It Has Put It under a Microscope," *Adweek*, April 14, 2020, https://www.adweek.com/brand-marketing/no-coronavirus-isnt-the-end-of-influencer-marketing-but-it-has-put-it-under-a-microscope/2/; Lerman, "Social Media Influencers"; Neff, "How Brands Can Still Do Influencer Marketing."

114. Kristina Monllos, "'Everyone Is Grasping for Nostalgia and Happiness': Why Marketers Are Ringing in the Holiday Season with More Influencers," *Digiday*, December 2, 2020.

115. Nickalls, "Influencers Are Bigger Than Ever"; Klear, "The State of Influencer Marketing 2019," 2019, https://klear.com/blog/2019-state-of-influencer-marketing-report-instagram-trends/.

116. Young; Duffy, "The Romance of Work," 444.

117. Karwowski; Subramanian; Quinn.

118. Karwowski; Duffy, 443; Hund, "The Influencer Industry," 3.

119. Duffy, *(Not) Getting Paid to Do What You Love*, 79.

120. Alison J. Clarke, "Tupperware," in *Visions of Suburbia*, ed. Roger Silverstone (London: Routledge, 1997), 142.

121. Karwowski.

122. Dubrofsky and Wood, "Posting Racism and Sexism," 283.

123. Georgia Wells, Jeff Horwitz, and Deepa Seetharaman, "Facebook Knows Instagram Is Toxic for Teen Girls, Company Documents Show," *Wall Street Journal*, September 14, 2021, https://www.wsj.com/articles/facebook-knows-instagram-is-toxic-for-teen-girls-company-documents-show-11631620739.

124. T. Sullivan.

125. Kaye, "Love Connection."

126. Duffy and Hund, "Gendered Visibility on Social Media," 4988.

127. van Driel and Dumitrica, "Selling Brands While Staying 'Authentic,'" 2, 4; Wellman et al., "Ethics of Authenticity," 69.

128. Hund, "The Influencer Industry," 67, 156.

129. McRae, "'Get off My Internets,'" 21.

130. Subramanian.

131. DiCapua; Assayag.

132. Hund, "The Influencer Industry," 85.

133. Nat Ives, "Holiday Ad Creep Comes to Influencer Marketing," *Wall Street Journal*, November 22, 2019, https://www.wsj.com/articles/holiday-ad-creep-comes-to-influencer-marketing-11574452919.

134. van Driel and Dumitrica, "Selling Brands While Staying 'Authentic,'" 4.

135. Duffy, *(Not) Getting Paid to Do What You Love*, 175; Audrezet, de Kerviler, and Guidry Moulard, "Authenticity under Threat," 1.

136. DiCapua.

137. Marrs; Santangelo.

138. Marrs.

139. Mackenzie Newcomb, "How to Cultivate the Best Influencer Partnerships Based on Organic Love," Traackr Blog, 2020, https://www.traackr.com/blog/how-to-cultivate -best-influencer-partnerships-based-on-organic-love.

140. Newcomb, "How to Cultivate the Best Influencer Partnerships."

141. Jacob Feldman, "NFL Turns to Digital Influencers in Fight to Win over Young Fans," *Sportico*, October 21, 2020, https://www.sportico.com/leagues/football/2020/nfl -influencer-marketing-strategy-gen-z-1234615235/.

142. Ilyse Liffreing, "How 'Influencers' Became 'Creators' and What It Means for Brands," *Advertising Age*, September 14, 2021, https://adage.com/article/digital-market ing-ad-tech-news/how-influencers-became-creators-and-what-it-means-brands /2363261.

143. Quinn.

144. Marrs; Santangelo; DiCapua.

145. Maheshwari, "Are You Ready for the Nanoinfluencers?"

146. Wittebols, "Crisis and Contradiction," 60.

147. Neff and Stein, "Peer Pressure."

148. Liao and Ma, "Conceptualizing Consumer Need," 108, 110; Chelsea Fives, "Numbers Don't Lie: 10 Stats That Explain Why Influencer Marketing Will Dominate in 2019," Obviously Blog, 2018, https://www.obvious.ly/blog/numbers-dont-lie-10-stats -that-explain-why-influencer-marketing-will-continue-to-dominate-in-2019.

149. Ellie Jenkins, "Shift Your Perspective and Think about Influencers as Strategic Consultants," Mavrck Blog, 2020, https://www.mavrck.co/influencer-marketing-influ encers-as-strategic-consultants/.

150. Fives, "Numbers Don't Lie"; Mark Pollard, "The Crucial Challenges Facing Brands and Their Marketers Right Now," 2019, https://player.fm/series/sweathead-with -mark-pollard/the-crucial-challenges-facing-brands-and-their-marketers-right-now -jason-lonsdale-cso.

151. DiCapua.

152. Wellman et al., "Ethics of Authenticity," 72.

153. Serazio, *Your Ad Here*.

154. Serazio, "How News Went Guerrilla Marketing," 123.

155. Federal Trade Commission, "FTC Publishes Final Guides Governing Endorsements, Testimonials," October 2, 2009, https://www.ftc.gov/news-events/news/press -releases/2009/10/ftc-publishes-final-guides-governing-endorsements-testimonials.

156. Sapna Maheshwari, "Endorsed on Instagram by a Kardashian, but Is It Love or Just an Ad?," *New York Times*, August 30, 2016, https://www.nytimes.com/2016/08/30/ business/media/instagram-ads-marketing-kardashian.html?module=inline; Wellman

et al., "Ethics of Authenticity," 77; Federal Trade Commission, "FTC Revises Online Advertising Disclosure Guidelines," 2013, https://www.ftc.gov/news-events/press-re leases/2013/03/ftc-staff-revises-online-advertising-disclosure-guidelines.

157. Lesley Fair, "Three FTC Actions of Interest to Influencers," 2017, https://www.ftc .gov/news-events/blogs/business-blog/2017/09/three-ftc-actions-interest-influencers; Kaye, "Love Connection"; Federal Trade Commission, "FTC Puts Hundreds of Businesses on Notice about Fake Reviews and Other Misleading Endorsements," 2021, https://www.ftc.gov/news-events/press-releases/2021/10/ftc-puts-hundreds-businesses -notice-about-fake-reviews-other.

158. Martineau, "The WIRED Guide to Influencers"; Martineau, "Inside the Weird, and Booming, Industry."

159. Schram; Maheshwari, "Endorsed on Instagram by a Kardashian."

160. Nicholas Confessore et al., "The Follower Factory," *New York Times*, January 27, 2018, https://www.nytimes.com/interactive/2018/01/27/technology/social-media-bots .html?module=inline.

161. Kapner and Terlep, "Online Influencers Tell You What to Buy"; Martineau, "Inside the Weird, and Booming, Industry."

162. Confessore et al., "The Follower Factory."

163. Diana Pearl, "How Brands Are Combatting Influencer Fraud in an Ever-Changing Social Landscape," *Adweek*, August 25, 2019, https://www.adweek.com/ brand-marketing/how-brands-are-combatting-influencer-fraud-in-an-ever-changing -social-landscape/; Kapner and Terlep, "Online Influencers Tell You What to Buy"; Neff, "Clean Break."

164. Young; Sapna Maheshwari, "Uncovering Instagram Bots with a New Kind of Detective Work," *New York Times*, March 12, 2018, https://www.nytimes.com/2018/03 /12/business/media/instagram-bots.html?module=inline; *Obviously*, "Curating the Right Creators at Scale," n.d.

165. Johan Lindquist and Esther Weltevrede, "Negotiating Authenticity in the Market for Fake Followers on Social Media," *Social Science Research Council*, October 5, 2021, https://items.ssrc.org/beyond-disinformation/negotiating-authenticity-in-the -market-for-fake-followers-on-social-media/.

166. Neff, "Clean Break."

167. Confessore et al., "The Follower Factory."

168. Duffy, "The Romance of Work," 441, 443, 446; Hund, "The Influencer Industry," 44.

169. Duffy, "The Romance of Work," 442.

170. van Driel and Dumitrica, "Selling Brands While Staying 'Authentic,'" 2, 9; Duffy, *(Not) Getting Paid to Do What You Love*, 151; Duffy, "The Romance of Work," 449.

171. Marwick, *Status Update*, 5, 6, 15, 166, 169, 186.

172. Jennings, "A Celebrity Endorsement, for $500"; Kati Chitrakorn, "Poparazzi, BeReal: Social Media's New Generation," *Vogue Business*, June 8, 2021, https://www. voguebusiness.com/companies/social-media-trends-2021-poparazzi-capcut-bereal -newnew.

173. Banet-Weiser, *Authentic*, 17, 56, 118.

174. Hund, "The Influencer Industry," 28.

175. Whitmer, "You Are Your Brand," 4; Tom Peters, "The Brand Called You," *Fast Company*, August 31, 1997, https://www.fastcompany.com/28905/brand-called-you.

176. Ruth Whippman, "Everything Is for Sale Now: Even Us," *New York Times*, November 24, 2018, https://www.nytimes.com/2018/11/24/opinion/sunday/gig-economy-self-promotion-anxiety.html.

177. Hund, "The Influencer Industry," 52; Whitmer, "You Are Your Brand," 1, 6, 7.

178. Whitmer, "You Are Your Brand," 1; Susie Khamis, Lawrence Ang, and Raymond Welling, "Self-Branding, 'Micro-Celebrity' and the Rise of Social Media Influencers," *Celebrity Studies* 8, no. 2 (2017): 2,.

179. Peters, "The Brand Called You."

180. Khamis, Ang, and Welling, "Self-Branding, 'Micro-Celebrity'," 1, 4, 5, 10; Hearn, "Verified," 67.

181. Assayag.

182. Hearn, "Verified," 194.

183. Lorenz, "For Creators, Everything Is for Sale."

184. Bartholomew, *Adcreep*, 2, 5, 37.

185. Karwowski.

186. Cummings.

187. Silverstein; Lonsdale; Coles; Martin; H. Sullivan.

188. Karwowski.

189. Serazio, *Your Ad Here*, 120, 121.

190. Hearn and Schoenhoff, "From Celebrity to Influencer," 208; Banet-Weiser, *Authentic*, 54.

191. Bartholomew, *Adcreep*, 7.

Chapter 6: Performative Politics

1. Umbach and Humphrey, *Authenticity*, 4.

2. Potter, *The Authenticity Hoax*, 114.

3. Fordahl, "Authenticity," 300; Umbach and Humphrey, *Authenticity*, 2.

4. Enli, *Mediated Authenticity*, 29–32.

5. Kathleen Hall Jamieson and Paul Waldman, *The Press Effect* (Oxford: Oxford University Press, 2003), 29; John Corner and Dick Pels, "Introduction: The Re-Styling of Politics," in *Media and the Re-Styling of Politics* (London: Sage, 2003), 11; Erica J. Seifert, *The Politics of Authenticity in Presidential Campaigns, 1976–2008 (Jefferson, NC: McFarland)*, 23.

6. David Greenberg, *Republic of Spin* (New York: W.W. Norton, 2016), 300.

7. Seifert, *The Politics of Authenticity*, 2, 15.

8. Seifert, *The Politics of Authenticity*, 21, 25.

9. Jeffrey P. Jones, *Entertaining Politics*, 2nd ed. (Lanham, MD: Rowman & Littlefield, 2010), 11.

10. Seifert, *The Politics of Authenticity*, 191–92, 205.

11. Joana Weiss, "Reality TV Has Remade Our Politics: But Just for One Party," *Politico*, July 17, 2021, https://www.politico.com/news/magazine/2021/07/17/where-are-all-the-democrats-in-reality-tv-499897.

12. Gabrielle Grow and Janelle Ward, "The Role of Authenticity in Electoral Social Media Campaigns," *First Monday* 18, no. 4 (2013), https://firstmonday.org/article/view/4269/3425.

13. Shane, "The Semiotics of Authenticity," 2.

14. T. Sullivan; Wickers.

15. Edelman, "Authenticity Just Means Faking It Well."

16. Margolis.

17. Fordahl, "Authenticity," 301.

18. Seifert, *The Politics of Authenticity*, 28.

19. Jamieson and Waldman, *The Press Effect*, 29.

20. Simon M. Luebke, "Political Authenticity: Conceptualization of a Popular Term," *International Journal of Press/Politics* 16, no. 3 (2020): 8.

21. Shane, "The Semiotics of Authenticity," 3; Gaden and Dumitrica, "The 'Real Deal.'"

22. Luebke, "Political Authenticity," 5.

23. Christine Bachman, "Democratic Caucus Series" (Campaigns & Elections, 2021), https://app.livestorm.co/c-e/democratic-caucus-series?s=aba988cd-0b70-4a92-9dc8-cfcf65b5b0a3.

24. Delia Dumitrica, "Politics as 'Customer Relations,'" *Javnost* 21, no. 1 (2014): 56.

25. Jeffrey C. Alexander, *The Performance of Politics* (Oxford: Oxford University Press, 2010), 12.

26. Umbach and Humphrey, *Authenticity*, 79.

27. Shrum.

28. Michael Serazio, "Encoding the Paranoid Style in American Politics," *Critical Studies in Media Communication* 33, no. 2 (2016): 191.

29. Timur Kuran, "The Authenticity Deficit in Modern Politics," *Cato Unbound*, March 7, 2016, https://www.cato-unbound.org/2016/03/07/timur-kuran/authenticity-deficit-modern-politics.

30. Serazio, "Encoding the Paranoid Style," 190.

31. Kenneth Vogel, *Big Money* (New York: PublicAffairs, 2014), x; Shane Goldmacher, "The 2020 Campaign Is the Most Expensive Ever (by a Lot)," *New York Times*, October 28, 2020, https://www.nytimes.com/2020/10/28/us/politics/2020-race-money.html.

32. Serazio, "Encoding the Paranoid Style," 187.

33. Shane Goldmacher, "Michael Bloomberg Spent More Than $900 Million on His Failed Presidential Run," *New York Times*, March 20, 2020, https://www.nytimes.com/2020/03/20/us/politics/bloomberg-campaign-900-million.html.

34. Alexander, *The Performance of Politics*, 41.

35. Rocha.

36. Michael Serazio, "Branding Politics," *Journal of Consumer Culture* 17, no. 2 (2017): 237, 238.

37. Serazio, "Encoding the Paranoid Style in American Politics," 187.

38. Enli, "'Trust Me, I Am Authentic!'" 133.

39. Trippi.

40. Bill Scher, "You Say You Want a Revolution? Sorry, Bernie, Not for 27 Dollars Apiece," *Politico*, August 31, 2016, https://www.politico.com/magazine/story/2016/08/bernie-sanders-27-dollars-revolution-activists-214202/.

41. Jacob Bernstein, "Pete Buttigieg and the One Percent," *New York Times*, January 3, 2020, https://www.nytimes.com/2020/01/03/us/politics/pete-buttigieg-celebrity-donors.html; Nick Daggers, "The Risks of a Purity-Driven Fundraising Strategy," *Campaigns & Elections*, January 13, 2020, https://campaignsandelections.com/industry-news/the-risks-of-a-purity-driven-fundraising-strategy/.

42. Scaramucci.

43. Harry Gantz, "Harry Gantz Communications," accessed September 8, 2021, https://www.hgantzcom.com/.

44. Murphy; Paul Starr, "Spare Us from Authenticity," *Cato Unbound*, March 9, 2016, https://www.cato-unbound.org/2016/03/09/paul-starr/spare-us-authenticity.

45. Jamieson and Waldman, *The Press Effect*, xiv; Michael Serazio, "The New Media Designs of Political Consultants: Campaign Production in a Fragmented Era," *Journal of Communication* 64, no. 4 (2014): 755.

46. Tamar Liebes, "'Look Me Straight in the Eye,'" *Communication Review* 4, no. 4 (2001): 503.

47. Alexander, *The Performance of Politics*, 12.

48. Compton.

49. Serazio, "Branding Politics," 232.

50. Michael Serazio, "Producing Popular Politics," *Journal of Broadcasting and Electronic Media* 62, no. 1 (2018): 141.

51. Serazio, "Producing Popular Politics," 141.

52. Holst.

53. Ludwig.

54. Al Tompkins, "The 'Hire a Crowd' Business Operates Openly and Makes Journalism Even More Difficult," *Poynter*, May 21, 2018, https://www.poynter.org/reporting-editing/2018/the-hire-a-crowd-business-operates-openly-and-makes-journalism-even-more-difficult-2/.

55. Charles Barbour, "3 Production Tips for Your Next Shoot," *Campaigns & Elections*, November 24, 2021, https://campaignsandelections.com/creative/3-production-lessons-for-your-next-shoot/; Serazio, "Branding Politics," 237.

56. Serazio, "Branding Politics," 236.

57. Murphy.

58. DuHaime.

59. Jones.

60. Will Feltus, Kenneth M. Goldstein, and Matthew Dallek, *Inside Campaigns* (Thousand Oaks, CA: CQ Press, 2017), 5, 180.

61. Serazio, "The New Media Designs," 754.

62. Luebke, "Political Authenticity," 6; Louden and McCauliff, "The 'Authentic Candidate'," 91; Jamieson and Waldman, *The Press Effect*, xv.

63. Shawn J. Parry-Giles, *Hillary Clinton in the News* (Urbana: University of Illinois Press, 2014), 179.

64. Jamieson and Waldman, *The Press Effect*, 28.

65. Clare Malone, "Lis Left Standing," *New York*, February 1, 2020, https://nymag.com/intelligencer/2020/02/lis-smith-pete-buttigieg-2020-campaign.html.

66. Jones.

67. Corner and Pels, "Introduction"; Greenberg, *Republic of Spin*, 219–221.

68. McKinnon.

69. Enli, *Mediated Authenticity*, 111.

70. Seifert, *The Politics of Authenticity*, 16; Enli, *Mediated Authenticity*, 112–113.

71. Stevens.

72. Gantz.

73. Varoga.

74. Umbach and Humphrey, *Authenticity*, 68.

75. Kuran, "The Authenticity Deficit in Modern Politics"; Starr, "Spare Us from Authenticity."

76. Spicer.

77. Varoga; Joe Fuld, "7 Questions with 'The Campaign Doctor' Craig Varoga," *Campaign Workshop*, August 18, 2016, https://www.thecampaignworkshop.com/7-questions-campaign-doctor-craig-varoga.

78. Trippi; Megan McArdle, "For Good or Ill (Probably Ill), at Least Bernie Sanders Is Sincere," *Washington Post*, February 11, 2020, https://www.washingtonpost.com/opinions/2020/02/11/good-or-ill-probably-ill-least-bernie-sanders-is-sincere/.

79. DuHaime.

80. Montgomery, "The Uses of Authenticity."

81. Shane, "The Semiotics of Authenticity," 2.

82. Jamieson and Waldman, *The Press Effect*, 27.

83. Edelman, "Authenticity Just Means Faking It Well."

84. Luebke, "Political Authenticity," 10.

85. David Smith, "AOC's Cooking Live Streams Perfect the Recipe for Making Politics Palatable," *The Guardian*, December 13, 2020, https://www.theguardian.com/us-news/2020/dec/13/aoc-cooking-live-streams-politics.

86. Jim Newell, "The Surge," *Slate*, October 25, 2019, https://link.slate.com/view/5d0d13d42c885e2efa0030c7ayz41.1lv/8c5aff8f; Glenn Thrush and Sydney Ember, "The Bernie Sanders Personality Test," *New York Times*, March 6, 2020, https://www.nytimes.com/2020/03/06/us/politics/bernie-sanders-image.html.

87. Murphy.

88. Louden and McCauliff, "The 'Authentic Candidate'," 87.

89. Luebke, "Political Authenticity," 10, 11.

90. Serazio, "Encoding the Paranoid Style," 190.

91. Rocha.

92. Sean Sullivan, "At His Presidential Campaign Kickoff, Sanders Gets Personal," *Washington Post*, March 2, 2019, https://www.washingtonpost.com/politics/at-his-cam paign-kickoff-bernie-sanders-will-emphasize-his-personal-story/2019/03/02/1244c2e0 -3cd9-11e9-aaae-69364b2ed137_story.html.

93. Daniel Kreiss, Regina G. Lawrence, and Shannon C. McGregor, "In Their Own Words," *Political Communication* 35, no. 1 (2018): 14.

94. Grazian, "Demystifying Authenticity," 191.

95. Wickers.

96. Linehan.

97. Loeser.

98. Skidmore.

99. Serazio, "Branding Politics," 231–32.

100. Seifert, *The Politics of Authenticity*, 1, 17.

101. DuHaime.

102. Stevens.

103. McKinnon.

104. Hamburger.

105. Serazio, "Branding Politics," 232.

106. Seifert, *The Politics of Authenticity*, 1.

107. Enli, *Mediated Authenticity*, 129.

108. "The Art of Authenticity in Voiceover: Matching Voice and Audience to Boost Your Ad Campaigns" (Campaigns & Elections, 2020), https://campaigncreativesummit .com/.

109. Delany; Skidmore.

110. T. Sullivan.

111. Shepardson.

112. Kennedy and Kolb, "The Alchemy of Authenticity," 318; Corner and Pels, "Introduction," 7.

113. Potter, *The Authenticity Hoax*, 188.

114. Simon Dumenco, "The Lincoln Project's Rick Wilson on the Ads That Actually Worked," *Advertising Age*, December 9, 2020, https://adage.com/article/campaign-trail /lincoln-projects-rick-wilson-ads-actually-worked/2300051.

115. Serazio, "Branding Politics," 233.

116. Seifert, *The Politics of Authenticity*, 18.

117. Sean Trende, "The Perils and Promise of Authenticity," *Cato Unbound*, March 11, 2016, https://www.cato-unbound.org/2016/03/11/sean-trende/perils-promise-authen ticity.

118. Holst.

119. Michael Serazio, *The Power of Sports* (New York: New York University Press, 2019), 238.

120. Serazio, "Producing Popular Politics," 142–43.

121. Neil Swidey, "If the Elites Go Down, We're All in Trouble," *Boston Globe*, Octo-

ber 5, 2017, https://www.bostonglobe.com/magazine/2017/10/05/elites-down-all-trouble /TSyELMqod5a9AtooPRhXEP/story.html.

122. Adam Chandler, "Fast Food Is Totally Artificial: No Wonder Politicians Eat It to Seem Real," *Washington Post*, October 20, 2020, https://www.washingtonpost.com/ outlook/2020/10/20/biden-dairy-queen-fast-food/.

123. Swidey, "If the Elites Go Down."

124. Ben Zimmer, "Elizabeth Warren and the Down-to Earth Trap," *The Atlantic*, January 5, 2019, https://www.theatlantic.com/entertainment/archive/2019/01/why-eliza beth-warrens-beer-moment-fell-flat/579544/.

125. Chandler, "Fast Food Is Totally Artificial"; Seifert, *The Politics of Authenticity*, 19.

126. DuHaime.

127. Murphy.

128. Serazio, "Branding Politics," 225.

129. Alexander, *The Performance of Politics*, xii, 9, 18.

130. Shannon C. McGregor, Regina G. Lawrence, and Arielle Cardona, "Personalization, Gender, and Social Media," *Information Communication and Society* 20, no. 2 (2017): 265.

131. Rocha.

132. Serazio, "Branding Politics," 230.

133. Serazio, "Branding Politics," 233.

134. Serazio, "Branding Politics," 231.

135. Serazio, "Producing Popular Politics," 140.

136. Serazio, "Branding Politics," 235.

137. Luebke, "Political Authenticity," 12.

138. Potter, *The Authenticity Hoax*, 74; McCarthy, "Emotional Performances as Dramas," 241.

139. Potter, *The Authenticity Hoax*, 175.

140. Corner and Pels, "Introduction," 8, 9; Lewin and Williams, "The Ideology and Practice of Authenticity," 65.

141. Serazio, "Branding Politics," 234.

142. Drew Westen, *The Political Brain* (New York: PublicAffairs, 2007).

143. Wickers.

144. Michael Serazio, "Managing the Digital News Cyclone," *International Journal of Communication* 9 (2015): 1921.

145. Hamburger.

146. Serazio, "Branding Politics," 238, 239.

147. Liebes, "'Look Me Straight in the Eye,'" 502.

148. Serazio, "Producing Popular Politics," 144.

149. Geoffrey Craig, *Performing Politics* (Cambridge: Polity, 2016), 1; Serazio, "Branding Politics," 227.

150. Neil Postman, *Amusing Ourselves to Death* (New York: Penguin, 1985).

151. Jason Zengerle, "We Expect Sports Stars to Be Heroes: What about Our Politi-

cians?," *New York Times Magazine*, March 31, 2021, https://www.nytimes.com/2021/03/31/magazine/damian-lillard-interview.html.

152. Serazio, "Branding Politics," 226, 232.

153. Alexandra Alter and Elizabeth A. Harris, "Dr. Seuss Books Are Pulled, and a 'Cancel Culture' Controversy Erupts," *New York Times*, March 4, 2021, updated October 20, 2021, https://www.nytimes.com/2021/03/04/books/dr-seuss-books.html.

154. Serazio, "Branding Politics," 234.

155. Dan Brooks, "Montana's Greatest Cultural Export: Inane Campaign Ads," *New York Times Magazine*, September 10, 2020, https://www.nytimes.com/2020/09/10/magazine/montanas-greatest-cultural-export-inane-campaign-ads.html.

Chapter 7: Populist Politics

1. Megan McCluskey, "'Don't Post a Meme If You Don't Know What a Meme Is': Alexandra Ocasio-Cortez Schools Stephen Colbert on Her Social Media Strategy," *Time*, January 22, 2019, https://time.com/5509391/alexandria-ocasio-cortez-stephen-colbert-social-media/.

2. Kirsten Theye and Steven Melling, "Total Losers and Bad Hombres," *Southern Communication Journal* 83, no. 5 (2018): 330.

3. Ryan Broderick, "Here's Everything the Mueller Report Says about How Russian Trolls Used Social Media," *BuzzFeed*, April 18, 2019, https://www.buzzfeednews.com/article/ryanhatesthis/mueller-report-internet-research-agency-detailed-2016.

4. Ashley Bryant, "Combatting the Disinformation Campaign Targeting Black and Latinx Voters," *Campaigns & Elections*, July 20, 2020, https://campaignsandelections.com/industry-news/combatting-the-disinformation-campaign-targeting-black-and-latinx-voters/.

5. Gunn Enli and Linda Therese Rosenberg, "Trust in the Age of Social Media," *Social Media and Society* 4, no. 1 (2018): 7; Claes H. de Vreese et al., "Populism as an Expression of Political Communication Content and Style," *International Journal of Press/Politics* 23, no. 4 (2018): 423.

6. Jessica Baldwin-Philippi, "The Technological Performance of Populism," *New Media & Society*, 2018, 2, 3.

7. Sven Engesser, Nayla Fawzi, and Anders Olof Larsson, "Populist Online Communication," *Information Communication and Society* 20, no. 9 (2017): 1286; Baldwin-Philippi, "The Technological Performance of Populism," 3.

8. Engesser, Fawzi, and Larsson, "Populist Online Communication," 1286.

9. Homero Gil de Zúñiga, Karolina Koc Michalska, and Andrea Römmele, "Populism in the Era of Twitter," *New Media and Society* 22, no. 4 (2020): 586.

10. de Vreese et al., "Populism as an Expression," 428.

11. Engesser, Fawzi, and Larsson, "Populist Online Communication," 1282, 1283; Gil de Zúñiga, Koc Michalska, and Römmele, "Populism in the Era of Twitter," 587.

12. de Vreese et al., "Populism as an Expression," 428; Mattia Zulianello, Alessandro Albertini, and Diego Ceccobelli, "A Populist Zeitgeist? The Communication Strategies of Western and Latin American Political Leaders on Facebook," *International Journal*

of Press/Politics 23, no. 4 (2018): 441; Sven Engesser et al., "Populism and Social Media," *Information Communication and Society* 20, no. 8 (2017): 1109.

13. Lozada, *What Were We Thinking*, 221.

14. Joseph Lowndes, "Populism in the United States," in *The Oxford Handbook of Populism* (Oxford: Oxford University Press, 2017), 232–47.

15. de Vreese et al., "Populism as an Expression," 424, 428.

16. Serazio, "Producing Popular Politics," 133; Seifert, *The Politics of Authenticity*, 26; Gil de Zúñiga, Koc Michalska, and Römmele, "Populism in the Era of Twitter," 587.

17. Alexander, *The Performance of Politics*, 9.

18. Richard Hofstadter, *The Paranoid Style in American Politics and Other Essays* (New York: Alfred A. Knopf, 1965), 4, 14.

19. Jeffrey M. Jones, "Confidence in U.S. Institutions Still below Historical Norms," 2015, http://www.gallup.com/poll/183593/confidence-institutions-below-historical -norms.aspx.

20. Edelman, "2020 Edelman Trust Barometer," 2020, https://www.edelman.com/ trust/2020-trust-barometer; Natasha Kennedy, "Covid-19 Mindset: The Collison of Issues," 2020, https://fleishmanhillard.com/wp-content/uploads/2021/03/COVID-19 -Mindset-The-Collision-of-Issues.pdf.

21. Shepardson.

22. Theda Skocpol and Vanessa Williamson, *The Tea Party and the Remaking of American Conservatism* (Oxford: Oxford University Press, 2012), 53, 99.

23. Swidey, "If the Elites Go Down"; Michael Lewis, *The Fifth Risk* (New York: W. W. Norton, 2018).

24. Starr, "Spare Us from Authenticity."

25. Umbach and Humphrey, *Authenticity*, 72; Engesser, Fawzi, and Larsson, "Populist Online Communication," 1283.

26. Geoffrey Skelley, "Why More Inexperienced Candidates Are Running—and Winning," *FiveThirtyEight*, January 24, 2022, https://fivethirtyeight.com/features/why -more-inexperienced-candidates-are-running-and-winning/.

27. Engesser, Fawzi, and Larsson, "Populist Online Communication," 1285.

28. de Vreese et al., "Populism as an Expression," 432.

29. Judith S. Trent, Robert V. Friedenberg, and Robert E. Denton, *Political Campaign Communication*, 7th ed. (Lanham, MD: Rowman & Littlefield, 2011).

30. Bruce Bimber, "How Information Shapes Political Institutions," in *Media Power in Politics*, ed. Doris A. Graber, 6th ed. (Washington, DC: CQ Press, 2011), 7; W. Lance Bennett and Shanto Iyengar, "A New Era of Minimal Effects?" *Journal of Communication* 58, no. 4 (December 2008): 708–9.

31. McKinnon.

32. Baldwin-Philippi, "The Technological Performance of Populism," 4; Enli and Rosenberg, "Trust in the Age of Social Media"; Gil de Zúñiga, Koc Michalska, and Römmele, "Populism in the Era of Twitter," 585.

33. Kreiss, Lawrence, and McGregor, "In Their Own Words," 13; Frenkel and Kang, *An Ugly Truth*, 106.

34. Serazio, *Your Ad Here*, 104–5.

35. Daniel Kreiss, *Taking Our Country Back* (Oxford: Oxford University Press, 2012).

36. Trippi.

37. Dawn R. Gilpin, Edward T. Palazzolo, and Nicholas Brody, "Socially Mediated Authenticity," *Journal of Communication Management* 14, no. 3 (2010): 261, 267; Gaden and Dumitrica, "The 'Real Deal'"; Dumitrica, "Politics as 'Customer Relations,'" 64; Gunn Enli, "Twitter as Arena for the Authentic Outsider," *European Journal of Communication* 32, no. 1 (2017): 52.

38. Grow and Ward, "The Role of Authenticity."

39. Skidmore.

40. Serazio, "The New Media Designs," 750.

41. Engesser et al., "Populism and Social Media," 1113; de Vreese et al., "Populism as an Expression," 428.

42. Skidmore.

43. Sean J. Miller, "The Midterm Cycle Saw 'Record' Digital Content Production as Strategists Worked to 'Feed the Beast,'" *Campaigns & Elections*, November 21, 2022, https://campaignsandelections.com/campaigntech/the-midterm-cycle-saw-record-digital-content-production-as-strategists-worked-to-feed-the-beast/.

44. T. Sullivan.

45. Serazio, "Managing the Digital News Cyclone," 1913.

46. DuHaime; "A New Reality for Video Production: Creating Socially-Distanced Content," *Campaigns & Elections*, August 5, 2020.

47. Mark Deuze, *Media Work* (Cambridge: Polity, 2007); Henry Jenkins, *Convergence Culture* (New York: New York University Press, 2006); Baldwin-Philippi, "The Technological Performance of Populism," 6.

48. Serazio, "Managing the Digital News Cyclone," 1919.

49. Serazio, "Managing the Digital News Cyclone," 1919.

50. "4 Campaign Questions as the 2020 Cycle Officially Gets Underway," *Campaigns & Elections*, January 22, 2020, https://campaignsandelections.com/industry-news/4-campaign-questions-as-the-2020-cycle-officially-gets-underway/.

51. John F. Harris, "What We Know about the Democratic Primary," *Politico*, September 3, 2019, https://www.politico.com/magazine/story/2019/09/03/what-we-know-about-the-democratic-primary-227996/.

52. Jeff Horwitz and Georgia Wells, "Bloomberg Bankrolls a Social-Media Army to Push Message," *Wall Street Journal*, February 19, 2020, https://www.wsj.com/articles/bloomberg-bankrolls-a-social-media-army-to-push-message-11582127768.

53. Sean J. Miller, "Two Early Takeaways from Biden's Digital Program," *Campaigns & Elections*, November 17, 2020, https://campaignsandelections.com/campaigntech/two-early-takeaways-from-biden-s-digital-program/.

54. Tate Ryan-Mosley, "Why Political Campaigns Are Sending 3 Billion Texts in This Election," *MIT Technology Review*, October 28, 2020, https://www.technologyreview.com/2020/10/28/1011301/why-political-campaigns-are-sending-3-billion-texts-in-this-election/.

55. Kevin Roose, "How Joe Biden's Digital Team Tamed the MAGA Internet," *New York Times*, December 6, 2020, updated January 16, 2021, https://www.nytimes.com /2020/12/06/technology/joe-biden-internet-election.html.

56. Karine Nahon and Jeff Hemsley, *Going Viral* (Cambridge: Polity, 2013), 62.

57. "Most Influential Emotions on Social Networks Revealed," *MIT Technology Review*, September 16, 2013, https://www.technologyreview.com/2013/09/16/176450/ most-influential-emotions-on-social-networks-revealed/.

58. Gil de Zúñiga, Koc Michalska, and Römmele, "Populism in the Era of Twitter," 588.

59. Serazio, "Managing the Digital News Cyclone," 1914.

60. Enli, "'Trust Me, I Am Authentic!'" 121, 127.

61. Enli, "'Trust Me, I Am Authentic!'" 130.

62. Holst.

63. Kreiss, Lawrence, and McGregor, "In Their Own Words," 21; McGregor, Lawrence, and Cardona, "Personalization, Gender, and Social Media"; Gaden and Dumitrica, "The 'Real Deal.'"

64. Gaden and Dumitrica, "The 'Real Deal.'"

65. Schuller, *The Trouble with White Women*, 225, 235.

66. Grow and Ward, "The Role of Authenticity."

67. Dumitrica, "Politics as 'Customer Relations,'" 61–62.

68. Dumitrica, "Politics as 'Customer Relations,'" 56.

69. Skidmore.

70. Margolis.

71. Enli, "Twitter as Arena," 57.

72. Shepardson; Stevens.

73. Nick Daggers, "The Risks of a Purity-Driven Fundraising Strategy," *Campaigns & Elections*, January 13, 2020, https://campaignsandelections.com/industry-news/the -risks-of-a-purity-driven-fundraising-strategy/.

74. Adam Goldstein, "6 Ways to Improve Your Campaign's Smartphone Video," *Campaigns & Elections*, May 8, 2019, https://campaignsandelections.com/creative/6 -ways-to-improve-your-campaign-s-smartphone-video/?utm_medium=newsletter& utm_source=email&utm_campaign=content.

75. Harry Gantz, "The Democratization of Video Production for Political Campaigns," *Campaigns & Elections*, February 26, 2020, https://campaignsandelections. com/creative/the-democratization-of-video-production-for-political-campaigns/?utm _medium=newsletter&utm_source=email&utm_campaign=content.

76. Compton.

77. Sydney Ember and Jonathan Martin, "Bernie Sanders Is Making Changes for 2020, but His Desire for Control Remains," *New York Times*, March 1, 2019, https://www. nytimes.com/2019/03/01/us/politics/bernie-sanders-president-2020-brooklyn.html.

78. Jason Zengerle, "These Republicans Have a Confession: They're Not Voting for Trump Again," *New York Times Magazine*, August 5, 2020, https://www.nytimes.com /2020/08/05/magazine/republicans-confess-against-trump.html.

79. Delany.

80. Baldwin-Philippi, "The Technological Performance of Populism," 15.

81. Ludwig.

82. Kevin Roose, "How Joe Biden's Digital Team Tamed the MAGA Internet," *New York Times*, December 6, 2020, https://www.nytimes.com/2020/12/06/technology/joe -biden-internet-election.html.

83. Holst.

84. "A New Reality for Video Production."

85. "Republican Caucus Series: Ad Creative and Production," *Campaigns & Elections*, January 14, 2021, https://campaignsandelections.com/videos/republican-caucus -series-ad-creative-and-production/.

86. "Compelling Content from Concept to Execution: Lessons from Creative Directors," *Campaigns & Elections*, August 5, 2020.

87. "A New Reality for Video Production."

88. Fordahl, "Authenticity."

89. Tim Alberta, "'Complete This Sentence: Donald Trump Wins Releection If . . . ,'" *Politico*, June 26, 2019, https://www.politico.com/magazine/story/2019/06/26/ trump-2020-democrats-campaign-election-strategy-227210/.

90. T. Sullivan.

91. Theye and Melling, "Total Losers and Bad Hombres," 322, 326, 328.

92. Margolis.

93. Scaramucci.

94. Theye and Melling, "Total Losers and Bad Hombres," 329; Glenn Kessler, Salvador Rizzo, and Meg Kelly, "Trump's False or Misleading Claims Total 30,573 over 4 Years," *Washington Post*, January 24, 2021, https://www.washingtonpost.com/politics /2021/01/24/trumps-false-or-misleading-claims-total-30573-over-four-years/.

95. Fordahl, "Authenticity," 308.

96. Lozada, *What Were We Thinking*, 137; Theye and Melling, "Total Losers and Bad Hombres," 322.

97. Serazio, "Encoding the Paranoid Style," 191.

98. Poniewozik, *Audience of One*, 196.

99. Matt Terrill, "$8 Billion Was Spent on Political Ads during 2020: The Election Proved That Money Was Mostly Wasted," *Business Insider*, December 26, 2020, https:// www.businessinsider.com/2020-election-confirmed-free-media-is-better-than-politi cal-ads-2020-12?utm_source=reddit.com.

100. Theye and Melling, "Total Losers and Bad Hombres," 323.

101. Theye and Melling, "Total Losers and Bad Hombres," 324.

102. Fordahl, "Authenticity," 309.

103. Umbach and Humphrey, *Authenticity*, 71.

104. Stevens.

105. Theye and Melling, "Total Losers and Bad Hombres," 329.

106. Theye and Melling, "Total Losers and Bad Hombres," 331.

107. Edelman, "Authenticity Just Means Faking It Well."

108. Varoga.

109. Dietrich.

110. DuHaime.

111. Spicer.

112. Scaramucci.

113. Greg Sargent, "Who Is the 'Authenticity' Candidate of 2016? Yup: It's Donald Trump," *Washington Post*, December 11, 2015, https://www.washingtonpost.com/blogs/plum-line/wp/2015/12/11/who-is-the-authenticity-candidate-of-2016-yup-its-donald-trump/.

114. McKinnon.

115. Kessler, Rizzo, and Kelly, "Trump's False or Misleading Claims."

116. Daniel Dale, "The 15 Most Notable Lies of Donald Trump's Presidency," *CNN*, January 16, 2021, https://www.cnn.com/2021/01/16/politics/fact-check-dale-top-15-donald-trump-lies/index.html.

117. Scaramucci.

118. Fordahl, "Authenticity," 308.

119. Lozada, *What Were We Thinking*, 233.

120. Salena Zito, "Taking Trump Seriously, Not Literally," *The Atlantic*, September 23, 2016, https://www.theatlantic.com/politics/archive/2016/09/trump-makes-his-case-in-pittsburgh/501335/.

121. Lozada, *What Were We Thinking*, 57.

122. Colin Delany, "How Trump Will Fight Impeachment Online," *Campaigns & Elections*, October 2, 2019, https://campaignsandelections.com/campaigntech/how-trump-will-fight-impeachment-online/.

123. Enli, "Twitter as Arena," 50, 58.

124. Baldwin-Philippi, "The Technological Performance of Populism," 17, 18.

125. Baldwin-Philippi, "The Technological Performance of Populism," 10–12.

126. Baldwin-Philippi, "The Technological Performance of Populism," 6; Enli, "Twitter as Arena," 54.

127. Shane, "The Semiotics of Authenticity," 6.

128. Shane, "The Semiotics of Authenticity," 6–7.

129. Shane, "The Semiotics of Authenticity," 8.

130. Shane, "The Semiotics of Authenticity," 2.

131. David Weinberger, "How Donald Trump Hijacked the Authenticity of the Web," *Wired*, June 3, 2016, https://www.wired.com/2016/06/how-donald-trump-hijacked-the-authenticity-of-the-web/.

132. Jason Lemon, "Fox News Guest Defends Trump Twitter Typos, Saying They Make the President 'Feel Personal' and 'Connected' to Supporters," *Newsweek*, November 5, 2019, https://www.newsweek.com/dilbert-creator-praises-trump-twitter-presence-1469920.

133. Baldwin-Philippi, "The Technological Performance of Populism," 3.

134. Parry-Giles, *Hillary Clinton in the News*, 1.

135. Elrod.

136. Hendrik Hertzberg, "Second Those Emotions," *New Yorker*, January 13, 2008, https://www.newyorker.com/magazine/2008/01/21/second-those-emotions.

137. Tori Bedford, "Mark McKinnon: Politics, Predictions, and Producing the Circus," *WGBH*, February 5, 2016, https://www.wgbh.org/news/2016/02/05/boston-public-radio-podcast/mark-mckinnon-politics-predictions-and-producing-circus.

138. Parry-Giles, *Hillary Clinton in the News*, 51, 52, 100.

139. Parry-Giles, *Hillary Clinton in the News*, 27, 37, 40, 92, 98, 99.

140. Kennedy and Kolb, "The Alchemy of Authenticity," 320; Parry-Giles, *Hillary Clinton in the News*, 156.

141. McGregor, Lawrence, and Cardona, "Personalization, Gender, and Social Media," 264.

142. Umbach and Humphrey, *Authenticity*, 83.

143. Shrum.

144. Seifert, *The Politics of Authenticity*, 207.

145. Edelman, "Authenticity Just Means Faking It Well."

146. Amy Chozick, "Hillary Clinton to Show More Humor and Heart, Aides Say," *New York Times*, September 7, 2015, https://www.nytimes.com/2015/09/08/us/politics/hillary-clinton-to-show-more-humor-and-heart-aides-say.html?_r=0.

147. Margolis.

148. Holst.

149. Compton.

150. Shane, "The Semiotics of Authenticity," 9; Enli, "Twitter as Arena," 56.

151. Helen Rosner, "The Pure American Banality of Donald Trump's White House Fast-Food Banquet," *New Yorker*, January 15, 2019, https://www.newyorker.com/culture/annals-of-appearances/the-pure-american-banality-of-donald-trumps-white-house-fast-food-banquet.

152. David Caplan, "President Trump Climbs into an 18-Wheeler and Pretends to Be a Trucker," *ABC News*, March 23, 2017, https://abcnews.go.com/Politics/president-trump-climbs-18-wheeler-pretends-truck-driver/story?id=46337896; Ashton Marra, "'Trump Digs Coal' at Charleston Rally," *West Virginia Public Broadcasting*, May 5, 2016, https://www.wvpublic.org/news/2016-05-05/trump-digs-coal-at-charleston-rally.

153. Nicholas Kristof, "The Black Eyes in Donald Trump's Life," *New York Times*, September 8, 2016, https://www.nytimes.com/2016/09/08/opinion/the-black-eyes-in-donald-trumps-life.html.

154. Lozada, *What Were We Thinking*, 3, 9.

155. Poniewozik, *Audience of One*, 262.

156. Serazio, "Encoding the Paranoid Style," 190.

157. Kennedy and Kolb, "The Alchemy of Authenticity," 316.

158. Thomas Frank, *What's the Matter with Kansas?* (New York: Henry Holt, 2005).

159. Much of the past two paragraphs is drawn from a previous article on the subject. Serazio, "Encoding the Paranoid Style," 181, 182, 183, 188, 192.

160. Serazio, "Encoding the Paranoid Style," 193.

Conclusion: The Business of Keeping It "Real"

1. Guignon, *On Being Authentic*, 151.

2. Enli, *Mediated Authenticity*.

3. Eric Grundhauser, "Did a Silent Film about a Train Really Cause Audiences to Stampede?," *Slate*, January 5, 2017, https://slate.com/human-interest/2017/01/the-silent -film-that-caused-audiences-to-stampede-from-the-theater.html.

4. Serazio, *Your Ad Here, 7–8.*

Index

A$AP Ferg, 94
Abidin, Crystal, 138
Ad Age, 72, 79, 116, 124
Adams, Scott, 193
Adidas, 94
advertising: ad creep, 149; Big Data and, 108; digital developments of, 106; disclosure and, 145–46; emotion and, 113; five senses within, 118; food in, 171; forecasting in, 107; garage myth origin story and, 61–62; immateriality regarding, 172; mass intimacy and, 107; moral authenticity within, 116; in music, 95–99; narcissism of small differences and, 110; native, 145; nostalgic populism within, 116; origin stories for, 117; overview of, 29–30, 106; in politics, 160–61, 167–70; rough cut in, 113–15, 160; on social media, 76–81, 106; sports in, 170–71; statistics regarding, 131–33; vacations in, 171–72; vintage aesthetics within, 116. *See also* branding; influencers/influencing
Adweek, 3, 120, 121–22, 141

Alaska, 155
Alexander, Jeffrey, 159–60, 172
Alfano, Kim, 187
Alger, Horatio, 42
algorithm, 57, 65, 71–72, 183
Allocca, Kevin, 57, 60, 62, 67, 68, 75, 76, 80
alternative music, 87
amateurism, 57–62, 74–76, 142
Amazing Race, 40, 41
American Eagle, 115
American Idol, 38, 42
American Influencer Council, 147
America's Next Top Model, 40
anger, 183
anonymity, weight of, 9
Apple, 61–62, 95, 110, 113
applications, spontaneity on, 66. *See also* specific apps
The Apprentice, 47, 155, 163
archetypes, for casting process, 42
art, authenticity in, 19
aspirational labor, 147–48
aspirational ordinariness, 142

Bully Pulpit Interactive, 181
Burnett, Mark, 40
Burning Man, 17
Bush, George H. W., 171
Bush, George W., 1, 31, 155, 162, 163, 168, 170–71, 204
Busta Rhymes, 95
Buttigieg, Pete, 153, 158–59, 162, 182–83
buzz marketing, 129

calculated authenticity, 23, 63–64
calibrated amateurism, 142
camera work, strategies for, 44–45
capitalism, 8, 11, 12, 16, 73, 97, 108, 149–50, 205
Cardi B, 83, 93, 205
Cash, Johnny, 5
cash, power of, 11–13
Castelaz, Jeff, 85, 86, 88, 100
casting: archetypes for, 42; emotion experts within, 46; of influencers, 54–55, 74, 136; preferences within, 53; process of, 40–41, 48, 52–53; therapist façade within, 50
Castro, Julian, 153
celebrities: authenticity among, 3; availability expectations on, 37–38; crafting and micromanaging of, 37; endorsements of, 129; fame of, 36–39; influence of, 129; on Instagram, 60; micro, 37; proximity of, 37; on social media, 60. See also specific persons
Cesarkas, Yael, 61, 116
Chamberlain, Emma, 67–68, 204
Charli XCX, 90
Chase, Meredith, 108, 113, 114, 122
children, as influencers, 138–39
Chili's, 110, 117
Chopra, Deepak, 5
Christie, Chris, 171
The Circle, 3, 54
Citi, 96
Citizens United, 157

class conventions, authenticity and, 42–43
Clinton, Hillary, 31, 155, 158, 176, 185, 188, 190, 192–93, 194–97
Clorox, 145
Cobain, Kurt, 82, 88, 99–100
Coca-Cola, 109, 121
Cohn, Roy, 192
Colbert, Stephen, 173
Coles, Margaret, 112
Combs, Sean, 145
commercialization, 8
commodity activism, 120–27
communication, advancement in, 179–80
Compton, Matt, 160, 196
confessions, 48–49, 50
Conlin, Shelia, 40, 49, 50–51
consumerism, 11–12, 29–30
consumer products: commodity activism of, 120–27; gender and, 141; immaterial qualities to, 110–11; perceived intentions regarding, 112; personal details for, 118–19; rough cut of, 113–15; uniqueness of, 15–16; utility of choice regarding, 206; vintage aesthetics for, 116
context collapse, 64
Converse, 97
Coors, 116
Cops, 39
Costolo, Dick, 56
country music, 18, 20, 82, 90, 91
COVID-19 pandemic, 2, 59, 67, 70, 79, 187, 204
craft ideal, 15
Craig, David, 60
Crichton, Michael, 11
crowdsourcing, 182–83
Cruz, James, 93, 94, 95, 102
cultural industries, defined, 23
Cummings, Chris, 62, 149
Cunningham, Stuart, 60
curated imperfection, 142

within, 48–49; emotion experts within, 46; emotion within, 50; familiarity with, 53; foresight within, 45; Franken-editing on, 46; genealogical authentic-ity and, 41–42; ice method within, 45; inauthenticity within, 45; nonverbal accompaniments, 49; overview of, 28, 38; paradox of, 52; political figures on, 155; rough cut concept within, 44–45; self-disclosure within, 47–52; spatial bias and, 42–43; surveillance for, 43–44

The Real World, 35–36, 38–39, 49

Reckwitz, Andreas, 14

record labels, 87, 98. *See also* music

Reels (Instagram), 58

Reider, Adam, 49, 53

religion, 20

Republican Party, 178–79

Republican Voters Against Trump, 186

Revenge Body, 49

Rey, Lana Del, 83

Reynolds, Catherine, 121

Richards, Denise, 45

Richardson, Bailey, 59–60, 68, 76, 77–78

Ricki Lake, 52

Rifkind, Steve, 91, 94, 129

Ringel, Matt, 91, 96–97, 101

Rocha, Chuck, 158, 166–67, 172

rock music, 88–90

Roetter, Alex, 71, 78–79

Rolling Stone (magazine), 88, 99

Rolling Stones, 95

Romney, Mitt, 110, 155, 185

Roosevelt, Franklin, 154

rough cut: in advertising/branding, 113–15; of influencers, 140–41; in music, 89; overview of, 66–70; in political advertising, 160, 183–87; in reality television, 44–45; in social media, 66–70, 183–84; on vlogging, 67

Rousseau, Jean-Jacques, 7–9, 14, 18, 22, 29, 31, 36, 47, 63, 77, 84, 87, 91, 108, 112, 126, 139, 156, 157, 159, 182, 188, 189, 190,

191, 201, 206

Rubber Tracks, 97

Rubin, Rick, 93

Rule, Ja, 128

Run-DMC, 93

Salisbury, Meredith, 8, 66, 72

Sandberg, Sheryl, 4, 64, 140

Sanders, Bernie, 5, 123, 154, 158, 166–67, 172, 185–86, 198

Santangelo, Lisa, 135

Santos, Joah, 123, 124

Sasso, Joey, 3

Scaramucci, Anthony, 159, 171, 189, 191–92, 197

Schram, Ryan, 114

Schuller, Kyla, 133, 184

Schultz, Howard, 105, 118, 119–20

Schwartz, Tony, 172

Scion, 97

Scott, Travis, 91

self-actualization, 83, 107, 201

self-branding, 148–49

self-disclosure, 47–52, 62–64, 65, 83, 155

self-expression, 84

self-marketing, 54

selling out: currency of, 12–13; defined, 30, 87; of influencers, 142–44, 149; in music, 94, 95–102; reluctance of, 205–6; as scarlet letter, 142; as success, 149

Shandling, Garry, 35

Shepardson, Rob, 169, 178

Shorts (YouTube), 58, 74

Shrum, Bob, 195

side hustle, 148

Silicon Valley, 3–4, 29, 61, 78

Silverstein, Rich, 5, 61, 110

Singh, Lilly, 74

single-identity authenticity, 62–66

singularities, 14

Siwa, JoJo, 63

Skocpol, Theda, 179

Milton Keynes UK
Ingram Content Group UK Ltd.
UKHW011951111023
430421UK00006B/47/J